Organized Interests and Self-Regulation

FEEM Studies in Economics

Fondazione Eni Enrico Mattei (FEEM) is a non-profit, non-partisan research institution established to carry out research in economics with special reference to sustainable development. The volumes in this series are the main results of FEEM's research activities and conferences in economics. They are approved on the basis of the standard Oxford University Press refereeing procedure. The series is guided by the following Scientific Advisory Board:

Organized Interests and Self-Regulation

An Economic Approach

EDITED BY

BERNARDO BORTOLOTTI AND GIANLUCA FIORENTINI

OXFORD

UNIVERSITY PRESS

OXFORD
UNIVERSITY PRESS

Great Clarendon Street, Oxford OX2 6DP

Oxford University Press is a department of the University of Oxford.
It furthers the University's objective of excellence in research, scholarship,
and education by publishing worldwide in

Oxford New York

Athens Auckland Bangkok Bogotá Buenos Aires Calcutta
Cape Town Chennai Dar es Salaam Delhi Florence Hong Kong Istanbul
Karachi Kuala Lumpur Madrid Melbourne Mexico City Mumbai
Nairobi Paris São Paulo Singapore Taipei Tokyo Toronto Warsaw

with associated companies in Berlin Ibadan

Oxford is a registered trade mark of Oxford University Press
in the UK and in certain other countries

Published in the United States
by Oxford University Press Inc., New York

British Library Cataloguing in Publication Data

Data available

Library of Congress Cataloging in Publication Data

Data available

ISBN 0–19–829652–5

1 3 5 7 9 10 8 6 4 2

Typeset in Minion and Rotis
by BookMan Services
Printed in Great Britain
on acid-free paper by
Biddles Ltd., Guildford and King's Lynn

Preface

This volume collects together selected contributions from a research project sponsored by Fondazione Eni Enrico Mattei. The papers were presented at the conference 'Pressure Groups, Self-Regulation, and Enforcement Mechanisms' also organized by the Fondazione Eni Enrico Mattei.

The editors would like to thank the referees, the OUP Delegates for useful comments, and the series editor, Giorgio Barba Navaretti, for valuable suggestions. Barbara Racah and Roberta Ranzini provided excellent editorial assistance.

B.B.
G.F.

Contents

List of contributors   ix

1. Introduction   1
   BERNARDO BORTOLOTTI AND GIANLUCA FIORENTINI

Part I: Organized Interests Produce Legislation

2. Political institutions as screening devices   15
   GIANLUIGI GALEOTTI

3. Electoral rules and interest groups:
   the mix of direct and indirect taxation   30
   GIANLUCA FIORENTINI

4. Endogenous regionalism's free-trade bias:
   special interests in the EEC, 1968–1983   51
   STEPHEN P. MAGEE and HAK-LOH LEE

Part II: Organized Interests Enforce Legislation

5. Self-regulation of the medical and legal professions:
   remaining barriers to competition and EC law   89
   ROGER VAN DEN BERGH

6. Barriers to entry and the self-regulating professions:
   evidence from the market for Italian accountants   131
   BERNARDO BORTOLOTTI AND GIANLUCA FIORENTINI

7. Imperfect competition in certification markets   158
   LUIGI ALBERTO FRANZONI

Part III: Private Ordering and Self-Regulation

8. Trust under endogenous transaction costs   179
   PIER LUIGI SACCO

9. Self-regulation of pollution:
the role of market structure and consumer information 206
DEVON GARVIE

10. The theory of quality regulation and self-regulation:
towards an application to financial markets 236
CARLO SCARPA

Index 261

Contributors

BERNARDO BORTOLOTTI, University of Turin, Italy, and Fondazione Eni Enrico Mattei, Milan, Italy

GIANLUCA FIORENTINI, University of Bologna, Italy

LUIGI ALBERTO FRANZONI, University of Bologna, Italy

GIANLUIGI GALEOTTI, University of 'La Sapienza', Rome, Italy

DEVON GARVIE, Queen's University, Kingston, Ontario, Canada

HAK-LOH LEE, Ministry of Trade, Industry, and Energy, Government of Korea

STEPHEN P. MAGEE, University of Texas at Austin, USA

PIER LUIGI SACCO, University of Florence, Italy

CARLO SCARPA, University of Bologna, Italy

ROGER VAN DEN BERGH, Erasmus University, Rotterdam

1
Introduction

BERNARDO BORTOLOTTI AND GIANLUCA FIORENTINI

1. The revival of political economy

After at least a century of division, political theory and economics are finding a common ground in modern political economy. The separation of the two disciplines has been functional to specialization: economics developed price theory and formal analytical tools to tackle the complexity of market interactions, while political science focused on the analysis of the working of existing political institutions.[1] Despite the advantages of specialization, a problem arises when economists investigate different types of government intervention. Typically, the normative approach to policy analysis from an economic standpoint is based on some sort of social welfare function to be maximized via policy instruments, under a given set of feasibility constraints. If no special attention is devoted to political institutions, the 'technical' approach to policy-making, embedded in traditional welfare economics, fails at the implementation stage when the economist's prescription should turn into factual political decisions. Indeed, within the traditional normative approach the functioning of institutions is seldom an object of analysis, and this may explain the limited success of some policy recommendations despite the almost unanimous consent within the economic profession.[2]

It is surely difficult to provide a comprehensive definition of modern political economy. To start with, its basic tenet is that separating the study of the economy from the study of the political institutions is not conducive to a proper understanding of the social system. At the core of the discipline lie two crucial assumptions: (1) politics and policymaking can be interpreted and analysed as rational decision-making processes; (2) legislation is the outcome of the interaction between economic and political forces.

In order to study the complex interactions between economic and political institutions in their entirety one needs either to abandon a formal modelling strategy or to drastically restrict the field of analysis. While the former strategy is adopted by most of the literature in political science, the most influential contributions related to modern political economy build on the latter option using a reduced form model of the political institutions. This gives rise to a large number of models each emphasizing specific elements of the political setting under the assumption that what is left in the background does not play a crucial role in shaping the legislative outcome. In other words, economists argue that the gains stemming from analytical tractability more than compensate the losses from a sketchy description of the institutional setting. Political scientists maintain that following the economist's approach one obtains results that are necessarily sensitive to small changes even in relatively minor assumptions, such as the information set of the agents or the sequence of the interaction between agents, that are not likely to be tested empirically. As a consequence, the economic approach is regarded as relatively useless to investigate outcomes determined by the interaction of constitutional rules, political institutions, and economic interests.

The criticisms from the political scientist's standpoint are well taken; as a matter of fact, a 'grand' economic model able to capture all the relevant political interactions in the economic system is obviously not available and it is very likely to remain so for a long time. Nevertheless, the achievements of modern political economy—including public choice, constitutional economics, and new institutional economics—cannot be underestimated. The next sections are intended to provide a brief and necessarily in-complete survey of the main achievements of the literature, and to single out the thread linking the contributions of this volume, namely the role of organized interests in collective decision-making.

2. Research directions in modern political economy

Constitutions define the basic principles of a polity, provide the rules to issue legisla-tion and to choose who should govern. In the attempt to organize the various fields of modern political economy, a very broad distinction that can be made is between models in which constitutional rules are an object of analysis or just in the background and not explicitly modelled.

We therefore start our survey with a highly influential literature, albeit relatively limited as to the number of contributions, addressing the normative issue of how agents should select the basic constitutional rules to take collective decisions. Here the focus of the analysis is basically on the properties of constitutional rules in terms of fairness and efficiency.[3] These models make explicit reference to agents who ignore their actual role in the political arena: constitutional rules should be chosen only with reference to the long-term interests and not to pursue specific distributive aims. Due to the focus on the fairness of the procedures, this literature is not particularly concerned with the analysis of specific legislative outcomes. This does not mean that authors such as Buchanan or Tullock had little interest in ascertaining the likely effects of different constitutional rules on the economy or on specific groups of agents. On the contrary, one of the main recurring themes in this literature is that constitutional rules—selected behind a veil of ignorance—should constrain the discretion of the agents active on the supply side of the political mechanism precisely to minimize the coercive elements of collective action.

Most work has been carried out in settings where constitutions—in a broad sense—are given, but none the less represent a crucial element of analysis. The literature dealing with exogenous constitutions can be roughly subdivided according to whether the analysis focuses on the link between constitutional rules and (1) the working of the political game among voters, politicians and lobbyists or (2) the legislative outcomes in terms of economic policies. In the former area, which includes most contributions in the public choice tradition, authors investigate different electoral rules, or other features of the political mechanisms such as the relations between institutions in a federal setting, exploring the properties of the equilibria reached at the political stage (i.e. existence, stability, efficiency). This approach has been pursued in several strands of literature where collective decisions are analysed as the outcome of voting schemes, competition among lobbies or agency relationships between politicians and voters.[4] In the contributions belonging to the public choice tradition, one can still detect an interest in normative issues although not in terms of fairness of the *procedures* established for the working of the political mechanisms, but of comparison of their *outcomes*.

The basic message of the second area is that constitutional rules also play a role in terms of economic policymaking. For instance, an influential tradition in the positive theory of international trade studies the interaction between voting schemes, lobbies, and bureaucracies to explain the emergence of tariffs and other trade-limiting institutions. Subsidies to specific industries, cost-sharing rules to finance the provision of public goods, income tax rates, and the size of government are instead the object of analysis in the positive approach to public economics.[5] Moreover, a related line of research in macroeconomics takes into account relatively general features of the political system (single party vs. coalitional governments) or more circumscribed rules (viz. central bank independence, fixed policy rules vs. discretion), showing the effects of institutional credibility and political commitment on economic variables.[6] More recently, the same research strategy yielded interesting results when applied to the relations between constitutional provisions, regulatory commitments, and long run investments.[7]

As stated at the beginning of this section, several studies in modern political economy shift the focus of the analysis from constitutional rules to the working of the political process. In this field, constitutions are exogenous and, moreover, they are not explicitly modelled: the behaviour of political actors (voters, parties, organized interests, and the government) is the main object of analysis.

The idea that the political mechanism can be described in terms of competing pressure groups, outbidding each other to obtain favourable legislation, prompted the Stigler–Peltzman capture theory of regulation and, with very different normative implications, the Becker approach to legislation as a competitive process for political influence (Stigler 1971, Peltzman 1976 and Becker 1983). From a different perspective, the relations between voters and the government are at the core of the 'political macroeconomics' which has studied how the outcome of the political game at general elections affects economic policy. This approach analysed issues like the politico-economic business cycle, where policymaking is manipulated to increase the likelihood of re-election of incumbent governments, the politics of budget deficits, inflation and stabilization (Nordhaus 1975, Alesina 1995). More recent developments have introduced the assumption of rational expectations of voters, who therefore become knowledgeable about the incentives of politicians (Cukierman and Meltzer 1986). Political parties are instead the key players in partisan models. The basic assumption of these models is that political interests matter: politicians select platforms maximizing the utility of given groups of voters. In this framework, partisan forces affect macroeconomic variables like unemployment and inflation (Hibbs 1992).

The principles we introduced to organize the literature revolved around the concept of constitutions and constitutional rules. Constitutions establish principles through which agents obtain formal legislation. While the output of the political process is typically a 'top-down' legislation enacted according to constitutional rules and enforced by the state, norms, conventions, and informal legislation emerge spontaneously among coalitions of agents. The incentives to the production of private norms has been the object of a strand of research in new institutional economics that we include in a broad definition of modern political economy. The starting point of this literature is the recognition that parties engage in economic activities in contexts with incomplete information and positive transaction costs. In particular, parties anticipate the negative consequences of opportunistic behaviour, and try to overcome possible inefficiencies via private ordering and self-enforcing contracts. In this framework, agents may establish private governance systems designed to enforce contract provisions.[8] Clearly private orderings interact with the political mechanism in a complex way. In some cases, such as in the professions, the legislative body delegates the enforcement of legislation to private parties. In other circumstances, coalitions of agents decide to abide by special standards of conduct, as in self-regulation of environmental performance and financial markets.

3. The theme of the book

Within this plurality of fields of research, the present book aims at exploring the role of organized interests in shaping collective action and in the emergence of self-regulation.[9] Organized interests are usually active not only at the legislative and administrative stages of the political process; they are closely related to the working of the economic mechanism, often promoting the enactment of self-enforcing codes aimed at reducing transaction costs. Accordingly, focusing on their role, one could provide a more integrated view of the reciprocal influence of economic and political forces. Hence, political institutions cannot be regarded as neutral bodies, whose role is to transform individual preferences into collective decisions.[10] On the contrary, legislators, bureaucrats, and organized interests are all active in becoming pivotal players in the political arena. In this respect, although political scientists have always worked on this very topic, the use of economic tools to investigate the role of organized interests in shaping economic policies and/or in enforcing regulations represents a relatively innovative research strategy.

Most contributions which focus on the working of organized interests at the legislative stage stress the negative consequences of lobbying in terms of rent creation and/or protection leading to inefficient policies (Tullock 1980, Bhagwati and Srinivasan 1980). However, a few, but influential, authors stress that organized interests improve the efficiency of the political market because they convey information about the intensity of preferences toward legislation. In view of such a basic contrast of opinions, legislative outcomes should be carefully evaluated particularly in those industries (industrial, financial, professional) which are most likely to be influenced by organized interests, not only to deter possible inefficiencies, but also to favour their role as institutional channels to gather specific information at relatively low cost.[11]

Moreover, even if the organized interests are seen as institutional bodies to represent the demand for legislation, their relations with the actors and bodies active on the supply side of the political market should also be considered. Indeed, at that stage it is more likely that the competition between organized interests bring them to collude with political representatives.[12] In this respect, one may pose the question of how to regulate such interests in order to make a proper use of the information they provide and to call upon them when public administrations are unable to cope with the growing amount of information needed to provide an efficient enforcement.

Arriving at the stage where legislation is implemented, regulated economic activities sometimes turn out to be monitored by groups that are active in the supply side of the market, that is under self-regulation. Obviously, the rationale for these non-standard regulatory regimes lies in the fact that information on quality is often not contractible when it is asymmetrically distributed, such as in the market for professional services. Under these circumstances, delegating the control over quality to those who are better suited to evaluate it might partially fulfil the asymmetry. Nevertheless, this informational advantage has to be traded-off with the possible costs of self-serving behaviour, whenever producers engage in rent-seeking activities with a public interest alibi.

This trend toward a greater reliance on professional bodies and industrial associations at the administrative stage is rapidly gaining momentum in Europe and especially in those countries and industries where the public administration seems unable to cope with the growing amount of information needed to enforce legislation effectively. Accordingly, several economists are worried about the possible rents which can be created by delegating growing regulatory functions to the organizations who represent private economic agents. Indeed, organized interests might represent a multiple source of inefficiency: at the legislative stage, where some laws might be enacted although they do not generate any allocative improvement, and at the administrative stage, when pressure groups display conflicting interests with the parties they should allegedly defend from opportunistic behaviour.

To respond to these inefficiencies, one should invest resources in designing more sophisticated institutional settings where the beneficial role of organized interests is enhanced, while the costs arising from their attempt to manipulate regulation are kept under control. The research collected in this volume tries to suggest under which conditions organized interests may contribute to improve the efficiency of legislative outcomes and of enforcement mechanisms.

4. Structure of the volume

Part I: Organized interests produce legislation

The first part addresses the role of organized interests in political institutions. More specifically, Galeotti analyses two of the classic problems of collective action: how to avoid free-riding in the expression of collective interests and how to control rent-seeking by political representatives. The author posits organized interests at the centre stage of the political mechanism as they provide information on the demand for collective action and reduce the politicians' discretion in agenda setting. In this direction, Galeotti sets forth a distinction between the vertical and horizontal dimension of politics, that is collecting and processing information vs. selecting interests. In the former, the emergence of organized interests contributes to defining the dimensions of the market for political influence. In this respect, the comparative advantage of groups with more concentrated interests does not hinder the positive role of competition between organized interests. In fact, the author argues that when voters realize the full extent of distributive effects of the bias against more diffused interests, they will take action by either promoting institutional innovations aimed at reducing their influence or by investing more resources in such competition. On the contrary, in the horizontal dimension of politics, where the priorities between different interests are set, the possibility of trades between agents on the supply side and organized interests may be less easily detected, and the conditions for competition among the latter are relatively more difficult to enforce. In this respect, the trend towards the creation of a more diffuse network of institutional actors able to shape legislation (parliamentary committees) or to influence its enforcement (independent authorities, special judiciaries) creates more room for collusive practices.

In the second paper, Fiorentini proposes a model where the policy mix between direct and indirect taxation emerges from the interaction between organized interests active at the legislative stage where different electoral rules are enforced. In this setting, the fiscal structure of a community represents an equilibrium of a non-cooperative game where members of different organized groups—characterized by conflicting interests—compete to get distributive gains. Their choice of participation in the activity of the organized groups is constrained by a set of constitutional rules which are embodied in a reduced-form model of electoral competition. Accordingly, the paper develops a positive analysis of the effects of different institutional rules regulating the interaction between citizens as voters and as members of organized interests (electoral rules and competition rules between organized interests) on the resulting fiscal equilibrium. In this setting, when an effective ban on organized interests' activities is enforced, fiscal rules are shown to be strictly determined by the features of the electoral rules for the legislative body. On the contrary, when transaction costs to organize dispersed interests are low enough to make it possible to overcome free-riding, small groups can shift the fiscal equilibrium to their advantage. However, such comparative advantage decreases if binding agreements can be enforced inside the organized groups to coordinate the supply of contributions.

The last paper, by Magee and Lee, dealing with the organized interests' activities at the legislative stage, investigates the hypothesis that the creation of a more integrated European market leads to an increase in the level of protectionism. The theoretical reasoning hinges upon the endogenous protection literature where the organized interests are seen as the crucial actors in the bargaining taking place in a relatively black-boxed political setting. More specifically, Magee and Lee build their empirical analysis on a general equilibrium model of endogenous protection in a custom union where tariffs are determined by the relative size of free-riding in the producers' association versus the consumer groups. To estimate their model, the authors approximate the degree of free-riding of the producers' association with an inverse proxy of industrial concentration and the strength of the consumers' groups by the overall expenditure in the same industry. Two effects are singled out. First, a tariff diversion effect resulting in a fall of the unions' external tariffs caused by two main factors: an increase in the growth of the domestic markets reinforcing consumers' pressure to lower tariffs and a decrease of the concentration index at the EC level, after the creation of the union, at a much lower level than those at the country levels. Second, a tariff creation effect resulting in a rise in the external tariff level, due to an increase in the intra-EC trade and in a process of mergers. The latter has a positive impact on the EC concentration index and therefore on the endogenous tariff level. The empirical results show that the tariff creation effect dominates the tariff diversion effect in the EC during the period 1963–83.

Part II: Organized interests enforce legislation

Private parties are sometimes called upon to enforce existing legislation. In the market for professional services, regulators have realized that information asymmetries are difficult to fulfil via public intervention and have often resolved to discipline the market involving professionals in regulation. In certification, third parties act as gatekeepers in charge of verifying the conformity of products and production processes to specified standards. This kind of activity is typically carried out by underwriters and auditors in financial markets, and by independent intermediaries accredited to award quality labels.

In this framework, professional bodies are among the most influential organized interests which are also delegated to enforce regulation. In his paper, Van den Bergh presents a comparative survey of the regulatory framework for the legal and medical professions in most European countries. Such a survey explores the main areas of convergence which may constitute the legislative basis to build a more integrated market for professional services. On this basis, Van den Bergh applies the economic analysis of law to evaluate the current state of the regulatory measures, with special reference to the width of the self-regulation provisions. In doing so, the author considers the relative merits of the public interest approach—based on the limits of contractual solutions in the professional services—and of the private interest approach—based on rent protection. Overall, Van den Berg concludes that most specific features of the self-regulation regime adopted in the two above professions (ban on advertising, minimum tariffs, restriction on mobility) cannot be regarded as the less costly institutional solutions to ensure quality standards.

Bortolotti and Fiorentini develop an empirical analysis focused on the market for Italian accountants trying to provide some insights about the overall welfare effects of self-regulation. Two major stylized facts emerge: first, the convergence in incomes of the two professions operating with different licensure requirements; second, the existence of a substantial earning differential between the two professions despite the recent trends. The rate of entry, and in particular, the admission policy in the profession implemented each year by boards, provides some interesting insights to explain this evidence. First, lagged admission rates represent an important factor to explain professional incomes. Second, admission rates are deeply influenced by past level of incomes. These results cast some doubt on the view that professional boards are benevolent institutions that strive to preserve high quality standards of active professionals and raise the question of whether they might represent a possible guideline for an intervention by anti-trust authorities.

Franzoni studies certification in a traditional Cournot setting under the assumption that the gatekeepers' function is to prevent the production of a negative externality. Under some conditions, it is shown that (1) an increase in competition in the certification market has adverse consequences since the expected harm from the activity by non-compliant firms is negatively related to the certification fee; (2) the highest gatekeepers' liability is socially desirable. These results shed some light on the welfare properties of the private enforcement of law, suggesting the need for careful design of the implementation of forms of market regulation.

Part III: Private ordering and self-regulation

In a purely decentralized setting with no public institution in charge of the enforcement of contracts and legislation, private parties still have incentives to establish self-regulation and private orderings. Self-regulation is often a more formal definition of private legislation and governance structures by coalitions of agents, typically firms, while private orderings usually refer to self-enforcing of implicit contracts bringing about the spontaneous emergence of trust.

Scarpa provides a critical survey of the existing literature in the attempt to draw some lessons for the implementation of self-regulation in financial markets. Theory seems to suggest that self-regulation is desirable when the coalition of agents is small and homogeneous, when the mobility of investors is high and public regulation is unable to identify the firms' true cost structures. When reputation matters, typically a multiplicity of equilibria exists, since (1) many different models are plausible candidates for representing particular features of self-regulation and (2) even within a given model, there is a large number of equilibrium solutions with different qualitative properties. The multiplicity of equilibria poses problems when normative prescriptions should be drawn from theory. Nevertheless, what appears to be inescapable is the trade-off between guarantees and fairness—under public regulation—and riskiness and efficiency—probably enhanced under self-regulation.

Garvie addresses the key question of whether environmental self-regulation provides sufficient incentives for the correction of externalities in a cost-effective manner. Environmental self-regulation is a regime under which private firms voluntarily control their pollution emission levels. Several options are available to firms in that respect: they can reduce output, shift the product mix toward 'green' products, or improve the environmental impact by installing pollution abatement technologies. Building a model in which firms are restricted to reducing emissions only by reducing output or installing an emission control input, the complex interactions among market structure, consumer demand and environmental factors are evaluated. In particular, consumer demand is supposed to be affected—among other factors—by (1) environmental quality so that the willingness to pay is influenced by the marginal damage stemming from the production of the pollution-generating good and (2) consumers' knowledge about the true environmental consequences of production. An important trade-off emerges in this context: firms can exploit the consumers' environmental preferences to raise profits so that when firms have monopoly power, the incentives to effective environmental self-regulation are the strongest. Voluntary codes may therefore have strong anti-competitive effects. The overall welfare properties of self-regulation are evaluated comparing Pareto efficient outcomes with oligopolistic solutions. In a simulation analysis, voluntary regimes are shown to work best in controlling cumulative pollutants in highly concentrated industries.

Sacco studies the emergence of trust which represents the basic pre-condition for the emergence of voluntary codes of conduct. The framework is very general, but an R&D joint-venture is set forth as a reference case. In this setting, incentives to cheat are high since each party can sell the common property asset to a rival firm despite the sequential investment by the initial partner. The value of the investment therefore depends crucially on whether the partner will cooperate or not. Parties can monitor the partner's type at a cost depending on the actual diffusion of cooperation across the economy. Transaction costs are therefore endogenous to the co-evolution of different patterns of behaviour among firms. Under this set of assumptions, an evolutionary game theory model is developed to explore whether and under what conditions trust —that is cooperation without any investment in monitoring—is the social standard of behaviour. The results of a simulation analysis show that the emergence of trust as the equilibrium social standard crucially depends on the completion value of the partnership and on the initial distribution of behaviour across the population.

Notes

1. Myerson (1997) provides a thorough discussion of the gains from a closer interaction between economists and political scientists in the analysis of political institutions. See also Banks and Hanushek (1996).

2. Recently Dixit (1996) explored rather diffusely the relative weaknesses of the normative approach common in welfare economics and of the positive perspective of the public choice tradition in the analysis of policymaking.

3. In this area of constitutional economics the most influential work is Buchanan and Tullock (1962) and more recently Brennan and Buchanan (1980). A recent discussion of the reasons why economists find it difficult to accept a constitutional approach to policymaking is in Dixit (1996).

4. See Mueller (1989) and Wittman (1995) for recent surveys of the contributions in this area. Notwithstanding the influence of the work on constitutional rules, most of the public choice literature takes such rules for granted and does not discuss the procedures through which a specific mechanism has been chosen in order to reach a collective decision.

5. For a recent survey on the contributions on endogenous tariffs in a rent-seeking setting one can see Magee (1997) and, in a more critical perspective, Wittman (1995). For a broad review of the applications of the public choice theory to microeconomic policies, the most complete reference is still Mueller (1989). More specifically on the debate on the size of government the classic references are Peltzman (1980), Olson (1982) and North and Wallis (1982).

6. Macroeconomic policy analysis has particularly benefited from this approach, with important insights about the effects of dynamic commitment on economic variables (Persson and Tabellini 1990).

7. For an instance of this type of work with reference to the effects of constitutional rules limiting the discretion of the collective decision-maker on private investment in utilities see Spiller (1993).

8. This framework of analysis is very general and may help to elucidate the emergence of agreements like contracts with hostages, ownership concentration, or vertical integration within firms (Williamson 1983 and 1996, Greif 1993, Ogus 1994).

9. We adopt the term 'organized interests' even if most economic literature on this topic prefers 'pressure groups' (Becker 1983, Austen-Smith 1987, Mueller 1989, Wittman 1995). This is because, in the political science literature, 'pressure groups' are specialized in lobbying the legislature or the government while 'organized interests' are characterized by more broadly defined objectives. They typically include political representation for political parties, categorical representation for industry associations, self-regulation functions for professional associations, etc.

10. This observation obviously is not new. A long tradition of studies in positive political economy has questioned the neutrality of the state towards organized interests and stressed the fundamental role of economic forces in shaping legislative activity. Beard, Pareto, Mosca, Schumpeter, just to mention a few, undermined the conventional wisdom that institutions are designed to transform the preferences of the public at large into collective actions.

11. See Wittman (1995) for a complete survey of the role of organized interests in shaping the working of the political mechanism at the legislative stage.

12. As we have seen, almost all areas of public interventions have been investigated making use

of models where organized interests play a relevant role in shaping legislation. In this respect, the problem of how voters process information is a crucial one in the literature on pressure groups. Authors like Becker (1983) and Magee, Brock and Young (1989) implicitly or explicitly adopt the Downesian idea of rational ignorance. On the contrary, Austen-Smith (1987), Hinich and Munger (1989), and Baron (1994) model how voters make use of the political information produced by politicians and by organized interests.

References

Alesina, A. (1995) 'Elections, Party Structure, and the Economy', in Banks, J. S. and Hanushek, E. A. (eds.), *Modern Political Economy*. Cambridge: Cambridge University Press.

Austen-Smith, D. (1987) 'Interest Groups, Campaign Contributions and Probabilistic Voting', *Public Choice*, 54: 123–39.

Austen-Smith, D. (1997) 'Interest Groups: Money, Information, and Influence', in Mueller, D. (ed.), *Perspectives on Public Choice*. Cambridge: Cambridge University Press.

Banks, J. and Hanushek, E. (eds.) (1996) *Modern Political Economy*. Cambridge: Cambridge University Press.

Baron, D. (1994) 'Electoral Competition with Informed and Uninformed Voters', *American Political Science Review*, 88: 33–47.

Becker, G. (1983) 'A Theory of Competition among Pressure Groups for Political Influence', *Quarterly Journal of Economics*, 98: 371–400.

Bhagwati, J. and Srinivasan, T. (1980) 'Revenue Seeking: A Generalization of the Theory of Tariffs', *Journal of Political Economy*, 88: 1069–87.

Brennan, G. and Buchanan, J. (1980) *The Power to Tax: Analytical Foundations for a Fiscal Constitution*. Cambridge: Cambridge University Press.

Breton, A. (1997) *Competitive Governments*. Cambridge: Cambridge University Press.

Buchanan, J. and Tullock, G. (1962) *The Calculus of Consent*. Ann Arbor: University of Michigan Press.

Cukierman, A. and Meltzer, A. (1986) 'A Positive Theory of Discretionary Policy, the Cost of Democratic Government, and the Benefits of a Constitution', *Economic Inquiry*, 24: 367–88.

Dixit, A. (1996) *The Making of Economic Policy*. Cambridge, MA: MIT Press.

Greif, A. (1993) 'Contract Enforceability, and Economic Institutions in Early Trade: The Maghribi Traders' Coalition', *American Economic Review*, 83: 525–48.

Hibbs, D. (1992) 'Partisan Theory after Fifteen Years', *European Journal of Political Economy*, 8: 361–74.

Hinich, M. and Munger, M. (1989), 'Political Investment, Voter Perceptions, and Candidate Strategy: An Equilibrium Spatial Analysis', in Ordeshook, P. (ed.), *Models of Strategic Choice in Politics*. Ann Arbor: University of Michigan Press.

Magee, S. (1997) 'Endogenous Protection: The Empirical Evidence', in Mueller, D. (ed.), *Perspectives on Public Choice*. Cambridge: Cambridge University Press.

Magee, S., Brock, W., and Young, L., (1989), *Black Hole Tariffs and Endogenous Policy Theory*. Cambridge: Cambridge University Press.

Mayer, W. and Li, J. (1994) 'Interest Groups, Electoral Competition, and Probabilistic Voting for Trade Policies', *Economics and Politics*, 6: 59–77.

Mueller, D. (1989) *Public Choice II*. Cambridge: Cambridge University Press.

Mueller, D. (1997) *Perspectives on Public Choice.* Cambridge: Cambridge University Press.

Myerson, R. (1997) 'Economic Analysis of Political Institutions: An Introduction', in Kreps, D. and Wallis, K. (eds.), *Advances in Economic Theory and Econometrics.* Cambridge: Cambridge University Press.

Nordhaus, W. (1975) 'The Political Business Cycle', *Review of Economic Studies,* 42: 169–90.

North, D. (1990) *Institutions, Institutional Change, and Economic Performance.* Cambridge: Cambridge University Press.

North, D. and Wallis, J. (1982) 'American Government Expenditures: A Historical Perspective', *American Economic Review,* 72: 336–40.

Ogus, A. (1994) *Regulation: Legal Form and Economic Theory.* Oxford: Clarendon Press.

Olson, M. (1982) *The Rise and Decline of Nations: Economic Growth, Stagflation, and Social Rigidities.* New Haven, CT: Yale University Press.

Peltzman, S. (1976) 'Toward a More General Theory of Regulation', *Journal of Law and Economics,* 19: 211–40.

Peltzman, S. (1980) 'The Growth of Government', *Journal of Law and Economics,* 23: 209–88.

Persson, T. and Tabellini, G. (1990) *Macroeconomic Policy: Credibility and Politics.* Reading: Harwood Academic Publishers.

Shepsle, K. and Weingast, B. (1995), *Positive Theories of Congressional Institutions.* Ann Arbor: University of Michigan Press.

Spiller, P. (1993) 'Institutions and Regulatory Commitment in Utilities' Privatization', *Industrial and Corporate Change,* 2: 387–450.

Stigler, G. (1971) 'The Theory of Economic Regulation', *Bell Journal of Economics,* 4: 114–44.

Tullock, G. (1980) 'Efficient Rent-Seeking', in Buchanan, J., Tollison, R., and Tullock, G. (eds.), *Towards a Theory of Rent-Seeking Society.* College Station: Texas A&M Press.

Williamson, O. (1983) 'Credible Commitments: Using Hostages to Support Exchange', *American Economic Review,* 73: 507–40.

Williamson, O. (1996) *The Mechanism of Governance.* Oxford: Oxford University Press.

Wittman, D. (1995) *The Myth of Democratic Failure: Why Political Institutions Are Efficient.* Chicago: University of Chicago Press.

Part I

Organized Interests Produce Legislation

2
Political institutions as screening devices

GIANLUIGI GALEOTTI

1. Continuity and novelty in political history

Daily news as well as the conventional analysis on rent-seeking often gives the impression that pressure groups are the woodworms generated by modern democracy. The emphasis on the informational value of their activities does not dispel the doubt that the promotion of special interests contradicts a basic tenet of democracy, the pursuit of general interest. Is that a failure of democracy? The reply has to avoid the pitfall of reading political history at its face value, as discontinuities are more apparent than real, and innovations occur within a continuity that can be appreciated later on, when the reference points find the proper perspective. Karl Popper provides a significant, though radical, illustration of this point, when he suggests re-reading the traditional normative search for political legitimacy: who should rule? The question asked from Plato to Karl Marx, put in the more worldly Popperian words becomes: 'how is the State to be constituted so that rulers causing too much harm can be dismissed without bloodshed and violence?' If democracy loses some of its rhetoric charm in the reply, it gains an indisputable point of merit. In a similar vein, this paper takes for granted that in all polities pressure lobbies represent the crucial nexus between the vertical dimension of politics—related to problems of information processing—and the horizontal dimension dealing with the selection of interests worth protecting.

We start by recollecting how public action is set in motion, and is always influenced by interests strong enough to make themselves heard. The ensuing market for political influence is characterized by a balance of interests affected not only by the institutional context—who is in charge of the public choices—but also by social expectations concerning the how of those choices *vis-à-vis* their eventual outcomes. We interpret those expectations in terms of shared ideologies supplying terms of reference, weight and meaning in the classification of interests. Being perceived as sets of implicit promises, ideologies help to make people comply, but at the same time orient and somehow constraint the behaviour of the decision-makers. The management of the ideologies, by those in charge of the screening of political demands, is a factor that comes to be assessed in terms of eventual outcomes and that, in the long run, moulds the very evolution of political institutions.

The emphasis on ideologies is not new—see Douglas North's (1981) hint at their role in controlling free-riding and its rediscovery by Melvin Hinich and Michael Munger (1994)—but they have to be seen in connection with the behaviours of those in charge of their application. Richard Musgrave has recently (1996) stressed the English, American and Scandinavian evolution from the *Service State*, aimed at correcting market failures, to the *Welfare State* designed to modify the market-determined distribution of resources. However, Musgrave integrates that normative clear-cut evolution with reference to the positive notion of the *Communal State*—based on the distinction between the public and the private needs of its members—and of the *Flawed State* infested by the self-serving behaviour of its controlling agents. If the former directs attention to the notion of a shared set of values, the latter recalls the Italian traditional concern with public action biased in favour of powerful interests: think of Vilfredo Pareto on the pursuit of minority interests and of Amilcare Puviani on fiscal illusion. Although we can read those authors as anticipating contemporary criticisms of democratic politics reduced to a battleground of rent-seekers, that anticipation is more descriptive than analytical.[1] We can obtain a better reconciliation of those different models, if we accept that different regimes are characterized by specific solutions to the problems of asymmetric information and signalling that feature the market for political influence. In our suggested approach, the study of those solutions is the study of how ideologies and institutions combine in processing the information and selecting the interests. In the long run the evaluation of the outcomes reduces to an evaluation of the efficiency of the selection performed by different institutions, in terms of their impact on the welfare of the people who represent the passive yet eventually decisive side of the game, *à la* Popper. We could reinterpret a famous remark pronounced by Pareto and consider history as a graveyard of crashed screening devices.

Once we have clarified the essential framework, it becomes possible to single out a number of biases affecting the identification of focal interests within the combination of horizontal and vertical relationships, and in this way to assess the continuity and the novelty of what happens under the different arrangements of contemporary representative democracies. It is in that framework that an assessment of new virtues and old vices of the democratic performance becomes possible. The paper is therefore arranged in the following way. Section 2 underlines how the economic interpretation considers public action plagued by free-riding and opportunism from its very conceptual beginnings. Section 3 analyses the two structural components of political screening devices, the ideological syntax and the institutional architecture that identifies those in charge of articulating that syntax. Section 4 discusses a number of flaws that affect the processing of information and the two following sections consider more closely democratic innovations in terms of electoral rules and party organizations. Finally, the fall of information costs and the parallel reduction of the role played by ideologies are discussed in Section 7, where the tendency towards a judgementalization of politics is discussed.

2. The Scylla and Charybdis of public action

According to a saying, when an economist sees something working in practice she or he starts wondering whether it could work in theory. A case in point is supplied by the analysis of collective action which is seen poised in mid-air, weighed down with the sloth of free-riders and stirred up by the activism of strong interests. Modern scholars have reinterpreted old analytical issues, from Thomas Hobbes' pact between worried warring individuals ready for an unconditional surrender to the supply-oriented saga of rulers all too willing to oblige.[2] Leaving aside aetiologic accounts, economics invites reflection about the twin dangers which make the navigation of public action difficult. In a nutshell, we can say that because of individual free-riding, public action requires a measure of coercion (Baumol 1952); because of coercion, whoever is in control of that action is tempted to exploit it to his own advantage (Brennan and Buchanan 1980). It is the trade-off between the Scylla of free-riding and the Charybdis of the leaders' opportunism that makes the notion of a Flawed State not so much a deviation, as a kind of congenital setting: as soon as the control of free-riding allows the development of a collective action, that action becomes a tool in the hands of those powerful enough to control it.

The implication of that result—interest-groups belong to the genetic code of public action—does not change substantially if we follow the less dramatic reflection of a number of scholars (from Anthony Downs to Douglass North) on how information problems compel any government, whatever its nature and its scope, to rely on inter-mediaries to take the pulse of the people. That hidden information issue represents the *vertical dimension* of politics, involving the activity of what Breton (1996) comprises under the label of 'demand lobbies'. As it happens, the intermediaries—whether ruler's agents, sycophants, favour-buyers, pressure-groups or political parties—provide the information at a price, cashed in terms of influence over policy formation. An import-ant issue faced by any polity is therefore that of controlling the opportunism of those agents, an opportunism made easier by the discretion they enjoy and by the collusive exchanges they can arrange with the *policy suppliers* which incarnate public power: civil servants, judges, central and local authorities, the army, advisors and courtesans, high, middle, and low officers, etc. Breton (1996) stresses how all those *elected and non-elected* centres of power have to conquer consent and to impose repression in order to exercise their authority. The many ways through which the constituents of each centre can call their consent back and forth—voting is just one of the many channels ex-pressing peoples' reactions—can be interpreted in terms of the *horizontal dimension* of politics, a dimension characterized by a hidden action issue involving the behaviours of the decision-makers. The policy suppliers respond to the interests of different com-binations of citizens, while engaged in a reciprocal competition that helps them check each other's behaviour in a sort of reversed *divide and rule* pattern. The information and monitoring problems of the market for political influence can be interpreted in terms of the interaction between those vertical and horizontal dimensions, roughly expressing the demand and the supply sides of politics. It is the complexity of that interaction to prevent the reduction of politics to a mere recording of the economic interests of the better organized groups.[3]

Within that framework, sources of inefficiency relate to the lack of competition along either the vertical or the horizontal dimension of politics, or both. A first source occurs when lobby leaders can use their information advantages against the interests of their principals, the lobby members: this is related to the reduced competition brought about by the control of internal free-riding. A second source occurs when the centres of power are able to reduce their reciprocal competition thanks to stable and strong horizontal relationships: the less biting the horizontal competitive check, the more they are able to shift the burden of their collusive agreements to the shoulders of citizens. A third source occurs when an opportunity for collusion between centres of power and lobby managers is capable of generating rents that can be shared between them. That broader collusion is what Breton considers should be properly defined as rent-seeking (1996, 65–6).

For an illustration, consider a certain economic activity—the location of a pharma-ceutical firm—that falls under the regulations of a number of centres of power (a Ministry, a Parliamentary Committee, a number of local Governments), and assume that the political bargains are over the returns generated by the control of that activity. When there are strong horizontal links—nurtured, say, by party loyalty or by any other device restricting competition—it becomes possible to coordinate the actions of those centres in ways which allow the collection of rents which would be reduced to zero in a competitive setting. A second illustration is provided by the Corporatist State, defined as 'a mode of social organization in which functional groups rather than discrete indi-viduals wield power and transact affairs' (Bruno and Sachs 1985). Though appreciated in terms of macroeconomic performance, a Corporatist setting is often plagued by collusion. Take the case of professional regulations, where privileges of various kinds (including those in terms of a statutory definition of professional negligence) and a tight control of internal competition can nurture a collusive climate that is extremely hard to change, as we shall see later on. For the moment, having identified the market for political influence and the role played by collusion, we have to discuss how the political institutions have evolved in handling the selection of the interests to be satisfied.

3. Structural features of the 'screening' process

Ordinary political activity comprises many competing demands that substantiate the market for political influence. When the decisions to be enforced are mutually in-compatible, criteria to process the information and rules to reach decisions are needed. In this paper, the combination of information processing and interest selection is referred to in terms of a *screening process*, not in the now conventional sense of sorting out the good from the bad, but in that of selecting those who receive benefits from those who do not. We submit that the screening of demands to be satisfied occurs through two intertwined components: an ideological and an institutional one. Though the latter represents the focus of the economic analysis of politics, we maintain that it cannot work without a shared set of beliefs about public interest and the values to be respected and promoted. Those beliefs represent an important operational feature that keeps the political system going (Calvert 1995), as they are perceived by citizens as implicit promises—helping to nurture political legitimacy—and at same time they come to limit the discretion of the decision-makers in more or less precise ways.

At times the ideology is ethical or religious, and at other times more definite in their contents with the inclusion of standards, up to the point of stating rights written down in a formal constitution. In the suggested approach, we should speak of an ideological syntax in order to stress its guiding role in ranking requests, supplying criteria of discrimination between acceptable and non-acceptable goals, and establishing benchmarks which allow the evaluation of what has been decided. Though traditionally considered outside rational choice analysis, ideologies—however defined[4]—are attracting new attention.[5] For those who are inclined to deem all non-democratic regimes, of the present or of the past, as a synonym for absolute power, the importance of participation in ideological syntax can appear questionable. But 'no leadership is absolute' and no ruler has ever enjoyed a complete discretion in his or her choices, not only because of the economic logic of demand but because of the mix of repression and loyalty any government has to adopt (Wintrobe 1998). To respect that syntax and to take note of side effects and non-voiced needs is in the interest of rational rulers in order to gain loyalty and to nurture in their subjects a feeling of moral obligation to comply.[6] Traditional confidence in legitimate authorities was based upon shared values experienced as pledges that not only reduced uncertainty but also provided benchmarks restricting absolute power. Max Weber's very definitions of the charismatic and the traditional bases of political authority imply that warranty. And the combination of ideology and institutional rules represents the backbone of the returning appeal to the 'rule of law', an appeal that in its early statements (Plato) could only refer to a broad view of what a good society should be. Because of that, the respect of criteria and rules represents some sort of constraint setting limits to the power of the decision-makers.

The authorities are identified by an institutional architecture[7] stating who has to process the information, and how to apply the syntax and select the interests. It could be an individual, a group, a bureaucracy, or a plurality of centres that have to agree in order to get the decision acted upon.[8] All political engines—in Schumpeter's term—make use of ideology and structure, with a formal emphasis often inversely related to the most effective input.[9] As 'the allocating of resources through the political process provides ample opportunity for ideological conviction to dominate the decision-making process' (North 1981, 56), controlling the ideological syntax has always been the most direct way of controlling the screening. Hence the need to cultivate the horizontal links in order to keep the relevant behaviours under control, and the ideology represents a reunifying factor to check the behaviour of different authorities. Nobody has to display his or her power by direct intervention if he or she is influential enough to manipulate the ideological paradigm and control the agenda, by allowing the emergence only of the expedient issues and by keeping annoying items away from the discussion. Because of that manipulation, the real set of implicit promises can sometimes become very different from what it appears. It follows that many power struggles are fought in terms of interpreting and altering the paradigm, with a historical acceleration which is bringing about the growing irrelevance of the ideologies (see below).

In conclusion, within the ideological syntax, it is the set of more or less formal procedures that define, and therefore limit the autonomy of those in charge of taking decisions. Because of that, the evolution of the relative impact of those two inputs (ideological paradigms and institutional architecture) allows a better appreciation of the forces in action and what happens when they evolve at a different pace. Think of Pareto's disappointment on seeing the new political institutions dominated by the traditional syntax, or—conversely—of the very notion of lobby, contrived when the behaviours which had always accompanied public action appeared in conflict with the new syntax of an equal representation of interests. Those observations would suggest a plan of research on contents and evolution of those ideological paradigms and how their development combine and interact with the evolution of political institutions and the vested interests they come to protect. As in the case of scientific revolutions, inconsistencies between experience and ideologies must accumulate before individuals react, by changing either their ideologies or the political institutions. Such inquiry, however, is beyond the limits of this paper, and in the following we confine ourselves to the identification of a number of biases that affect the screening procedures, first along the vertical dimension as they evolve from pre-democratic to democratic politics. Secondly, the devices aiming at reducing political competition along the horizontal dimension are discussed in Section 6.

4. Flaws affecting the vertical dimension of politics

A general feature of pre-democratic politics is that of recognizing sectional interests, up to the point of having the ideological paradigm built on them (from the apologue of Menenius Agrippa told by Titus Livius to the Indian caste system). Scholars of different backgrounds have underlined the evolution of group aggregation from 'natural' links (kinship and neighbourhood) to functional ones, based on trade, profession and otherwise defined interests. The legacy of those early links is still alive (when not nurtured by the media) in terms of the strong and special ties between a leader and 'his' people which grant the leader the power of interpreting the paradigm and taking decisions. However, the double-edged nature of that deepening of consent deserves attention. The stronger the trust in the leader, the greater the opportunity for his opportunistic behaviours. As the followers are encased in a relationship that does not provide any easy alternative, we have a *loyalty trap* better illustrated shortly in connection with voting rules.

When the collective subjects entitled to representation were defined by the social structure itself, all interests accounted for were by definition 'special' interests. The only bearer of a general interest was assumed to be the sovereign, himself a former bearer of a special interest who had become 'general' by defeating other special interests in a given territorial area, in the period of time roughly coincident with the formation of the European national states (Pizzorno 1981). But that was more a convenient assumption than a fact, as the better organized interests—around dynastic, educational or professional lines: the nobility, the clergy, the city tradespeople—yielded to the absolute power of the kings by getting special protection, and a substantial influence on the interpretation and administration of the paradigm. Still, the old notion that the ruler was in charge of the protection of the ordinary folk survived. And that early accomplishment of Director's Law reinforced the mediating role of the king, allowing him to answer for other people's respect of the privileged groups' requests. On both accounts, that intermediate position—a kind of *pledge bias*—allowed the closeness between the business community and national state that featured the mercantilism, with a wealth accruing more to the rulers and to the mercantile elite than to the people at large.

Remnants of those historical roots can be still found in the *corporatist bias*. Following our previous reference, we can corroborate it by mentioning the case of the regulation of the Italian chemist's shops, paradigmatic in revealing how the professional associations are ready to protect each other in a collusive web. The protective regulation of chemists survives the decline of their professional responsibility due to the industrial production of drugs. Today not only is the chemist remunerated on a fixed percentage basis of the final price of the drugs (a price regulated itself), but the number of city shops is established by a body controlled by shop owners, a university degree is required to own (not to run!) a shop that, in due time, is bequeathed to the offspring with the title pending for years until one of the children gets the proper qualification. Some time back, a proposal for the elimination of those privileges in order to reduce the National Health bill was soon dropped by the government, notwithstanding its economic and (at face value) electoral advantages. Why? The only explanation can be traced back to the implicit threat that the proposal represented for all the other professional regulations.

It is a fact that the formal denial of association rights did not reduce the effective influence on policymaking exerted by special interests, as the institutional setting was still the old one. That led to what could be called the *pretended invisibility bias*, that is the voiced denial of any political pressure, still claimed in a number of democratic countries. The protection of the traditional interests therefore become latent, and brings about the formation of concealed groups operating across party lines, which influence the screening process through a shrewd management of the formal lines of power.

As the estates gradually lost power until their formal abolition by the liberal regime, the early democratic experience was characterized by the narrowness of suffrage and, following the French revolution, by the denial of association rights. Still, new rules of political representation applied within the logic of the old paradigm and of the traditional links, pushed the incumbent politicians to try to manufacture their own electorate. That explains the attempts to influence the composition of the constituencies for partisan purposes, thus inverting the logic of political representation. The presence of this *reverse democracy bias* is shown by the British experience of the rotten boroughs, by the American gerrymandering, and by the Italian electoral results merrily arranged by the Government appointed Prefects until the outbreak of the First World War. In the latter case at least, a number of reasons combined to make that bias worthwhile for both sides: the moderate Italian voters of the time expected that indication in order to avoid the risk of 'wasting' their vote and of losing the contacts required by the loyalty links.

The geographical definition of the units of political representation has remained formally unchanged, though accompanied by the rhetoric of universal representation. Certainly better than any explicit aggregations according to functional or interest lines, that persistence is somehow puzzling and it is not easy to identify the bias that it could induce, especially if we take into account how such a quasi-random selection increases the transaction costs of interests in search of protection. Some authors distinguish geographical from electoral constituencies, by identifying the latter in terms either of pivotal subgroups of constituents (Peltzman 1984) or along functional or ideological lines, an occurrence made easier by proportional representation (invoked by John Stuart Mill for that purpose). On the other hand, the question of whether all members of a constituency are weighted equally is handled by Lohman's (1995) elaboration of Down's passionate minorities: representatives do not react mechanically to the power in numbers, but take into account differential participation incentives. And it is noteworthy how modern party politics retains most of those biases, though making the underlying relationships clearer.

5. A detour on the rise, and decline, of political parties

The liberal attempt to limit the political relationships to the direct ones between the individual and the state was soon overcome with the recognition that any group of people sharing the same interest could get organized to promote that interest. Given the traditional ideological syntax, it took time before the new institutions were able to express new interests with the organization of mass political parties. Although representing a fraction of the population, those parties adopted broad platforms strongly emphasizing the representation of general interests. After all, the notion of a lobby as of a group of persons who attempt to influence legislators at the expense of more general interests has been made clear by modern democracy. However, though recognizing the biases of the former syntax, the new party ideologies had to be flexible enough to establish new loyalties while retaining the old ones. At the same time, the multiplication of ideologies and their ensuing competition anticipated a decline soon to be speeded up by the fall of information costs. It was with representative institutions that a distinction of capacities was introduced, with an explicit identification of interests that modified the interaction between the ideology and the decision process, a modification far from settled.

For the moment, let us observe how that ideological competition brought about the need of new procedural and value-empty rules that gave substance to the notion of the rule of law. The constitutionalization and the extension of competition have accompanied the evolution, first, over a range of institutional environments. The separation of powers, the independence and guarantees that protect many bodies, decentralization (upward or downward) re-enforced the competitive push, providing each centre of influence with more capacities to control and limit the set of other centres' choices. In addition, and this is the second innovation, the democratic state introduced special ties of an electoral nature that helped to steer the entire competitive dynamics explicitly towards the people's demands. However, the strengthening of the vertical dimension revealed new ways of shielding politicians from voters' control. A brief reflection on the logic of political representation will help the analysis of how collusion can creep back and influence the working of democratic institutions.

In order to reflect on the role of political parties, let us recall how the notion of political exchange—voting and other forms of political support in exchange for opinion representation[10]—poses three problems relative to the rational calculations of the participants: Why are people politically active? What does the exchange consist of? What are the guarantees that make it possible? Either when the main concern is with the choice of the government (the Schumpeterian approach) or with the representation of opinions (the Millian approach), the issue is how to guarantee both sides' performances and to protect their expectations against possible non-fulfilment: How to be sure that the candidate, once elected, will carry out what he or she promised over a period of time and on often unpredictable matters? And, vice versa, how can the representative be guaranteed against any fickleness on the part of the voters? The property rights that make the political exchange viable are provided by political parties, seen as an organization characterized by a temporal horizon that is much broader than that of single candidates and voters. By reducing the risks and the costs of political activity,[11] the vertical relationship of voter/representative, crucial for the vitality of the system, is encouraged. However, to carry out that vertical support function, a party uses an organizational structure based on horizontal relations which on one hand involve the cadres at various levels, and on the other involve the relationship between leaders, elected representatives and in general those chosen to occupy positions at the top of the various centres of power.

In doing what it is supposed to in the social division of work—represent opinions and influence public decisions—a party can use various combinations of vertical and horizontal inputs.[12] If two extremes at once come to mind—a party that exists solely in its function of the vertical relationship against a hierarchical party in which the leadership has a predominant role—there are institutional factors that tend to reinforce the horizontal links. For example, with the broadening of state activity and of the complexity of the matters involved, the platforms become more articulate and intricate, thus expanding the discretion of the leadership in the choice of solutions to adopt, priorities to follow, compromises to accept, etc. We have therefore to consider the factors that generate a collusive environment favourable to lobby pressure through the weakening of the vertical spur and the strengthening of the horizontal links.

Consider, for example, the impact of *electoral rules*. As shown elsewhere (Galeotti 1994), a proportional rule helps to generate what was previously identified as the loyalty trap, by reducing the possibility for swing voters to 'punish' the incumbents.[13] Moreover, and contrarily to the market case, a large number of parties reduces electoral competition as the gain in terms of a better representation of opinions is offset by a lower political substitution rate that locks the voters into their own choices.[14] In both cases the relationship of voters to representatives gets hardened, and that reduces the uncertainty about voters' reactions and limits the working of competition. Other voting rules, such as the-first-past-the-post one, score better in spurring legislators' attention towards their constituencies, though they present other features able to protect the horizontal links. Apart from the high costs of entry for new parties, it is the length of incumbency that deserves attention. This phenomenon appears in many representative systems, especially in the USA, where the tenure in office of Congressional members has increased by 50 per cent in the first 60 years of this century (Scully 1993) with a reelection rate of over 90 per cent for fifteen of the last nineteen elections (Reed and Schansberg 1992). We do not yet have satisfactory explanations for that lengthening (it could be due to the growth of the public budget, following one of our previous inferences). However, when that longer tenure is associated with other sources of horizontal loyalty (as those described by Coker and Crain 1994), the implications in terms of rent extraction deserve reflection.

6. Horizontal exchanges and demand lobbies

What are the institutions that enforce the allocation agreements among the decision-makers inside each centre of power (the Parliament, the Congress, or other corporate decision-makers)? The question is not simple, because the risk of conspiracy against the public is always present, whilst stable outcomes are necessary to avoid abrupt policy twists and inconsistencies. The previous discussion in terms of party influence reminds one of Schumpeter's remark that 'party and machine politicians . . . constitute an attempt to regulate political competition exactly similar to the corresponding practices of a trade association'. And are the risks of collusion lower when the property rights supporting the horizontal exchanges are provided by the Committee system in the US Congress (Weingast and Marshall 1988) or by a permanent and non-partisan bureaucracy in parliamentary systems, as submitted by Breton (1996)? The recognition of that supporting function is not as neutral as it appears, since it could spill over and be used to protect collusive agreements leading to excessive returns. The suspicion is fully confirmed by the attention that powerful demand lobbies appear to pay for the activities of congressional committees. Staying with the US evidence—though the same happens elsewhere[15]—if campaign contributions do not seem to affect the vertical

relationships between voters and representatives,[16] things are different at the committee level. When Hall and Wayman (1990) conclude that 'House members and interest
group representatives are parties to an implicit cooperation agreement', it not only
confirms the presence of a horizontal exchange, but it shows that an efficient vertical
framework does not represent sufficient protection.[17] That can happen because in the
Congress—as in any legislature

only a small fraction of the decisions that shape a bill ever go to a vote, either in committee or on
the floor. The vast majority are made in authoring a legislative vehicle, formulating amend-
ments, negotiating specific provisions or report language behind the scenes, developing legislative strategy, and in other activities that require substantial time, information, and energy on the
part of member and staff (Hall and Wayman 1990, 814).

And that explains why it is the buying of politicians' time and attention, as well as the
number of lobbying contacts (Wright 1990), that is relevant in affecting decision-
making. The effective neutrality of that apparently neutral supply of information
depends on the competitiveness of the environment.

Still within the same logic, the apparent paradox of campaign contributions going
to legislators already favourable to a group's position disappears. True, there can be
uncertainty about the distribution of preferences inside the lobbying group so that the
opportunity of access is a prerequisite for later influence (Austin-Smith 1995), but in
general contributions enshrine relationships and convergence that are already present.
Those results confirm how there are interests that tend to remain more prominent than
others, both when the issue at stake evokes high salience in the geographical constituency and when it does not (Hall and Wayman 1990). And here the occurrence of
politicians' opportunism (reverse-shirking in Breton's language) becomes true when a
representative is able to exploit a loyal and imperfectly informed constituency. Bender
and Lott (1996) are right in underlining that the efficiency of the screening performance of a political system cannot be limited to the study of how candidates solve the
trade-off between serving voters and serving interest groups, as what is needed is a
more general analysis of the efficiency of the political market as a whole, a theme that
in this paper we have tried to handle in its historical perspective. However much more
specific research is required.

7. Political information and the judgemental twist of politics

Collective action is difficult to set in motion because of individual shirking, and once
there with its paraphernalia of centralized decision-making and coercion, it is difficult
to constrain because of the opportunism of political leaders. Given that basic two-
faceted problem of knowing demand and controlling supply, we approached the study
of interests' influence by considering a political system in its structural role of sifting
out which demands deserve satisfaction. If democracy is different in selecting the
interests to protect, it is not because of the wishful notion of a government 'of the

people, by the people and through the people', but rather because of the efficiency of its screening performance. We sketched the ingredients of an analytical framework attempting to assess the virtues and limits of different screening regimes. As a general scheme, we submitted that the regulation of the market for political influence is performed through an ideological syntax and an institutional architecture, to reduce communication costs and appointees' shirking. The reduction of information costs and stronger competitive settings characterize the evolution of the screening devices, reducing the relevance of the ideological component and entrenching the rights of the different centres of power. If our frame captures a basic trend towards a reduction of the space for political collusion, two consequences should follow, related to the activities of pressure groups and to the evolution of the monitoring role played by citizens.

Defining pressure groups in terms of demand lobbies underlines their basic task of providing information, be it through social mobilization, favour buying, ideological pressure or campaign contributions. The political impact of that vertical information depends on how the degree of competition[18] affects the application of the ideological syntax. Better levels of information and the statutory protection of competition make explicit the confrontation among competing interests and reduce the relevance of the ideological component. It is in a world implicitly assumed to be devoid of any ideology such that Stigler (1972) saw the elimination of unnecessary returns to the incumbents as the specific role of political competition. But, then, the role of citizens and the features of politics itself undergo a change.

That brings us to the second consideration concerning what can be interpreted as a judgemental twist of politics, a twist that expands the role of voters as political judges (thus different from any normative claim to give power to the judges as guardians of the political constitutions). Scattered contemporary evidence seems to support that inference. Think of the testimonies and hearings before legislative committees and the comments appending to the statutes in order to put the measure in the context of the avowed interests of the various groups: in Sweden the 'comments' of outside interests are attached to government's bills, even when they contradict the bill's purposes. The growing request to introduce independent agencies dealing with matters traditionally belonging to the political mediation (consumers' and environmental protection, ombudsmen, etc.) can be interpreted as a search for a more technical and better-informed balance of interests.

The role of voters as judges is not new in that Pericles remarked 'if few of us are originators, we are all sound judges of a policy' (Hornblower 1991, p. 295). The people always had the last word in passing judgement on the eventual impact of political screening devices, and they, of course, can never be fooled in the *ex post* evaluation of what has been achieved by the chosen policies. In that sense, Popper's point quoted at the beginning of this paper underlines how the cost of enacting a negative judgement qualifies different political regimes. The presence of that *ex post* assessment involving the entire population is a matter of historical evidence, and the apparent nature of popular quiescence represents the more or less founded wager of many would-be revolutionaries. Modern elections allow politicians to anticipate citizens' reactions, and it is easy to understand why politicians prefer to encourage a prospect voting that gets citizens involved *ex ante* in the screening process. Voters oblige, but they retain intact their freedom to change their minds.

Notes

The author is grateful to Kimberley Scharf for her comments on a preliminary version of this paper, to Ron Wintrobe for useful discussions which helped to make a number of points clearer, and to three referees for their perceptive comments.

1. Pareto and the other scholars working in his tradition dismissed the alleged novelty of a majority rule, denied any specifics to democracy and deemed different forms of government as mere facades for the continuity of the oligarchic power.
2. The latest episode of which is the story of the bandit turned autocrat told by McGuire and Olson (1996).
3. As some authors have been tempted to do, from Mancur Olson to Gary Becker. Olson's emphasis on the positive relationship between group size and the relevance of the interest it pursues is neither necessary nor sufficient to qualify the evenness of the outcome. The fact that a strong lobby of physicians promoted and got approved a public health plan with a view to personal gain does not impinge upon the social value of that plan. Moreover, putting the thrust of the solution on large groups pursuing more encompassing interests represents a *petitio principii*, as public action itself is called, exactly for that purpose.
4. 'A sense of what the good society should and can be like' (Musgrave 1996); 'an internally consistent set of propositions that make both proscriptive and prescriptive demands on human behavior. All ideologies have implications for . . . where power appropriately resides' (Hinich and Munger 1994).
5. Calvert (1995) underlines how phenomena such as rhetoric, ritual, and symbolic speech can help to transmit messages—though purely cheap talk—essential to the development of co-ordination.
6. See the words used by Walter Bagehot, as quoted in Breton (1996, 125).
7. We use the term in the sense suggested by Sah and Stiglitz (1986) in reference to the distribution of decision-making authority and the ability to process information.
8. Remember, for example, the Parliament of Paris which registered the royal decrees in France before the Revolution.
9. In medieval Europe, when the Christian creed was pervasive, the attention was on power-holders; in the Communist Soviet Union, where the party was dominant, the formal attention was on ideological correctness.
10. Galeotti and Breton (1986) develop John Stuart Mill's remark that people vote so as to be able to count on the presence in that 'Congress of opinions' which is the Parliament of their own 'political opinion'.
11. The party has every interest in investing and protecting its reputation and avoiding short-term gains at the expense of long-term ones. It is therefore motivated to control the activities of the representatives and to offer instruments for voters' participation.
12. For example, it can mobilize public opinion (by organizing debates, campaigns and protest

meetings) or insert (or withdraw) a topic from the political agenda, ask for more power for parliamentary commissions, re-affirm the political nature of certain appointments etc.

13. When votes are translated into seats, the different electoral systems can magnify or reduce the impact of variations of vote shares with different effects on vertical bonds: for the same expected variation of votes, the less proportional systems generate larger risks of failure.

14. Galeotti and Merlo (1995) show that in some instances the stability of electoral results can prompt political parties to Cabinet reshuffles associated with a permanent partisan control of key ministries in order to maximize kickbacks from contractors.

15. For the Italian case, see Visco 1991; it could be submitted that breaking the horizontal networks of power producing 'unnecessary returns' has been the target of the recent prosecution undertaken by the Italian Courts.

16. The efficiency of the US electoral market is confirmed in the review work of Bender and Lott 1996.

17. The authors conclude the above sentence with the remark that 'the constraints on member behavior and the rational calculations of group strategists limit the extent to which votes become the basis for exchange'.

18. That recalls the proposal of Galbraith (1990) turned novelist when he speaks of a Maecenas funding any lobby ready to support the opposite position voiced by any actual lobby.

References

Austin-Smith, David (1995) 'Campaign Contribution and Access', *The American Political Science Review*, 89: 566–81.

Baumol, William (1952, revised 1965) *Welfare Economics and the Theory of the State*. London: Longmans.

Bender, Bruce and Lott, John R. (1996) 'Legislator Voting and Shirking: A Critical Review of the Literature', *Public Choice*, 87: 67–100.

Brennan, Geoffrey and Buchanan, James (1980) *The Power to Tax*. Cambridge: Cambridge University Press.

Breton, Albert (1996) *Competitive Governments*. Cambridge: Cambridge University Press.

Bruno, Michael and Sachs, Jeffrey (1985) *The Economics of Worldwide Stagflation*. Boston, MA: Harvard University Press.

Calvert, Randall L. (1995) 'The Rational Choice Theory of Social Institutions: Cooperation, Coordination and Communication', in Banks, Jeffrey S. and Hanushek, Eric A. (eds.), *Modern Political Economy*. Cambridge: Cambridge University Press, 216–67.

Coker, David and Crain, Mark (1994) 'Legislative Committees as Loyalty-Generating Institutions', *Public Choice*, 81: 195–221.

Galbraith, John K. (1990) *A Tenured Professor*. Boston, MA: Houghton Mifflin.

Galeotti, Gianluigi (1994) 'On Proportional Non-Representation', *Public Choice*, 80: 359–70.

Galeotti, Gianluigi and Breton, Albert (1986) 'An Economic Theory of Political Parties', *Kyklos*, 39: 47–65.

Galeotti, Gianluigi and Merlo, Antonio (1994) 'Political Collusion and Corruption in a Representative Democracy', *Public Finance/Finance Publique*, 49: 232–43.

Hall, Richard and Wayman, Frank (1990) 'Buying Time: Moneyed Interests and the Mobilization of Bias in Congressional Committees', *American Political Science Review*, 84: 797–820.

Hinich, Melvin and Munger, Michael (1994) *Ideology and the Theory of Political Choice*. Ann Arbor: University of Michigan Press.

Hornblower, S. (1991) *A Commentary on Thucydides*. Oxford: Oxford University Press.

Lohmann, Susanne (1995) 'A Signaling Model of Competitive Political Pressure', *Economics and Politics*, 7: 181–206.

McGuire, Martin C. and Olson, Mancur (1996) 'The Economics of Autocracy and Majority Rule: The Invisible Hand and the Use of Force', *Journal of Economic Literature*, 34: 72–96.

Musgrave, Richard A. (1996) 'The Role of the State in Fiscal Theory', *International Tax and Public Finance*, 3: 247–58.

North, Douglass (1981) *Structure and Change in Economic History*. New York: Norton.

North, Douglass (1990) *Institutions, Institutional Change and Economic Performance*. Cambridge: Cambridge University Press.

Peltzman, Sam (1984) 'Constituent Interest and Congressional Voting', *Journal of Law and Economics*, 27: 181–210.

Pizzorno, Alessandro (1981) 'Interests and Parties in Pluralism', in Berger, Suzanne (ed.), *Organizing Interests in Western Europe*. Cambridge: Cambridge University Press, 247–84.

Reed, Robert and Schansberg, Eric (1992) 'The Behavior of Congressional Tenure Over Time: 1953–1991', *Public Choice*, 73: 183–203.

Sah, Raays Kumar and Stiglitz, Joseph (1986) 'The Architecture of Economic Systems: Hierarchies and Polyarchies', *American Economic Review*, 76: 716–27.

Scully, Gerard (1993) 'Congressional Tenure: Myth and Reality', *Public Choice*, 83: 203–19.

Stigler, George (1972) 'Economic Competition and Political Competition', *Public Choice*, 13: 91–106.

Visco, Vincenzo (1991) 'Alcune osservazioni sulla formazione delle decisioni legislative in materia di politica fiscale', *Rivista di diritto finanziario e scienza delle finanze*, 50: 261–87.

Weingast, Barry R. and William, J. Marshall (1988) 'The Industrial Organization of Congress, or, Why Legislatures, like Firms, are not Organized as Markets', *Journal of Political Economy*, 96: 132–63.

Wintrobe, Ronald (1998) *The Economics of Dictatorship*. Cambridge: Cambridge University Press.

Wright, John (1990) 'Contributions, Lobbying, and Committee Voting in the U.S. House of Representatives', *American Political Science Review*, 84: 417–38.

3
Electoral rules and interest groups: the mix of direct and indirect taxation

GIANLUCA FIORENTINI

1. Introduction

This paper describes the fiscal structure of a community as an equilibrium of a non-cooperative game where members of different interest groups—characterized by conflicting objectives—compete to get distributive gains. Their interaction is regulated by a constitution setting the electoral rules and the regulatory framework for the competition between interest groups. In terms of specific economic policies, we focus on how the equilibrium mix of direct and indirect taxation is determined in a community divided into two groups working respectively in the *regular* and *shadow* sectors. In the former agents are subjected both to income and to expenditure taxation while in the latter agents are subjected only to expenditure taxation.[1]

There are two main purposes in the paper. First, to investigate the relations between the number of agents in a given group (workers in the shadow and regular sectors) and its relative influence at the legislative stage under different electoral rules and regulatory frameworks. Second, to understand how these different political mechanisms affect the outcome of the legislative process (mix of direct and indirect taxation). In this respect, among other results, we show that when a small minority of agents work in the shadow sector its political influence is highest under strictly proportional electoral rules and when there are no limits to the contributions of interest groups. In its turn such an institutional setting brings about a fiscal mix which relies heavily on income taxation and therefore provides further incentives to enlarge the shadow sector.

In Section 2 we discuss the relevant literature on the interaction between the activities of the interest groups and the features of the electoral rules. In Section 3, we introduce the basic elements of the model and analyse the resulting fiscal equilibria in a relatively general setting. To develop the analysis for specific functional forms, Section 4 investigates the working of the electoral model with a ban on interest groups' activities. Section 5 deals with the effects of such activities when members are unable to undertake binding commitments in supplying contributions. This allows us to quantify the extent of the comparative advantage enjoyed by agents in the shadow sector in the competition between interest groups. A closer analysis of the sources of such comparative advantage is presented in Section 6 which investigates the effects of cooperative agreements between members due to the emergence of well-established interest groups. Section 7 concludes the paper with a summary of the main results.

2. The background literature

The issue of the relative weight of electoral rules and interest groups in the political mechanism has always been a central topic in political science and, more recently, in public choice. The literature in this field presents two opposite viewpoints. The demand-side theorists stress the exclusive role of the competition among interest groups in shaping legislation.[2] In this approach, the institutions involved in the electoral competition, as well as in the competition between interest groups, are fully responsive to the intensity of preference expressed by different groups demanding legislation. Votes can be bought, political preferences can be manipulated, and even constitutional constraints can be violated provided that there is a sufficient willingness to pay for producing political pressure. In other words, the transaction costs to obtain desired legislation imposed by the existing institutions do not represent a significant obstacle to competition in the market for legislation. On the contrary, the supply-side theorists argue that interest groups' activities are rigidly constrained by electoral and political institutions.[3] In this approach, the actors and bodies (assemblies, committees and bureaus) that supply collective decisions can impose transaction costs to interest groups in such a way as to make them virtually ineffective.[4] It follows that the agents active on the supply side—politicians, bureaucrats and judges—end up having substantial discretion over legislation and its enforcement.

Becker's (1983, 1985) models of competition among interest groups are among the most influential contributions in the demand-side literature. Such models avoid the analysis of electoral or constitutional rules and the political mechanism is entirely described in terms of the interaction between members of the interest groups. More precisely, agents finance their groups' activity, and the groups then compete between themselves to bid for favourable legislation (or to avoid unfavourable legislation). Becker shows that in equilibrium the members' investment in lobbying crucially depends on the dead-weight costs imposed on different groups by the legislation at stake. Hence, the competition between interest groups brings about efficient outcomes since the emergence of heavy dead-weight costs on other groups would elicit their reaction and would not represent an equilibrium.

Becker's approach has been criticized for different reasons.[5] The most straightforward criticism is that in his model the institutional framework plays no role. This would not be a decisive point *per se*, since Becker's focus on agents' behaviour inside the interest groups can justify a black-boxed version of the institutional setting in which they compete. However, the objection becomes more serious given that Becker's con-clusion on the efficiency of the legislative outcome depends on the exclusion from the analysis of the institutions—legislative bodies and committees—which can increase the costs of political transactions. Accordingly, Becker's approach tends to overestim-ate the ability of interest groups in responding to the intensity of preferences of their members.

More recently, at least two lines of research have tried to explore models where both demand and supply elements coexist in the analysis of collective decision-making.[6] First, Coughlin et al. (1990a, 1990b) build a Downsian model of electoral competition where an incumbent faces a rival and voters are divided into different interest groups whose members have the same utility function over the candidates' proposals.[7] The two candidates maximize their expected plurality as they know only the distributions of the ideological bias affecting voters' decisions. In such a framework, interest groups represent an analytical device to sort out voters in homogeneous groups as for the welfare consequences of the policies chosen, but they do not invest economic resources to influence legislation. In this respect, Coughlin et al. emphasize the supply-side elements in the analysis of collective decision-making.

Secondly, Magee et al. (1989), building on a research project begun in the early 1970s, analyse the competition between interest groups. In their approach the latter do not represent large sections of the electorate, but more narrowly defined groups of economic agents investing resources in contributions to electoral campaigns. Votes can be bought as the electorate is assumed to be rationally uninformed over the con-sequences of the legislation at stake. Accordingly, the institutional features of the electoral competition do not influence the economic policies which emerge as the outcome of the political process. Indeed, the only reference to institutional elements is a measure of the effectiveness of the contributions to candidates in shifting their prob-ability of success. In this respect, Magee et al. underline the demand-side elements in the analysis of collective decision-making.

3. The basic model

In this section we present a model which builds on the electoral competition described in Coughlin et al. (1990a, 1990b), but which integrates such analysis with a richer de-scription of the interest groups' activities such as that provided in Magee et al. (1989). Moreover, with respect to each of the above approaches we introduce some new elements. First, in the Coughlin et al. (1990a) model, candidates are the only players in the electoral competition which leads to collective decisions since voters—as members of interest groups—play no active role other than to cast their votes. However, we believe that decentralized agents, mainly through the activity of interest groups, play a more relevant part in collective decision-making than is the case in standard Downsian models. Therefore, we allow for a strategic interaction between agents contributing to interest groups' activities which then influence the electoral competition. Second, we differentiate our approach from Magee *et al.* (1989) since we pay greater attention to the institutional elements of the competition between interest groups.

In our model, the outcomes of the electoral competition and of the competition between interest groups depend on two major institutional features: the electoral rules for the legislative body which regulate the access to political representation for groups of different sizes, and the transaction costs incurred in transforming economic resources into political influence.

The model consists of two hierarchically linked games. In the former, which describes the competition between interest groups, each member of a group chooses how much to contribute, given the other members' contributions, in order to modify the candidates' policies. In the latter, two candidates compete in a probabilistic electoral context, selecting such policies to maximize their expected plurality.[8]

3.1. The electoral competition

Following Coughlin *et al.* (1990a, 1990b), in the competition between candidates the government (g) and the opposition (o) choose $z_g \in Z$ and $z_o \in Z$, respectively, in order to maximize their expected plurality, where $Z \subseteq R$ is a non-empty, compact, and convex set of feasible economic policies. Voters are exogenously sorted into m interest groups, where group i has n_i members with identical interests on the single issue on which the elections are contested. The probability that an individual j in group i votes for candidate g (o) depends on two elements.

First, the utility level under the two policy proposals is described by the following functions: $U_{ij}(z_g) \equiv U_i(q_i, s_{ij}, z_g)$ and $U_{ij}(z_o) \equiv U_i(q_i, s_{ij}, z_o)$, where q_i is the given endowment of a private good—equal across members of the same group—and s_{ij} is the individual contribution to the activity of the organized interest, which is taken as given by the two candidates. By assumption, $U_i(\cdot)$ are continuous and concave functions in z and q_i. The second component is an *ideological bias* defining the value voters in group i attach to having g elected which is not related to the proposed policies. Such bias is randomly distributed across members of each group. Hence, candidates cannot be sure to capture all votes of the members of an interest group even if the proposed policy maximizes their payoffs.

The two candidates take into account the probabilistic nature of the ideological bias looking at the distribution of the random variable b_i which is assumed to be uniform over a real interval, symmetric around the value 1 and with density a_i.[9] For the voter j in group i the conditional probability for the event '*i will vote for o given g's choice of z_g and o's choice of z_o*', conditional on the value b_i, is given by:[10]

$$p_{ij}^g(b_i, z_g, z_o) = \begin{cases} 1 & \text{if} \quad b_i U_{ij}(z_g) > U_{ij}(z_o) \\ 0 & \text{if} \quad b_i U_{ij}(z_g) < U_{ij}(z_o). \end{cases}$$

On this basis, to link the electoral game with the competition between interest groups, we assume that the density of the rectangular distribution of b_i for agents in group i is:

$$a_i = \frac{1}{n_i}\left(\frac{n_i^\gamma \sum\limits_{j=1}^{n_i} s_{ij}}{\sum\limits_{i=1}^{m} n_i^\gamma \sum\limits_{j=1}^{n_i} s_{ij}}\right),$$

where γ is a measure of the comparative disadvantage for small groups to reach political representation in the legislative body. The idea is that members' contributions are used to produce and distribute information concerning the effects of policy proposals on members' payoffs and to mislead non-members on how their payoffs depend on the issue at stake.[11] Hence, the investment in the activities of the interest group i reduce the relevance of the ideological bias in the voting decisions of its members. This is reflected in a reduction in the dispersion of the distribution of b_i as well as in an increase in the dispersion of the distributions of b_k for $k \neq i$.

Moreover, a_i is also affected by the specific features of the electoral mechanism which differentiates the costs of political representation for agents in groups of different size. Such features can be measured in terms of the degree of disproportionality of the electoral rules or the degree of concentration of the political parties in the legislative body.[12] The reason for including such a parameter is that the relative ability of groups with different size to produce information concerning the effects of given policies depends on the features of the electoral system. More specifically, we assume that systems where only few large political parties are represented in the legislative body (higher γ) give a comparative advantage to larger groups because they can establish a closer relationship with such parties. In its turn this provides easier access to multiple financial sources ranging from public funding at the legislative level to bribes at the administrative level.

Under the above assumptions, for any $z_g \in Z$ and $z_o \in Z$:

$$\Pr(ij \text{ votes for } o) = \Pr\left(b_i < \frac{U_{ij}(z_o)}{U_{ij}(z_g)}\right)$$

and the cumulative distribution function for b_i becomes:

$$F_{ij} = \Pr(b_i < x) = \begin{cases} 1 & \text{if } x \geq 1 + \frac{1}{2a_i} \\ a_i x & \text{if } 1 - \frac{1}{2a_i} < x < 1 + \frac{1}{2a_i}. \\ 0 & \text{if } x \leq 1 - \frac{1}{2a_i} \end{cases} \tag{1}$$

In order to solve the electoral competition model one needs to consider only the case in (1) where the ratio between the utilities U_{ij} under the two alternative policies belongs to the domain of the ideological bias term. This is because if this were not the case one of the two candidates' expected number of votes would be zero, which is in contradiction with the assumption that they are both maximizing their expected plurality. Using (1) and the assumptions above Coughlin *et al.* (1990a) show that:

$$\Pr(ij \text{ votes for } o) = a_i(U_{ij}(z_o)/U_{ij}(z_g)),$$
$$\Pr(ij \text{ votes for } g) = (1 - a_i)(U_{ij}(z_o)/U_{ij}(z_g)),$$

which, summed across agents in different interest groups allow the expected number of votes for the opposition and the government to be predicted and therefore the expected plurality functions to be obtained. Coughlin *et al.* prove that a Nash equilibrium for this electoral game exists and, on the basis of a result in Coughlin and Nitzan (1981), that the necessary conditions to obtaining such an equilibrium are equivalent to those required to maximize the following fictitious social welfare function:

$$\sum_{i=1}^{m} a_i \sum_{j=1}^{n_i} \log(U_{ij}(z)), \tag{2}$$

with $\sum_{i=1}^{m} n_i a_i = 1$. Hence, an asymmetric Nash bargaining between interest groups—where payoffs at the threat point are normalized to zero for both players—can be regarded as the reduced-form of a model of electoral competition where different institutional features are explicitly dealt with. This equivalence will be used in the analysis of the competition between interest groups, where voters invest in their activities in order to obtain more favourable legislation. Indeed, the constitutional constraint in (2) will allow us to analyse how interest groups affect legislation in different ways according to the institutional setting where they operate as defined by the type of electoral rules and of the regulation of their activities.

3.2. The competition between interest groups

We can now investigate the competition between interest groups.[13] In the above electoral game interest groups aim at reducing the dispersion of the ideological bias among their members, making them more aware of the effects of different policies on their utilities. A reduced dispersion benefits a group because it makes the candidate's equilibrium platforms more receptive to the group's preferences. As we have seen, the dispersion of the bias depends on the members' contributions to the group and on the possibility for groups of different sizes to acquire political representation in the legislative body. Thus, contributions do not directly influence the electoral competition as if they were used for buying votes. On the contrary, the voters, who are also members of interest groups, and not the candidates, are the principals in the agency problem inherent to representative democracies.[14]

We consider a community made up of a finite number (N) of agents exogenously distributed into two groups. Agents in group b work in the shadow (*black*) sector of the economy where they pay no income taxes, whereas agents in group r work in the *regular* sector where such taxation is enforced. There is no mobility across sectors. Agents in both sectors are subjected to the same expenditure taxation. To rationalize this situation one can think that in the labour market the contractual agreements undertaken in sector r allow for fiscal inspections at zero cost while monitoring costs are infinite in sector b.

Both sectors produce the same homogeneous commodity, whose price is normalized to one, using the following linear technology:

$$Q = n_r l_r + n_b l_b,$$

where n_i is the number of agents active in each sector, l_i is their exogenous labour supply ($i = r, b$), Q is the total output. The net equilibrium wage in the regular sector is equal to the value of the labour's marginal productivity $w_r = (1 - t_l)$ where t_l is the tax rate on labour income. The output can be either consumed or invested in contributions to interest groups. Assuming that the investment in contributions to interest groups, as well as the direct consumption, is subjected to expenditure taxation, the fiscal constraint can be written as:

$$T = t_l l_r n_r + t_y [l_b n_b + (1 - t_l) n_r l_r],$$

where t_y is the tax rate on expenditures and T is the exogenously given level of fiscal revenue to be collected. Since T is exogenous, the above expression for the fiscal constraint can be written as:

$$(1 - t_y) = \frac{Y}{L_r (1 - t_l) + L_b},$$

where $Y = Q - T$ is the disposable aggregate income gross of the contributions to interest groups, and $L_i = l_i n_i$. In what follows we assume that the candidates in the electoral competition ignore the contributions of individual agents, and treat them as if they all contribute equally ($\bar{s}_i$). Accordingly, the problem faced by a representative agent j of group i in the game between members of different interest groups, can be written as follows:[15]

$$\max_{s_{rj} \in S_{rj}} \quad U_{rj} = U((1 - t_l)(1 - t_y)l_r - c(s_{rj})) \quad \forall j, \tag{3}$$

s.t.

$$t_l = \arg\max \quad C = N_{sr} \log U((1 - t_l)(1 - t_y)l_r - c(\bar{s}_r)) +$$
$$+ N_{sb} \log U((1 - t_y)l_b - c(\bar{s}_b)), \tag{3a}$$

$$t_y = (T - t_l L_r) / (L_r (1 - t_l) + L_b), \tag{3b}$$

where $N_{sr} = n_r^{\gamma+1} \bar{s}_r / (n_r^{\gamma+1} \bar{s}_r + n_b^{\gamma+1} \bar{s})$ and $N_{sb} = n_b^{\gamma+1} \bar{s}_b / (n_r^{\gamma+1} \bar{s}_r + n_b^{\gamma+1} \bar{s}_b)$. In (3) U_{ij} are assumed to be defined, continuous, and bounded for $\forall s_{ij} \in S_{ij}$, where $S_{ij} \subseteq R$ is a compact and convex set for $\forall i, j$. Moreover, $c(s_i)$, with $c' > 0$, and $c'' > 0$, is the transaction cost for the unit of contributions to an interest group.[16]

The constraint (3a) shows how the individual maximization problem is linked with the rules for collective decision-making. Its adoption underlines the fact that although voters (members of interest groups) are the principals in the collective decision mechanism, they are subjected to the constitutional constraints embodied in (3a). In the welfare economics approach to public decision-making (3a) represents the collective objective function and (3) is an incentive compatibility constraint. Indeed, such a format could also be adopted here, where the possibility for decentralized agents to act through contributions to interest groups results in an additional constraint for the collective decision-maker. However, such a format would obscure the strategic elements introduced by (3a) in the agents' choice of contributing to their interest groups.

This approach allows us to characterize the fiscal rules with respect to changes in the following exogenous variables: (1) the individual labour supply, (2) the distribution of agents across sectors, (3) the features of the electoral rules for the legislative body, and (4) the regulation of the contributions to interest groups. Given these variables, the model determines the level of contributions to each interest group, the fiscal rules, and the relative after-tax allocations.

We first deal with a generic form of the utility function in (3) to determine a few general features of the equilibrium in the contributions to interest groups. In the following sections we will adopt a more specific form in order to derive further results. The necessary condition for equilibrium in the electoral competition is:

$$n_r^{\gamma+1}\bar{s}_r\left(\frac{\partial U_r}{\partial t_l}U_b\right) - n_b^{\gamma+1}\bar{s}_b\left(\frac{\partial U_b}{\partial t_l}U_r\right) = 0, \tag{4}$$

which allows us to characterize the relations between the fiscal policy chosen at the electoral equilibrium and the exogenous variables of the model. Implicitly differentiating (4):

$$\frac{dt_l}{dn_r} < 0, \ \frac{dt_l}{dn_b} > 0, \ \frac{dt_l}{dl_r} > 0, \ \frac{dt_l}{dl_b} < 0,$$

$$n_r \gtrless n_b \ \Rightarrow \ \frac{dt_l}{d\gamma} \lessgtr 0, \ n_r \gtrless n_b \ \Rightarrow \ \frac{dt_y}{d\gamma} \gtrless 0,$$

$$\frac{dt_l}{d\bar{s}_r} < 0, \ \frac{d^2t_l}{d\bar{s}_r^2} > 0, \ \frac{dt_l}{d\bar{s}_b} > 0, \ \frac{d^2t_l}{d\bar{s}_b^2} < 0.$$

An increase in the number of agents active in a given group reduces their fiscal burden while an increase in their labour supply has the opposite effect. Moreover, irrespective of the relative size of a group, a growth in the individual contributions leads to a more favourable fiscal equilibrium for its members while an increase in γ makes the fiscal burden heavier for agents in the smaller group.

Let us now go back to the analysis of how the fiscal mix affects agents' utilities. To understand the incentives for members of different groups to invest in contributions, we observe that:

$$\frac{\partial U_r}{\partial t_l} = U_r'(\cdot)\left(\frac{-L_b l_r Y}{D}\right) < 0, \quad \frac{\partial U_b}{\partial t_l} = U_b'(\cdot)\left(\frac{L_r l_b Y}{D}\right) > 0, \tag{5}$$

where $D = L_r(1 - t_l) + L_b$. From the two expressions in (5), if the utility functions are the same across groups, workers in the larger one are characterized by a lower marginal utility from a variation of t_l because the effects of a change in the fiscal mix are shared by a greater number of agents (recall that $T = \bar{T}$).

We can now analyse the equilibrium in the competition between interest groups. The necessary conditions for an equilibrium for agents in the two groups are as follows:[17]

$$F_r = U_r'(\cdot)\left(\frac{-\partial t_l}{\partial \bar{s}_r} \frac{1}{n_r} \frac{l_r L_b Y}{D^2} - c'(s_{rj})\right) = 0,$$

$$F_b = U_b'(\cdot)\left(\frac{\partial t_l}{\partial \bar{s}_b} \frac{1}{n_b} \frac{l_b L_r Y}{D^2} - c'(s_{bj})\right) = 0. \tag{6}$$

PROPOSITION 1. *At least one Nash equilibrium exists.*

PROOF. $S_{ij} \subseteq S$ is compact and convex for all agents, and U_{ij} are assumed as defined, continuous, bounded, and quasi-concave in s_{ij} for $\forall s_{ij} \in S_{ij}$ and for all agents. This ensures that the best reply function of each agent is upper semicontinuous, and by a fixed point argument, that the competition between interest groups has at least one equilibrium. ∎

As all agents in the same group are equally affected by t, face the same cost function in contributing to their group's activities, and their marginal contributions have the same effect on s_i, heuristically, one can show that the intra-group equilibrium is symmetric ($s_{ij} = s_i, i = b, r$). Indeed, from the literature on linear Cournot oligopoly one recalls that if all firms face the same cost and demand functions this is not sufficient to ensure that the equilibrium is symmetric. However, asymmetric equilibria typically arise when fixed costs create discontinuities in the reaction functions. In the present case such discontinuities are ruled out by our assumptions on the cost functions for contributing to interest groups.

PROPOSITION 2. *The Nash equilibrium is unique and stable.*

PROOF. Notice that:

$$F_{rr} = U_r''(\cdot) + U_r'(\cdot)\left(\left(\frac{-\partial^2 t_l}{\partial \bar{s}_r^2} - \frac{2L_r}{D}\left(\frac{\partial t_l}{\partial \bar{s}_r}\right)^2\right)\frac{Y l_r L_b}{n_r^2 D^2} - c''(s_{rj})\right) \tag{7}$$

$$F_{bb} = U_b''(\cdot) + U_b'(\cdot)\left(\left(\frac{-\partial^2 t_l}{\partial \bar{s}_b^2} - \frac{2L_r}{D}\left(\frac{\partial t_l}{\partial \bar{s}_b}\right)^2\right)\frac{Yl_b L_r}{n_b^2 D^2} - c''(s_{bj})\right)$$

are both negative, given (5) and our comparative statics results on (4). Differentiating (6) with respect to s_b and s_r, respectively, we get:

$$F_{rb} = U_r''(\cdot) + U_r'(\cdot)\left(-2\frac{\partial t_l}{\partial \bar{s}_r}\frac{\partial t_l}{\partial \bar{s}_b}\frac{L_r L_b l_r Y}{n_r n_b D^3}\right)$$

$$F_{br} = U_b''(\cdot) + U_b'(\cdot)\left(2\frac{\partial t_l}{\partial \bar{s}_b}\frac{\partial t_l}{\partial \bar{s}_r}\frac{L_b L_r l_b Y}{n_b n_r D^3}\right).$$

(8)

From (7) and (8), the Jacobian of the implicit form of the best reply functions in (6) is negative quasi-definite. This and the assumptions used to prove proposition 1 are sufficient to prove uniqueness and stability.[18] ∎

Expression (6) allows us to characterize more fully the Nash equilibrium in the contributions to interest groups.

PROPOSITION 3. *At the non-cooperative equilibrium we have that*:

$$\frac{s_b^N}{s_r^N} = \frac{n_r^2(\partial U_r / \partial c)c'(s_r)}{n_b^2(\partial U_b / \partial c)c'(s_b)}.$$

PROOF. From the implicit differentiation of (4):

$$\frac{dt_l / ds_r}{dt_l / ds_b} = \frac{n_r^{\gamma+1}(\partial U_r / \partial t_l)U_b}{n_b^{\gamma+1}(\partial U_b / \partial t_l)U_r}.$$

(9)

Equating the necessary conditions (6) for agents in the two sectors:

$$\frac{(dt_l / ds_r)}{(dt_l / ds_b)} = \frac{(\partial U_b / \partial t_l)n_r(\partial U_r / \partial c)c'(s_r)}{(\partial U_r / \partial t_l)n_b(\partial U_b / \partial c)c'(s_b)}.$$

Substituting the latter in (6), and recalling (4), the proposition follows. ∎

Proposition 3 does not allow us to isolate the two different effects at work in determining the differences in interest groups' contributions. First, the *organizational effect* has to do with a problem of intra-group coordination due to the incomplete appropriability of the effects of individual contributions on the fiscal mix. Second, the *institutional effect* reflects the fact that agents in larger groups are individually less affected by a marginal variation in the fiscal mix, when the revenue is kept constant.

To distinguish between these two effects, we assume that interest groups can coordinate their members' investments as they can efficiently control free-riding. In other words, we assume that agents can undertake intra-group binding agreements on how to contribute to their group. The agent's problem in such a cooperative setting is modified as follows:

$$\max_{s_{i1},...,s_{in_i}} \sum_{j=1}^{n_i} U_{ij} = U(l_i, t_l(s_{ij}, S_{-ij}), s_{ij}), \qquad (3')$$

under the constraint (3a) and (3b). Implicitly differentiating (3'), and equating the necessary condition for a maximum for both groups, proposition 3 can be re-written as:

PROPOSITION 4. *If a Nash equilibrium exists, it is such that*:

$$\frac{s_b^c}{s_r^c} = \frac{n_r(\partial U_r / \partial c)c'(s_r)}{n_b(\partial U_b / \partial c)c'(s_b)}.$$

PROOF. See, *mutatis mutandis,* proof of proposition 3. ■

Here, the gap between contributions by members of different groups becomes smaller due to the disappearance of the organizational effect. However, members of the larger group are still characterized by lower contributions in equilibrium. This further asymmetry is due to the institutional effect for which members of the larger group have a lower intensity of preferences towards variations in the fiscal mix when the fiscal revenue is constant.

Finally, let us now examine how different forms of $c(s_i)$ influence the relations shown in propositions 3 and 4. To do so, we assume that all agents in group r are characterized by the following linear utility function $U_r = ((1 - t_l)(1 - t_y)l_r) - cs_r^\lambda)$. Accordingly, the relation in propositions 3 and 4 can be written as:

$$\frac{s_r^N}{s_b^N} = \left(\frac{n_b}{n_r}\right)^{\frac{2}{\lambda}} \quad \text{and} \quad \frac{s_r^C}{s_b^C} = \left(\frac{n_b}{n_r}\right)^{\frac{1}{\lambda}}. \qquad (10)$$

The more convex is the cost function for contributing to interest groups (higher λ), the lower the asymmetry between individual contributions in groups of different sizes. This is irrespective of the existence of organizations whose purpose is to control free-riding. In such a case, however, one can quantify the differences in the equilibrium level of contributions passing from a cooperative to a non-cooperative setting. Moreover, if the value of λ can be set at the constitutional level, it becomes a tool to regulate the competition between interest groups.

4. The regulated setting

To develop the logic of the model for specific functional forms, let us begin with an analysis of the *regulated* setting where a ban against the contributions to interest groups is enforced or, alternatively, the transactions costs for transforming contributions into political pressure are prohibitively high. As for the specific utility function chosen for the analysis, we assume that agents in both sectors maximize their incomes net of taxation and of the costs of contributing to the activity of interest groups.

In the regulated setting, there are no strategic choices left for the decentralized agents so that the fiscal equilibrium can be derived as in a command and control case:

$$\max_{t_l} \quad C = N_{rr} \log((1-t_y)(1-t_l)l_r) + N_{rb} \log((1-t_y)l_b), \tag{11}$$

$$s.t. \quad t_y = \frac{T - t_l L_r}{L_r(1-t_l) + L_b},$$

where $N_{rr} = n_r^{\gamma+1}/(n_r^{\gamma+1} + n_b^{\gamma+1})$ and $N_{rb} = n_b^{\gamma+1}/(n_r^{\gamma+1} + n_b^{\gamma+1})$. From (11) the tax rates are:

$$(1-t_l^R) = \frac{n_r^\gamma l_b}{n_b^\gamma l_r}, \tag{12}$$

$$(1-t_y^R) = \frac{Y n_b^\gamma}{(n_r^{\gamma+1} + n_b^{\gamma+1})l_b}.$$

A few comments on (12) are helpful to compare this model to more complex ones. We shall focus on two analytical elements: the distribution of agents across sectors and the features of the electoral rules for the legislative body. We examine the role of each element, keeping the other constant.

Suppose that $\gamma = 0$, so that the electoral rules are neutral with respect to the distribution of agents across sectors because they are given the same representation in the legislative body irrespective of the size of their group. Under this assumption we can derive some interesting results. First, differences in number do not affect the income tax rate and the distributive role of income taxation becomes clearer. Indeed, t_l vanishes if the pre-distribution incomes are equal and becomes negative when agents in the shadow sector are better off than those working in the regular sector ($l_b > l_r$). Secondly, the tax rate on expenditure depends not only on the difference between pre-distribution incomes, but also on the share of agents active in the regular sector. This is because, for a given fiscal budget, the larger the revenue of agents subjected to income taxation, the lower t_y. Thirdly, the expenditure tax rate depends positively on fiscal revenue. This is not the case for the income tax rate. Hence, although expenditure taxation has an opposite distributive effect to income taxation, the former can hardly become a subsidy, unless for limited fiscal revenues T and for pre-tax income distribution which is very favourable to agents in the regular sector ($l_r > l_b$). Fourthly, the different role of income and expenditure taxation can be better seen when no distributive concerns ($l_r = l_b$) are at work. In such a case only expenditure taxation is used to collect T ($t_l = 0$ and $t_y = (T/Q)$).

PROPOSITION 5. *The electoral equilibrium in the regulated setting is such that*:

$$\gamma > 0, \quad n_r \gtrless n_b \quad \Rightarrow \quad U_r \gtrless U_b,$$
$$\gamma = 0, \quad U_r = U_b \quad \forall n_r, n_b.$$

PROOF. Substituting (12) into (11) we get:

$$U_i = \frac{Yn_i^\gamma}{n_i^{\gamma+1} + n_k^{\gamma+1}} \quad i \neq k = r, b \tag{13}$$

from which the proposition follows. ∎

Differences in the equilibrium utilities depend only on how agents are distributed across sectors and on the features of the electoral rule.[19] When agents are divided equally among groups ($n_r = n_b$) utility levels are equated for all values of γ. More generally, when economic resources cannot be transformed into political pressure, for given n_r and n_b, the equilibrium allocation is mainly determined by the features of the electoral rules. The results obtained in this section are now compared with other settings under which the competition between such groups can take place.

5. The non–cooperative setting

Let us now assume that there is no ban on the supply of contributions to interest groups so that agents in both sectors solve the maximization problem in (3). Assuming that the cost function is quadratic ($c(s_{ij}) = cs_{ij}^2$), and proceeding as in the previous section, one obtains the tax rates as functions of the average contributions to the interest groups ($\bar{s}_i$):

$$(1-t_l) = \frac{l_b \bar{s}_r (Yn_r^\gamma - cn_b \bar{s}_b A)}{l_r \bar{s}_b (Yn_b^\gamma - cn_r \bar{s}_r A)}, \tag{14}$$

$$(1-t_y) = \frac{\bar{s}_b (Yn_b^\gamma - cn_r \bar{s}_r A)}{l_b (n_b^{\gamma+1} \bar{s}_b + n_r^{\gamma+1} \bar{s}_r)},$$

where $A = n_r^\gamma \bar{s}_b - n_b^\gamma \bar{s}_r$. If the average contribution is the same across sectors, the fiscal equilibrium in (14) does not differ from (12). More generally, the possibility of collecting contributions shifts the fiscal equilibrium to the advantage of the group with a larger average supply.

Plugging (14) into the utility functions, the utility levels of agents in both sectors become functions of their average contributions to interest groups:

$$U_{ij} = \frac{n_i^\gamma \bar{s}_i (Y - c(n_i \bar{s}_i^2 + n_k \bar{s}_k^2)) + n_k \bar{s}_k c(\bar{s}_i^2 - s_{ij}^2)}{n_i^{\gamma+1} \bar{s}_i + n_k^{\gamma+1} \bar{s}_k} \quad i \neq k = r, b. \tag{15}$$

The role played by the contributions should now be clearer. Let us assume that $s_{ij} = \bar{s}_i$ and that $\gamma = 0$. In such a case, the individual utilities are the share of the overall income Y equal to the average share of each group's contributions. If the latter are equal across agents in different groups, each agent gets an equal proportion of the aggregate net income.[20] If γ increases, the agents in the larger group, *ceteris paribus*, get larger utility levels through the working of the fiscal mechanism. Moreover, the last term in (15) measures the gains from the opportunistic behaviour inside the interest groups increasing with the difference between the individual and the average contribution.

Under the assumption of Nash conjectures with respect to the decisions of both the $n_i - 1$ agents in the same sector and the agents in the other sector, from (15) one derives the following necessary condition (for agents in sector i):[21]

$$\frac{n_i^{\gamma-1} n_k^{\gamma+1} \bar{s}_k (Y - c(n_k \bar{s}_k^2 + n_i \bar{s}_i^2))}{(n_k \bar{s}_k^{\gamma+1} + n_i \bar{s}_i^{\gamma+1})^2} - 2c s_{ij} = 0 \quad i \neq k = r, b. \tag{16}$$

In (16) the marginal cost of contributing to the activities of interest groups is equated to its marginal revenue.[22] Imposing symmetry within each sector after this point, the individual contribution becomes:

$$s_i^N = \left(\frac{Y n_i^{\gamma-2} n_k^{\gamma}}{cB} \right)^{\frac{1}{2}} \quad i \neq k = r, b, \tag{17}$$

where $B = (n_i^{\gamma-1} n_k^{\gamma-1} N + 2(n_k^{\gamma} + n_i^{\gamma})^2)$ and the subscript j is no longer needed. From (17), for any γ:

$$s_i^N = s_k^N (n_k / n_i) \quad i \neq k = r, b.$$

Here the asymmetry in the contributions across groups is due to the co-existence of the aforesaid organizational and institutional effects. From the equilibrium conditions in (16) one understands the reasons behind the emergence of the organizational effect. A marginal increase of the contribution of agent j in sector i also increases the denominator in the LHS of (17) proportionally to the number of agents in sector i. Hence, the marginal benefits from such investment for agents in the smaller groups fall much more slowly than for those in the larger, while the marginal cost is equal across groups. Agents in the smaller group are therefore in a better position to increase the proportion of contributions of the group as a whole and therefore to increase their utility levels.[23]

Differentiating (17) one can show that $\partial s_i^N / \partial \gamma \leq 0$ which holds with strict equality when $n_r = n_b$. Hence, an institutional setting that creates a comparative disadvantage to reach political representation for small groups decreases the incentives to supply contributions. This is more so the more uneven the distribution of agents across groups. This inverse relation between γ and the individual supply of contributions holds true for agents in both sectors and irrespective of the fact that agents in the smaller group invest more heavily in contributions.

The most direct way to see how the distribution of agents and of shares of contributions affects the fiscal equilibrium is substituting (17) into (14) so that the equilibrium tax rates become:

$$(1-t_l^N) = \frac{l_b n_r^{\gamma-2}(n_r B - n_b^{\gamma-1}C)}{l_r n_b^{\gamma-2}(n_b B - n_r^{\gamma-1}C)}, \tag{18}$$

$$(1-t_y^N) = \frac{n_b^{\gamma-2}Y(n_b B + n_r^{\gamma-1}C)}{l_b B(n_r^\gamma + n_b^\gamma)},$$

where $C = n_r^{\gamma+1} - n_b^{\gamma+1}$.

PROPOSITION 6. $n_r \gtreqless n_b \;\Rightarrow\; t_l^N \gtreqless t_l^R \;\; and \;\; t_y^N \lesseqgtr t_y^R.$

PROOF. By comparing (12) and (18). ∎

For $n_r = n_b$, the regulated and non-cooperative regulated settings bring about the same fiscal equilibrium. In this specific case the equilibrium supply of contributions does not differ between agents of different groups and the distributive implications do not differ from those in the previous section. However, in the more general case of an uneven distribution of agents across sectors, for any given γ, the fiscal equilibrium under a non-cooperative setting is more favourable to agents in the smaller group than under the regulated setting.

PROPOSITION 7. *The electoral equilibrium in the non-cooperative setting is such that:*

$$n_r^{\gamma-1} \gtreqless n_b^{\gamma-1} \;\Rightarrow\; U_r \gtreqless U_b.$$

PROOF. Substituting (18) into (15) we get:

$$U_i = \frac{Y n_i^{\gamma-1}}{(n_i^\gamma + n_k^\gamma)} \left(\frac{2(n_i^\gamma + n_k^\gamma)^2}{n_i^{\gamma-1} n_k^{\gamma-1} + 2(n_i^\gamma + n_k^\gamma)^2} \right) \quad i \neq k = r, b, \tag{19}$$

from which the proposition follows. ∎

For any γ, agents in the smaller group are better off than those in the larger one because of the working of the institutional and organizational effects. However, the level of utility reached in (19) is smaller than that obtained in the regulated setting in (13) due to the assumed wastefulness of the contributions.

The above results allow us to draw some implications for the fiscal structure under the assumption that $n_r > n_b$. First, when non-cooperative agents supply contributions to interest groups, the resulting fiscal equilibrium is shifted to the advantage of those working in the shadow sector. This has as a benchmark the regulated setting, and keeps constant the features of the electoral rules for the legislative body. Secondly, such bias of the fiscal equilibrium in favour of those working in the shadow sector decreases as the electoral rules make it more difficult for small groups to reach representation in the legislative body. Thirdly, as we noticed before, the supply of contributions to interest groups is negatively affected by the degree of convexity of the transaction cost function, (which is here assumed to be quadratic).

6. The cooperative setting

In this section agents in each group can costlessly coordinate their actions, as is approximately the case when well-rooted political institutions (e.g. unions, producers' associations) are at work. As a consequence, we assume that agents maximize the group utility function with respect to their own individual contributions. Following the steps described in the previous sections, the new individual contributions become:

$$s_i^C = \sqrt{\frac{Y n_i^{\gamma+1/2} n_k^{\gamma+3/2}}{2cB'}} \qquad i \neq k = r, b, \tag{20}$$

where $B' = n_i^{\gamma+3/2} n_k^{\gamma+3/2} + (n_k^{\gamma+1/2} + n_i^{\gamma+1/2})^2$. The main features of the non-cooperative supply functions are preserved in the cooperative setting. As before, the supply of contributions to interest groups is inversely related to γ and the marginal transaction costs, while it depends positively on Y. An interesting implication of (20) is that:

$$s_i = s_k \sqrt{(n_k / n_i)} \qquad i \neq k = r, b. \tag{21}$$

The individual supply for agents in the smaller group is still greater than that in the larger group providing a measure of the institutional effect on the contribution to the activity of interest groups. However, it is now possible to isolate such an effect as the difference between cooperative and non-cooperative settings is entirely due to the organizational effect.

PROPOSITION 8. $s_i^C > s_i^N$.

PROOF. Comparing (17) and (20):

$$s_i^C > s_i^N \quad \Leftrightarrow \quad 2(n_i / n_k)^{\gamma+1/2}\left(1 - n_i^{1/2} n_k^{3/2}\right) +$$
$$+ 2(n_k / n_i)^{\gamma+1/2}\left(1 - n_k^{1/2} n_i^{3/2}\right) < (2n_i n_k - 3) \quad i \neq k = r, b, \tag{22}$$

which holds for $n_i > 1$. ∎

The cooperative supply of contributions for agents in sector i is larger than the non-cooperative one. Moreover, from (22) $\partial(s_i^C - s_i^N)/\partial\gamma > 0$ so that an increase in the advantage of larger groups in the electoral system has a positive effect on the difference between the cooperative and non-cooperative supply of contributions. Hence, a change towards electoral rules that reduce the political representation of small groups in the legislative body decreases the individual incentives to supply contributions, particularly in a setting where agents in the same sector do not coordinate themselves.

Substituting (20) into (14), the equilibrium tax rates become:

$$(1-t_l^C) = \frac{l_b n_r^{\gamma-1/2}(2YB' - n_r n_b^{\gamma+3/2}C')}{l_r n_b^{\gamma-1/2}(2YB' + n_r^{\gamma+3/2}n_b C')}, \tag{23}$$

$$(1-t_y^C) = \frac{n_b^{\gamma-1/2}Y(2B' - n_r^{\gamma+3/2}n_b C')}{2l_b(n_r^{\gamma+1/2} + n_b^{\gamma+1/2})B'},$$

where $C' = n_r^{\gamma-1/2} - n_b^{\gamma-1/2}$.

PROPOSITION 9. $n_r \gtrless n_b \implies t_l^N \gtrless t_l^C \gtrless t_l^R$ and $t_y^R \gtrless t_y^C \gtrless t_y^N$.

PROOF. Comparing (12), (18) and (23). ∎

For any γ and distribution of agents across sectors, the fiscal equilibrium under the regulated setting is intermediate between the non-cooperative and the cooperative settings.

PROPOSITION 10. *The electoral equilibrium in the cooperative setting is such that*:

$$n_r^{\gamma-1/2} \gtrless n_b^{\gamma-1/2} \implies U_r \gtrless U_b.$$

PROOF. Substituting (23) into (15) we get:

$$U_i = \frac{Yn_i^{\gamma-1/2}}{n_i^{\gamma-1/2} + n_k^{\gamma-1/2}}\left(\frac{(n_i^{\gamma+1/2} + n_k^{\gamma+1/2})^2}{n_i^{\gamma+3/2}n_k^{\gamma+3/2} + (n_i^{\gamma+1/2} + n_k^{\gamma+1/2})^2}\right) \quad i \neq k = r, b, \tag{24}$$

from which the proposition follows. ∎

The utility levels in (24) are on average smaller than those obtained in the regulated and in the non-cooperative settings (see (13) and (19)). Moreover, the switching in the ranking between agents in different groups now occurs for a lower level of γ with respect to the non-cooperative setting. Though agents in the smaller group individually supply more contributions, their relative advantage with respect to the regulated setting is lower because they cannot exploit the organizational effect. Moreover, the general increase in the supply of wasteful contributions reduces further the advantage of agents in the smaller group. This notwithstanding, the cooperative setting is still more favourable for the smaller group than the regulated setting.

The comparison of cooperative and non-cooperative supplies of contributions has brought forward some new features of the collective decision mechanism and of its implication for the fiscal equilibrium. First, when binding agreements take place not only are the contributions generally higher but they are also more evenly distributed across groups. Secondly, when contributions to interest groups are somehow institutionalized, their supply becomes less subjected to decline, at the individual level, in response to an increase in the costs of political representation in the legislative body for small groups. Thirdly, the aggregate supply of contributions is equal across groups so that individual agents in the smaller group supply more contributions. Fourthly, in terms of fiscal equilibrium, agents in the shadow sector are worse off with respect to the non-cooperative case, but fare better than in the regulated setting where smaller groups are more damaged by non-proportional electoral rules.

As for the constitutional implications of these results, the second point suggests that an increase of γ—which can reduce the comparative advantage of smaller groups in lobbying—plays a minor role when interest groups are able to control free-riding.

7. Conclusions

This paper analyses the fiscal mix between direct and indirect taxation as an equilibrium of a non-cooperative game where members of different interest groups compete to get distributive gains. Their contributions to the activity of interest groups is constrained by a set of constitutional rules which are embodied in a reduced-form model of electoral competition. Hence, the focus is on the relations between different political mechanisms and the features of the fiscal equilibrium.

Our main results are the following. First, when institutional rules enforce a ban on interest groups' activities, the fiscal mix is mainly determined by the features of the electoral rules for the legislative body. In these circumstances if the electoral rules are highly disproportional, small groups suffer from a comparative disadvantage in obtaining political representation. Accordingly, if we assume that agents in the regular sector are the larger group, the fiscal mix relies heavily on expenditure taxation that cannot be avoided by agents in the shadow sector. Secondly, when the transaction costs to transform contributions into political pressure are relatively low, small groups gain a comparative advantage. This is because the supply of contributions to interest groups has effects on the fiscal equilibrium which are not completely appropriable. It follows that there will be a shift in the fiscal mix towards income taxation which is avoided by agents in the shadow sector. Thirdly, such comparative advantage of smaller groups is reduced if there is the opportunity to undertake binding agreements inside groups to coordinate the supply of contributions. Accordingly, when well-established interest groups are active, the fiscal equilibrium is less favourable to agents in the shadow sector. However, the advantage of smaller groups is not cancelled because, even without free-riding, members of a larger group are individually less affected by changes in the fiscal mix and therefore contribute less to their interest groups' activities.

Notes

1. We are not interested in the analysis of fiscal evasion in the shadow sector, and we ignore the analysis of agents' behaviour in violation of fiscal rules—taking it as given for technological reasons (e.g. excessively high costs of enforcement)—to concentrate on their behaviour in the legislative competition from which the fiscal rules emerge.

2. See Ordeshook (1992) for a survey of both positions. Ordeshook labels the authors who privilege the analysis of constitutional details as 'institutionalists' and those who stress the activity of organized interests as 'pluralists' or, and perhaps less benevolently, 'populists'. Among the latter are: Dahl (1956), Olson (1965), and Becker (1983), (1985). On this topic see also Mitchell and Munger (1991).

3. Brennan and Buchanan (1977), Riker (1982) and Ostrom (1987) are among the most influential 'institutionalists'.

4. See Twight (1992) for a survey of the obstacles which are usually imposed on the process of revision of constitutional rules as well as of other institutions involved in collective decision-making.

5. See Mitchell and Munger (1991) and Wittman (1995) for a survey of such criticisms. Wittman also provides an exhaustive survey of the arguments against the view that the markets for political transactions are less efficient than economic ones.

6. For non-analytical approaches one should also see Hayes (1981), Miller and Moe (1983), and Ordeshook (1992).

7. Enelow and Hinich (1989) investigate an electoral equilibrium where the features of the electoral platform depend on how interest groups' ideological bias is perceived by the candidates. In their model, however, they do not focus on an active role played by such interest groups. See also Austen-Smith (1987).

8. The expected plurality is often assumed to be a sensible proxy for the candidates' maximand. Indeed, the latter are often professional politicians, and a large margin in the present election is likely to have a positive effect on the margin in the following one. The logic is that a narrow victory is a sign of weakness that can provide incentives for rivals to invest more intensively in the following election. Cf. Stigler (1972).

9. The realization of b_i is the same for all members of group i.

10. The probability p_{ij}^o of voter ij voting for candidate o is equally obtainable (with g and o interchanged).

11. Most representative democracies explicitly forbid large contributions to some pressure groups or put different limits to their amount. However, since it is extremely difficult to give account of such institutional details, we prefer to introduce them as shown above. On this point see also Stratman (1992).

12. These measures, both as concentration or as disproportionality indexes, are such that $0 < \gamma < 1$. For detailed definitions and a discussion of their properties, see Rae (1971), Bogdanor and Butler (1983) and Grofman and Lijphart (1986).

13. We assume that agents can participate in only one pressure group, and that their membership is exogenously given.

14. This in contrast with most voting models where a clear distinction is drawn between un-organized voters and pressure groups whose interests are opposed to those of the former.

15. A generic agent j in sector b is faced by a slightly different objective function (3) in which $t_i = 0$.

16. The shape of such a cost function is a second institutional element—other than the electoral rule for the legislative body—on which the normative analysis can focus. The larger $c''(s_i)$, the more costly for the individual agent to increase his investment in political pressure. This may reflect the presence of rules making it more difficult to transform economic resources into political pressure.

17. We do not analyse the possibility of corner solutions.

18. See Friedman (1986, 45).

19. For $\gamma = 0$, (13) describes the equilibrium utilities even for $n_r \neq n_b$ because the constitutional constraint becomes equivalent to a standard social welfare function.

20. One can interpret the investment in contributions as an investment in shares of the social capital, whose ownership allows an increase in the investor's control over collective decisions. Compare this notion with that of social capital used in Coleman (1990).

21. The equality in (16) holds for large n_i for which it is reasonable to assume that n_i approximates to $n_i - 1$.

22. Differentiating (16) with respect to s_{ij}, one can check that U_i is concave (and therefore also quasi-concave) in s_{ij} and therefore satisfy such a condition for the existence of Nash equilibria.

23. In other words, when agents in the larger group invest in contributions, they generate aggregate benefits shared by a greater number of agents.

References

Austen-Smith, D. (1987) 'Interest Groups, Campaign Contributions and Probabilistic Voting', *Public Choice*, 54: 123–39.

Becker, G. (1983) 'A Theory of Competition among Pressure Groups for Political Influence', *Quarterly Journal of Economics*, 98: 371–400.

Becker, G. (1985) 'Public Policies, Pressure Groups, and Dead Weight Costs', *Journal of Public Economics*, 28: 329–47.

Bogdanor, V. and Butler, D. (1983) *Electoral Systems and Their Political Consequences.* Cambridge: Cambridge University Press.

Brennan, G. and Buchanan, J. (1977) 'Towards a Tax Constitution for Leviathan', *Journal of Public Economics*, 8: 255–74.

Coleman, J. (1990) *Foundations of Social Theory.* Cambridge, MA: Harvard University Press.

Coughlin, P. and Nitzan, S. (1981) 'Electoral Outcomes with Probabilistic Voting and Nash Social Welfare Maxima', *Journal of Public Economics*, 15: 113–21.

Coughlin, P., Mueller, D., and Murrell, P. (1990a) 'A Model of Electoral Competition with Interest Groups', *Economics Letters*, 32: 307–11.

Coughlin, P., Mueller, C., and Murrell, P. (1990b) 'Electoral Politics, Interest Groups and the Size of Government', *Economic Inquiry*, 28: 682–705.

Dahl, R. (1956) *A Preface to Democratic Theory.* New Haven, CT: Yale University Press.

Enelow, J. and Hinich, M. (1989) 'A General Probabilistic Spatial Theory of Elections', *Public Choice*, 61: 101–13.

Fiorentini, G. (1993) 'A Model of Electoral Competition with Pressure Groups', *Sticerd Discussion Papers*, London School of Economics.

Friedman, J. (1986) *Games Theory with Applications to Economics.* Oxford: Oxford University Press.

Grofman, B. and Lijphart, A. (1986) *Electoral Laws and Their Political Consequences.* New York: Agathon Press.

Hayes, M. (1981) *Lobbyists and Legislators: A Theory of Political Markets.* New Brunswick, NJ: Rutgers University Press.

Magee, S., Brock, A., and Young, W. (1989) *Black Hole Tariffs and Endogenous Policy Theory: Political Economy in General Equilibrium.* Cambridge: Cambridge University Press.

Miller, G. and Moe, T. (1983) 'Bureaucrats, Legislators, and the Size of Government', *American Political Science Review*, 77: 297–322.

Mitchell, W. and Munger, M. (1991) 'Economic Models of Interest Groups: An Introductory Survey', *American Journal of Political Science*, 35: 512–46.

Olson, M. (1965) *The Logic of Collective Action*. Cambridge, MA: Harvard University Press.

Ordeshook, P. (1992) 'Constitutional Stability', *Constitutional Political Economy*, 3: 137–75.

Ostrom, V. (1987) *The Political Theory of the Compound Republic*. Lincoln: University of Nebraska Press.

Rae, D. (1971) *The Political Consequences of Electoral Laws*. New Haven, CT: Yale University Press.

Riker, W. (1982) *Liberalism against Populism*. San Francisco: W.H. Freeman.

Stigler, G. (1972) 'Economic Competition and Political Competition', *Public Choice*, 13: 91–106.

Stratman, T. (1992) 'Are Contributors Rational?', *Journal of Political Economy*, 100: 647–64.

Twight, C. (1992) 'Constitutional Renegotiation', *Constitutional Political Economy*, 3: 89–112.

Wittman, D. (1995) *The Myth of Democratic Failure: Why Political Institutions are Efficient*. Chicago: University of Chicago Press.

4
Endogenous regionalism's free-trade bias: special interests in the EEC, 1968–1983

STEPHEN P. MAGEE AND HAK-LOH LEE

1. Introduction

Recent work on economic integration and endogenous protection by Bhagwati (1993), Bilal (1998), Grossman and Helpman (1995), Melo *et al.* (1993), Panagariya and Findlay (1994) and Richardson (1993, 1994, 1995) yields mixed results on whether regionalism promotes protectionism. In this paper, we find that both the creation and the existence of regions is free-trade biased.

In a full general-political equilibrium, both regionalism and protection are endogenous so that the research challenge is to explain the underlying causes of both. We explore qualitatively endogenous regionalism and the exogenous forces which led to the formation of the European Economic Community (the EEC) in the 1950s and 1960s. We also explain why the EEC countries may have chosen to be a customs union rather than a more protectionist free-trade area, such as EFTA.

We then explain movements in the common external tariff after the EEC was formed. We borrow language from Viner (1950) who analysed 'trade creation' and 'trade diversion'. Trade creation increases welfare because intra-union trade expands with the abolition of tariffs on imports from member countries. Trade diversion decreases welfare because importers switch from low-priced world sources to higher priced member country sources after tariffs drop to zero on intra-union trade. This paper is a positive analysis describing the evolution of the endogenous common external tariff after a customs union is formed rather than Viner's welfare questions. A shorter version of this paper appears in Magee and Lee (1999).

Our work here builds upon Brock and Magee's (1977, 1978) work on endogenous free-riding, Magee, Brock and Young's (1989) work on endogenous protection and Lee and Magee's (1996) model of endogenous free-riding.[1] Lee and Magee showed how endogenous free-riding in protectionist lobbies can be modelled as a mixed-strategy equilibrium. We use this model to explain changes from 1968 to 1983 in the common external tariff following the creation of the EEC in 1968. Endogenous industry tariff changes cannot be properly modelled at a time of custom union formation without properly accounting for free-riding changes from the country to the customs union level.

We suggest that after a customs union is formed, the endogenous common external tariff will rise because of 'tariff creation' effects and fall because of 'tariff diversion' effects.

Tariff diversion are those post-customs union forces leading to declines in the endogenous common external tariff. To date, we have identified four forces, including (1) endowment effects reflecting capital deepening (a growing ratio of the abundant factor to the scarce factor weakens the relative political power of protectionists); (2) increased free-riding within protectionist industry lobbies because of their operation within the larger political arena of the EEC; (3) decreased political pressure from protectionists whose industries had grown rapidly due to overall EEC prosperity; and (4) increased specialization away from import-competing activities.

Tariff creation forces are those forces causing increases in the endogenous common external tariff. These include (1) greater motivation to increase the terms of trade; (2) decreased industry free-riding from higher industry concentration due to firm mergers and economies of scale; and (3) increased political pressure from protectionists harmed by rapid growth in intra-EEC imports.

Whether tariff creation or tariff diversion will predominate is an empirical question. The formation of the European Economic Community (EEC) is a good experiment. The common external tariff set in 1968 was a simple average of the pre-existing tariffs of the six member countries[2,3]—Belgium, the Netherlands, and Luxembourg plus Germany, France, and Italy.[4] Thus, every change in the common external tariff from the inception of the EEC is, by definition, a change relative to the preunion average of country tariffs. Recall that we measure the tariff-creating and tariff-diverting effects on the common external tariff of the EEC between 1968 and 1983, using pre-EEC data from two of the three largest countries in the EEC, France and Italy.

Our data indicates that tariff diversion exceeded tariff creation on protection against non-member imports in the first fifteen years after tariffs were eliminated on intra-EEC trade in 1968.

2. A review of the literature

Custom unions and free-trade areas have been discussed widely in the press in recent years because of the regionalism versus globalization debate. Grossman and Helpman (1995) argue that free-trade areas are more likely than customs unions because they enhance protection. This observation may explain evidence from the early 1990s from de la Torre and Kelly (1992) that there were only eight customs unions in the world compared to thirty-three free-trade areas.

The regionalism debate is part of a broader question of what defines a 'country'. Mundell (1961) defined a optimum currency area as a region within which there is factor mobility and between which there is not. Friedman (1977) introduced a 't-nation' as the largest political unit within which tax policy is effectively coordinated. According to this theory, countries exist to maximize total revenue, inclusive of the tax. Magee *et al.* (1989, ch. 6) provide a general equilibrium model of endogenous protection with some speculations on whether country mergers would increase or decrease external protection. Krugman (1991a) says that political boundaries are relevant to the study of trade only if they are effective barriers to movements of goods and factors. Hanson (1994) says in his analysis of the North American Free Trade Agreement (NAFTA) that regions rather than nations should be the unit of analysis in international trade. Carneiro (1970) provides an interesting history of country formation, based on pre-Christian anthropological evidence. For a theoretical treatment of endogenous regions, see Yi (1994).

There is a growing body of literature which applies endogenous policy theory to international trade. The application of the interest-group lobbying model with an emphasis on free-riding in a setting of the private provision of a public good is especially relevant here. See Magee *et al.* (1989) and Helpman (1995) for a survey of endogenous tariff theory and Magee (1997) for a survey of the empirical evidence.

Tharakan (1991) proposes a lobbying effect hypothesis that the lobbying power of professional associations representing industries having a higher degree of concentration is likely to be greater. In his study of the anti-dumping proceedings of the EEC, the hypothesis is that the more concentrated an EEC industry, which is the *de facto* plaintiff, the more likely is a definitive anti-dumping duty, which is disadvantageous to the defendant exporting firms, and the less likely are price undertakings, which are more advantageous to the defendant exporting firms. Schuknecht (1991) also takes a similar approach in his study of EEC protectionist policy, where the number of total complaints by member countries or the approval rate of a national protective measure are explained by political economic variables such as changes in the EEC unemployment rate and the GDP growth rate of the EEC.

A size-of-country-factor would lead us to expect that formation of a customs union would have a common external tariff that is lower than the average of the pre-union country tariffs. The reason is that the more distant the circumscribing boundaries from the centre of a country, the greater the natural economic protection from foreign goods. For example, almost all of the trade of one city block in a city is external while none of the trade of the entire globe is external. By implication, large countries should require lower political protection.

An offsetting factor is the terms of trade effect. Large countries can exploit their smaller trading partners to get terms of trade gains, so this would dictate that larger countries would have greater politically created protection.

Since the formation of a customs union is like the formation of a large country, the size-of-country effect would suggest a decline of the common external tariff of a customs union while the terms of trade effect would dictate an increase. Krugman (1993) suggests casual empirical evidence that larger countries have greater political protection than small ones. However, we find in our empirical evidence below that size of country and endowment effects more than offset terms of trade effects in the first fifteen years after final EEC formation in 1968. Our evidence does not support Krugman's assumption that the EEC would lead to trade gains. Magee *et al.* (1997) have shown that the United States is also a small country in world trade.

3. Endogenous regionalism: the EEC's formation

Whether the common external tariff of a customs union will rise or fall after union formation is part of a larger picture. Creation of a customs union itself is an endogenous event. The formation of any regional trade arrangement is a major change, meaning changes must have occurred in the exogenous determinants of the pre-existing political equilibrium.

With hindsight, the formation of the EEC as a customs union is no surprise. Free-trade areas are the usual means of trade integration. Recall that a customs union is a preferential trading arrangement within which members enjoy free trade and maintain a common external tariff.[5] A free-trade area maintains free trade within but member countries maintain their own individual tariffs *vis-à-vis* non-member countries. The EEC is a customs union while the European Free Trade Area (EFTA) and the North American Free Trade Area (NAFTA) are free-trade areas. According to de la Torre and Kelly (1992), there were about thirty-four FTAs and there are nineteen prospective FTAs as of the end of 1991.[6] Table 4.1 reports the numbers by region.

Why the dominance of free-trade areas? Richardson (1994) argues that in a free-trade area, domestic industries only need to lobby the national government for external tariffs, whereas in a customs union they need to negotiate with larger government bodies to get the same level of tariff. It is free-riding on the firms' side that shapes the protection level because free-riding amongst firms is more severe under a customs union than under a free-trade area, which makes the tariff under a customs union lower than that under a free-trade area. Protectionist firms clearly prefer a free-trade area over a customs union. We note below why pro-export interests and con-

Table 4.1. Regional trading blocs

	Existing arrangements			Prospective arrangements		
	FTA	CU	Other	FTA	CU	Other
Europe	8	1	1	7	1	1
W. Hemisphere	9	2		2		5
Africa	5	2	1			
Asia-Pacific and Middle East	2	2	1			3
Total	24	7	3	9	1	9

Key: FTA = free-trade area; CU = customs union.

Source: de la Torre and Kelly (1992, Tables 1–4).

sumers will prefer customs unions. Panagariya and Findlay (1996) show rather general conditions under which a customs union Pareto dominates a free-trade area.[7]

Richardson (1994) argues that preferential trading arrangements can package tariff reductions that might not be accepted by individual sectors but which are, on aggregate, welfare improving. Also, a new regime with large changes in tariffs might be possible even when small changes would not be accepted on an individual basis if there were fixed costs of participation in politics. In this case, large changes could cover the fixed political costs and yield large welfare gains.

In general, both customs unions and free-trade areas are moves toward freer trade. In 1963, imports from member EEC countries were 56 per cent of total imports. Tariffs on this intra-EEC trade were cut to zero between 1959 and 1968. The initial common external tariff of the EEC in 1968 was 15.1 per cent in our sample, which was a simple average of the previous country tariff rates. Thus, formation of the EEC created a large decline in average protection.

The EEC could have come into existence only if there was a pre-union decline in protectionist forces relative to pro-export forces and generalist voter sentiments. This is particularly true taking into account the post-1968 movements toward freer trade described in this paper.

Why the decline in the relative power of protectionists and what other forces led the six EEC countries to merge? The most obvious explanations are the monolithic economic threat of the USA, geographic contiguity and the decreases in transport and information costs which have increased optimum country size world-wide since the Second World War. But three other forces were at work, two suggested by the theory of endogenous protection and one by Mancur Olson.

The first endogenous tariff explanation of EEC formation is the endowment effect of capital deepening from Magee *et al.* (1989, ch. 15). The physical capital structures of the EEC countries were especially devastated by the Second World War. The rapid rebuilding of both the physical and human capital structures of these countries greatly increased the size and political clout of the abundant factors relative to the scarce factor, unskilled labour. The endowment effect means that increases in the ratio of the abundant to the scarce factor increase the economic clout of export interests. This results in decreases in tariffs because there is greater lobbying power for export interests who favour freer trade. The endogeneity of EEC creation reflects this decline in the relative political power of the scarce factor, unskilled labour.

A second explanation comes from the compensation effect of the theory of endogenous protection from Magee *et al.* (1989, ch. 11). The compensation effect dictates that politics compensates for economic weakness. Anything that lowers (raises) the economic return of a factor of production also lowers (raises) the opportunity cost of its lobbying the government for favourable policies, which increases (decreases) its lobbying activity. This effect grows out of Stolper–Samuelson factor prices effects, as the following example illustrates. When an industry contracts, the price of its intensive factor is pushed down. Factors typically employ their own factor in lobbying. For example, capitalists use capital (money) to lobby while labour unions use their

membership to take people to the polls, etc. Contraction by import-competing industries which are unskilled-labour intensive leads to a decline in wages which lowers
the opportunity cost of lobbying for labour. Thus, lobbying for protection should
increase as the prices of imports fall according to the compensation effect.

Consider the terms of trade. A decrease in the terms of trade of a country is a decrease in the price of the country's exportables relative to its importables. This increase
in the price of the country's importables on world markets means that import-
competing firms face less competition from imports and hence will decrease their
lobby efforts for protection. We have measurements of the terms of trade for the USA.
The US terms of trade for manufactures increased from an index of 82 in 1948 to 89 in
1958 to 104 in 1968, the year in which the EEC adopted the common external tariff. If
the USA traded only with the EEC, the EEC index would have been the mirror image of
the USA and would have displayed manufacturing terms of trade declines. A terms of
trade decline is a rise in the relative price of importables. If the pre-EEC terms of trade
did decline, the higher relative price of imports would have reduced the political opposition of protectionists to the formation of the EEC via the compensation effect.

A third potential explanation of EEC formation can be adapted from the late
Mancur Olson (1982). Olson argued that cataclysmic political events, such as the
Second World War, largely destroy the pre-existing interest group influence over governments in war-torn countries. Protectionists are usually better organized than are
the opponents of protectionism, namely, consumers and pro-export interests. Thus,
the Second World War was disproportionately disadvantageous to protectionist interests in Europe. Further, the greatest political devastation occurred in Germany and
Italy, the losers in the war, two of the three largest principals of the EEC. To summarize,
the EEC opted for a customs union rather than the weaker political affiliation of a free-
trade area for both economic and political factors.

To summarize this entire paper, we find that free-trade bias accompanied regionalism, at least for the EEC. We speculate at the end that these results may carry over to
other advanced countries. What does the theory of endogenous tariffs have to offer in
the way of speculations about regional trading blocs among developing countries?
Foroutan (1993) points out that many south–south regional economic integration
schemes have failed. Empirical work by Magee offered weak evidence of an inverted U-
shaped relationship between capital–labour endowment ratios across countries and
their tariff rates. Why is this? Endogenous tariff theory predicts that capital deepening
in developing countries has a pro-protectionist bias while capital deepening in developed countries has an anti-protectionist bias. In a Stolper–Samuelson framework,
the growth of capital builds political support for protection in developing countries,
where protection enriches capital, the scarce factor. The growth of capital in developed
countries reduces political support for the scarce factor, labour, and hence reduces
protection. This effect would predict growing regional trading arrangements which
reduce tariffs in developed countries. However, attempts to reduce protection through
regionalism in developing countries will encounter this offsetting endowment force
for greater protection, which may explain their failure.

We turn now to the question of what happens to the common external tariff of a customs union such as the EEC after it is formed. The results can go either way. Tariffs fall because of tariff diverting effects and rise because of tariff creating effects.

4. Trade creation and trade diversion vs. tariff creation and tariff diversion

There is a welfare gain from trade creation from a customs union à la Viner (1950) but we find that this will be offset by a welfare loss from the associated tariff creation. Trade creation expands trade and increases welfare for a customs union because tariffs drop to zero on trade which is already from member countries. But this increase in trade harms import-competing firms in the union. This harm stimulates the compensation effect[8] from endogenous tariff theory: import-competing firms will increase their lobbying efforts against imports from non-member countries. The resulting increase in the common external tariff will lower welfare. Thus, the welfare gains from trade creation will be partially offset by welfare losses from tariff creation.

Panagariya and Findlay (1994) report a related effect. A customs union will eliminate tariff lobbying for a good previously imported from a member country. Elimination of lobbying against member countries makes lobbying against non-member countries more attractive, which results in increased protection against the rest of the world.

Contrasted with the compensation effect is the result of Hillman (1982), Cassing and Hillman (1986), van Long and Vousden (1991), and Richardson (1993) that political support for domestic industries decreases with increased import competition, because the industry becomes smaller and weaker. According to this view, politics reinforces the downfall of declining industries rather than compensating for their economic disadvantage. Cassing and Hillman (1986) argue that decreasing government support for declining industries stops abruptly at a certain point. Brainard and Verdier (1994) modify this prediction and say that government protection fades out more gradually. Richardson (1993) shows in an endogenous tariff setting model that trade diversion is less severe in the case of a free-trade area than in a customs union. The reason is that declining industries will simply face tariff elimination, following the insurance argument, so that tariff diversion may not occur.

Consider now the broader welfare question of trading blocs. Krugman (1991b) extends the optimal tariff discussion to explore the welfare consequences of trading blocs where blocs produce differentiated goods and affect world prices by setting optimal tariffs on imports from other blocs. Adding additional members to the trading bloc has a different effect on intra-bloc and extra-bloc welfare. The increasing size of a bloc allows a greater variety of products to be available duty-free within the bloc, but leads to higher optimal tariffs on inter-bloc trade. As a result, the welfare consequences of a movement towards the bigger sized trading blocs will depend on just how important within-bloc varieties are relative to varieties from outside the bloc.

Yi (1994) analyses the different effects of a customs union and a free-trade area on the members and non-members by maximizing the aggregate welfare of the countries involved, which consists of consumer surplus, domestic and export profits, and tariff revenue. The major results are supportive of the optimal tariff argument that the common external tariff of a customs union will rise and the individual tariff of free-trade area will fall. These results depend crucially on the ability to exercise collective market power in setting external tariffs.

The General Agreement on Tariffs and Trade (GATT), whose aim is global trade liberalization, reserves room for regional trade arrangements. Article XXIV of the GATT permits regional trading blocs, with some conditions, and suggests that after-bloc tariffs should not be increased compared with the before-bloc average level.[9]

Bhagwati (1991, 1993) and Krueger (1995) mention the coercive feature of trading blocs. A trading bloc is conducive to global free trade through its power to push countries to the negotiation table for multilateral trade cooperation in order to avoid potential retaliatory trade wars. However, it reduces world trade to the extent that it is tempted to exploit its monopoly power in world trade.

They compare the welfare implications of different types of preferential trading arrangements with endogenous protection. The free-riding opportunism within a customs union makes the common external tariff of a customs union lower than a trade area members' national tariff levels. Further, the level of the common external tariff will be lower as the number of member countries increases in a customs union. In this sense, a customs union is Pareto-superior to a free-trade area.

Thus, endogenous politics predicts that free-trade areas would be more common while welfare analysis suggests that there should be more customs unions. Here politics appears to dominate welfare considerations. The evidence from de la Torre and Kelly (1992) in Table 4.1 indicates a total of thirty-three free-trade areas compared to only eight customs unions.

We summarize the effects of trade creation and trade diversion on tariff creation as follows. Consider a fixed world price and an initial pre-customs union tariff. If the member country price of the product were equal to the world price plus the pre-customs union tariff, then there would be complete trade diversion and no trade creation. While there would be maximum welfare harm from creation of the customs union, there would be no change in the economic situation facing import-competing firms: they face the same price from foreign competition as they faced pre-union.[10] All that has changed is that, say, a 20 per cent tariff on the most efficient world supplier has been replaced by the same good coming from a partner country whose price is 20 per cent higher than the most efficient world supplier. The absence of domestic partial equilibrium price and quantity effects for import-competing industries means no endogenous political reactions by them.

To summarize, large trade diversion effects generate no tariff creation effects for the common external tariff after the customs union is formed.[11] At the other extreme, if the partner country suppliers were already the most efficient world providers, then customs union formation would cause import-competing firms to face large price decreases and an expanded quantity of imports. In the Magee *et al.* (1989) world, this reduction in economic returns relative to political returns induces increased lobbying for a higher common external tariff.

To summarize, large trade creation effects generate the largest tariff creation for the common external tariff after the customs union is formed.[12]

Proponents of economic integration tend to emphasize the dynamic advantages over the static benefits.[13] The removal of trade barriers leads to trade creation and greater specialization in areas of comparative advantage. This will be offset by trade diversion, which encourages intra-union specialization in areas of competitive disadvantage relative to the rest of the world.

We are persuaded by Krugman's speculation that trade creation will dominate trade diversion because countries typically form unions with contiguous neighbours, with whom they already have large fractions of trade. For example, in 1963, imports into EEC countries from member countries were 56 per cent of total imports.

Thus, there is a presumption that trade creation will exceed trade diversion. If so, customs union formation causes resources to concentrate in the areas in which they are more competitive.[14] There is a reduction in the domestic production of import-substituting goods and greater specialization in export commodities. Overall, comparative advantage is strengthened. The removal of trade barriers should increase the intensity of competition, leading to an increase in the share of the market by exporters and more competitive producers.[15]

A customs union also permits industry concentration to increase[16] and the larger market allows for greater economies of scale.[17] Peck (1989) argues that a major source of the 1992 EEC economic gains is a reorganization of European industry to take advantage of economies of scale, thereby allowing the number of plants and firms in the Community be reduced.

Table 4.2 reports simulation results from Smith and Venables (1988) which show that for ten industries, the number of firms in the EEC is expected to decline in all

Table 4.2. Simulation result for the number of firms after market integration

Industry	Before	After	Change
Cement	119	120	+1
Pharmaceuticals	390	343	−47
Artificial, synthetic fibre	43	42	−1
Machine tools	646	628	−18
Office machines	66	66	0
Electric motors	471	439	−32
Electrical appliances	141	82	−59
Motor vehicles	14	6	−8
Carpet	287	178	−109
Footwear	737	530	−207

Note: The assumptions for this simulation are that there is no price differentiation and there is a reduction in trade barriers.

Source: Smith and Venables (1988, Tables 1 and 5, arranged).

industries except cement and office machinery out of ten major industries. Increased industry concentration after economic integration should reduce protectionist lobby free-riding and thereby increase common external protection, that is promote tariff creation.

5. The endogenous tariff with endogenous free-riding

We assume the endogenous tariff is determined by the size of free-riding in the producer group relative to the consumer group and the relative size of production and consumption proxied by the stakes of the producer and consumer group, respectively. Denote n, m: number of producers and consumers, respectively; S, C: shipments, consumption; H: industry Herfindahl index $(= 1/n)$; a, b, (A, B): producer group's free-riding coefficient, perceived effectiveness coefficient, (consumer group's free-riding coefficient, perceived effectiveness coefficient); α, β, α': size parameters; $a + b \leq 1$, $a \geq 0$, $b \geq 0$.[18] The parameter a is the probability of free-riding in the lobby mixed strategy equilibrium.

Lee and Magee (1996) show that the endogenous tariff equation can be written as follows:[19]

$$t = \alpha \left[\frac{\left(\frac{a}{n} + b\right)}{\left(\frac{A}{M} + B\right)} \frac{S}{C} \right]^{\beta} = \alpha \left[\frac{aH + b}{B} \frac{S}{C} \right]^{\beta}$$

$$= \alpha \left[(aH + b) \frac{S}{C} \right]^{\beta} B^{-\beta} = \alpha' \left[(aH + b) \frac{S}{C} \right]^{\beta}. \tag{1}$$

While this equation looks complicated, the last term is simple. It states that tariffs increase with industry concentration (H), with the ratio of industry shipments (S) over consumption (C). The latter says that tariffs increase with the stake of import-competing shipper interests but decline with consumer stakes. Without loss of generality, the number of consumers, m, is assumed to be big enough to make the term A/m vanish. In our regressions below, this assumption is violated; whatever power consumers do have will be reflected in the tariff and captured in the constant. From this discussion of the tariff equation with the free-riding and perceived effectiveness coefficients, we derive a theoretical specification, which links industry concentration to the tariff level as follows:

$$t = \alpha' \left[(aH + b) \frac{S}{C} \right]^{\beta}, \tag{2}$$

where the symbols remain the same. For empirical tractability, let α' in (2) be equal to one. We also add variables suggested by endogenous tariff theory such as various compensation variables. The basic tariff equation to be estimated is as follows:

$$Tariff = \left[(aH + b)\frac{S}{C} \right]^\beta + eP, \tag{3}$$

where P denotes other control variables.

Lee and Magee (1996), following Brock and Magee (1977), Magee *et al.* (1989, Appendix to ch. 6) and Gawande (1994), show how the degree of free-riding within industry lobbies can be estimated from industry data. They interpret a as the degree of free-riding and assume that $a + b = 1$. As the Herfindahl approaches zero with large numbers of firms, the effect of the economic stake S and campaign contributions on the election will also approach zero because of free-riding. If $a = 0$ and $b = 1$, then there will be no free-riding and the tariff will be proportional to the economic stake of the industry, S.

We proceed with the restriction of $a + b = 1$. Therefore,

$$\begin{aligned}
Tariff &= \left[(aH + b)\frac{S}{C} \right]^\beta + eP, \\
&= \left[(aH + 1 - a)\frac{S}{C} \right]^\beta + eP, \\
&= \left[(a(H - 1) + 1)\frac{S}{C} \right]^\beta + eP,
\end{aligned} \tag{4}$$

$$\frac{dTariff}{dt} = \beta \left[a\frac{d((H-1)(S/C))}{dt} + \frac{d(S/C)}{dt} \right]^{\beta-1} + e\frac{dP}{dt}. \tag{5}$$

Assuming linearity of the first term (i.e. $\beta = 2$) yields a tractable estimating equation

$$\frac{dTariff}{dt} = \beta \left[a\frac{d((H-1)(S/C))}{dt} + \frac{d(S/C)}{dt} \right] + e\frac{dP}{dt}. \tag{6}$$

6. Endogenous tariff creation and tariff diversion with trade bloc formation

The interest group model has been applied both to the USA (e.g. Snyder (1993)) and to Europe (e.g. Fiorentini (1993) and Weiss (1987)).[20] Weiss (1987) argues that interest groups in Europe are well organized, and the political economy explanatory variables can be used with confidence in regression analysis to show the direction of influence of the interest group in trade protection.

Andersen and Eliassen (1991) document increasing lobbying in Europe. The number of lobbyists increased ten times from the early 1970s to the end of 1980s, and has increased four times since 1985. After the European Customs Union proposal in 1957, pressure groups moved beyond national boundaries to affect EEC policies. Vaubel

(1994) also notes the active role of EEC-wide interest groups in policies. He argues that along with EEC formation, local interest groups may become weaker, but groups with EEC-wide interests can increase their influence because of advantages such as lobbying cost savings and they can lobby one instead of several governments.

Does a tariff against outsiders rise or fall with trade regionalism and formation of a customs union? Apply equation (2) to regionalism. If we let $\alpha' = \beta = 1$ for simplicity, then

$$t = (aH + b)(S/C). \tag{7}$$

Suppose two countries, A and B, form a customs union. From equation (7), country A's tariff is constructed as follows:

$$t_A = \left(\frac{a_A}{n_A} + b_A \right) \frac{S_A}{C_A}. \tag{8}$$

Similarly, country B's tariff is

$$t_B = \left(\frac{a_B}{n_B} + b_B \right) \frac{S_B}{C_B}. \tag{9}$$

First, assume that the two countries are identical in the sense that the numbers of producers and consumers are the same and the sizes of production and consumption are the same in both countries. Also assume that the free-riding and perceived effectiveness coefficients are the same: $n_A = n_B$, $S_A = S_B$, $C_A = C_B$, $a_A = a_B$, $b_A = b_B$. It follows that $t_A = t_B$. The post-customs union common external tariff will be

$$t_{CU} = \left(\frac{a_{CU}}{n_{CU}} + b_{CU} \right) \frac{S_{CU}}{C_{CU}}, \tag{10}$$

which might vary according to the number of producers, n_{CU}, as well as S_{CU} and C_{CU}. Even though a certain level of tariffs appears in the end, we can break the resulting tariff into two effects.

Consider a short-term perspective, and assume that every producer remains after the customs union is formed and maintains their production and consumption. In equation (10), $n_{CU} = n_A + n_B$, and

$$\frac{S_{CU}}{C_{CU}} = \frac{S_A + S_B}{C_A + C_B} = \frac{S_A}{C_A} \left(= \frac{S_B}{C_B} \right).$$

Let

$$\frac{S_{CU}}{C_{CU}} = \frac{S_A}{C_A} = \frac{S_B}{C_B} = \lambda.$$

Then

$$t_{CU,SHORT-TERM} = \left(\frac{a_{CU}}{n_A + n_B} + b_{CU} \right) \lambda. \tag{11}$$

For tractability, let $a + b = 1$. In this case, the post-customs union tariff should decrease because free-riding opportunities will be stronger with more members because of tariff diversion.[21] The initial tariff diversion effect is caused by the decrease from the country Herfindahl $H_{C,63}$ to the European Community Herfindahl, $H_{E,63}$.

If there were no free-riding, a would equal 0 in equation (11) and hence industry concentration would be irrelevant to the tariff level. If $a = 1$, free-riding is complete and the tariff would be proportional to the inverse of the number of firms. Estimates by Lee and Magee (1996) indicate from US data that free-riding over protectionist lobbying is pervasive, with estimates of the free-ride parameter $a = .8$.

After the short-term tariff, we have the long-term tariff, as follows:

$$t_{CU,LONG-TERM} = \left(\frac{a_{CU}}{n_{CU}} + b_{CU} \right) \lambda. \tag{12}$$

The tariff creation phase is the longer period over which the Herfindahls evolve from their value initially, $H_{E,63}$, to $H_{E,83}$, the Herfindahl index in 1983 for the European union. Integrated and adjusted EEC industries can have higher long-term tariffs, $t_{CU,LONG-TERM}$, bigger than the short-term tariffs, $t_{CU,SHORT-TERM}$, if this were a period of consolidation and mergers. Comparing (11) and (12), if n_{CU} in (12) is smaller than $n_A + n_B$, then the long-term tariff rises and tariff creation occurs. If rapid growth of the EEC brings sufficient small firm growth, then the Herfindahl can decrease and tariff diversion results.

The common external tariff will also be affected by other variables in both pre-union countries A and B, such as shipments and consumption. If the ratio of import-competing shipments to consumption rises in the larger trade bloc, the stake is higher for protectionists relative to consumer groups and the endogenous common external tariff rises.

7. The data

We use the model above to measure tariff-creating and tariff-diverting changes in the common external tariff between 1968 and 1983 in the EEC. We proxy pre- and post-EEC industry conditions using three digit industry data from two of the three largest countries in the EEC (France and Italy). Industry data were not available for this level of aggregation from Germany.

Yamawaki *et al.* (1989) studied the effect of the EEC formation on EEC-wide concentration and subsequently, on the effect of EEC-wide concentration on the price–cost margin for EEC industries. Following Yamawaki *et al.* we also choose 1963 as the year to represent the pre-integration year for the original member countries because it is the first year when comparable industry data were published, such as the number of firms and employees from which a Herfindahl index may be calculated. In addition, as Sleuwaegen and Yamawaki (1988) note, since the tariff reduction process in the EEC started in 1959 and did not end until 1968, 1963 offers a reasonable representation of pre-integration characteristics.

For the post-integration era, the appropriate year should be selected to minimize the effect of the addition of new members to the EEC and changes in the world trade environment. France, Italy, West Germany, Belgium, the Netherlands, and Luxembourg were the original six members which formed the EEC in 1957. In 1973, Ireland, Denmark, and the UK joined the EEC and in 1981 Greece was admitted. The year 1978 is chosen mainly because the data are available for 1978 and beyond.[22] The change in membership, however, complicates matters because the three new members might derogate the purity of the data. As with Yamawaki *et al.* (1989), this problem is minimized by excluding the new members in calculating the degree of industry concentration. Furthermore, some data have been obtained for years other than 1978 in case the data for 1978 are either not available or their quality is low owing to so many missing values for 1978. For these reasons, post-integration industry data were chosen between the years 1978 and 1982.

7.1. Tariffs

It would be desirable to estimate the level of protection through import duties, but it is impossible to find data regarding EEC import duties. We have to construct data on pre-integration tariffs from the 1968 EEC autonomous tariff rates; 'base' rates mean the data are from the Official Journal of the European Communities. Those tariff rates are assumed to represent the pre-integration status of the tariff structure of member states because the post-integration tariff levels, such as 1968, are equal to the simple arithmetic average of pre-integration tariff levels.[23] The 1983 EEC concession rates to the GATT members or the 'conventional rates', Most Favoured Nation (MFN) rates from now on, as post-integration tariff rates are from the Official Journal of 1983. The raw tariff rates data in the Official Journal by Brussels Tariff Nomenclature (BTN) have been converted to the three-digit level of EEC Industrial Classification, 'la Nomenclature générale des activités économiques dans les Communautés Européennes (NACE)', which is the classification used for the present research. For the method used to construct the concordance table used in this study, see Lee (1996). The tariff variables used in the empirical study are as follows:

$$\text{Tariff base } 1968 = \frac{\sum_{i=1}^{I} t_i, 1968, base}{n_I}, \quad \text{Tariff MFN } 1983 = \frac{\sum_{i=1}^{I} t_i, 1983, MFN}{n_I},$$

where t_i denotes the tariff rate by four-digit BTN and n_I denotes the number of BTN in an NACE.

The absolute tariff rates may not accurately reflect the size of the change in the protection level due to the fact that the NACE tariff rates are the average of the composed tariff rates of the BTN. For example, suppose that there are two tariff items in the BTN also belonging to the same NACE. The tariff rate of the first item changed from 100 per cent to 50 per cent and that of second item changed from 2 per cent to 1 per cent. It is clear from this example, that the more approximate status of the tariff change would be 50 per cent down, the mean of each tariff reduction, 50 per cent and 50 per cent, rather than 25.5 per cent down, subtracting the post-CU simple mean of 25.5 per cent from the pre-CU simple mean of 51 per cent. Therefore, the change in tariffs was constructed based on the following formula:

$$\text{Tariff MFN 1983 / Tariff base 1968} = \frac{\sum \frac{t_i,1983,MFN}{t_i,1968,base}}{n_I}.$$

Hereafter, we refer to this dependent variable as 'tariff 1983/tariff 1968'. Data show that MFN 1983 tariff rates were 48 per cent of 1968 base tariff rates (i.e. a 52 per cent reduction).

7.2. Trade creation and trade diversion

Kreinin (1981) estimates the trade creation (TC) and trade diversion (TD) effects of enlarging the EEC from six to nine members and launching free trade between the EEC and the rest of the European Free Trade Association (EFTA). The enlargement is therefore viewed as a fusion of the two blocs into one. He calculates trade creation and trade diversion as follows:[24]

TC: increase in total imports (= external imports + internal imports),
TD: decrease in external imports.

Alternatively, Kreinin offers an approach based on the growth rates between the preintegration base year and the post-integration years:

TC: growth rate in the ratio of 'total imports/consumption',
TD: growth rate in the ratio of 'external imports/consumption'.

As Neven and Roeller (1991) indicate, the question is whether the observed decreases in non-EC imports are due to a change in the fundamental factors underlying trade patterns or whether it is induced by the formation of the EEC. We assume that changes in trade creation and trade diversion arise purely from the integration factor. Our indicator of trade diversion—measured by the share of external imports in total consumption—increased from 8.7 per cent in 1963 to 10 per cent in 1979. Trade creation, equal to total imports/consumption, increases from 21.6 per cent in 1963 to 23.4 per cent in 1979.

Table 4.3. Mean of external imports/consumption

1963	1979	Difference
0.08685	0.10145	+0.01459

Besides the Kreinin method, we can measure trade diversion and trade creation in a different way. We measure trade diversion as the change in external imports during the period divided by external imports in 1963 and trade creation as the change in internal imports during the period divided by internal imports in 1963. A potential problem with this method is that both external and internal imports should increase due to the increase of the economy and trade size.

7.3. Concentration

In their study of the effects of the EEC's formation on market structure and competitive performance in member countries, Yamawaki *et al.* (1989) estimate EEC-wide concentration by taking the average of the maximum of the four largest firms' share in total employment and the minimum of it. First, they find that removing intra-EEC trade barriers has led to a more concentrated industry structure. Secondly, they show that the EEC-wide concentration is a significant variable in explaining the price–cost margin in national markets of member countries. In their estimation of EEC-wide concentration, Yamawaki *et al.* subtract the employment of Great Britain, Ireland, and Denmark from the total EEC employment in 1978 to eliminate possible distortions related to the 1973 accession of these three countries.

We estimate concentration using the Herfindahl index. Sales data would be most desirable but only data about the number of firms and employees of the member countries are available. The classified categories of the raw data are different between the pre-integration period and post-integration period. This problem is handled by combining categories. A more serious problem is that the firms' and employees' data for member countries other than France and Italy have quite a few missing values in many industries, which derogates the quality of the data. To solve this problem, we only use the most accurate information, that is French and Italian data, to construct the Herfindahl index. Even then, we were only able to make a very preliminary cut at the data. We calculated the Herfindahl index using only the 100 largest firms in France and Italy. See Lee (1996, Appendix K) for a detailed method for calculating the Herfindahl index.

The degree of concentration after EEC integration measured by the Herfindahl index increased very modestly from 137.5 in 1963 to 140.8 in 1983.[25] Out of fifty-one industries in the study, the number of industries with an increased Herfindahl index is thirty-one, while twenty industries show the decreased concentration ratio. The Herfindahl indices for individual industries are available in Lee (1996).

8. Preliminary estimation results

Marvel and Ray (1983) studied US tariff cuts in the Kennedy Round of GATT negotiations and found that tariff cuts were more severe in less concentrated industries. Cheh (1974) studied the exemptions from the across-the-board 50 per cent tariff cut imposed in the Kennedy Round awarded to US industries. He showed that reductions in tariff and non-tariff trade barriers may be explained by variables such as labour adjustment costs. In particular, declining industries with a high proportion of unskilled

Table 4.4. Mean of the EEC Herfindahl index

1968	1983	Difference
137.5	140.8	+3.3

Note: Unweighted means for 51 three-digit manufacturing industries.

Table 4.5. Number of industries by change in concentration

Increase (+)	Decrease (−)	Total
31	20	51

Table 4.6. Effect of trade diversion on protection

Independent variable	Regression 1	Regression 2	Regression 3	Regression 4
Constant	0.4833*** (25.212)	0.4834*** (26.505)	0.4899*** (21.454)	0.4497*** (16.174)
TD: ΔExternal import penetration	0.0231 (0.130)	−0.0662 (−0.382)		
TD: External import penetration ratio			−0.0044 (−0.501)	−0.0063 (−0.752)
HDif: ΔHerfindahl EEC index = $H_{E,83} - H_{E,63}$		3.4783** (2.475)		
Concentration ratio = $H_{E,83}/H_{E,63}$				0.0285** (2.345)
Adjusted R^2	−0.020	0.07	−0.01	0.07
F value	0.017	3.072	0.251	2.888
Sample size	51	51	51	51

Dependent variable: tariff 1983/tariff 1968.

Note: The numbers of observations may differ due to exclusion of outliers. *t*-values appear in parentheses below coefficients.

Key: ** significant at the 5% level; *** significant at the 1% level.

workers are associated with low reductions. Riedel (1977) applied the methodology of Cheh to West Germany between 1964 and 1972.

We analyse industry tariffs in this paper. However, we know that overall tariff declines could have been expected in Europe from the 1960s to the 1980s for two reasons. First, the average effective country size increased, meaning that geographically driven changes could have occurred as described above. Secondly, there were GATT rounds of tariff negotiations during this period. The GATT effect can be seen in the US tariff reductions. The average US tariff rates in 1967 and 1968 were 7.5 and 7.1 per cent, respectively, and in the later years of 1982 and 1983 they were 3.6 and 3.7 per cent, respectively.[26] From this, we know that tariff reductions were approximately halved internationally.[27] The estimated constants in our regressions are around 0.4 to 0.5, which means 50–60 per cent tariff reductions occurred in the EEC.

Consider now the effects of trade creation (TC) and trade diversion (TD) on the common external EEC tariffs over this period. Kreinin estimated trade diversion by the growth rate in the ratio of 'external imports/consumption'. We construct two variables, the *external import penetration ratio* for 1979 relative to 1963 (= IMETCON79: Imports from non-EC, 1979/Consumption, 1979)/(IMETCON63: Imports from non-EC, 1963/Consumption, 1963) and the difference of the two import penetrations, Δ*external import penetration* [= IMETCON79 − IMETCON63]. We expect a weak positive sign for the trade diversion effect. The *t*-values in regressions 1 to 4 are very low and show different signs except in regression 1. Recall that our dependent variable is the ratio of the 1983 common external tariff divided by the 1968 common external tariff.

In Table 4.7 we use different measures for trade diversion and trade creation. Trade diversion here is the change in external imports during the period divided by external

Table 4.7. Effect of trade diversion and trade creation on protection

Independent variable	Regression 5	Regression 6
Constant	0.4924*** (20.277)	0.4226*** (13.03)
Trade diversion		
TD: ΔExternal imports/External imports$_{63}$ = ΔIMET/IMET63	−0.0009 (−0.58)	
Trade creation		
TC: ΔInternal imports/Internal imports$_{63}$ = ΔIMIN/IMIN63		0.0038** (2.268)
Adjusted R^2	−0.01	0.07
F value	0.336	5.144
Sample size	51	51

Dependent variable: tariff 1983/tariff 1968.

Note: The numbers of observations may differ due to exclusion of outliers. *t*-values appear in parentheses below the coefficients.

Key: ** significant at the 5% level; *** significant at the 1% level.

imports in 1963, ΔIMET/IMET63, but is insignificant. However, trade creation as the change in internal imports during the period divided by internal imports for 1963, ΔIMIN/IMIN63, is significant at the 5 per cent level.

Regression 6 confirms the compensation effect of Magee *et al.* (1989) compared to the accelerated declining support hypothesis of Hillman (1982), Cassing and Hillman (1986), van Long and Vousden (1991), and Richardson (1993). The accelerated declining support hypothesis says that political support for domestic industries decreases with increased import competition, because the industry becomes smaller and weaker. Magee *et al.* (1989), in contrast, asserts that the causes of industry decline vary and the causes of industry decline determine whether the industry lobbies more or less. For example, if an unskilled-labour intensive industry declines because the country's endowment of unskilled labour declines relative to human and physical capital, capital endowment for the entire country, then a lower tariff results because of lower total political clout. However, if an unskilled-labour intensive industry declines because of lower prices for its products, it lobbies more for a tariff because the price of labour, its intensive factor, falls and it has a lower opportunity cost of lobbying.

Regression 6 confirms the Magee *et al.* result because it shows that trade creation results in a higher external tariff. That is, the more rapid the growth of imports from member countries, the higher the resulting industry tariff. Even though the import-competing industries face greater import competition and may be declining, they struggle nevertheless to get relief through higher tariffs because lower prices and lower wages lower their opportunity costs of lobbying.

In Table 4.8, we estimate the coefficients for the free-riding coefficient in the EEC, *a*. If equation (6) is linear, then $\beta = 2$ and the estimated coefficients on the two equation (6) terms are equal to $a/2$. Notice that the smallest two coefficients are in regression 9 and equal to about 3.0, yielding an estimate of $a = 1.5$. The coefficients are positive as expected, significant, but both are considerably greater than 1. A coefficient of $a = 1$ is a high free-riding parameter. When $a = 1$, notice in equation (4) that the tariff is directly to the Herfindahl. We conclude that free-riding in Europe over tariff protection is high. It is higher than in the USA, where Lee and Magee (1997) estimate that the free-riding parameter $a = .8$. Table 4.8 also estimates the coefficients in equation (6) above, along with other control variables.

The sign of the *internal imports ratio* (= Internal imports, 1983/Internal imports, 1963) needs some explanation. The imports among member countries should be the same *ex post* as the exports among member countries. Therefore the *internal imports ratio* is thought to be equal to the internal export ratio. We may interpret this as meaning that more intra-customs union exports result in a higher external tariff because the higher ratio of intra-EC exports tends to alleviate risk exposure to a foreign country's retaliatory tariff once the EEC sets the higher tariff. Another regression result, with the addition of the ratio of two period shipments, S_{83}/S_{63}, and the difference of export intensity between the comparison times, $(EX/S)_{83} - (EX/S)_{63}$, is also presented. Greater shipments after integration mitigates the sentiment toward protection. Therefore, the sign of S_{83}/S_{63} is negative as expected. The *export intensity* variable (EX/S) denotes the

Table 4.8. Estimates of the free-riding parameters in equation (6)

Variables	Regression 7	Regression 8	Regression 9
Constant	0.41***	0.387***	0.605***
	(12.39)	(12.0)	(17.53)
Estimates for equation (6)			
Individual stake: $(H_{83}-1)(S/C)_{83}-(H_{63}-1)(S/C)_{63}$	3.53***	7.14***	2.96***
	(2.814)	(3.571)	(2.661)
Group stake: $(S/C)_{83}-(S/C)_{63}$	3.44***	6.99***	3.0***
	(2.78)	(3.551)	(2.70)
Other variables			
Internal imports ratio:	0.004***	0.005***	0.005***
Internal imports$_{83}$/Internal imports$_{63}$	(2.69)	(3.3)	(3.464)
Compensation effect: Shipment$_{83}$/Shipment$_{63}$			−0.01**
			(−2.39)
ΔExport intensity: $(Export/Shipment)_{83}-(Ex/S)_{63}$			−0.47*
			(−1.84)
Adjusted R^2	0.18	0.26	0.24
F value	4.728	6.614	4.207
Sample size	51	49	51

Dependent variable: tariff 1983/tariff 1968.

Note: The numbers of observations may differ due to exclusion of outliers. *t*-values appear in parentheses below coefficients.

Key: * significant at the 10% level; ** significant at the 5% level; *** significant at the 1% level.

Table 4.9. The effect of industry concentration on protection

Independent variable	Regression 10	Regression 11	Regression 12	Regression 13	Regression 14
Constant	0.4825***	0.4141***	0.4769***	0.4380***	0.44183***
	(26.922)	(6.524)	(26.195)	(6.728)	(17.225)
HDif: ΔHerfindahl EEC	3.3668**	3.0543**	6.6412**	5.7275**	
index = $H_{E,83}-H_{E,63}$	(2.471)	(2.202)	(2.811)	(2.207)	
Concentration ratio =					0.0276**
$H_{E,83}/H_{E,63}$					(2.293)
Tariff$_{68}$		0.0045		0.0027	
		(1.123)		(0.624)	
Adjusted R^2	0.0926	0.00975	0.1257	0.1142	0.0784
F value	6.105	3.7	7.903	4.095	5.256
Sample size	51	51	49	49	51

Dependent variable: tariff 1983/tariff 1968.

Note: The numbers of observations may differ due to exclusion of outliers. *t*-values appear in parentheses below coefficients.

Key: ** significant at the 5% level; *** significant at the 1% level.

Table 4.10. Regression results of tariff diversion and tariff creation

Independent variable	Regression 15	Regression 16	Regression 17	Regression 18	Regression 19
Constant	0.4446***	0.4287***	0.4112***	0.4036***	0.5256***
	(7.004)	(13.077)	(12.036)	(11.122)	(6.675)
$Tariff_{68}$	0.0015				
	(0.373)				
Tariff diversion					
Tariff diversion: D2	0.4577	1.6012[a]	3.4104[b]	3.5943[c]	3.4882[d]
Hdivert $= H_{E,63} - H_{C,63}$	(0.331)	(1.278)	(1.657)	(1.622)	(1.611)
Tariff diversion: D3		−0.0081***			
Shipments ratio $=$		(−2.158)			
$Shipments_{83}/$					
$Shipments_{63}$					
Tariff diversion: D4		−0.3759***	−0.1952*	−0.2326*	−0.2416*
ΔExport intensity:		(−2.801)	(−1.706)	(−1.874)	(−1.911)
$(Exports/Shipments)_{83}-$					
$(Exports/Shipments)_{63}$					
Tariff creation					
Tariff creation: C2	6.8915***	6.6976***	7.6420***	8.0836***	6.7472***
Hdif: ΔHerfindahl EEC	(2.949)	(2.764)	(3.011)	(2.912)	(2.412)
index $= H_{E,83} - H_{E,63}$					
Tariff creation: C3		0.0063***	0.0049***	0.0057***	0.0042***
Internal imports		(4.246)	(3.303)	(3.543)	(2.355)
growth $=$					
Internal $imports_{83}/$					
Internal $imports_{63}$					
Control variable:					−0.1713*
Initial internal imports					(−1.736)
share $=$					
Internal $imports_{63}/$					
Total $imports_{63}$					
Adjusted R^2	0.163	0.312	0.259	0.259	0.293
F value	4.057	5.278	4.849	5.038	4.827
Sample size	48	48	45	47	47

Dependent variable: tariff 1983/tariff 1968.

Note: The numbers of observations may differ due to exclusion of outliers. *t*-values appear in parentheses below coefficients.

Key: [a] significant at the 20.8% level; [b] significant at the 10.6% level; [c] significant at the 11.2% level; [d] significant at the 11.5% level; * significant at the 10% level; ** significant at the 5% level; *** significant at the 1% level.

ratio of extra-regional exports to shipments. A higher ratio means more risk related to the EEC's import protection policy because the region's exports will be the target of retaliation. The sign of Δ*export intensity* is negative as expected.

Table 4.10 reports the industry regressions which are the basis of our tariff creation and tariff diversion calculations. Table 4.13 provides summary statistics for the data which we use in the regressions. We use the results in regression 16 of the summary work on tariff creation and tariff diversion in what follows. The average of the country tariff rates for the 47 industries which we report in regression 16 was 15.1 per cent in 1968. After 1968, these tariffs, which have become the EEC common external tariffs, declined to 7.0 per cent in 1983. The 1963 average country Herfindahl indices for France and Italy were .0253. These Herfindahls declined to .0138 when recalculated at the EEC level in 1963. These Herfindahls then rise, albeit microscopically, to .0141 by 1983. Note the 16.9 times increase in imports from member countries over the period 1963 to 1983, compared to the 6.9 increase in industry shipments over the same period. The exports (to non-member countries) to shipments ratio declined from 1963 to 1983.

Table 4.10 provides the results of different regressions across 47 to 51 industries. The dependent variable for all of the regressions is the ratio of the industry's common external tariff in 1983 to the same tariff rate in 1968 (the mean value of which is .4836).

Four of the coefficients in regression 16 may be subject to simultaneous equation bias because the variables include values for 1983. Table 15 discussed in the Appendix performs Hausman (1978) tests for the exogeneity of the four variables of the right-hand side of regression 16 which contain 1983 data in them and reports two-stage least squares estimation of regression 16. Only one of the variables suffers from simultaneity problems.

8.1. Estimates of tariff diversion

Regression 16 in Table 4.10 permits measurement of the two principle tariff-diverting effects. We will discuss the first tariff-diverting effect, D1, below. The second, D2, captures the tariff-reducing effects of the initial drop in the Herfindahl industry concentration. The positive coefficients on the Herfindahl changes indicate that the dependent variable (the ratio of the 1983 to the 1968 common external tariff) falls more the greater the initial decline in the industry Herfindahl. Recall this is caused by protectionist industries being less concentrated in their lobbying of the EEC in Brussels for protection after 1968 than they were before in lobbying their individual country governments. This D2 effect was not statistically significant in any of the regressions. It came close in regression 17, being significant there at the .106 level.

The third measure of tariff diversion, D3, captures the higher opportunity cost of lobbying in more prosperous industries. The more rapid the growth of the industry, the less the industry lobbies for a higher common external tariff. The regression results for D3 confirm this effect, indicating that the higher the ratio of 1983 shipments over 1963 shipments, the lower the 1983 tariff. These results are statistically significant and have the right sign in two of the five equations.[28]

The fourth measure of tariff diversion, D4, captures the growth of intra-industry comparative advantage through greater export specialization. The regression results for D4 indicate that the higher the ratio of 1983 exports over 1963 exports, the lower the 1983 tariff. This effect is statistically significant in three out of four equations.

8.2. Estimates of tariff creation

Consider the tariff-creating effects. The first, C1, is discussed below. Secondly, an increase in EEC country size allows firms to achieve the minimum efficient scale. As weaker companies merge into stronger ones, the Herfindahl measure of industry concentration increases, lobbies have decreased free-rider problems and become more effective in increasing the common external tariff of the EEC. This effect is confirmed in measure C2, which is the change in the industry Herfindahl index from 1963 to 1983. It has the right sign and is significant at the .01 level.

Third, formation of the EEC causes a surge in imports from EEC member countries, whose products now enter free of duties. This reduces the profitability of import-competing firms, lowers their opportunity costs of lobbying and causes them to press for higher common external tariffs against non-member countries. The tariff-creating measure, C3, captures the ratio of imports in 1983 compared to 1963 from EEC member countries. That is, industries with higher increases in internal imports (i.e. imports from EEC member countries) did succeed in having higher common external tariffs in 1983 compared to 1968. The C3 variable has the right sign and is significant at the .01 level in four of the five equations. For both of the tariff-creating effects, the Hausman test later fails to reject exogeneity, despite the presence of 1983 data on the right-hand side of the equation.

8.3. Estimates of the terms of trade and endowment effects in the constant of the equations

There are several effects captured in the constants in the regressions in Table 10. We must first eliminate the non-customs union effect of GATT tariff reductions. GATT tariff negotiations over this period reduced the common external tariff of the EEC. For example, US average tariff rates dropped from 7.1 per cent in 1968 to 3.7 per cent in 1983.[29] Second, we would expect tariff diversion because of continuation of the same endowment and other changes which led to the EEC itself: capital deepening will lead to continuous decreases in the common external tariff. Third, there is a tariff creating force, which is the ability of the EEC to exercise its market power by raising tariffs to improve its terms of trade.

The constants tell us how much the EEC's common external tariffs fell for all reasons other than the variables on the right-hand side of our equations. Regression 16, in which the tariff diverting and tariff creating effects were estimated unconstrained, has the greatest explanatory power of the regressions and is later estimated using two-stage least squares to avoid simultaneity. Regressions 16 through 18 and the later version estimated using two-stage least squares have constants in the neighbourhood of .4, suggesting that tariffs fell about 60 per cent due to the three effects above and other unmeasured forces.[30]

We use tariff reductions in the USA over the 1968–83 period as proxies for GATT effects. The US tariff in 1968 was .52 of its 1968 value while the EEC industry tariffs were .4 of their 1968 value. Thus, after adjustment for GATT, the net of all of the effects captured in the constants are tariff diverting (i.e. tariff reducing). That is to say, the tariff-creating terms of trade effects are more than offset by the tariff diverting endowment and other effects. The details are explained in the notes to Table 4.11.

9. A summary of the empirical results

A summary of the overall changes in EEC external tariffs from 1968 to 1983 is presented in Table 4.11. We apply the regression coefficients in regression 16 of Table 4.10 to the means of the variables in Table 4.13 to derive the results. The common external tariff of the EEC on manufactures in our sample dropped from 15.1 per cent in 1968 to 7.0 per cent in 1983. Using the USA as a benchmark, the decline as explained by GATT tariff negotiations is about 7.2 percentage points.

After adjusting for GATT effects, the common external tariff of the EEC fell by another .9 percentage point. This suggests that the feared 'Fortress Europe' increases in protection discussed in recent years is unfounded, in the EEC and may be in advanced countries generally. We find that in the EEC, tariff diversion accounted for tariff decreases of 2.5 percentage points while tariff creation forces explain tariff increases of 1.6 percentage points. Both sides can be theoretically right in this regionalism debate. But, in general, the results depend on empirical work. The constant in our regressions indicate that Krugman's much speculated protectionist terms of trade effects coming from a large trading bloc were more than offset by capital-deepening endowment effects and other freer trade forces.

In both the formation and for the first full fifteen years of the EEC, regionalism was accompanied by endogenous forces which generated freer trade. We speculate that these results generalize to other advanced countries, although not to developing countries.

Table 4.11. Percentage point changes in the common external tariff in the first fifteen years of the EEC, 1968–1983, caused by tariff creation and tariff diversion ($n = 47$ industries)

Actual common external tariff of the EEC, 1968	**15.1%**
Changes due to GATT tariff reductions and other non-customs union effects[a]	–7.2%
Tariff increases due to tariff creation[b]	+1.6%
C2 Less free-riding due to mergers after 1968[c] (firm mergers cause Herfindahls to rise following creation of EEC)	+0.03%
C3 Tariff increases caused by increased internal imports[d] (import growth increases lobbying in Brussels)	+1.6%
Tariff declines due to tariff diversion[e]	–2.5%
D1 + C1 Net endowment effects (endowment effects > terms of trade)[f] (endowment effects offset terms of trade tariff increases)	–1.4%
D2 Increased free-riding in EEC compared to country lobbying[g] (EEC Herfindahls are smaller than pre-EEC country Herfindahls)	–0.3%
D3 Reduced tariffs due to rapid industry growth[h] (rapid EEC industry growth reduces industry dependence on external protection)	–0.8%
D4 Reduced tariffs due to greater export specialization[i] (free intra-EEC trade permits greater intra-industry specialization on exports)	0.0%
Actual common external tariff of the EEC, 1983[j]	**7.0%**

Notes: The coefficients of the effects come from Regression 16 in Table 4.10; the mean values of the independent variables come from Table 4.13.

[a] We use the United States as the benchmark for the effect of GATT and other non-customs union effects on tariffs. US tariffs declined from 7.1% in 1968 to 3.7% in 1983. The US 1983 tariff is .5211 of the 1968 tariff, for a tariff ratio change of –.4789. Multiply this tariff change by the 1968 EEC tariff, which gives –7.2% (–.4789 × 15.1%).

[b] This is the sum of tariff creation effects C2 plus C3. Large country effect C1 could not be separated from D1. The net of the two large country effects, C1 plus D1, is presented as a tariff diversion because the sum of the two effects is negative.

[c] Multiply the coefficient on C2 (6.6976) by the mean of C2 (.0003) = .002; multiply this by 1968 tariff of 15.1% = +.03%.

[d] Multiply C3 coefficient (.0063) by the mean of C3 (16.9447) = .1068; multiply this by the 1968 tariff of 15.1% = +1.6%.

[e] This is the sum of the net effects (D1 + C1), D2, D3, and D4.

[f] The constant in the regression equation (.4287) incorporates (1) GATT reductions and all other changes; (2) reductions in tariffs due to the large country effect of greater natural protection (higher transport costs to the common external border reduce the need for policy-induced protection); and (3) increases in tariffs due to the large country effect of the EEC attempting to improve its terms of trade. But effect (1) has already been captured: the 1983 tariff is .5211 of the 1968 tariff because of GATT and other effects. Thus, the net large country effects (2) plus (3) must be the difference between .4287 and .5311, or –.0924. Multiplying –.0924 by 15.1% yields –1.4%.

[g] Multiply D2 coefficient (1.6012) by the mean of D2 (–.0115) = –.0184; multiply this by the 1968 tariff of 15.1% = –.3.

[h] Multiply D3 coefficient (–.0081) by the mean of D3 (6.9372) = –.0562; multiply this by the 1968 tariff of 15.1% = –.8.

[i] Multiply D4 coefficient (–.3759) by the mean of D4 (–.0045) = +.002; multiply this by the 1968 tariff of 15.1% = .03%

[j] The difference between the two actual tariffs (15.1% less 7.0%) equals the sum of the three changes of –8.1% (–7.2%, +1.6%, and –2.5%).

Appendix

The beta coefficients for selected equations are estimated in the standardized regressions. In Table 4.12, a change of one standard deviation in the variable *HDivert*, is expected to change the dependent variable, *Tariff1983/Tariff1968*, by 0.1619 times the standard deviation of the dependent variable. Using the real value reported in Table 4.13, a change of 0.0134 in *HDivert* is expected to change *Tariff1983/Tariff1968* by 0.0217 (= 0.1619 × 0.1343). A change of 0.0133 in the variable *HDif* is expected to change the dependent variable, *Tariff1983/Tariff1968*, by 0.0505 (= 0.3766 × 0.1343). Similarly, in regression 18, the sizes of change in the dependent variable due to a change of one standard deviation in the variables *HDivert* and *HDif* are 0.0289 (= 0.2154 × 0.1343) and 0.0570 (= 0.4249 × 0.1343), respectively.

Table 4.12. Beta coefficients in selected regressions

Independent variable	Regression 16	Regression 18
Constant	0.0	0.0
HDivert	0.1619	0.2154
HDif	0.3766	0.4249
Internal imports ratio	0.5913	0.4519
Shipments ratio	−0.3659	
ΔExport intensity	−0.4711	−0.2493

Table 4.13. Summary statistics for the industries in the regressions

Variable	N	Mean	Standard Dev.
Tariff_{68}	51	15.10904	4.563298
Tariff_{83}	51	7.371824	4.007021
$\text{Tariff}_{83}/\text{Tariff}_{68}$	51	0.4836	0.134321
Herfindahl, France	51	0.024324	0.033628
Herfindahl, Italy	51	0.026264	0.033117
$H_{C,63}$ (= Pre-EC Herfindahl)	51	0.025294	0.031332
Herfindahl, EEC, 1963	51	0.013759	0.018974
Herfindahl, EEC, 1983	51	0.014087	0.015392
$\text{HDif} = H_{EC,83} - H_{EC,63}$	51	0.000329	0.01328
$\text{HDivert} = H_{EC,63} - H_{C,63}$	51	−0.011535	0.013379
$\text{Internal imports}_{83}/\text{Internal imports}_{63}$	51	16.94468	10.8135
$\text{Shipments}_{83}/\text{Shipments}_{63}$	51	6.937188	5.155767
$\text{Internal imports}_{63}/\text{Total imports}_{63}$	51	0.5648	0.1893
$(\text{Exports/Shipments})_{83} - (\text{Exports/Shipments})_{63}$	51	−0.004477	0.143584

We address the simultaneity problem in two ways. We first estimate the tariff with variables predetermined before 1968 (Table 4.14). The signs are as expected and are not different from previous regressions. However, we still have low *t*-values for *Tariff1968* as before and for $H_{E,63}$. Table 4.14 provides a list of variables that are candidates for instrumental estimation.

A second approach is to apply the Hausman (1978) test to those variables in Table 4.10 with 1983 subscripts. The results indicated that the Shipments Ratio (= Shipments$_{83}$/Shipments$_{63}$) was predetermined at the 5 per cent level but not at the 10 per cent level, which leaves the issue to the reader. Table 4.15 reports the original regression 16 in Table 4.10 and the estimation of regression 16 using instrumental estimates.

Table 4.14. Regressions using pre-determined variables only

Independent variable	Regression 20	Regression 21	Regression 22	Regression 23
Constant	0.4653***	0.4118***	0.480***	0.5422***
	(4.367)	(3.475)	(4.274)	(6.560)
Tariff$_{68}$		0.004		0.0057
		(1.208)		(1.477)
$H_{E,63}$			−0.4338	
			(−0.452)	
Shipments–consumption ratio:	0.2703*	0.2511*	0.2557*	
Shipments$_{63}$/Consumption$_{63}$	(1.980)	(1.824)	(1.835)	
Initial internal imports share:	−0.3545***	−0.3443***	−0.3537***	−0.2564***
Internal imports$_{63}$/Total imports$_{63}$	(−3.345)	(−3.236)	(−3.308)	(−2.753)
Export intensity:	−0.5554**	−0.4988**	−0.523**	
(Exports/Shipments)$_{63}$	(−2.307)	(−2.021)	(−2.071)	
Adjusted R^2	0.177	0.168	0.163	0.142
F value	4.583	3.204	3.430	5.130
Sample size	51	51	51	51

Dependent variable: tariff 1983/tariff 1968.

Note: The numbers of observations may differ due to exclusion of outliers. *t*-values appear in parentheses below coefficients.

Key: * significant at the 10% level; ** significant at the 5% level; *** significant at the 1% level.

Table 4.15. Regression results of tariff diversion and tariff creation using two-stage least squares

Independent variable	Regression 16	Regression 16A	Hausman test significance
Constant	0.4287*** (13.077)	0.3981*** (10.043)	
Tariff_{68}			
Tariff diversion: Hdivert = $H_{E,63} - H_{C,63}$	1.6012[a] (1.278)	1.9097** (1.431)	
Tariff diverting: shipments ratio = $\text{Shipments}_{83}/\text{Shipments}_{63}$	−0.0081*** (−2.158)	−0.0011 (−0.192)	.0983[b]
Tariff diverting: Initial internal imports share = Internal imports$_{63}$/Total imports$_{63}$			
Tariff diverting: $(\text{Exports/Shipments})_{83} - (\text{Exports/Shipments})_{63}$	−0.3759*** (−2.801)	−0.2292* (−1.353)	.2101
Tariff creation: Hdif: ΔHerfindahl EC index = $H_{E,83} - H_{E,63}$	6.6976*** (2.764)	7.8405*** (2.367)	.7817
Tariff creating: Internal imports ratio = Internal imports$_{83}$/Internal imports$_{63}$	0.0063*** (4.246)	0.0054*** (3.207)	.9854
Adjusted R^2	0.312	0.237	
F value	5.278	3.924	
Sample size	47	47	

Dependent variable: tariff 1983/tariff 1968.

Note: The numbers of observations may differ due to exclusion of outliers. *t*-values appear in parentheses below coefficients. Equation (16A) is a two-stage least squares estimation of equation (16) using the predicted value of the shipments ratio. The first-stage estimators were SHCON63, EXINT63, DHERFT, HDIF, IMINRAT, and EXINTDIJ.

Key: [a] significant at the 20.8% level; [b] significant at the 10% level; * significant at the 18.3% level; ** significant at the 16% level; *** significant at the 1% level.

Notes

1. For a discussion of the 1977 paper on endogenous free-riding, see Magee, Brock and Young (1989, Appendix to ch. 6, pp. 278–91).
2. See Lasok and Cairns (1983, 143).
3. GATT (1955) XXIV also stipulates, '[paragraph] 8. For the purpose of this Agreement: (a) A customs union shall be understood to mean the substitution of a single customs territory for two or more customs territories, so that (i) ... (ii) ..., substantially the same duties and other regulations of commerce are applied by each of the members of the union to the trade of territories not included in the union; ...'.
4. The EEC, which became the main body of the EC, was created by the Treaty of Rome in 1957. The original six members were Belgium, the Netherlands, Luxembourg, Germany, France, and Italy. In 1973, Denmark, Ireland, and the UK joined. Greece followed them in 1981 and Spain and Portugal joined the EC in 1986. With the accession of Austria, Finland, and Sweden

in 1995, the EC has become the European Union (EU) of 15 members. The tariff reduction started in 1959 and ended in 1968. The first EEC census was published in 1963.

5. See Whalley (1996) for the reasons that countries seek preferential trade areas.

6. See WTO (1995) for more recent regional arrangements notified to GATT.

7. Krueger (1995) argues that an FTA is dominated by a CU for two reasons. First, a common external tariff of a CU is set between the high pre-CU level of a member A, and the low level of another member C, so that the post-CU tariff should not be increased after the CU, while FTA members do not change their pre-FTA levels. This lowered tariff under a CU forces the production of A to reduce, which creates trade creation. In contrast, A's production is sustained under an FTA and thus, there is less trade creation. Secondly, it is costly to implement the rules of origin (ROO) under an FTA, which is necessary to prevent export circumvention via a partner country with lower external tariff rates. Taking this into consideration leads Krueger to conclude that an FTA is likely to incur a greater welfare loss.

8. For a detailed discussion of the compensation effect, see Magee *et al.* (1989, ch. 11).

9. Article XXIV (Territorial Application—Frontier Traffic—Customs Unions and Free-trade Areas) of the GATT(1955) reads, '[Paragraph] 4. [The contracting parties] also recognize that the purpose of a customs union or of a free-trade area should be to facilitate trade between the constituent territories and not to raise barriers to the trade of other contracting parties with such territories. 5. Accordingly, the provision of this Agreement shall not prevent, as between the territories of contracting parties, the formation of a customs union or of a free-trade area . . .; Provided that: (a) with respect to a customs union, or an interim agreement leading to the formation of a customs union, the duties and other regulations of commerce imposed at the institution of any such union or interim agreement in respect of trade with contracting parties not parties to such union or agreement shall not on the whole be higher or more restrictive than the general incidence of the duties and regulations of commerce applicable in the constituent territories prior to the formation of such union or the adoption of such interim agreement, as the case may be; (b) with respect to a free-trade area, or . . . the duties and other regulations of commerce maintained in each of the constituent territories . . . shall not be higher or more restrictive than the corresponding duties and other regulations of commerce existing in the same constituent territories prior to the formation of the free-trade area, . . .'.

10. There will be general equilibrium effects coming from the negative welfare effects of transfer of tariff revenue from the country to the less efficient member country suppliers.

11. We are ignoring pre-union partner country lobbying for the union based on these expected trade diversion gains. Krueger (1995) mentions the possibility that newly grown intra-customs union firms apply protectionist efforts against third countries in order to keep now established intra-market shares. Trade diversion does economic harm to foreign suppliers, but it is to non-members of the customs union.

12. There is an offsetting reason to expect lower tariffs from trade creation. If a tariff increases with the share of non-customs union imports in consumption, then the lowered non-union import share due to economic integration will lead to lower protection against non-member countries. Neven and Roeller (1991) take a similar position: 'A high common external tariff seems to be associated with a higher import share from the rest of the world and a lower import share of EEC origin. This finding is possibly explained by the "political economy" of protectionism, such that industries that are not competitive seek protectionism more than others' (p. 1304).

13. The Commission of the EC (1988) emphasizes the dynamic aspect of EC 1992. For example,

see Chapter 5 in volume 2, Basic Findings by Smith and Venables and Chapter 8 in the same volume by Cawley and Davenport.

14. High concentration and larger market share per firm after integration may be argued as a good sign because competitive firms have increased their market shares at the expense of the less efficient firms even though the costs of large firms such as numerous X-inefficiencies are forthcoming. This consideration leads to research of the relationship between concentration and price–cost margin after economic integration. See Yamawaki *et al.* (1989) and Sleuwaegen and Yamawaki (1988) for this study.

15. See Neven (1990) for these dynamic aspects.

16. The EEC-wide Herfindahl index increases because of mergers.

17. Smith and Venables (1988) share the same opinion: 'With EC market integration, shares in 'national' markets are no longer of economic significance' (p. 304).

18. See Magee *et al.* (1989) for the reason for these restrictions.

19. Pincus (1975) says 'the ratio of imports plus domestic production to production is proxy for the loss to gain' (footnote 10).

20. See Kirchner and Schwaiger (1981) for a detailed study of interest groups in the EC. See Magee (1996) for applications to a number of countries, including the USA.

21. The tariff reductions started in 1959 and ended in 1968. The first EEC census was published in 1963.

22. Emerson *et al.* (1988) mention 10 years for industry adjustment (p. 201).

23. Article 19 of the Treaty of Rome in 1957, reprinted in EC (1967), stipulates: '1...., duties in the common customs tariff shall be at the level of the arithmetical average of the duties applied in the four customs territories comprised in the Community.'

24. Kamera and Koo (1994) use different methods for trade creation and trade diversion, modifying Baldwin and Murray (1977). They calculate trade creation and trade diversion as $TC_i = M_i \times n_i \times (\Delta t_i/1 + t_i)$ and $TD_i = TC_i \times (MN_i/V_i)$, where TC_i (TD_i) is trade creation (trade diversion) effect for good i in a country, M_i is the initial level of imports from the beneficiary country, t_i is an initial level of tariffs for good i from the beneficiary country, Δt_i is tariff cuts in good i and MN_i is imports of good i from non-beneficiary countries, V_i is total domestic production of commodity i in a country, and n_i is price elasticity of import demand for good i. We do not adopt this method because of the limitation of elasticity data.

25. For reference, the average Herfindahl index of 50 firms for 1980 in the USA is about 600, which shows US industries to be more concentrated than European ones.

26. Magee *et al.* (1989, Appendix to ch. 13).

27. Lasok and Cairns (1983) mention the several rounds of the GATT tariff reduction: in the 1962 Dillon Round, a 20% tariff reduction was decided. The Kennedy Round starting in 1962 reached average tariff reductions of 35% and the Tokyo Round from 1973 resulted in an average tariff reduction of 30% on industrial products (pp. 144–6). If tariffs were reduced according to these rounds, the final tariff level would be 36.4% $[= ((100 \times 0.8) \times 0.65) \times 0.7]$.

28. The Hausman test marginally rejects the exogeneity of the shipments ratio variable (at the .098 level). However, endogeneity bias does not suggest a spurious finding of tariff diversion in our results. That would happen only if external tariff declines to 1983 caused the industry's output to rise (which is opposite to the effect that tariffs have on industry output). The puzzling result is the failure of D2 to be significantly negative after simultaneity is accounted for in regression 5.

29. Magee *et al.* (1989, Appendix to ch. 13). The GATT effect can be seen in the US tariff reductions: for the numerical values, see note 27.

30. Three of the four control variables on the right-hand side of the equations have the expected signs. Industries which are increasingly export oriented (Δ*export intensity*) or which had a high initial export intensity have greater drops in the common external tariff. Industries in which shippers dominate consumers politically (have high shipments–consumption ratios) have higher common external tariffs in 1983 relative to 1968. The puzzle is that industries with high initial internal import shares have lower tariffs in 1983 relative to 1968. We would expect the industries to face a flood of imports from member countries after the EEC is formed, which should drive them to Brussels to get greater protection against imports from non-members. Two potential explanations are that (1) the EEC may possess a comparative advantage in these industries, so there were few non-member countries for the common external to protect against or (2) that free intra-industry trade wiped out these industries, so there was little industry left to protect.

References

Andersen, Svein S. and Eliassen, Kjell A. (1991) 'European Community Lobbying', *European Journal of Political Research*, 20: 173–87.

Bagwell, Kyle and Staiger, Robert W. (1993) 'Multilateral Tariff Cooperation During the Formation of Regional Free Trade Areas', Working Paper no. 4364 (May). Cambridge, MA: NBER.

Baldwin, Robert E. (1985) *The Political Economy of U.S. Import Policy*. Cambridge, MA: MIT Press.

Baldwin, R. E. and Murray, T. (1977) 'MFN Tariff Reductions and LDC Benefits Under GSP', *Economic Journal*, January: 30–46.

Bhagwati, Jagdish (1991) *The World Trading System at Risk*. Princeton, NJ: Princeton University Press.

Bhagwati, Jagdish (1993) 'Regionalism and Multilateralism: An Overview', in de Melo, Jaime and Panagariya, Arvind (eds.), *New Dimensions in Regional Integration*. New York: Cambridge University Press.

Bilal, Sanoussi (1998) 'Why Regionalism May Increase the Demand for Trade Protection', *Journal of Economic Integration*, 13: 30–61.

Brainard, Lael S. and Verdier, Thierry (1994) 'Lobbying and Adjustment in Declining Industries', *European Economic Review*, 38: 586–95.

Brock, William A. and Magee, Stephen P. (1977) 'Understanding Collective Action: A Formal Analysis of the Voluntary Provision of Public Goods', mimeo, University of Chicago.

Brock, William A. and Magee, Stephen P. (1978) 'The Economics of Special-Interest Politics: The Case of the Tariff', *American Economic Review*, 68: 246–50.

Carneiro, Robert L. (1970) 'A Theory of the Origin of the State', *Science*, 169: 733–8.

Cassing, James H. and Hillman, Arye L. (1986) 'Shifting Comparative Advantage and Senescent Industry Collapse', *American Economic Review*, 76: 516–23.

Caves, Richard E. (1985) 'International Trade and Industrial Organization: Problems, Solved and Unsolved', *European Economic Review*, 28: 377–95.

Cawley, Richard and Davenport, Michael (1988) 'Partial Equilibrium Calculations of the Impact of Internal Market Barriers in the European Community', in Commission of the European Communities (ed.), *Research on the 'Cost of Non-Europe'—Basic Findings*, vol. 2: *Studies on the Economics of Integration*. Luxembourg: Office of Official Publications of the European Communities.

Cheh, John H. (1974) 'United States Concessions in the Kennedy Round and Short-Run Labor Adjustment Costs', *Journal of International Economics*, 4: 323–40.

Chiu, Y. Stephen (1994) 'Public Goods Provision, International Trade, and Economic Integration', paper presented at the autumn 1994 Meeting of the Mid-West International Economics Group, University Park: Penn State University, October.

Commission of the European Communities (ed.) (1988) *Research on the 'Cost of Non-Europe'—Basic Findings*, vol. 2: *Studies on the Economics of Integration*. Luxembourg: Office for Official Publications of the European Communities.

Connor, John M. and Peterson, Everett B. (1992) 'Market-Structure Determinants of National Brand–Private Label Price Differences of Manufactured Food Products', *Journal of Industrial Economics*, June: 157–71.

Deardorff, Allan V. and Stern, Robert R. (1993) 'Multilateral Trade Negotiations and Preferential Trading Arrangements', in Deardorff, Allan V. and Stern, Robert M. (eds.), *Analytical and Negotiating Issues in the Global Trading System*. Ann Arbor: University of Michigan Press.

de la Torre, Augusto and Kelly, Margaret R. (1992) 'Regional Trade Arrangements', Occasional Paper no. 93 (March), Washington, DC: International Monetary Fund.

de Melo, Jaime, Panagariya, Arvind, and Rodrik, Dani (1993) 'The New Regionalism: A Country Perspective', in de Melo, Jaime and Panagariya, Arvind (eds.), *New Dimensions in Regional Integration*. Cambridge: Cambridge University Press.

Emerson, Michael, Aujean, Michel, Catinat, Michel, Goybet, Philippe, and Jacuemin, Alexis (1988) *The Economics of 1992: The European Commission's Assessment of the Economic Effects of Completing the Internal Market*. Oxford: Oxford University Press.

European Communities (1957) *Treaty Establishing the European Economic Community* (Treaty of Rome). Brussels, Belgium: Publication Services for the European Communities. Reprinted Washington, DC: European Community Information Service.

European Communities (1964a) *Foreign Trade: Analytical Tables—Export, 1963*. Luxembourg: Statistical Office of the European Communities (SOEC; Eurostat).

European Communities (1964b) *Foreign Trade: Analytical Tables—Import, 1963*. Luxembourg: Statistical Office of the European Communities (SOEC; Eurostat).

European Communities (1969) *Etudes et enquêtes statistiques: 2/1969*. Luxembourg: Statistical Office of the European Communities (SOEC; Eurostat).

European Communities (1975) *Etudes et enquêtes statistiques: 2/1975*. Luxembourg: Statistical Office of the European Communities (SOEC; Eurostat).

European Communities (1976) *Common Nomenclature of Industrial Products: NIPRO, edition 1975*. Luxembourg: Statistical Office of the European Communities (SOEC; Eurostat).

European Communities (1979) *Analytical Tables of Foreign Trade: Nimexe 1977*. Luxembourg: Statistical Office of the European Communities (SOEC; Eurostat).

European Communities (1980) *Analytical Tables of Foreign Trade 1979: Series A to L*. Belgium: Statistical Office of the European Communities (SOEC; Eurostat).

European Communities (1981) *Structure and Activity of Industry: Main Results—1979/1980*. Luxembourg: Statistical Office of the European Communities (SOEC; Eurostat).

European Communities (1983) *Structure et activite de l'industrie: data by size of enterprises 1983—Theme 4 (Energy and Industry) Series C (Accounts, Surveys and Statistics)*. Luxembourg: Statistical Office of the European Communities (SOEC; Eurostat).

Findlay, Ronald (1994) 'Towards a Model of Territorial Expansion and the Limits of Empire', Columbia University (May).

Fiorentini, Gianluca (1993) 'A Model of Electoral Competition with Pressure Groups', London School of Economics Suntory–Toyota International Centre for Economics and Related Disciplines Working Paper no. 35.

Foroutan, Faezeh (1993) 'Regional Integration in Sub-Saharan Africa: Past Experience and Future Prospects', in de Melo, Jaime and Panagariya, Arvind (eds.), *New Dimensions in Regional Integration*. Cambridge: Cambridge University Press, 234–71.

Friedman, David (1977) 'A Theory of the Size and Shape of Nations', *Journal of Public Economics*, 85: 59–77.

Gawande, Kishore (1994) 'Measuring Free-Riding', mimeo, Department of Economics, University of New Mexico.

Gawande, Kishore (forthcoming) 'US Nontariff Barriers as Privately Provided Public Goods', *Journal of Public Economics*.

General Agreement on Tariffs and Trade (GATT) (1955) *Basic Instruments and Selected Documents: Texts of the General Agreement, as Amended, and of the Agreement on the Organization for Trade Cooperation*, vol. 1 (revised). Geneva: The Contracting Parties to the GATT.

Grossman, Gene and Helpman, Elhanan (1994) 'Protection for Sale', *American Economic Review*, 84: 833–50.

Grossman, Gene and Helpman, Elhanan (1995) 'The Politics of Free Trade Agreements', *American Economic Review*, 85: 667–90.

Hanson, Gordon H. (1994) 'Regional Adjustment to Trade Liberalization', NBER Working Paper 4713 (April). Cambridge, MA: NBER.

Hausman, J. A. (1978) 'Specification Tests in Econometrics', *Econometrica*, 46: 1251–71.

Helpman, Elhanan (1995) 'A Survey of Rent Seeking and Trade Policy', mimeo.

Hillman, Arye L. (1982) 'Declining Industries and Political-Support Protectionist Motives', *American Economic Review*, 72: 1180–7.

Hillman, Arye L. (1991) 'Protection, Politics, and Market Structures', in Helpman, Elhanan and Razin, Assaf (eds.), *International Trade and Trade Policy*. Cambridge, MA: MIT Press.

Jacquemin, Alexis (1990) 'Horizontal Concentration and European Merger Policy', *European Economic Review*, 34: 539–50.

Kamera, David and Koo, Won W. (1994) 'Trade Creation and Diversion Effects of the US–Canadian Free Trade Agreement', *Contemporary Economic Policy*, 12: 12–23.

Kemp, Murray C. and Wan, Henry Y. (1976) 'Elementary Proposition Concerning the Formation of Customs Unions', *Journal of International Economics*, 6: 95–7.

Kirchner, Emil and Schwaiger, Konrad (1981) *The Role of Interest Groups in the European Community*. Aldershot: Gower.

Kreinin, Mordechai E. (1981) 'Static Effect of EEC Enlargement on Trade Flows in Manufactured Products', *Kyklos*, 34: 60–71.

Krueger, Anne (1995) 'Free Trade Agreements versus Customs Unions', Working Paper no. 5084 (April). Cambridge, MA: NBER.

Krugman, Paul R. (1991a) *Geography and Trade*. Cambridge, MA: MIT Press.

Krugman, Paul R. (1991b) 'Is Bilateralism Bad?', in Helpman, Elhanan and Razin, Assaf (eds.), *International Trade and Trade Policy*. Cambridge, MA: MIT Press.

Krugman, Paul R. (1993) 'Regionalism versus Multilateralism: Analytical Notes', in de Melo, Jaime and Panagariya, Arvind (eds.), *New Dimensions in Regional Integration*. Cambridge: Cambridge University Press, 58–79.

Krugman, Paul R. and Obstfeld, Maurice (1994) *International Economics: Theory and Practice*, 3rd edn. New York: HarperCollins.

Lasok, D. and Cairns, W. (1983) *The Customs Law of the European Economic Community.* Deventer, Netherlands: Kluwer Law and Taxation Publishers.

Lee, Hak-Loh (1996) 'The Effect of the Industrial Structure on Trade Policy'. Ph.D. Dissertation, Department of Economics, University of Texas at Austin, December.

Lee, Hak-Loh and Magee, Stephen P. (1996) 'Endogenous Free-Riding in Protectionist Lobbies: Theory and Evidence', mimeo, Department of Finance, University of Texas at Austin, December.

Magee, Stephen P. (1997) 'Endogenous Protection: The Empirical Evidence', in Dennis Mueller (ed.), *Perspectives on Political Economy.* New York: Cambridge University Press, 526–61.

Magee, Stephen P. and Lee, Hak-Loh (1999) 'Endogenous Tariff Creation and Tariff Diversion in a Customs Union', forthcoming, *European Economic Review*, 1999.

Magee, Stephen P., Brock, William A., and Young, Leslie (1989) *Black Hole Tariffs and Endogenous Policy Theory: Political Economy in General Equilibrium.* Cambridge: Cambridge University Press.

Magee, Stephen P., Yoo, Kwang-Yeol, and Choi, Nakgyoon (1997) 'The United States is a Small Country in World Trade', mimeo, Department of Finance, University of Texas at Austin.

Marvel, Howard P. and Ray, Edward J. (1983) 'The Kennedy Round: Evidence on the Regulation of International Trade in the United States', *American Economic Review*, 73: 190–7.

Meade, James E. (1955) *The Theory of Customs Unions.* Amsterdam: North-Holland.

Moore, Michael O. and Suranovic, Steven M. (1993) 'Lobbying and Cournot–Nash Competition: Implications for Strategic Trade Policy', *Journal of International Economics*, 35: 367–76.

Mundell, Robert A. (1961) 'A Theory of Optimum Currency Areas', *American Economic Review*, 51: 657–64.

Neven, Daimen J. (1990) 'Gains and Losses from 1992: Some Distributional Aspects', *Economic Policy*, April: 13–62.

Neven, Daimen J. and Roeller, Lars-Hendrik (1991) 'European Integration and Trade Flows', *European Economic Review*, 35: 1295–1309.

Olson, Mancur (1982) *The Rise and Decline of Nations.* New Haven: Yale University Press.

Owen, Nicholas (1983) *Economies of Scale, Competitiveness, and Trade Patterns within the European Community.* Oxford: Clarendon Press.

Panagariya, Arvind and Findlay, Ronald. (1994) 'Political Economy Analysis of Free Trade Areas and Customs Unions', Policy Research Working Paper no. 1261 (March). Washington, DC: World Bank, Trade Policy Division, Policy Research Department.

Peck, Merton J. (1989) 'Industrial Organization and the Gains from Europe 1992', *Brookings Papers on Economic Activity*, 2: 277–99.

Pincus, J. J. (1975) 'Pressure Groups and the Pattern of Tariffs', *Journal of Public Economics*, 83: 757–78.

Richardson, Martin (1993) 'Endogenous Protection and Trade Diversion', *Journal of International Economics*, 34: 309–24.

Richardson, Martin (1994) 'Why a Free Trade Area? The Tariff also Rises', *Economics and Politics*, 6(1) (March): 79–96.

Richardson, Martin (1995) 'Tariff Revenue Competition in a Free Trade Area', *European Economic Review*, 39: 1406–37.

Riedel, James (1977) 'Tariff Concessions in the Kennedy Round and the Structure of Protection in West Germany', *Journal of International Economics*, 7: 133–43.

Rodrik, Dani (1986) 'Tariffs, Subsidies, and Welfare with Endogenous Policy', *Journal of International Economics*, 21: 285–99.

Schuknecht, Ludger (1991) 'The Political Economy of EC Protectionism: National Protectionism Based on Article 115, Treaty of Rome', *Public Choice*, 12: 37–50.

Schwalbach, Joachim (1988) 'Economies of Scale and Intra-Community Trade', in Commission of the European Communities (ed.), *Research on the 'Cost of Non-Europe'—Basic Findings*, vol. 2: *Studies on the Economics of Integration*. Luxembourg: Office of Official Publications of the European Communities.

Skaperdas, S. (1992) 'Cooperation, Conflict, and Power in the Absence of Property Rights', *American Economic Review*, 82: 720–39.

Sleuwaegen, Leo and Yamawaki, Hideki (1988) 'The Formation of the European Common Market and Changes in Market Structure and Performance', *European Economic Review*, 32: 1451–75.

Smith, A. and Venables, A. (1988) 'The Costs of Non-Europe: An Assessment Based on a Formal Model of Imperfect Competition and Economies of Scale', in Commission of the European Communities (ed.), *Research on the 'Cost of Non-Europe'—Basic Findings*, vol. 2: *Studies on the Economics of Integration*. Luxembourg: Office of Official Publications of the European Communities.

Snyder, James M. (1993) 'The Market for Campaign Contributions: Evidence for the U.S. Senate 1980–1986', *Economics and Politics*, 5: 219–40.

Tharakan, P. K. M. (1991) 'The Political Economy of Anti-Dumping Undertakings in the European Economy', *European Economic Review*, 35: 1341–59.

Trandel, Gregory A. and Skeath, Susan E. (1994) 'Playing Favorites: A Political–Strategic Model of Interest Groups and Trade Policy', paper presented at the autumn 1994 Meeting of the Mid-West International Economics Group, University Park: Penn State University, October.

van Long, Ngo and Vousden, Neil (1991) 'Protectionist Responses and Declining Industries', *Journal of International Economics*, 30: 87–103.

Vaubel, Roland (1994) 'The Public Choice Analysis of European Integration: A Survey', *European Journal of Political Economy*, 10: 227–49.

Viner, Jacob (1950) *The Customs Union Issue*. Washington, DC: Anderson Kramer Associates. Reproduced by Permission of the Carnegie Endowment for International Peace in 1961.

Weiss, Frank D. (1987) 'A Political Economy of European Community Trade Policy against the Less Developed Countries?' *European Economic Review*, 31: 457–65.

Weiss, Leonard W. (1989) *Concentration and Price*. Cambridge, MA: MIT Press.

Whalley, John (1996) 'Why Do Countries Seek Regional Trade Agreements?' Working Paper no. 5552 (April). Cambridge, MA: NBER.

World Trade Organization (1995) *Regionalism and the World Trading System*. Geneva: World Trade Organization (April).

Yamawaki, Hideki, Sleuwaegen, Leo, and Weiss, Leonard W. (1989) 'Industry Competition and the Formation of the European Common Market', in Weiss, Leonard W. (ed.), *Concentration and Price*. Cambridge, MA: MIT Press.

Yi, Sang-seung (1994) 'Endogenous Formation of Trading Blocs', Working Paper no. 94-11 (May). Hanover, NH: Dartmouth College.

Part II

Organized Interests Enforce Legislation

5
Self-regulation of the medical and legal professions: remaining barriers to competition and EC law

ROGER VAN DEN BERGH

1. Introduction

Traditionally, medicine and law have not been subjected to the competitive forces that operate in commercial sectors. This policy of distinguishing professional practice from commercial trade reflects a traditional concept that due to the specialized, personal, and important nature of the professional services and the need to uphold and preserve the quality and integrity of the professions, competition would not guarantee a socially optimal outcome. Medicine and law can be seen as the prototypes of a profession.[1] Ideally, the advice of the lawyer and the doctor is impartial, of the highest quality and always in the best interests of the client. Much of this archetype has been developed by the professional societies in an effort to gain public trust.

Regulation of the medical and legal professions has, by tradition, been achieved through a combination of direct government regulation and, to a large extent, through rules adopted by professional associations. These associations enjoy public law status; they are called 'Orders' (France, Italy, Belgium, Netherlands) or 'Chambers' (Germany). Their self-regulatory powers enable them to establish both entry requirements and rules regarding professional conduct. The professional bodies are composed of practising professionals only; there are no lay members representing consumers' interests. In the legal and medical professions the self-regulatory powers have been used to promulgate 'ethical rules' which aim at protecting professional integrity and dignity. Instead of benefiting the consumers of medical and legal services, professional ethics may substantially hinder competition by imposing restrictions on advertising, establishing fee schedules and regulating the business structures of professionals. Since Milton Friedman's seminal early work on the professions (Friedman and Kuznets 1945), it has been widely recognized that a policy of giving professions powers of self-regulation carries with it the danger that the professions will thereby be enabled to pursue the interests of their members to the detriment of the public interest.

In recent years policymakers have become increasingly aware of the danger that self-regulation may excessively restrain competition and promote the interests of the professions, without yielding corresponding benefits to the public. The broader deregulation movement has also led to efforts seeking to liberalize markets for professional services. First, rules of competition law (prohibition of cartel agreements and abuse of a dominant position) have been applied to the professions. For example, regulation of fees by self-regulatory professional bodies has been held to violate the competition laws of some of the EC member states. Secondly, alternatives for the current self-regulatory frameworks have received particular attention from policymakers. In some countries, the preference of the legislator is shifting towards other instruments of control. For example, proposals have been made to replace the current self-regulatory system of licensing by certification, a procedure which reserves only the exclusive right to use the title to members of the profession, but does not exclude others from offering similar services. Thirdly, the scope of the professional monopoly is inclined to decrease. Very radical reforms took place in the UK. In order to develop a wider range of legal services and to improve consumer choices, several monopoly rights of the traditional legal professions (barristers and solicitors) have been abolished by the 1990 Courts and Legal Services Act. Also in other countries, efforts are being undertaken to broaden the supply of legal services. For example, in the Netherlands the professional body of attorneys has been forced to admit employed lawyers (e.g. legal counsellors of enterprises, lawyers working with insurance companies and lawyers representing unions) as members. Although the deregulation movement may be seen as a response to the growing criticism that self-regulation may be abused, the term 'deregulation' is still somewhat misleading. In spite of the recent efforts towards liberalization, regulation largely remains in place: the move towards less interventionist measures does not necessarily imply that the new degree of regulation will be optimal. Rules relaxing entry conditions may also have adverse effects if they simultaneously increase the control powers of the self-regulatory bodies.

In this paper it is investigated how EC law copes with the abuse of self-regulation. It could be expected that the competent EC authorities have assumed actions to set aside or modify restrictive practices, similar to the measures which have been undertaken at the member states' level. However, liberalization of entry conditions in the sector of the professions has been slow and not entirely successful. The implementation of the freedom of establishment (Article 52 EC Treaty) and the freedom to provide services (Article 59 EC Treaty) has posed serious difficulties. Compulsory membership of professional bodies, if required by member state law, has never been abolished. Additionally, the case law of the European Court of Justice—as it has developed in the 1990s—shows a remarkable (and somewhat unexpected) change of direction. In the *Hünermund* judgment[2] ethical rules restricting advertising in the pharmacists' profession were not considered to be against the principle of free movement of goods (Article 30 EC Treaty). Given the current state of EC law, liberalization thus largely remains the responsibility of member states. Therefore, a global assessment of the anti-competitive effects of self-regulation in the EC requires an extensive overview of the relevant provisions and their enforcement in the 15 EC member states. Such a survey cannot be offered within the scope of this paper. Interested readers are advised to consult other publications (Faure 1993, OECD 1985).

This paper is structured as follows. In the legal part of the paper an overview is given of the current state of market integration in the legal and medical professions. Both the EC Directives and the case law on the right of establishment and the freedom to provide services are examined. Then consideration is given to how far the competition laws of the EC member states and the EC competition rules are effective instruments in combating restrictions on competition in the medical and legal professions. After the legal analysis, an attempt is made to explain the current state of the law, using economic theories of regulation. Can the current degree of self-regulation be understood, from a 'public interest' perspective, as a set of rules needed to correct market failures (asymmetric information, principal–agent problems, externalities)? Or does the 'private interest' approach, stressing the role of pressure groups in decision-making, offer a more powerful explanation? Thereafter, the last section of the paper combines the legal and economic approaches. It is shown how economic insights may be made useful for the assessment of controversial legal issues in the domain of self-regulation. In particular, economic criteria prove to be helpful in interpreting the proportionality requirement, which is crucial under EC law. Finally, some concluding remarks are presented.

2. Legal analysis

2.1. Rules regarding access to the medical and legal professions

European law distinguishes between the right of establishment and the freedom to provide services. This difference is economically arbitrary and fluid in practice. Because the freedom to provide services does not entirely rest on the same principles as those governing establishment, the distinction will be kept in the legal part of the paper (but will be abandoned in the other parts). When professionals invoke the right of establishment they seek a permanent right to exercise an economic activity. In contrast, the freedom to provide services involves the exercise of an economic activity on a temporary basis in another EC member state while remaining established in a home country.[3]

Full market integration requires the removal of several obstacles to the free flow of professional services. Self-regulation may undermine some key principles of the EC Treaty in various ways. Rules which are discriminatory on grounds of nationality are blatant efforts to restrict entry. The argument that the removal of such discriminations suffices to guarantee a free flow of professional services, because nationals of other member states are free to obtain the requisite qualifications, would hardly be to the point. On the assumption that consumers' needs (and therefore appropriate minimum standards) do not vary significantly across member states, lawyers and doctors licensed in one state should be free to practise in another (Ogus 1994, 222). Therefore, provisions stipulating that the pursuit of a particular activity is restricted to holders of a diploma, certificate or other evidence of formal qualifications must equally be scrutinized.

Besides nationality requirements and the diplomas' barrier, market integration demands the removal of still another obstacle. National rules may lay down the conditions for the use of professional titles, such as *Rechtsanwalt* (Germany), *avvocato* (Italy) or the indication of a medical speciality (e.g. 'surgeon', 'dermatologist' or 'gynaecologist'). In EC countries there are differences in the scope of the protection of professional titles and the definition of the activities pursued by professions holding the title is not common to all member states.[4] In addition to the protection of the title, the pursuit of the regulated activity will usually be restricted to persons belonging to a professional body. Entry into the profession may thus be controlled by the professions themselves by establishing particular rules and/or supervision. For example, establishment may be contrary to 'ethical rules', prohibiting the opening of a second office.

The question arises whether the above measures are in conformity with EC law. First we will deal with the issue of discrimination on grounds of nationality. Secondly, the restriction of access to the profession benefiting holders of a diploma will be examined. Thirdly, the conditions for the use of professional titles and compulsory membership of professional bodies will be investigated. Finally, the ethical rules prohibiting the keeping of more than one office will be addressed.

2.1.1. *Discrimination on grounds of nationality*

Discrimination on grounds of nationality is an obvious and very serious impediment to market integration. In 1974 the European Court of Justice held the prohibition of discrimination contained in Article 52 EC Treaty 'directly applicable'. A national of a member state can directly invoke Article 52 when he or she wishes to establish himself or herself in another member state. This freedom applies even in the absence of implementing directives.[5] In the same year the direct effect of Article 59 EC Treaty, which guarantees freedom to provide services, was also confirmed.[6]

In several judgments the European Court of Justice made clear that the prohibition of discrimination on grounds of nationality is also to be respected by the self-regulatory bodies of the professions. With regard to the medical profession the European Court of Justice held in the *Broekmeulen* case that a national of a member state who has obtained a diploma of medical doctor in another member state and who, therefore, may practise general medicine in that other member state is entitled to establish himself in his own country, even if the latter makes entry into the profession subject to additional requirements. In this case the Dutch General Practitioners Registration Committee refused to register a Dutch doctor, having obtained his professional qualifications in Belgium, on the ground that he did not undergo a year's training in general medicine as required of any doctor holding a diploma of doctor in medicine awarded by a Dutch university. This refusal was considered contrary to Article 52 EC Treaty and Directive 75/362 concerning the mutual recognition of medical qualifications.[7] Another important judgment has dealt with the right of establishment for lawyers. In the *Thieffry* case the European Court of Justice held that when a national of one member state has obtained a diploma of doctor of law in his country of origin, which has been recognized as an equivalent qualification by the competent authority under the legislation of the country of establishment, the Bar cannot refuse permission to register for practical training. In these circumstances the act of demanding the prescribed national diploma constitutes a restriction incompatible with the freedom of establishment.[8] This judgment also showed the possibility of relying on the directly effective Article 52 EC Treaty without prior coordination of national professional requirements.

2.1.2. Diplomas

Freedom of establishment cannot be achieved solely by eliminating discriminatory rules with respect to entry into the profession. Non-discriminatory rules may form an even greater obstacle for foreigners than for the nationals of the member state of establishment. Rules regarding access to the professions often contain requirements which foreigners have great difficulty in meeting. The diplomas required for the exercise of medical and legal professions are a clear example. Where the taking-up or pursuit of a profession is subject to conditions regarding diplomas, a national of another member state intending to pursue that activity must in principle comply with them. It is for this reason that Article 57 EC Treaty stated that the Council had to issue directives for the mutual recognition of diplomas, certificates and other evidence of formal qualifications, in order to facilitate the exercise of the freedom of establishment. Mobility of professions may be enhanced also by a concomitant harmonization of education and training requirements. To achieve this goal, directives had to be adopted and implemented in the EC member states by the end of the transitional period (that was 31 December 1969). At the beginning of the 1970s there were still a lot of draft directives on the Council's table. During the 1970s the great backlog in the sector of the professions was partly removed by the adoption of the 1975 Directives with respect to the medical professions. However, as far as the legal profession is concerned, specific Directives on mutual recognition of diplomas and harmonization of education and training requirements have never been issued. On the one hand, legal professions come within the scope of the 1989 Directive on the mutual recognition of higher education diplomas by member states (see below). On the other hand, entry into the legal profession of host member states will be simplified from 2000 onwards for lawyers willing to practise under their home title (see 2.1.3).

Medicine. In the sector of the medical professions freedom of establishment has been realized through mutual recognition of medical qualifications and measures coordinating the training requirements.[9] The Directive on mutual recognition (75/362) applies to both self-employed and employed doctors. Directive 75/362 does not, however, affect national provisions which prohibit companies or firms from practising medicine or impose on them conditions for such practice.

Each member state is required to recognize the diplomas (listed in the Directive) awarded to nationals of member states by another member state, by giving these diplomas the same effect as those which the member state itself awards (Article 2 Directive 75/362). Where a specialty exists in the host member state, but diplomas leading up to such specialty are not awarded in the member state of origin, the host member state may require such person to fulfil the conditions of training as laid down in respect of that specialty by its domestic law, but must take into account the training periods completed by that person in the member state of origin as far as such training periods correspond to those required in domestic law (Article 8 Directive 75/362). Apart from training, other requirements for the taking up and the practice of a medical profession may consist of proof of good character, health certificate, membership of a professional body and (for the purpose of health insurance schemes) registration with a public social security body.

In order to ensure that the training of doctors is of equal standard in all member states, Directive 75/363 provides for a coordination of training requirements. This Directive imposes on the member states the obligation to require persons wishing to practise a medical profession to hold a diploma (as listed in Directive 75/362) awarded after a training which meets the requirements as set out in the Directive. Diplomas must be required from doctors and medical specialists where the specialty is listed in at least two member states. From 1995 on the activity of a general practitioner also requires specialized training.

Law. In the field of the legal profession a directive concerning the freedom to provide services was adopted in 1977. Progress with respect to the right of establishment has been much slower. The legal profession falls within the scope of the 1989 Directive on the mutual recognition of higher education diplomas by member states.[10] This Directive fits into the 'new approach' towards harmonization, which the Commission adopted in the mid-1980s. According to the principles of the new approach full harmonization is no longer a target to be achieved. With respect to the right of establishment of lawyers from other EC member states, the 1989 Directive kept the privilege of the host member state to require an additional examination intact. From 2000 onwards lawyers who can prove that they have been 'effectively and regularly active' in the law of the host member state for at least three years will be exempt from additional entry requirements.

Due to the allegedly national character of most legal problems, in the initial period only measures facilitating the provision of legal services have been taken. Directive 77/249 applies to the activities of lawyers pursued by way of provision of services. It states that a lawyer providing services is to adopt the professional title used in the member state from which he comes, expressed in the language or one of the languages of that state, with an indication of the professional organization by which he is authorized to practise or the court of law before which he is entitled to practise pursuant to the laws of that state. Services include both non-contentious (giving advice to clients and/or representation) and contentious activities (representation of clients in court proceedings). The Directive provides that

activities relating to the representation of a client in legal proceedings or before public authorities shall be pursued in each host member state under the conditions laid down for lawyers established in that State, with the exception of any conditions requiring residence or registration with a professional organisation, in that State.

Registration requirements would hinder the free flow of services. The temporary nature of the activities does not mean that the provider of services may not equip himself with an office, chambers or consulting rooms in the host member state insofar as such forms of infrastructure are necessary for the purposes of performing the services in question. If representation of clients in courts is mandatory, foreign attorneys must act in conjunction with national attorneys entitled to provide the service. According to Article 4(2) of Directive 77/2489, in pursuing activities relating to representation, the attorney must observe the rules of professional conduct of the host member state, without prejudice to his or her obligations in the member state from which he or she comes. As far as the pursuit of all other activities is concerned, the rules of professional conduct of the member state of origin apply, without prejudice to respect for the rules, whatever their source, which govern the profession in the host member state, especially incompatibilities and professional secrecy (Article 4(4) Directive 77/249). This rule of 'double ethics' imposes several behavioural controls whose cumulative effect may restrict competition substantially.

As far as the right of establishment is concerned, the legal profession falls within the scope of the Directive on the mutual recognition of higher education diplomas by member states. By virtue of Article 3 of this Directive all professional education qualifications acquired in the course of obtaining higher education diplomas are regarded as equivalent throughout the Community and the host member state may not require national diplomas. However, according to the same Directive the host member state is free to require an additional period of practice or an aptitude test, where the field covered by the higher education in the member state of origin differs substantially from the field covered by the higher education in the host member state. In the legal profession the choice between an examination or an additional period of practice is to be made by the member state and not by the applicant. The requirement to pass an examination in order to be allowed to practise under the professional title protected in the host country will be relaxed from 14 March 2000 onwards. In the future the right of establishment may be granted by the competent public bodies if they agree that the applicant has sufficiently proven that he or she has been effectively and regularly active in the law of the host member state during a period of at least three years (Article 10 Directive 98/5).[11]

2.1.3. *Professional titles and compulsory membership of professional bodies*

For a long time it was unclear whether lawyers willing to establish themselves in a host member state were free do to so under their home title. For example, an Italian lawyer could consider practising in other European countries using his home title *avvocato* and not titles protected by legislation of the host member state, such as *Rechtsanwalt* (Germany) or *advocaat* (the Netherlands). There were no clear-cut solutions to the problems raised by the use of home titles in the legal profession (Stuyck and Geens 1993, 85–6). The question whether the right to use the home title could be reserved to lawyers having obtained their professional qualifications in the state where they wish to practise was addressed by the European Court of Justice in the *Gebhard* judgment.[12]

In this case the question arose whether a German *Rechtsanwalt* who practised law in Italy (essentially by giving legal advice to German-speakers) could carry the title *avvocato*. Prior to the *Gebhard* judgment, the case law of the European Court of Justice with respect to non-discriminatory measures hindering freedom of establishment was not conclusive. In some cases freedom of establishment seemed to be restricted to a prohibition of discriminatory measures,[13] including cases of indirect or covert discrimination.[14] In other cases the Court went beyond a mere prohibition to discriminate.[15] The latter judgments seemed to bring the case law on the right of establishment in line with the key principles governing free movement of goods, which the Court developed in several well-known judgments (*Dassonville, Cassis de Dijon*). According to the 'rule of reason', developed in the latter case law, limitations on the free movement of goods may be justified for reasons of public interest if they do not go beyond what is necessary for attaining the public interest goal. An important, but not yet complete, step towards the convergence of both freedoms was taken in the *Kraus* case. For the first time, a clear reference to a 'rule of reason' appeared, but its formulation seemed to be restricted to the particular facts of the case.[16] In its *Gebhard* judgment the Court has formulated a general rule:

> It follows, however, from the Court's case-law that national measures liable to hinder or make less attractive the exercise of fundamental freedoms guaranteed by the Treaty must fulfil four conditions: they must be applied in a non-discriminatory manner; they must be justified by imperative requirements in the general interest; they must be suitable for securing the attainment of the objective which they pursue; and they must not go beyond what is necessary in order to attain it.

This sweeping statement lays down criteria without distinguishing the four freedoms (free movement of goods, persons, services and capital). The 'rule of reason' is formulated as a general test for all four freedoms: imperative requirements of public interest may justify restrictions on the key principles of free movement of goods, persons, services and capital if they are suitable for attaining goals of public interest and pass the proportionality test. Consequently, following the *Gebhard* rule, non-discriminatory rules restricting the right to bear a professional title and compulsory membership of public professional bodies must be justified by 'imperative requirements' in the general interest. In *Gebhard* the Court did not provide any indication about what may be considered such legitimate purposes. Assuming that the protection of consumers (and the public at large) from the harmful consequences of legal advice given by unqualified professionals is the goal of public interest to be aimed at, the analysis will then have to proceed with an investigation of both the suitability and proportionality of the contested measures.

The *Gebhard* judgment seemed to have opened the door for a proportionality test of the conditions for the use of professional titles and compulsory membership of public professional bodies. Older judgments of the Court of Justice gave clear support to the survival of entry restrictions existing in most member states and acknowledged the role of the Bar as the final supervisor of entry into the legal profession. In *Gullung*[17] the Court considered the case of a person who wished to practise as an *avocat* without being registered at a French Bar and held such a registration requirement not incompatible with Article 52 EC Treaty. Gullung was a member of the Bar in Germany and wanted to exercise his profession in France, where he was denied access to the Bar because of lack of proof of good character. The Court decided that a lawyer who had been denied access to the Bar in a member state because of failure to fulfil the necessary conditions of good character could not rely on Community law (being a member of the Bar in another member state) to exercise his profession in the entire Community. The *Gebhard* judgment, though, made membership of a professional body subject to the four conditions governing restrictions of the fundamental freedom of the right of establishment. Hence the question was raised whether membership of the Bar is suitable for securing the quality of professional services and, more importantly, whether such membership does not go beyond what is necessary. Unfortunately, from the viewpoint of liberalizing the market for legal services, the requirement of compulsory membership of the Bar has been accepted by the recent EC Directive 98/5, which also regulates the use of the home title. Hence, the criticism that protection of professional titles and compulsory membership of public bodies may not satisfy the proportionality test must be raised against the Directive, rather than against member state laws endorsing the self-regulatory powers of professional bodies of lawyers. The 'rule of reason' test, proposed in *Gebhard* seems to remain relevant only for other professions rather than those of medical doctor and lawyer.

Following Article 3 Directive 98/5 lawyers willing to practise in a host member state under their home title must register themselves with the professional body of the host member state. Such lawyers must practise under their home title and avoid confusion with the professional title of the host member state. Confusion between the latter title and the eventually homonymous home title must be avoided by adding additional information (e.g. 'avocat *au barreau de Paris*'). They may not use the title of the host country for as long as they do not fulfil the prerequisites of entry into the profession. It may also be required that mention be made of the public professional body of the member state of origin, to which the lawyer belongs (Article 4 Directive 98/5).

It may be asked whether the EC policy has been successful in removing the barriers to entry into the legal profession. The answer must be a balanced one. Only those lawyers having obtained their professional qualification in another member state, who are allowed to practise under the professional title of the host member state, will not suffer a competitive disadvantage. The professional body of the host member state still retains control over the exercise of the 'full' right of establishment. It must be added, however, that the activities reserved to domestic lawyers are very limited. Lawyers practising under their home title can give legal advice on all areas of European and national law, including the law of the host country. The restrictions which may remain in force are the following. Member states may not allow foreign lawyers to arrange documents for the administration of deceased persons' estates and for the transfer of real property.[18] If representation of clients in legal proceedings is compulsory, lawyers working under their home title may be forced to cooperate with a lawyer who is allowed to carry the professional title of the host country. Finally, member states may lay down specific requirements regarding access to higher courts in order to guarantee good administration of justice (Article 5 Directive 98/5). Since the scope of the professional monopoly is thus rather limited, the competitive disadvantages for migrant lawyers may remain minor.

This is not to say that EC policy on the right of establishment for lawyers could not be improved. According to the Directive on the mutual recognition of higher education diplomas by member states, the host country is free to require an additional period of practice or an aptitude test, where the field covered by higher education in the member state of origin differs substantially from the field covered by the higher education in the host member state. It is not easy to judge whether such 'substantial differences' exist to justify the additional examinations which migrant lawyers have to pass. There is thus a risk that differences in education will continue to serve as a general excuse not to allow free establishment. As far as the legal profession is concerned, legal systems are often grouped into two main families, depending upon whether they fit into the 'civil law' tradition or into the 'common law' tradition. Although there are indeed differences between both legal families, it may be asked whether these differences are substantial enough to abandon the principle of free establishment in the legal profession. The latter question has become particularly significant since the emergence of a common law of Europe (a new *ius commune*) has been documented in recent legal literature. Exceptions to the right of establishment will be even harder to justify in cases where attorneys may wish to move to another country whose legal system belongs to the same legal family as the system of his or her home country. It seems hard to justify additional examinations if the law of the host country is largely similar to the law of the country of origin (e.g. German and Austrian law), or if the migrant attorney is willing to handle cases involving only the law of his or her home country and European law. In spite of the increasing similarities between legal families, the ongoing harmonization of legal rules (either by EC Directives or spontaneously) and the presumably limited scope of the intended professional practice, the Directive excludes case-by-case adjudication by explicitly stating that additional requirements may be set for professions for which knowledge of the national legal system is required. Therefore it cannot be questioned that legal education covers 'substantially different' rules. Moreover—in contrast with the holders of other higher education diplomas, where the applicant who wishes to establish himself (herself) has the right to choose between having to pass examinations or to undergo additional practical training—in the case of the legal profession the host member state, eventually after consulting with the professional bodies of attorneys, will decide how the substantial differences in education must be overcome. As was to be expected, the overall preference went to the aptitude test. An additional training period is very cumbersome for the attorneys' profession: the number of trainee posts is limited and older practitioners ('patrons') may not wish to teach experienced attorneys coming from another EC member state.

It is clear that the ease with which attorneys can move between member states will depend upon the contents of the law examinations in the host countries. Even though there is a need to ensure that attorneys are familiar with laws and regulations of the host member states, examinations which are too rigorous may significantly limit freedom of establishment. In the USA, law examinations have been criticized as creating the potential for unreasonable exclusion of qualified attorneys, since the Bar examiners may possibly have an economic interest in limiting the number of successful applicants (OECD 1985, 35). It follows from the American experience that the drafting and grading of exams should not be assigned to practising attorneys and that excessive failure rates may indicate a wish to limit entry. European legislators do not seem to have learned the lessons from their American counterparts.

Some examples may suffice to illustrate how well established lawyers keep entry into the legal profession under control. Lawyers from other EC member states willing to establish themselves in Belgium will have to undergo an aptitude test, which is organized by the professional body of attorneys.[19] In some German states, diplomas acquired in another EC member state are not regarded as equivalent to the first German state examination.[20] Lawyers willing to establish themselves as a *Rechtsanwalt* in Germany may thus be required to pass two state examinations, including an aptitude test (*Eignungsprüfung*). Life is easier for lawyers who are already registered as an attorney in another EC member state. These attorneys may establish themselves in Germany if they confine themselves to conducting litigation in fields of foreign and international law (including European law) and if they are registered with the competent public professional body (*Rechtsanwaltskammer*). This distinction relating to the areas of law covered by the attorney's practice overcomes some of the criticisms which have been formulated above with respect to the lack of differentiation in EC Directive 89/48. For the sake of completeness, it may be added that attempts to limit entry are not only directed against attorneys coming from other member states but also against own nationals.[21] As mentioned above, the recent Directive 98/5 has opened the possibility (from 2000 onwards) that lawyers who have effectively and regularly practised the law of the host country may be exempted from the requirement to pass an examination. However, professional bodies of lawyers will keep control over entry since they will decide whether the applicant has 'effectively and regularly' been active in the law of the host member state.

Compulsory membership of public professional bodies may create additional problems. If membership can be denied to applicants who are not of 'good conduct', subjective decisions as to who will be permitted to practise can hardly be avoided. Hence the licensing process may operate to limit the numbers of new entrants and harm competition. To prevent abuse of the prerequisite of 'good character' as a condition of entry into regulated professions, an economic analysis of the proportionality requirement may be particularly helpful (see Section 4).

2.1.4. Second office

Professionals may wish to practise in more than one member state. Regarding the establishment of a second professional base, the Court of Justice had to decide upon the validity of ethical rules prohibiting the opening of a second office. Restraints on the opening of a second office are usually justified by the need to ensure that clients can easily reach their attorneys. Attorneys who keep more than one office, so it is said, would not be sufficiently available to their clients. In the *Klopp* case the single chambers rule of the Paris Bar, even though non-discriminatory, was held incompatible with Article 52 EC Treaty. The Court of Justice held that the right to enter the attorneys' profession may not be denied to a German 'Rechtsanwalt' wishing to establish himself as an attorney in Paris, on the ground that this registration would contravene the relevant French law as well as the internal rules of the Paris Bar, providing that an 'avocat' may not keep chambers in more than one place and that such place must be within the territorial jurisdiction of the court with which he or she is registered. With respect to the medical profession the same principle has been confirmed in the case *Commission v. France*. The rule of French professional ethics prohibiting medical doctors and dentists from keeping more than one practice was held incompatible with the freedom of establishment. In this judgment the Court stressed that restrictions on this freedom must, if they are to be acceptable, satisfy the requirement of proportionality. If professional ethics for the medical profession are defended for reasons of public health, it must be shown that the challenged rules really serve this purpose and that public health cannot be safeguarded by less restrictive means.[22]

It follows from the above judgments that non-discriminatory ethical rules prohibiting the keeping of more than one office or the entering into partnerships at more than one Bar are incompatible with Article 52 EC Treaty. The freedom of establishment implies that a national of another member state may not be denied entry into a profession solely on the ground that he or she already maintains an office in another member state.

2.2. Rules regarding conduct

The medical and legal professions have used their self-regulatory powers to restrict many types of conduct, which allegedly may endanger professional integrity and dignity. Rules requiring adherence to fee scales—so it is said, in order to guarantee the quality of the services offered—are overt restrictions of competition. Besides from fee schedules, restrictions on advertising and rules concerning business structure, which restrict multi-disciplinary practices, may equally harm the public interest. The question arises whether these restrictions are subject to challenge by the anti-trust authorities of the EC member states and/or the European Commission. The applicability of rules of competition law to professional ethics will be examined below. Additionally, the rules regarding free movement of services (Article 59 EC Treaty) will be investigated. It seems evident that restrictions on advertising and fixed fee scales may hinder the free flow of professional services. Therefore, one could expect that the European Court of Justice would complement the control exercised by the European Commission. Unfortunately, the current state of the law does not provide for a simple answer to the question whether the ethical rules are in conformity with the principle of free movement of services. The latter problem will be addressed in the second part of this section.

2.2.1. Competition law

The great degree of regulation covering the professions, both through government actions and self-regulation, also has an impact on the application of rules of competition law to the professions. The competition laws of the EC member states discussed below have not specifically addressed the question of the relationship between the professions and the national competition laws. None of the competition laws, however, has granted an exemption for cartel-like behaviour and monopolistic conduct in the sector of the professions. While the professions are not generally exempted from the provisions of competition law, in some member states restrictive practices may escape anti-trust scrutiny as long as they are mandated by government or are promulgated by a public or private professional association under the supervision or direction of the government.

Even though professions are thus generally subject to anti-trust scrutiny, professional regulations will not be controlled by the competition authorities if, according to national competition law, they can be understood as the consequence of state action or as government-authorized conduct. Under US anti-trust law this favourable treatment of restrictive practices directly arising from state or government action is known as the 'state action' doctrine. In the European Community the applicability of competition laws to the professions will depend upon two factors. First, it must be investigated whether the national competition laws provide for a 'state action'-like exemption and, if this is the case, how such exemption is construed. A narrow interpretation of the requirement that professional ethics must be based on statutory authority may bring most of the restrictions on competition within the scope of national cartel prohibitions. Second, even if the law of the member states allows restrictive practices, these rules must be analysed as far as their conformity with the EC Treaty is concerned. The Treaty provides for the possibility of attacking member states' laws which adversely affect the full applicability of the prohibitions contained in Articles 85 and 86 of the EC Treaty. Professional ethics may be challenged on the basis of the combined use of Articles 3(g), 5(2) and 85–86 EC Treaty. Given the primacy of European law, the member states have to reconcile their national regulations with the competition rules of the EC.[23] Let us now examine the competition law of six member states' 'state action'-like exemptions for liberal professions and the problem of their conformity with EC law in more detail.

Germany. In Germany competition is regulated by the Act against Restraints of Competition (*Gesetz gegen Wettbewerbsbeschränkungen*, abbreviated GWB). Professions are not generally exempted from the prohibition of cartels and monopolistic practices; they fall within the scope of the GWB if the general requirements are met. The German competition law applies to agreements entered into by 'undertakings'. The definition of 'undertaking' is broad enough to include liberal professions. According to German competition law the term includes any entity, regardless of size, which is engaged in trade with goods or services. Also professions come within this definition (Immenga in Immenga/Mestmäcker 1992: §1, Nr. 84–85). German case law shows some examples of practices which were held contrary to the principle of free competition. Price agreements between professionals and price recommendations issued by professional bodies were held to violate the prohibition of cartel agreements. For example, the Federal Supreme Court held that a Chamber of Architects violated the cartel prohibition by encouraging its members not to charge lower prices than the maximum indicated in the statutory scale of fees.[24] Another practice, which was prohibited by the German cartel authorities, related to attempts to exclude outsiders by means of a boycott. For example, the Berlin Court of Appeal confirmed fines imposed on certain medical societies for inciting members to boycott two drug manufacturers who offered laboratory services in competition with independent laboratory specialists.[25]

Although the German competition law thus applies to liberal professions and there is no general exemption from the said law, at the same time, however, rules governing entry into the professions and performance of the professional services will not be controlled to the extent that these practices are authorized by other legislation or are conducted pursuant to statutory directive. State regulations controlling entry or training in the professions are clear examples of rules which—in spite of their potential harmful effects on competition—escape from anti-trust scrutiny (Immenga in Immenga/Mestmäcker 1992: §1, Nr. 90). This leaves us with the question of whether rules of conduct, issued by professional bodies, may be attacked on the basis of the German competition law. In principle, restrictive practices do not violate the German competition law if they are authorized by other legislation. However, this exception in the German competition law is interpreted narrowly; rules restricting types of conduct will be challenged if they are not clearly based on statutory authority or exceed such authority. For example, price-fixing will be challenged if professional bodies have been empowered to generally safeguard professional duties, without giving them explicit power to establish fee schedules.[26] Even though the case law shows a clear tendency to interpret the exemption narrowly, some anti-competitive practices remain outside the scope of the German competition law because they are directly compelled by the state. With respect to attorneys the state imposes a fixed fees schedule. The attorney's fee has to be calculated on the basis of fixed percentages of the litigation value. Higher salaries can be agreed upon in a written contract, but lower salaries are permitted only in exceptional circumstances (e.g. limited means of the client). Fixed fees for attorneys' services are clearly based on statutory authority and do not exceed such authority. For this reason it does not seem possible to challenge these anti-competitive practices on the basis of the German competition rules only; the EC rules will have to fill this gap in the German control system.

France. In France the scope of competition law is very broad: it does not make any reference to agreements between 'undertakings'; moreover it applies to economic activities, irrespective of criteria relating to the size of the parties involved, such as market share. Both factors explain the great number of cases concerning professionals.[27] Several practices were considered contrary to French competition rules. Recommendations issued by the Paris Bar Council concerning fees were held to violate the French competition law because both professionals and clients could understand these recommendations as minimum fees to be respected. By fixing average and minimum fees in its Bulletins the Bar Council was restricting potential competition among lawyers. Recommended fee schedules were also condemned in other liberal professions. The Order of Pharmacists tried to prevent price competition in the market for pharmaceutical products by encouraging the use of recommended prices, to be set by producers, and threatening pharmacists with disciplinary sanctions, if they lowered retail prices. The Order of Architects distributed standard form contracts containing clauses concerning remuneration; the wording of the contracts gave the impression that it was not possible to alter the terms of the contract with respect to fees. Another decision concerned the Order of Dentists, which organized a survey among its members to acquire information about fees. The results of the survey could be claimed by the members, so that it became easier for them to engage in illegal price-fixing. In each of the above cases the professional bodies were instructed to desist from these various fee fixing practices.

United Kingdom. In the UK there is a long tradition in applying competition rules to the professions. Restrictions on competition by the professions may be subject to investigation by the Monopolies and Mergers Commission (MMC) on a reference by the Director General or a Minister, under the 'complex monopoly' provisions of the Fair Trading Act. A complex monopoly under the Fair Trading Act exists if two or more persons who together account for 25 per cent or more of the supply in the UK of a designated service so conduct their respective affairs that competition is prevented, restricted, or distorted. The Commission must report to the Minister on the effects upon the public interest, and may make recommendations. If its conclusions are accepted, remedial action may be taken either by negotiation with the parties or by statutory order. In 1970 the Monopolies Commission (after 1973 the Commission was renamed the Monopolies and Mergers Commission) published a general report on restrictive practices in the supply of professional services.[28] Following this report, many references of particular restrictions were made to the Commission. They concerned advertising restrictions (e.g. for barristers, solicitors, veterinary surgeons and accountants), collective fixing of fee scales (architects and surveyors) and the 'two counsel rule'[29] in the legal profession. In every case, with the exception of the restrictions on advertising applying to barristers, the Commission found that the restrictions operated against the public interest. In some professions implementation of the recommendations of the Monopolies and Mergers Commission has been achieved (e.g. solicitors, opticians, veterinary surgeons). In other cases, where the restrictions were enshrined in rules issued under the authority of statute, implementation proved to be more difficult. With respect to advertising restrictions, the Office of Fair Trading (OFT) published a report in 1986. The OFT reported that a great majority of the eighty-three professions, examined by the MMC in 1970, had abolished advertising restrictions. Some professional associations (twenty-two in total, of which thirteen in the health sector) still imposed rules concerning the content, 'style' and 'dignity' of the advertisements, as well as on the advertising media used. The OFT argued that loss of reputation would prohibit professionals from engaging in incredulous advertising and that the general rules on advertising (British Code of Advertising Practice), which apply to all economic activities, are sufficient to protect the integrity of the professions. This report has certainly contributed to a very marked softening of attitudes towards advertising by professionals, even in the medical profession. The General Medical Council now believes that information about services offered by general practitioners should be widely publicized (Bowles 1993).

Currently in the legal profession, fees are freely negotiated between the solicitor and his client or between the barrister and the instructing solicitor. There are no minimum fees set by the self-regulatory bodies. Controls on fees are possible for services financed by Legal Aid. Clients may also require a solicitor to obtain a remuneration certificate from the Law Society, to show whether a fee is 'fair and reasonable'; if the fee certified by the Law Society is lower than that charged, only the lower sum is recoverable from the client. Clients may also apply to the High Court for formal verification of the fairness and reasonableness of fees (Ogus 1993).

Other countries: Italy, Belgium, the Netherlands. In countries which do not have a long-standing tradition as far as competition policy is concerned, the fixing of fees has also been held to be contrary to the (recently enacted) competition laws. Italian and Belgian competition law applies to agreements between undertakings. When interpreting the rules guidance is sought in the case law of the European Commission and the European Court of Justice. Since European law uses broad definitions, in both countries professions come within the scope of the cartel prohibition and the rules banning abuse of dominant position.[30] Professions are considered to be 'undertakings' and the Orders of attorneys and doctors are qualified as associations of undertakings. In Italy the anti-trust authority (*Autorità garante della concorrenza e del mercato*) considers collective fixing of fees as a serious impediment to competition in the market for professional services and is not willing to accept the argument that price fixing is a means of guaranteeing quality. However, in the legal and medical professions the criteria for calculating fees are fixed by the public professional bodies and approved by the competent Minister.[31] In cases of restrictions of competition caused by state action, the *Autorità* cannot directly prohibit the restrictive agreements and may only signal the anti-competitive self-regulatory rules to parliament and propose changes (Article 21 legge n. 287/90). If anti-competitive behaviour is not explicitly supported by legislative provisions, the Italian anti-trust authority may directly apply the prohibition of cartel agreements. The *Autorità* decided that the fee schedules of the national association of companies of chartered accountants, which contained both minimum and maximum tariffs constituted infringements of the Italian competition law. The *Autorità* rejected the argument that price fixing was needed to guarantee a proper remuneration, the necessity of which was argued by reference to the protection of the independence and the quality of the services. Consequently, the *Autorità* refused to grant an exemption.[32]

In Belgium the first steps have been taken to apply the recent competition law to the liberal professions. Unfortunately, the recent Belgian experience is not a complete success story. The Belgian competition authority *Raad voor de Mededinging* (Competition Council) held minimum fee scales for architectural services contrary to the prohibition of cartels.[33] It is significant to add that in the architects' case the Council decided that a posterior approval of fee scales by a public authority does not affect the applicability of the Belgian competition law and thus ruled out the possibility of a 'state action' defence. Recent court decisions, however, have restricted the powers of the Competition Council. The illegality of collectively fixed fees must be invoked as an exception in the proceedings before the competent professional bodies; the Competition Council cannot suspend these proceedings.[34] In a case concerning attorneys the Belgian Arbitration Court (which decides on the conformity of Belgian laws with the constitution) decided that the validity of regulations issued by the Order of Attorneys must be controlled by ordinary courts; an administrative court such as the Competition Council has no powers in this respect since the Order has public law status. It goes without saying that these court decisions have seriously limited the effectiveness of the Belgian competition law as regards restrictions on competition in the market for liberal professions.

Finally, in the Netherlands liberal professions also come within the scope of the competition law.[35] In addition, there is a growing deregulation of many aspects of the performance of professional services. The Guidelines of the Bar for calculating fees have been abolished. As a general rule advertising in the legal profession is permitted. Dutch attorneys may advertise fees and their field of specialization.[36] Gradually the amount of advertising is increasing and the advertisements are becoming less sober. By contrast, in the medical profession there remains a general prohibition on advertising of professional skills or specialized methods of treatment (Den Hertog 1993).

EC law. In a limited number of cases restrictions on competition contained in codes of professional ethics may survive at the national level. However, those restrictions may still be subjected to anti-trust control by the European Commission. If member states maintain regulations which adversely affect the full applicability of the prohibition of cartel agreements, they violate the Treaty on the basis of the combined use of Articles 3(g), 5(2) and 85–86. Even if one takes a very narrow view and requires that the anti-competitive activities must be compelled by direction of the state acting as a sovereign,[37] national rules satisfying this requirement may continue to constitute a major hindrance for competition. Therefore it is of utmost importance to contest national rules hindering full market integration. National rules which uphold restrictions of competition in the medical and legal professions may successfully be challenged, but only if the conditions for applying Article 85 EC Treaty are satisfied. In this respect the requirement that interstate trade must be affected may form a major obstacle, since markets for professional services have largely remained local.[38]

The applicability of the prohibition of cartel agreements (Article 85 EC Treaty) in the sector of the liberal professions has been confirmed by the recent Decisions of the

European Commission in the cases *Consiglio nazionale degli spedizionieri doganali*[39] and *Colegio Oficial de Agentes de la Propriedad Industrial*.[40] In the latter decision, the Commission stated that Article 85 EC Treaty fully applies if a member state gives authority to a professional association to fix prices, thereby violating Articles 3(g), 5(2) and 85 EC Treaty. When professional associations promulgate fee schedules on the basis of such authority they will not be immune from anti-trust scrutiny. In both decisions price fixing was held to be illegal.

It may be asked whether these principles can be extended without difficulty to the medical professions. In the legal professions, increased price competition may have a positive impact on efficiency and innovation while exercising a downward influence on costs. In the medical profession, by contrast, fee schedules may be useful because they facilitate insurance reimbursements under government programmes. Even though collective price-fixing may be considered a very serious infringement of the EC competition rules, especially when membership is a condition to practise the profession and may lead to market segmentation, the features of the medical profession in particular with respect to remuneration schemes agreed upon in the framework of public health systems seem to warrant a somewhat different treatment. The large share of medical services provided under public reimbursement suggests that price competition is less likely to occur in this profession. Therefore, distributive justice considerations (provision of medical services at low prices for poor people) may conflict with efficiency considerations.

2.2.2. Freedom to provide services

Ethical rules regarding conduct may affect the free movement of goods and services. Therefore, Article 30 EC Treaty, which prohibits quantitative restrictions on import and measures having equivalent effect, and Article 59 EC Treaty, which protects the free movement of services, must briefly be discussed. Unfortunately, the case law of the European Court of Justice is very complex on this point and there is no clear-cut answer to the question whether ethical rules hindering the free flow of goods and services are contrary to the fundamental principles of the EC Treaty. The case law on goods and the case law on services seem to evolve in a different way. In the *Hünermund* judgment ethical rules of a German Chamber of Pharmacists restricting advertising for non-medical products sold in pharmacies were not considered to be against Article 30 EC Treaty.[41] This judgment followed the famous distinction made in the *Keck* decision[42] between measures regulating production and rules which restrict or prohibit certain 'selling arrangements'. Whereas rules of the first category remain within the reach of the prohibition contained in Article 30 EC Treaty (and the 'rule of reason'), rules of the latter category are, according to the new learning, no longer considered as measures having equivalent effect. Recent case law of the European Court of Justice shows many examples of what—quite apart from a prohibition of sales at loss prices, which was the contested measure in *Keck*—may be considered regulations of 'selling modalities': rules concerning the location where products may be sold,[43] opening hours of shops,[44] and also the prohibition of televised advertising in respect of certain sectors of economic activity.[45] It is still uncertain whether the Court of Justice would also qualify a *total* ban on advertising (e.g. a prohibition to advertise specialties) as a regulation of selling modalities.

In the *Alpine Investment* case an attempt was made to transpose the *Keck* rule to the field of services. The measure contested was the general prohibition, which applied to all financial intermediaries established in the Netherlands and operating within and/ or outside that territory, of contacting individuals by telephone without their prior written consent. The Court of Justice stated that the contested measure was not analogous to the legislation concerning selling arrangements in *Keck*. The prohibition of 'cold calling' covered not only the provision of services in the Netherlands but also in other member states. The Netherlands thus required compliance with its own rules of marketing not only for the provision of services in its territory but also in the territory of other member states. This 'export of national restrictions concerning the manner in which services are to be provided' was seen as a measure of equivalent effect, but justified under the 'rule of reason' as necessary to protect the good reputation of the financial sector and proportionate to this aim.[46]

As long as the European Court of Justice has not explicitly extended its *Keck* rule to the supply of services, national regulatory measures restricting the free movement of goods may be dealt with in a more lenient way than restrictions on the free provision of services. Regulations restricting selling modalities, such as prohibitions of certain forms of advertising, are not considered contrary to the goal of market integration if they relate to goods, but may be held to violate the EC Treaty if they relate to services. However, in the latter case the restrictions may be justified if they are appropriate to attaining a goal of public interest (e.g. consumer protection) and proportionate to the objective pursued. Professionals willing to offer their services outside the member state where they are established may have to cope with ethical rules set by the public professional bodies of the host country holding the envisaged crossborder advertising contrary to the 'dignity' of the profession. If one adopts a fairly restrictive reading of the *Alpine Investments* decision, it may be argued that the professional public bodies are not exporting restrictions concerning the manner in which services are to be provided, as the Dutch government did, so that there remains scope for a *Keck*-like limitation of the prohibition of measures hindering the free movement of services. If one accepts this interpretation, ethical rules prohibiting the 'marketing' of professional services will not violate the EC Treaty. In the other case, they will have to be justified under the 'rule of reason'. The legal distinctions made by the European Court of Justice will strike non-lawyers as difficult and obscure. To simplify EC law one could argue in favour of a similar treatment of goods and services, so that non-discriminatory rules concerning marketing would generally be in conformity with the EC Treaty. The price to be paid for this simplification is high, however. Restrictions on competition in the markets for professional services would no longer have to be justified on public interest grounds and substantial inefficiencies may ensue.

3. Economic analysis

3.1. Self-regulation and the 'public interest'

Both in the medical and legal professions, public professional bodies control entry through registration requirements and control conduct through 'ethical rules'. It follows from the legal analysis that, under current EC law, these remaining barriers to market integration can be upheld if it can be shown that imperative reasons of 'public interest' justify restrictions on free movement of professionals. The rationale for the policy of some EC member states that restrictive practices cannot be challenged upon the basis of the competition rules if they are mandated by government or promulgated by professional associations under the supervision of the government is the same. The underlying belief is that governments act in the best interests of their citizens and that therefore any anti-competitive effects of government regulations are outweighed by their benefits to society. Since quality improvement is the crux of the matter, the acute question is whether self-regulatory measures of the professions concerning access and performance further the public interest. Which arguments may be advanced to regulate the medical and legal professions and to distrust the market mechanism? An unregulated market, that is where the provision of services is governed solely by contracts freely struck by suppliers and purchasers would, it is alleged, give rise to significant social welfare losses as a result of the following problems.

First, markets for professional services are characterized by asymmetric information and, as a result, there is a risk of adverse selection. Lack of information on the part of the consumers is likely to be most severe with services (experience goods), which are not regularly purchased (no learning through the repeat-purchase-mechanism) and services whose properties can be assessed only with the help of highly technical standards (credence goods). If consumers cannot reliably judge the quality, neither *ex ante* nor *ex post*, trust in the professional becomes the only factor to allow economizing on information costs. Such goods create the conditions for the emergence of a 'market for lemons'. In his well-known study on quality uncertainty, Akerlof (1970) argues that asymmetric information, which cannot be eliminated by credible disclosure, attracts sellers of low quality.[47]

Secondly, informational asymmetries lead to conflicting agency relationships between the professionals and the consumers. The principal–agent problem increases the magnitude of the welfare losses. Given the superior expertise of the supplier, discretion must be conferred on the professionals to determine to a large degree what services are needed. This may lead to demand generation, that is the provision of services which the clients, if fully informed, would not have wanted.[48]

Thirdly, externalities may result from poor quality of service. The quality of the service may affect third parties as well as the client. Considerable losses may be thrown upon society if poorly trained professionals were allowed to perform the services. An incompetently drafted will may impose losses on individuals far removed from the negligent lawyer; and a failure by a doctor in treating a contagious disease may give rise to an epidemic. Externalities are especially worrisome in the health sector, where injuries to the body represent significant and inherently unrecompensable losses.

Even though the above arguments do provide reasons for government intervention, they should be limited to their right proportions. The argument relating to lack of information about quality should not be overstated. Although costly, it is not impossible to get unbiased estimates of quality levels. Klein and Leffler (1981) demonstrate that the existence of any method to evaluate the validity of supplier claims is sufficient to allow the production of high quality services without regulation. Thus, a supplier wishing to produce high quality services will not be driven out of the market by quacks (lemons) as long as reputations for quality can be established on criteria other than prices. As far as legal services are concerned, a distinction is to be made between occasional clients who consult an attorney and corporate clients. Large corporations are undoubtedly better able to find competent providers of professional services than small businesses or individual consumers. For consumers who do not often require legal assistance, especially those in middle-income brackets, finding and selecting an attorney can be difficult, especially where little information is provided to the public. Large customers, who can invest more funds in obtaining the information and for whom the amount at stake is often larger, are able to overcome asymmetric information by investing money in searching for information. It has also been pointed out above that the problem of asymmetric information is particularly severe with services that are not regularly purchased. If, on the contrary, services are purchased on a regular basis, quality control becomes possible through experience. For instance, a learning process will enable the patient to judge the quality of the treatment (the availability of the physician, his diligence and support); judgement on the appropriateness of the treatment to cure the disease may remain biased, however.

Additionally, it is not immediately clear that regulations are needed to reduce the agency problem. Supplier-induced demand in the health sector, if evident, can also be reduced by demand-side reductions in insurance coverage. To justify the restriction of the number of practitioners in the health sector, the argument is made that without these limitations excess consumption of medical services would occur. This problem is connected with the regulation of fees. If patients have to pay only a small part of their expenses and the largest part is reimbursed by health insurance, a serious moral hazard problem emerges (Arrow 1963). The way to solve this problem is not necessarily by limiting entry; introducing a deduction high enough to deter excess consumption could also be considered. If demand for medical care is price-elastic,[49] the moral hazard problem may be better solved by exposing the patient to risk than by introducing quantity controls.

Finally, the externalities' problem does not compel self-regulation in its current form either. Regulations are not needed as long as there exist natural inducements or private law incentives (liability rules) to keep quality levels above some minimum. Quality may be regulated directly, through standards, or indirectly, through liability rules. In the literature (Shavell 1984 and 1986) quality regulation is advanced whenever the government has better information on optimal safety standards than parties in a market-setting and there is a risk that the defendants in a liability suit will not be able financially to compensate the harm ('judgment-proof problem'). Neither of these problems occur in malpractice cases given the information advantage of the professionals and their sheltered income situation. A case could thus be made for liability rules,[50] but it remains unclear why self-regulation should be considered the only remedy.

Which arguments can be advanced to explain the existence of a self-regulatory framework to overcome the above mentioned problems? The leading advocate of self-regulation, Miller (1985), presents three advantages of self-regulation. First, a self-regulatory regime takes advantage of the fact that the members of the profession have better knowledge of the ways to guarantee quality and about the efficacy of various potential actions. A regulatory authority cannot acquire and maintain a specialized knowledge of each profession. Without this knowledge the performance of the professional services cannot be effectively regulated. Members of professions have access to information needed for effective regulation at lower costs than others. Therefore, the profession has the best capacity to control quality and recognize low standards. Secondly, self-regulation is more flexible and therefore less likely to stifle innovation or excessively limit consumer choice. Finally, self-regulation generally results in the costs of regulation being borne by the profession itself. Public regulation is costly to taxpayers, some of whom do not consume the product. Additionally, self-regulatory bodies have incentives to minimize costs of enforcement and compliance.

Miller's arguments are not entirely convincing. Against the advantages of self-regulation, one must point to a major disadvantage. Although the professions may indeed have better information, they may lack appropriate incentives to control and enforce quality standards. It may be assumed that professionals wish to exclude competition, so that they will aim at giving the consumers the impression that the services of all professionals are equally good. The advertisements for the attorneys' profession as a group, which are made in spite of the strict ethical rules regarding advertising, confirm this goal. It is, of course, obvious that differences in quality do exist. Whereas competitive pressures could improve quality, professional ethics may restrict the information available to consumers and harm competition. There is thus a serious risk that market failures due to asymmetric information, principal–agent problems and externalities will persist. In spite of the conceivable ineffectiveness of self-regulation as a remedy to market failures and the substantial costs associated with them, the advocates of self-regulation hold that the benefits in terms of cost efficiency remain crucial. According to Miller, the government's role should be restricted to its function as referee. The job is to prevent self-regulation from discouraging competition within the industry. The overview of the substantive legal rules and their (lack of) enforcement in the first part of this paper warrants caution with respect to the ability of governments to eliminate restrictions on competition in the sector of the professions. If the damages to society caused by the self-regulatory restrictions on competition are higher than they are for government regulation, the arguments asserting the cost efficiency of self-regulation may not hold.

It should be added that the contentions about greater flexibility and the division of the costs of self-regulation are not compelling. First, as far as self-regulatory measures cause efficiency losses, they be may hard to change. If the professions can limit competition with the support of government officials, they may be better able to successfully resist the competition from associations of newcomers offering more efficient rules. The resistance to change may be more effective when the rules are promulgated by self-regulation than when they are laid down by governmental regulation. Even if the rents[51] have been dissipated by competition between the privileged or by newcomers, the artificial restrictions on output give rise to what Tullock (1975) has called a 'transitional gains trap'. There is no politically acceptable way to abolish a policy that is inefficient both from the standpoint of consumers, who pay artificially high prices, and from the standpoint of the privileged, who no longer make exceptional profits. The persons who lose will not willingly compensate the capital losses of what they consider to be immoral gainers, even though these capital losses are smaller than the overall social welfare gains from removing the output restriction. On many occasions, only revolution will shake loose an economy's inefficient regulations.

Secondly, if Miller's argument that all of the costs of regulation are borne in the market in which it is imposed holds, it remains hard to see why the distribution of the costs of the regulation would be split in an efficient fashion between the sellers and the buyers (Curran 1993, 63). Professional bodies of doctors and attorneys, who consist only of members of the professions, may pass on the great bulk of the costs to the ultimate consumers. This leaves only the technological argument having to do with the costs of gathering information intact. On this point it should be noted that, under a tort system, judges may also hire experts (usually members of the regulated profession) to assist them in the assessment of negligence. The question is then whether the savings resulting by combining the judges' and the experts' roles into one are greater than the potential losses due to overinclusive self-regulation. Ultimately, the magnitude of the costs and benefits of self-regulation is an empirical issue. On a theoretical level the case for regulation in its strongest form (self-regulation of entry and conduct) is weak. However, before definitive conclusions may be reached, both advocates of self-regulation and their critics should produce empirical evidence to sustain their positions.

3.2. Self-regulation and the pursuit of private interests

In contrast to the public interest theory of regulation, which sees self-regulation as a quality enhancing mechanism, in a private interest approach professions are seen as well-organized cartels with strong lobbies. The private interest theory of regulation predicts that professional groups will oppose all measures that may enhance competition between professionals. Market integration increases competitive pressures. The efforts of pressure groups to delay EC-programmes aiming at harmonization of training and professional qualifications are understandable from this perspective. This may explain why progress on the programmes to harmonize national systems for professional qualifications was painfully slow.[52]

At the member states' level, it may be expected that the professions will resist all changes in the institutional structures changing the scope of their monopoly rights. As a consequence of the reform of the legal profession in the Netherlands, employed lawyers will be able to become a member of the Order of attorneys. At the same time, however, the scope of the attorneys' monopoly has been extended. For example, lawyers working with trade unions, who are not members of the Bar, will no longer be able to represent workers in court. The extension of the monopoly rights does not come as a surprise if one takes into account the composition of the Cohen Commission which suggested the reforms. Only professional lawyers (with one exception, a socio-logist) were members of this Commission (Bruinsma 1997). In the UK possibilities have been created to open the market for legal services to practitioners other than barristers and solicitors. Professional associations of other lawyers may apply for access, but the institutional structures are unlikely to generate full competition.

As a result of pressure brought to bear on politicians during the legislative process, existing practitioners' groups succeeded in gaining a significant influence over the newly established agencies. For example, rights of audience are to be determined by the Lord Chancellor and designated judges, all of whom were formerly barristers and retain strong connections with the Bar (Ogus 1994, 110–11). Under the new regulation rights of audience can be sought by the Law Society (being the professional body of solicitors), by bodies representing employed lawyers or by bodies representing non-lawyers. The right to conduct litigation is granted to practitioners by the professional bodies to which they belong, if the bodies can demonstrate that they can set and maintain rules of conduct which are appropriate and in the interests of the proper and efficient administration of justice. Consequently, competition for market access be-tween self-regulatory bodies has become possible. As a result of the reforms the mono-poly of barristers is no longer intact, since self-employed solicitors who passed an examination now have a right of audience in the higher courts. The question for the immediate future, however, is how many solicitors will qualify for rights of audience in the higher courts[53] and, even more, how many will use them.

Private interest theory also criticizes regulations serving producers' interests as 'rent-seeking'. Professions seem to meet all requirements mentioned in the Public Choice literature to be effective interest groups, which may engage in rent-seeking. Rents earned in political and bureaucratic markets are defined as increases in net revenues that do not result from growth of output, but from redistribution of wealth through the coercive power of the state. Rent-seeking and profit seeking have much in common, but in competitive markets competition between producers eliminates profits (rents). In the absence of such competition, above-cost payments made available through the granting of exclusive rights by the government will be received by privileged groups, which will be able to retain the rents. To the extent that regulation protects the professions from competition they acquire rents and some wealth is transferred to them from consumers. The rents imply dead-weight losses beyond the standard losses of consumer surplus usually depicted by Harberger triangles. They cause additional social waste to the extent that lobbying for rents (and protecting them) binds resources which have an opportunity cost in terms of forgone production.

The rent-seeking hypotheses may be supported by three lines of reasoning. First, the professions fit the description of effective pressure groups. Secondly, the self-regulation extends beyond the scope of rules needed to correct market failures. Thirdly, incomes of professionals are excessively high. Let us look at these arguments in more detail.

The most successful groups in obtaining wealth transfers are likely to be small, homogeneous and well organized (Stigler 1971). The suppliers of the rents are large groups in the general public, which are difficult to organize and which face information problems. Politicians can be seen as the brokers of the wealth transfers. In a seminal study Olson (1965) identified the factors which make a group more or less effective in influencing political decisions. Each interest group is subject to the classic public good problem of lobbying. Overcoming free-riding tends to be a decisive factor of a group's ability to organize itself as an effective pressure group. Therefore, the size of the coalition determines its potential as an effective interest group. Relatively small groups face lower costs of monitoring and controlling free-riding behaviour and will thus be more effective than larger groups. The size of the interest is another important determinant. Smaller coalitions with a strong community of interests will tend to have stronger political voices because each group member has a larger financial stake in the outcome, given that the potential gains will be divided among fewer hands. Therefore, a group will become an effective lobby if it is small enough in number and if the financial interests are sufficiently concentrated so that the potential benefits from organizing and lobbying for governmental favours will exceed the associated costs. Small cohesive groups are often successful in obtaining wealth transfers at the expense of the general public. Consumer interests are more diffuse and the costs of organizing consumers to avoid wealth transfers are relatively high and will exceed the expected gains from doing so.

The above observations help explain why the medical and legal professions are successful interest groups. To overcome free-riding, the professions have the strongest instrument at their disposal: coercion. Since they enjoy public law status, they do not only determine who may engage in the professional practice, but may also impose punishments on individuals not complying with professional ethics. The professional bodies require financial contributions, which may be quite substantial for newcomers, as a condition of membership. When membership is required to engage in potentially highly profitable undertakings, professional associations may become very effective interest groups. In addition, sanctions for not complying with ethical standards may be far-reaching and may even include prohibition from practice, either temporarily or permanently. Occupations which have no coercive power will try to overcome free-riding by positive selective incentives, that is private goods which an individual can only use as a member of the group. Examples are the provision of information, education programmes and pension schemes. Also the medical and legal professions are offering such services to their members, which may add to legitimizing compulsory membership, being in itself a very effective way of overcoming free-riding problems. The varying degree of homogeneity of the different professional groups may also explain the relative success in rent-seeking.

In the sector of the medical professions, pharmacists seem to be a more effective interest group than medical doctors. For example, in Belgium pharmacists enjoy territorial protection and their income is higher than the earnings of general practitioners (Van den Bergh and Faure 1991). This can easily be explained using the above insights from Public Choice. The pharmacists' group is clearly smaller than the doctors' group. The homogeneity criterion applies to the former group (protection of the monopoly of selling medicines) but not to the latter group, which contains a lot of heterogeneous subgroups.

Finally, it is worth noting that the costs of lobbying for the medical and legal professions are reduced considerably because most of the organizational costs must be spent anyway. A significant portion of the costs of engaging in rent-seeking activity are start-up costs. Once they have been borne, the cost of supplying additional collective effort is relatively low. Professional societies are well situated to act on political issues that affect their wealth because the costs of identifying and organizing a community of interests have already been incurred. For this reason they prove irrelevant when it comes to deciding whether to engage in lobbying activities or not. On the other side clients face high transaction costs in opposing wealth transfers. As far as the services of attorneys are concerned, there is no structured organization of clients' interests. In the medical sector one would expect that health care insurers defend the interests of patients on a structured and continuous basis. However, experience indicates that health insurers have not been able to counter the bargaining strength of doctors effectively. For instance, in Belgium they have agreed not to inform their members about the quality of physicians in return for co-decision powers regarding fixing of fees (Swennen 1989). Policies whose benefits are narrowly focused on small, well-organized interest groups are favoured by politicians, especially when the prospective gains (votes, campaign contributions and the like) are high and the transfers are not recognized by the general public. In the health sector patients get medical bills reimbursed and are therefore less sensitive to the real amount of fees and the rents involved.

A second argument supporting the rent-seeking hypothesis follows from the scope of self-regulation itself. The comprehensive self-regulation of the medical and legal professions is not fully justified by market failures. First, professional ethics offers many examples of rules which go further than necessary to correct market failures. Restrictions on advertising, such as ethical rules prohibiting attorneys to solicit clients by informing them about their specialties,[54] inhibit the free flow of information and competition. Instead of reducing the problem of informational asymmetry, these ethical rules create inefficiencies instead of eliminating them. Restrictions on advertising are blatant efforts to reduce price competition by constraining the flow of information. American and Canadian studies provide overwhelming evidence that advertising does not adversely affect quality. In at least one study restrictions on advertising are found to have actually reduced the quality of services provided (Muris and McChesney 1979).

In many countries advertising restrictions are now being relaxed, either as a consequence of increasing interprofessional competition or judicial intervention. Secondly, in some countries, there is evidence that ethical rules are mainly used (or abused) to discipline members for offences unrelated to quality of output. In Belgium sanctions are most often imposed for lack of dignity in private life or for improper behaviour towards the professional body, but rarely for professional malpractice. The Belgian public body seems not so much concerned with the supervision of the quality of the services performed, but rather with the public image of the attorney and its own privileges (Van den Bergh and Faure 1991, 174–5, Faure 1993, 108–9). The picture is somewhat different in the Netherlands, where a relatively greater number of cases concern the duty of care towards clients, although sanctions are not only imposed for assuring minimum quality but also for violation of ethical rules restricting competition (Hellingman 1993, 193).

High incomes on their own do not provide conclusive evidence of successful rent-seeking. At this point it should be recalled that asymmetric information on markets for professional services prevents competitive pricing. Given the experience goods (or credence goods) character of professional services regulation of fees may be favoured in order to guarantee minimum quality. A sufficiently high 'confidence premium' must be paid to the professionals, in order to avoid strategic behaviour (Schäfer and Ott 1995, 429). If the amount of the premium for opportunism exceeds the confidence premium, incompetent professionals may drive out good professionals (market for lemons). Although price regulation may overcome the problem of adverse selection, a major problem with the argument is that regulators are supposed to be sufficiently benevolent and omniscient to eliminate unproductive monopoly rents while still allowing quasi-rents (confidence premiums) as quality incentives. Under the current self-regulatory systems the professions may abuse fee regulation by accepting rewards for their monopoly without enforcing high standards. This danger is especially present given the existing entry barriers. Regulation of fees in combination with limitations on entry is dysfunctional in view of improving quality, since it is precisely the facilitation of market entry that raises the chances of a successful quality-enforcing policy (Schulenburg 1986, 142–5). Moreover, insofar as clients cannot reliably evaluate service quality even after treatment (credence goods), there seems to be a case for more comprehensive quality-enforcing regulation. Regulation of fees seems to be an answer to strategic behaviour only if search costs exist and quality uncertainty can be reduced through the repeat purchase mechanism. It may be concluded that high incomes are partly justified insofar as they are able to guarantee minimum quality of experience goods. Although the protection of quality rents through professional self-regulation in its current form is dysfunctional, the analysis of income levels should take account of the desirability of quality rents to avoid adverse selection.

It is very difficult to prove empirically that doctors' or attorneys' incomes are the result of successful rent-seeking. Figures about income are available, but these data are seldom analysed in relation to the variables of professional regulation.[55] The income situation of medical doctors may serve as an example to illustrate the difficulties in proving rent-seeking.[56] Clearly average doctors earn higher incomes than average self-employed workers. Salaries paid to UK doctors put them in the highest paid sector of the population (Bowles 1993, 335). Empirical work done on physicians' income in Germany also shows that incomes are 60 per cent higher than the reference income of a civil servant (Männer 1993) and that they have the highest relative incomes compared to their colleagues in the USA, UK and France.[57] In Belgium and the Netherlands the picture is the same. In both countries medical specialists are at the top of the income scale.[58] Generally, the empirical work seems to corroborate the excessive income hypothesis for doctors compared with the income of a control group of individuals. In spite of this evidence, efforts to identify rent-seeking remain rather controversial exercises. The trouble starts at the assessment of the incomes: different methods of cost accounting yield different outcomes. Next, to assess the excess return to human capital investment, figures are needed to estimate the costs involved in seeking rents. The long duration of the studies reduces the period in which income is earned. Finally, high incomes may just reflect appropriate quality rents. For all these reasons, it is hard to say to which extent high incomes are effects of the current self-regulation. Moreover, in recent years the relative income position of doctors is deteriorating while physician density increases (Trautwein and Rönnau 1993, 289, 303). Strong cartelization would reflect a rather weak correlation of increasing physician density and decreasing incomes. And yet, the weak empirical evidence on rent-seeking should not let us forget that the other party in the controversy is likewise obliged to furnish proof that the current level of income just reflects an appropriate confidence premium.

Finally, although the empirical evidence is not conclusive, it is not difficult to find qualitative evidence for monopoly rent protection. Grandfather clauses, exempting the current members of the profession from having to satisfy new licensing standards, are the best known technique for generating rents for current members of an occupation. In the sector of the liberal professions rents are generated and protected through effective limitations on entry and competition. The most prominent example for attempts at monopoly rent protection is the asymmetry in the quality checks of entrants and of established members of the medical and legal professions. Once entrants are licensed they will not—as a rule—lose their licences even if they lose elementary parts of their qualification owing to lack of practice and/or by negligence over keeping track of innovations. Even if ethical rules require ongoing education (and professional bodies offer education programmes to their members on a voluntary basis), the licence to practise as an attorney or a doctor is valid for the entire professional life (Finsinger 1993a, 371 and Finsinger 1993b, 389). The intra-professional transfers to a limited group of practitioners may be the most significant consequence of self-regulation. As the literature on rent-seeking has shown, the intra-industry distribution of rents may very well explain the struggle for regulations yielding these rents (Guttmann 1978, Maloney and McCormick 1982); self-regulation in the medical and legal professions seems to provide additional evidence for this hypothesis (Van den Bergh and Faure 1991, 180–1).

4. The legal and the economic approaches combined: the proportionality requirement revisited

The prerequisite that professional rules must serve the general good and the requirement of proportionality are crucial in the evaluation of the compatibility of divergent national professional rules, which equally apply to national and foreign professionals, with the principles of free movement of goods and services and the right of establishment guaranteed by the EC Treaty. To make a convincing case in favour of self-regulation in its current form, two things must be shown. First, it should be demonstrated that regulation is needed for imperative reasons of public interest. Rephrased in economic terms the first question relates to the necessity to cope with market failures. It should be shown that competition, due to the special characteristics of the professions, will not guarantee quality. Even if this first requirement is met, the question remains which form regulatory intervention should take. In legal terms this equals the analysis of the proportionality of the self-regulatory measures. To make a case in favour of an exemption for the medical and legal professions from the competition laws, similar evidence must be submitted. It needs to be shown that competition on the market for professional services is not able to generate outcomes improving social welfare and that the restrictions imposed by self-regulation are indispensable to the attainment of the alleged benefits in terms of quality improvement.[59]

It may be doubted that the current self-regulation in the medical and legal profession would survive the 'rule of reason' test if the European Court of Justice were willing to adopt an economic approach. First, some rules do not cure market imperfections but rather create them. Restrictions on advertising, which go further than a prohibition of deception, do not satisfy the criterion of necessity advanced by the European Court of Justice. It is hard to see why such a prohibition may be needed to cure a market imperfection. For example, rules preventing professionals from mentioning their specialties increase the search costs of consumers; instead of curing the informational asymmetry they protect less qualified professionals from competition. Economic analysis may help lawyers in deciding hard cases by unmasking the rhetoric supporting rules, which are allegedly serving the public interest. If it can be shown that self-regulatory rules serve to create inefficiencies rather than to cure market imperfections, the first question regarding the necessity of the contested measures may be answered negatively. Many ethical rules, such as advertising restrictions and the referral system,[60] will not survive the reasonableness test at this first stage because they restrict the flow of information between clients and professionals. In these cases it will be possible to challenge the self-regulatory measures successfully and there will be no need to further investigate their proportionality.

The second question concerning the proportionality of the self-regulatory measures, which do serve the public interest, is much more difficult to answer. Some rules issued by self-regulatory bodies (e.g. control on entry and sanctions for malpractice) may be justified for imperative reasons of public interest, but it may be questioned whether they also satisfy the proportionality test. With respect to the requirement of proportionality, the crucial question is whether a less interventionist measure may cope with market failures as effectively as the current self-regulatory rules, without causing the same inefficiencies. Regulatory techniques differ in the extent to which they impede freedom of activity. Ogus (1994, 150–1) has classified different regulatory techniques according to the degree of state intervention. He envisages a spectrum with information measures at one end and prior approval at the other end of the spectrum. Information measures require suppliers to disclose certain facts, but do not otherwise impose behavioural controls. Under a prior approval regime, by contrast, individuals or firms may be prevented from lawfully supplying a product or service without obtaining an authorization from a public agency. Standards occupy a middle position between information remedies and prior approval; they allow the activity to take place without any *ex ante* control, but the supplier who fails to meet standards of quality commits an offence. Self-regulation, which enables professional bodies to control both entry (prior approval) and performance, represents high intervention, whereas other forms, such as information remedies and standards, represent low or middle-range intervention. Given the availability of these alternative regulatory techniques, the question arises whether self-regulation does not go beyond what is necessary to cope with market failures.

The proportionality problem is ultimately an empirical issue. On a theoretical level the case for self-regulation is not convincing, but empirical evidence to support the theory remains limited (see Section 3). For a long time the regulation of the medical and legal professions in European countries was based upon the same principles. Hence it was not possible to collect sufficient evidence about the effects of an alternative less interventionist regime. The deregulation movement in some European countries will allow more empirical research in the near future. Cost–benefit analyses should be conducted to assess whether the benefits of self-regulation can be achieved at lower costs. If this is the case, the contested measures will not satisfy the proportionality criterion. Unfortunately, lawyers who have to decide hard cases cannot afford to wait for this information. Even in the absence of empirical evidence, the economic analysis remains useful because it will at least allow lawyers to ask the right questions. The answers to these questions will be helpful in assessing the proportionality requirement. Compulsory membership of professional bodies may be used as an example to illustrate how the proportionality requirement may be assessed from an economic perspective.

Compulsory membership of professional bodies may go beyond what is necessary to keep quality standards intact. Consequently it must be deplored that the Directives on the right of establishment for medical doctors and lawyers (see Section 2.1 of this paper) have confirmed the conformity of this requirement with the fundamental freedoms of the EC Treaty. It has been explained above that information asymmetries and externalities may justify regulation. To cure the market failure of asymmetric information a less interventionist measure, such as registration and certification should be considered first. Under a registration programme those wishing to practise a profession would need only to inform the state of their intent. Registration does not address the issue of information asymmetry and may therefore be ignored as an alternative policy option (Curran 1993, 52–3). Under certification the professions would enjoy protection of their title only. Nobody would be allowed to call himself an attorney or a medical doctor, without being registered with the professional bodies. Protection of titles equals an information remedy: the member of an occupation may only use a title if he or she meets certain standards involving some combination of education, on-the-job experience and successful completion of an examination. Certification possesses the advantage of preserving freedom of choice. Consumers can elect for a lower quality service at what will be a lower price. If the goal were to protect the individual preferring low quality who, in the opinion of the regulator is not acting in his or her own interest, then the justification for self-regulation would be paternalistic. The current self-regulatory licensing system would not conform to the proportionality requirement if certification were able to overcome the information deficit effectively and efficiently. As mentioned above, a comparison of the effectiveness and efficiency of both alternatives remains difficult because of lack of empirical evidence.

Also with respect to the externalities' problem it needs to be shown that less restrictive regulatory techniques are not adequate to cure the market imperfection. Tort liability suffers from important drawbacks. These include the limited capacity of the courts to deal with malpractice, the difficulties in establishing causation and quantifying harm when damages are sought. Moreover, before the quality levels are established through malpractice cases and the good professionals have driven out the bad professionals, high unrecompensable losses may have occurred. This brings us to the question of whether quality standards, set by a regulator (not necessarily self-regulation) may adequately cope with the externalities' problem. Quality standards are less interventionist than prior approval and should therefore, in the proportionality test, be considered first. Here the relevant question is whether input controls are to be preferred to output controls. Quality standards are imposed *ex post*, after the occurrence of the harm, whereas prior approval operates *ex ante*. It may be argued that input variables can more easily be measured and that they may be presumed to be closely correlated to quality. Prior approval may exclude *ex ante* manifest incompetence of a kind which can give rise to high social costs. The advantage of controlling entry through licensing is that this may ensure that professionals are properly trained and competent to practise in their fields. The alternative, *ex post* quality standards, may be a less effective response. Legislators will face a difficult task; to set quality levels they must decide how to measure quality, which is as difficult as it is for the courts to handle malpractice cases.

If certification is deemed insufficient to adequately cope with the externalities' problem (even though it may be an adequate response to the market failure of asymmetric information) prior approval in the form of licensing may be considered. At this point it should, however, be noted that there are remarkable differences between the current self-regulation in the medical and legal professions and licensing systems for other occupations. Under most licensing systems, the rules regarding entry are established by the government, after consulting with the professional associations. Licences are issued by public authorities.[61] Moreover, licensing laws do not contain specific rules regarding performance. Performance remains subject to less interventionist controls (tort liability, general standards concerning safety and health). The role of the occupations thus remains limited. Self-regulation in the medical and legal professions, by contrast, transforms the professional association into a public body. Entry and performance are regulated by the profession itself.

Generally public interest arguments, involving the need to correct information asymmetries and the externalities' problem, raise a strong presumption for regulation but not necessarily self-regulation in its current form. Even though it may be difficult to assess the proportionality of self-regulatory rules, which may be justified as remedies to cure market imperfections, the economic analysis has made clear that several less interventionist measures are available. This raises some doubts with respect to the appropriateness of the current self-regulation in the medical and the legal professions. If one takes a closer look at self-regulation, as it exists in the medical and legal profession, a more striking conclusion may be reached. It is remarkable that the current self-regulatory systems make a combined use of all possible regulatory techniques. Registration is required since future professionals have to become a member of the public bodies of attorneys and doctors. Certification applies since the professions enjoy protection of titles. At the same time membership of the professional body implies the duty to comply with ethical rules. These rules, which prohibit certain modes of conduct are similar to performance standards. Finally, compulsory membership of the professional bodies equals prior approval. It adds to the protection of the title the protection of the profession itself (licensing). The right to perform protected services is reserved to persons who meet quality requirements to be proven by registration with the professional body (license). In the medical and legal occupations admittance to the profession is a right granted by the professional body. Not only will it be impossible to carry the protected title, the supply of the professional services will be reserved for those who are members of the professional bodies. Moreover, control of performance is far-reaching: the sanctions include the prohibition to practise the profession, either temporarily or permanently.

Even if it cannot be convincingly proven that a given regulatory measure taken on its own is disproportionate, it seems very difficult to justify the current overregulation which makes a combined use of all possible remedies. Prior approval may be the most effective and efficient way to cope with the externalities' problem, but its combination with control of fees may turn it into a powerful anti-competitive weapon. Similarly, the combined use of prior approval and registration with a privileged professional body protects the position of an incumbent monopolist from erosion by new market entry. Adverse effects may occur if rules aiming at a relaxation of entry conditions force public professional bodies to accept individuals, who have been denied registration in the past, as new members. In the Netherlands the Order of Attorneys has recently been compelled to admit employed lawyers (Cohen 1996). This reform has kept the monopoly intact and has increased the control powers of the public professional body. To stimulate competition it would have been wise to introduce competition between different licensing bodies.

It may be required in the general interest that professionals are appropriately qualified and that they obey rules of conduct which are in the interests of the proper and efficient provision of the professional services. In this respect a far-reaching intervention, such as prior approval, may be needed. But the case for prior approval has its limits: it does not necessarily imply that entry control must be performed by self-regulatory professional bodies. The case law of the European Court of Justice and the national competition authorities (see Section 2) shows that Orders tend to abuse their powers by imposing inappropriate criteria not ensuring competence nor response to consumer needs. For example, if membership can be denied to applicants who are not of good conduct[62] subjective decisions as to who will be permitted to practise can hardly be avoided and the licensing process may operate to limit the number of new entrants and harm competition. The proportionality requirement does not seem to be met if somebody, who is considered to be honest in one member state, is refused access to the same profession in another member state for lack of good character. In these circumstances the principle of mutual recognition seems to imply that assessments of honesty are equally valid in all member states. Even when control of the entry process is based on objective criteria, grading of licensing examinations by professional bodies can indirectly serve to limit the number of new professionals in the interests of the existing members of the profession. Entry requirements designed to ensure quality can serve to indirectly impose quantitative limits on the number of new entrants, depending on the level at which quality is set. It would, therefore, seem that control of the entry process by professionals should be limited to an advisory function. A far-reaching involvement in the grading of exams (as is currently the case in Italy) or the absence of a possibility of appeal against a decision rejecting registration with the professional body (as is currently the case in Belgium) open the door wide for unjustified entry limitations. Prior approval can only perform its function if the permission to enter the profession is granted upon the basis of objective criteria, which are applied in a non-discriminatory and non-arbitrary manner. In this respect it may be questioned why licences, which could be issued by public authorities, should be replaced by membership of professional bodies, enjoying public law status. Such membership requirements may go beyond what is necessary to guarantee quality.

5. Concluding remarks

Self-regulation in the medical and legal professions is a highly complex problem and it is not easy to reach hard conclusions. However, the following remarks seem appropriate. The theoretical justification for self-regulation in its current form is weak. Legal analysis shows that current European law and national competition laws only provide a partial remedy to restrictions on entry and anti-competitive rules regarding conduct. Economic analysis may be helpful in interpreting the 'rule of reason' (in particular the proportionality requirement) and may thus contribute to pulling down regulations which harm the public interest. However, the question about the appropriateness of a more global reform remains. There are many alternatives to cope with existing market failures in the legal and medical professions, which would reduce the likelihood of regulations pursuing the interests of the professions to the detriment of the public interest. It is ultimately an empirical question how well these alternative devices will perform their task in curing market imperfections without causing severe restrictions on competition. In what follows the reader will find a few author's suggestions with respect to possible future developments.

To prevent abuses of self-regulation, a first step is to increase government involvement in the licensing process. The current system enables the professions to limit entry by determining the capacity for education and training. The free movement of lawyers across European countries may be hindered by the requirement to undergo aptitude tests controlled by the legal professions themselves. As has been pointed out above, licensing can be done by public bodies. This may avoid the erection of entry barriers and stimulate competition. Lawyers must not necessarily be required to join the Bar Association or Chamber in order to practise law; neither must there be a duty for physicians to become a member of the Order of Doctors. Since membership of the professional association of physicians is not required in the Netherlands, it is hard to see why such membership should be required in other countries. Compulsory membership in privileged self-regulatory bodies should be abolished and replaced by optional membership in competing organizations. An independent governmental agency may exercise control over these professional associations by requiring them to impose quality standards upon their members. The ethical rules issued by these competing associations would be guidelines and not be binding on non-members. Such an approach generates competition between self-regulatory systems. In the Netherlands several alternative associations have already developed (den Hertog 1993, 209). In the UK a first step has been taken in the direction of competition between professional associations in the legal profession, by making it possible for competing professional bodies and institutions to apply for rights of audience in the courts. The British experience, however, illustrates that full competition will not be achieved if existing practitioner groups succeed in gaining a significant influence over the agencies, which grant the right to perform professional services.

A further step is to increase consumer participation and to develop countervailing power. Again the Netherlands and the UK have taken the first steps. In the Netherlands there are more than 250 organizations of patients. In the UK a new body has been created, the Lord Chancellor's Advisory Committee on Legal Education, the majority of whose members are not practising lawyers. Professional bodies will have to submit regulations to the Advisory Committee for its endorsement (Ogus 1993, 309).

At the level of performance controls, the remaining restrictions on advertising should be abolished. These restrictions impede the free flow of information and seriously hinder competition. Serious doubts arise with respect to regulation of fees. Minimum prices may be seen as a means to guarantee quality, but they are dysfunctional in combination with existing entry controls. Fee scales set by public professional bodies should be held contrary to the cartel prohibition as far as standardized fees cannot be justified to facilitate reimbursements under public health insurance plans. It is equally important to increase inter-professional competition. This competition may act as a powerful deterrent to the lowering of professional standards. Creative tension between the different professions may be helpful in discovering abuses and in improving efficiency by introducing a new division of labour. The current compartmentalization prevents the creation of alternative markets, for example for the provision of simple or routine services. The proposed reforms may be able to cure the market imperfections in the sector of the legal and medical professions, without creating scope for self-regulatory rules harming the public interest.

Notes

1. There is currently no existing agreed-upon definition of the term 'profession', either generally or under law. Therefore, in some countries the list of professions may be restricted to less than five occupations and in other countries businesses may be considered as professional activities, even though they are seen as purely commercial in the first group of countries.
2. Case C-292/92, *Hünermund et al. v. Landesapothekerkammer Baden-Württemberg* [1993] ECR I-6787. See the discussion in section 2.2.2 of this paper.
3. One may notice the arbitrariness of the distinction by comparing on the one hand, the attorney established in a border area, who has a large clientele from another country but maintains a single office in his 'home country', and on the other hand, the attorney who decides to open a second office a few kilometres across the border.
4. A well-known example is the distinction, in the British legal profession, between barristers and solicitors. See Ogus (1993).
5. The leading case for the direct applicability of Art. 52 concerned the legal profession. A Belgian regulation had laid down discriminatory conditions for foreigners to practise law as an attorney in Belgium. The Court of Justice ruled that the prohibition of discrimination has direct effect (Case 2/74, *Reyners v. Belgian State* [1974] ECR 631.
6. Case 33/74, *Van Binsbergen v. Bestuur van de Bedrijfsvereninging voor de Metaalnijverheid* [1974] ECR 1299.
7. Case 246/80, *Broekmeulen v. Huisarts Registratie Commissie* [1981] ECR 2311.
8. Case 71/76, *Thieffry v. Conseil de l'Ordre des Avocats à la Cour de Paris* [1977] ECR 765.
9. Directive 75/362 of 16 June 1975 deals with the *mutual recognition of medical qualifications, Official Journal* (hereinafter abbreviated as *OJ*), 1975, L 167/1 modified by Directive 81/1057 of 14 December 1981, *OJ* 1981, L 385/25 and Directive 82/76 of 26 January 1982, *OJ* 1982, L 43/21. *Measures co-ordinating the training requirements* have been laid down in Directive 75/363 of 16 June 1975, *OJ* 1975, L 167/14, modified by Directive 82/76 of 26 January 1982, *OJ* 1982, L 43/21.
10. Directive 89/48 of 21 December 1988, *OJ* 1989, L 19/16.
11. Directive 98/5 of 16 February 1998, *OJ* 1998, L 77/36.
12. Case C-55/94, *Reinhard Gebhard v. Consiglio dell'ordine degli Avvocati e Procuratori di Milano* [1995] ECR I-4165.

13. Case 221/85, *Commission v. Belgium* [1987] ECR 719; Case C-61/89, *Bouchoucha* [1990] ECR I-3551.
14. Case C-340/89, *Vlassopoulou v. Ministerium für Justiz, Bundes- und Europaangelegenheiten Baden-Württemberg* [1991] ECR I-2357.
15. Case 107/83, *Ordre des Avocats au Barreau de Paris v. Klopp* [1984] ECR 2971; Case 96/85, *Commission v. France* [1986] ECR 1475; Case 81/87, *The Queen v. H.M. Treasury and Commissioner of Inland Revenue, ex parte Daily Mail and General Trust PLC* [1988] ECR 5483. The first two cases dealt with the right to set up a secondary establishment in another member state; the last case extends the freedom of establishment to a right to move away.
16. In the older *Kraus* case, by contrast, criteria were given to assess whether a procedure by which permission for the use of a foreign diploma is granted stands up to the principle of proportionality. The procedure must be restricted to the question whether the academic diploma has been correctly issued by the competent institution; moreover, it has to be easily accessible, may not be made dependent on excessive administration fees, and must be subject to judicial review. Criminal sanctions for neglecting the permission requirement may be imposed, but may not be disproportionately grave (Case C-19/92, *Kraus v. Land Baden-Württemberg* [1993] ECR I-1663.
17. Case C-292/86, *Gullung v. Conseil de l'Ordre des Avocats au Barreau de Colmar et al.* [1988] ECR 111.
18. Previously in England and Wales, besides their monopoly rights to conducting litigation, solicitors had statutory monopolies in relation to the drawing up of documents for the administration of deceased persons' estates (the 'probate monopoly') and for the transfer of real property (the 'conveyancing monopoly'). The two latter solicitors' monopolies have been abolished. Banks, building societies and insurance companies may now also arrange documents for the administration of deceased persons' estates. Similarly, the right to engage in conveyancing services is no longer restricted to solicitors, but determined by the Authorised Conveyancing Practitioners Board. Since the deregulation of the solicitors' monopoly licensed conveyancers have entered the market.
19. The Examination Commission is composed of two attorneys, a judge and a university professor. Both judges and university professors tend to have strong connections with the Bar (see Royal Decree 2 June 1996, *Belgisch Staatsblad*, 15 May 1996).
20. Bayerischer Verwaltungsgerichtshof München, 23 November 1994 (Az: 3 B 94.227).
21. Public professional bodies may abuse their power by organizing examinations aiming at a general reduction of the number of young professionals (not only migrant professionals). For example, in Belgium young attorneys must take courses during their training period and pass a bar examination. These courses are largely a rehearsal of what they learned at university and would, therefore, be more useful for older attorneys. The augmenting number of duties during the training period is clearly a response to the increasing number of young attorneys (see Faure 1993, 92–3 and 110–11). In Great Britain, the failure rate of the (relatively low) number of solicitors taking the advocacy tests to obtain rights of audience in higher courts is high and steadily increases. These experiences seem to indicate that the incumbent professionals try to keep control over entry by newcomers and that they may remain able to limit market entry.
22. Case 96/85, *Commission v. France* [1986] ECR 1475.
23. According to settled case law, member states are required not to introduce or maintain in force measures, even of a legislative or regulatory nature, which may render ineffective the

competition rules applicable to undertakings (see e.g. Case C-379/82 *Peralta* [1994] ECR I-3453). Such is the case, according to that case law: (1) if a member state requires or favours the adoption of agreements, decisions or concerted practices contrary to Art. 85 or reinforces their effects, or (2) deprives its own legislation of its official character by delegating to private traders responsibility for taking decisions affecting the economic sphere. An example of the first indent could be the approval by government of prices fixed by professional bodies. An example of the second might be the extensive delegation of powers to professional bodies by allowing them to set performance standards.

24. WuW/E BGH 1474 (Architektenkammer Niedersachsen). See also: WuW/E BKartA 50 (Vereidigte Buchprüfer), KG WuW/E OLG 322 (Vereidigte Buchprüfer II), OLG Stuttgart WuW/E OLG 545 (Rabattverbot der Apothekerkammer) and OLG Bremen WuW/E OLG 4367 (Proben apothekenüblicher Waren).
25. KG WuW/E OLG 1687 (Laboruntersuchungen). See also: WuW/E BKartA 357 (Berufsboxer) and with respect to veterinary surgeons: WuW/E BGH 647, 650 (Rinderbesamung).
26. WuW/E BGH 1474, 1476.
27. See e.g. Decisions of the Competition Council (Conseil de la Concurrence) in the cases 82-4/DC, BOCC, 1982, 268–9 (legal counsellors), 86-2/DC, BOCC, 1986, 5–8 and 87-D 15, BOCCRF, 1987, 177–9 (pharmacists); 87-D-53, BOCCRF, 1987, 360–3 (architects); 88-D-23, BOCCRF, 1988, 143–5 and 91-D-04, BOCCRF, 1991, 59–64 (opticians), 89-D-36, BOCCRF, 1989, 295–301 (dentists); 91-D-43, BOCCRF, 1991, 27–32 (medical specialists); 91-D-55, BOCCRF, 1992, 27–32 (geometrical experts); 92-D-39, BOCCRF, 1992, 281–3 (private investigators); 96-D-78 and 96-D-79 (attorneys) and Advice in the case 92-A-04, BOCCRF, 1992, 298–301 (veterinaries).
28. Monopolies Commission, *A Report on the General Effect on the Public Interest of Certain Restrictive Practices so far as they prevail in the Supply of Professional Services*, October 1970 Cmnd 4463.
29. This is the rule whereby a Senior Counsel or Queens Counsel may not appear in a case without a junior counsel.
30. Italy: legge 10.10.1990, n. 287; Belgium: Wet 05.08.1991 tot bescherming van de economische mededinging (entered into force on 01.04.1993).
31. The criteria for fixing attorneys' fees are determined by the Consiglio Nazionale Forense and approved by the Minister of Justice (Art. 57 R.D.L., 27.11.1933, n. 1578; legge 07.11.1957, n. 1051; D.M. n. 392/1990). The tariffs are binding; no derogation is possible (Art. 24 legge 13.06.1942, n. 794). Minimum fees for medical services are set by decree of the President of the Republic, following a proposal made by the Ministers of Health and Finances, after having obtained opinions from the State Council, the Superior Council for Health and the National Federation of the Orders of Doctors. The minimum prices are obligatory (legge 21.02.1963, n. 244).
32. Provvedimento *Assirevi*. For a comment, see Cornetta (1992).
33. Raad voor de Mededinging, 31 Oktober 1995, 95-VMP-3.
34. Hof van Beroep Brussel, 14 November 1996, *Belgisch Staatsblad*, 26 November 1996.
35. In 1987 the original anti-trust law (Wet Economische Mededinging) was amended to include liberal professions. Regulations restricting competition, such as the codes of conduct, must be reported and registered. When they are not in the public interest they may be declared invalid. A new competition law (Act of May 22, 1997), based upon the EC competition rules, has entered into force on 1 January 1998.
36. Some restrictions still apply: to use methods of direct mailing, comparative advertising,

rates of success, information on particular cases (without the client's consent), to mention names of clients and the fact that one holds a position as a judge.

37. *Goldfarb v. Virginia State Bar*, 421 U.S. 773 (Decision of the US Supreme Court, 16 June 1975). The American Supreme Court explicitly stated that attorneys play an important role in economic markets and that restrictions on competition agreed upon by attorneys may be prohibited upon the basis of §1 Sherman Act.
38. Ehlermann (1993, 143).
39. Decision 30 June 1993 [1993] *OJ* L 203.
40. Decision 30 January 1995 [1995] *OJ* L 122.
41. Case C-292/92, *Hünermund et al. v. Landesapothekerkammer Baden-Württemberg* [1993] ECR I-6787.
42. Cases C-267 and C-268/91, *Keck and Mithouard* [1993] ECR I-6097. To remain outside the scope of the prohibition the rules must apply to all affected traders operating within the national territory and they may not, in law or in fact, affect the marketing of imported and of domestic products in a different manner (paragraph 16 of the Court's judgment).
43. Case C-391/92, *Commission v. Greece* [1995] ECR I-1621 (sale of milk for babies in pharmacies only); Case C-387/93 *Banchero*, not yet published (sale of cigarettes in tobacco shops).
44. Cases C-69/93 and C-258/93 *Punto Casa and Boermans* [1994] ECR I-2355; Cases C-401/92 and C-402/92 *Tankstation 't Heukske and PPV* [1994] ECR I-2199.
45. Case C-412/93, *Leclerc-Siplec v. TF 1 Publicité and M6 Publicité* [1995] ECR I-179.
46. Case C-384/93, *Alpine Investments BV v. Minister van Financiën* [1995] ECR I-1141.
47. As a result of asymmetric information producers are unable to signal differences in their relative quality to consumers. The result is that professionals who depress quality are not punished by the market mechanism. The market price will reflect only the average quality level and thus attract average quality sellers. In turn, this will lead to a reduction in the average level of quality perceived by consumers, a further reduction of the market price and another dilution of quality. This process of adverse selection is cumulative and may in the limit destroy the market altogether.
48. For empirical evidence on demand generation, see Trautwein and Rönnau (1993, 295–7) with further references.
49. Evidence that the demand for medical care in Belgium is price-elastic can be found in Carrin and De Graeve (1986) and Pacolet and Wouters (1986).
50. To avoid the problems arising from the need to prove negligence on the part of the professionals, a rule of strict liability may be considered. This, however, will not be a perfect solution given the difficulties in proving causation and quantifying harm when damages are sought.
51. The concept of rent-seeking is explained below (see 3.2).
52. See Section 1.1 of this paper. In the case of architects it took 17 years to produce a Directive (64/222).
53. The number of solicitors taking the advocacy tests is low: in the three first tests 74, 46 and 53 respectively. The failure rate is high: for example, only 29% of candidates passed the third evidence and procedure test, compared to 41% in the second test and 60% in the first test. In February 1996 there were no more than 375 solicitor advocates in the UK (*Law Society Gazette*, 14 February 1996).
54. Such a rule still exists in Belgium, but has been abolished in other European countries (Germany, the Netherlands).

55. Canadian research has established a relationship between different variables of self-regulation in 20 professions (limitations on mobility, price restraints and advertising restrictions) and income. See Muzondo and Pazderka (1983). Although the relationship between self-regulation and income has not clearly been established in European studies, there is some evidence about price-discrimination. In the UK conveyancing (a monopoly right of solicitors which has meanwhile been abolished) led to price discrimination, which was enhanced by the fixed scale of conveyancing fees set by the Law Society. See Bowles and Phillips (1977). With respect to minimum fee schedules and price discrimination in the American legal profession, compare Latham (1979).

56. Income statistics show that the average income of attorneys is not very much higher than the average income of self-employed workers, so that the excessive income hypothesis seems to be falsified from the very beginning of the empirical analysis. See e.g. Van den Bergh and Faure (1991, 178–9).

57. Reinhardt (1985). For other empirical studies, see Zohlnhöfer and Schmidt (1985) and Zweifel and Eichenberger (1988), whose research somewhat contradicts Reinhardt's conclusions.

58. See for Belgium: Van den Bergh and Faure (1991, 178–9), and for the Netherlands: den Hertog (1993, 213).

59. See Art. 85(3) EC Treaty, which makes an exemption from the cartel prohibition dependent upon the fulfilment of four conditions: production must be improved; consumers must get a fair share of the resulting benefits; the restrictions must be indispensable to the attainment of the benefits; and competition may not be eliminated in respect of a substantial part of the products in question.

60. In the medical profession the referral system prevents direct contacts between patients and specialists; general practitioners have to act as a clearing house for specialists. This kind of arrangement has been challenged successfully within the legal profession in the UK. See Ogus (1993).

61. For a critical analysis of the Belgian licensing system in the retailing trade, see Van den Bergh (1986).

62. See the *Gullung* case, cited note 17.

References

Akerlof, G. (1970) 'The Market for "Lemons": Qualitative Uncertainty and the Market Mechanism', *Quarterly Journal of Economics*, 84: 488–500.

Arrow, K. (1963) 'Uncertainty and the Welfare Economics of Medical Care', *American Economic Review*, 941–73.

Bos, D. I. (1995) *Marktwerking en Regulering: Theoretische aspecten en ervaringen in Nederland en het buitenland*. The Hague: Ministerie van Economische Zaken.

Bowles, R. (1993) 'Regulation of the Medical Profession in England and Wales', in Faure, M., Finsinger, J., Siegers, J., and Van den Bergh, R. (eds.), *Regulation of Professions: A Law and Economics Approach to the Regulation of Attorneys and Physicians in the US, Belgium, The Netherlands, Germany and the UK*. Antwerp: Maklu, 331–55.

Bowles, R. and Phillips, J. (1977) 'Solicitor's Remuneration: A Critique of Recent Developments in Conveyancing', *Modern Law Review*, 40: 639–50.

Bruinsma, F. (1997) 'Marktwerking en deregulering in en rondom de advocatuur', *Sociale Wetenschappen*, 40: 60–71.

Carrin, G. and De Graeve, D. (1986) 'Patiënten en hun raadplegingen van huisartsen en specialisten: Een toepassing van het model van Grossman', *Acta Hospitalia*, 3ff.

Cohen, C. J. (1996) 'Het domein geherdefinieerd', *Advocatenblad*, 233–8.

Cornetta (1992) 'Tariffe professionali e disciplina antitrust', *Foro italiano*, 3: 562.

Curran, C. (1993) 'The American Experience with Self-Regulation in the Medical and Legal Professions', in Faure, M., Finsinger, J., Siegers, J., and Van den Bergh, R. (eds.), *Regulation of Professions: A Law and Economics Approach to the Regulation of Attorneys and Physicians in the US, Belgium, The Netherlands, Germany and the UK*. Antwerp: Maklu, 47–87.

den Hertog, J. (1993) 'An Economic Analysis of the (Self-)Regulation of Physicians in the Netherlands', in Faure, M., Finsinger, J., Siegers, J., and Van den Bergh, R. (eds.), *Regulation of Professions: A Law and Economics Approach to the Regulation of Attorneys and Physicians in the US, Belgium, The Netherlands, Germany and the UK*. Antwerp: Maklu, 195–215.

Doornbos, N. (1996) 'Klachten aan de Orde', *Advocatenblad*, 74–9.

Ehlermann, C. D. (1993) 'Concurrence et professions libérales: Antagonisme ou compatibilité?' *Revue du marché commun et de l'union européenne*, 136–44.

Faure, M. (1993) 'Regulation of Attorneys in Belgium', in Faure, M., Finsinger, J., Siegers, J., and Van den Bergh, R. (eds.), *Regulation of Professions: A Law and Economics Approach to the Regulation of Attorneys and Physicians in the US, Belgium, The Netherlands, Germany and the UK*. Antwerp: Maklu, 89–123.

Finsinger, J. (1993a) 'Attorneys: Summary of the Cross-National Comparison', in Faure, M., Finsinger, J., Siegers, J., and Van den Bergh, R. (eds.), *Regulation of Professions: A Law and Economics Approach to the Regulation of Attorneys and Physicians in the US, Belgium, The Netherlands, Germany and the UK*. Antwerp: Maklu, 359–76.

Finsinger, J. (1993b) 'Doctors: Summary of the Cross-National Comparison', in Faure, M., Finsinger, J., Siegers, J., and Van den Bergh, R. (eds.), *Regulation of Professions: A Law and Economics Approach to the Regulation of Attorneys and Physicians in the US, Belgium, The Netherlands, Germany and the UK*. Antwerp: Maklu, 377–94.

Friedman, M. and Kuznets, S. (1945) *Income from Independent Professional Practice*. New York: National Bureau for Economic Research.

Guttmann, J. (1978) 'Interest Groups and the Demand for Agricultural Research', *Journal of Political Economy*, 86: 467–84.

Hellingman, K. (1993) 'An Economic Analysis of the Regulation of Lawyers in the Netherlands', in Faure, M., Finsinger, J., Siegers, J., and Van den Bergh, R. (eds.), *Regulation of Professions: A Law and Economics Approach to the Regulation of Attorneys and Physicians in the US, Belgium, The Netherlands, Germany and the UK*. Antwerp: Maklu, 147–85.

Herrmann, H. (1993) 'Regulation of Attorneys in Germany: Legal Framework and Actual Tendencies of Deregulation', in Faure, M., Finsinger, J., Siegers, J., and Van den Bergh, R. (eds.), *Regulation of Professions: A Law and Economics Approach to the Regulation of Attorneys and Physicians in the US, Belgium, The Netherlands, Germany and the UK*. Antwerp: Maklu, 225–47.

Immenga, U. and Mestmäcker, E.-J. (eds.) (1992) *GWB: Kommentar zum Kartellgesetz*. Munich: Beck.

Klein, B. and Leffler, K. B. (1981) 'The Role of Market Forces in Assuring Contractual Performance', *Journal of Political Economy*, 89: 615–41.

Latham, R. J. (1979) 'The Price Structure of the Legal Service Industry: Minimum Fee Schedules and Price Discrimination', *Antitrust Bulletin*, 24: 43–62.

Maloney, M. and McCormick, R. (1982) 'Environmental Quality Regulation', *Journal of Law and Economics*, 25: 99–123.

Männer, L. (1983) 'Höhe und Divergenz der Arzteinkommen als Kontrollgrößen für Fehlallokation in der kassenärztlichen Behandlung bei Einzelleistungshonorierung', in Henke, K.-D. and Reinhardt, U. E. (eds.), *Steuerung im Gesundheitswesen: Beiträge zur Gesundheitsökonomie*, vol. 4. Gerlingen: Bleicher, 77–122.

Miller, J. C. (1985) 'The FTC and Voluntary Standards: Maximizing the Net Benefits of Self-Regulation', *The Cato Journal*, 4: 897–903.

Muris, T. J. and McChesney, F. S. (1979) 'Advertising and the Price and Quality of Legal Services: The Case for Legal Clinics', *American Bar Foundation Research Journal*, 1: 179–207.

Muzondo, T. R. and Pazderka, B. (1983) 'Income-Enhancing Effects of Professional Licensing Restrictions: A Cross-Section Study of Canadian Data', *Antitrust Bulletin*, 28: 397–415.

OECD (1985) *Competition Policy and the Professions*. Paris: OECD.

Ogus, A. I. (1993) 'Regulation of the Legal Profession in England and Wales', in Faure, M., Finsinger, J., Siegers, J., and Van den Bergh, R. (eds.), *Regulation of Professions: A Law and Economics Approach to the Regulation of Attorneys and Physicians in the US, Belgium, The Netherlands, Germany and the UK*. Antwerp: Maklu, 307–29.

Ogus, A. I. (1994) *Regulation, Legal Form and Economic Theory*. Oxford: Clarendon Press.

Olson, M. (1965) *The Logic of Collective Action*. Cambridge, MA: Harvard University Press.

Pacolet, J. and Wouters, R. (1986) 'Gezins en inkomensaspecten van de kostenbeheersing in de ziekteverzekering in België', *Acta Hospitalia*, 8 ff.

Reinhardt, U. E. (1985) 'Honorierungssysteme in anderen Ländern—Internationale Vergleiche', in Ferber, C., Reinhardt, U. E., and Schaefer, H., *Kosten und Effizienz im Gesundheitswesen II*. Munich: Oldenbourg, 67–94.

Schäfer, H.-B. and Ott, C. (1995) *Lehrbuch der ökonomischen Analyse des Zivilrechts*. Berlin: Springer.

Graf von der Schulenburg, J.-M. (1986) 'Regulatory Measures to Enforce Quality Production of Self-Employed Professionals—A Theoretical Study of a Dynamic Market Process', in Graf von der Schulenburg, J.-M. and Skogh, G. (eds.), *Law and Economics and the Economics of Legal Regulation*. Dordrecht: Kluwer, 133–47.

Shavell, S. (1984) 'Liability for Harm versus Regulation of Safety', *Journal of Legal Studies*, 14: 357–74.

Shavell, S. (1986) 'The Judgment Proof Problem', *International Review of Law and Economics*, 6: 43–58.

Stigler, G. J. (1971) 'The Theory of Economic Regulation', *Bell Journal of Economics*, 2: 3–21.

Stuyck, J. and Geens, K. (1993) 'La libre circulation des avocats dans l'Europe du Marché Unique', *Revue du Marché Unique Européen*, 71–92.

Swennen, H. (1989) 'Concurrentie in het medisch beroep', in Heyvaert, A., Kruithof, R., and Vansweevelt, T. (eds.), *Juridische aspecten van de uitoefening van de geneeskunde*. Antwerp: Kluwer, 91–162.

Swennen, H. (1993) 'The Medical Profession in Belgium', in Faure, M., Finsinger, J., Siegers, J., and Van den Bergh, R. (eds.), *Regulation of Professions: A Law and Economics Approach to the Regulation of Attorneys and Physicians in the US, Belgium, The Netherlands, Germany and the UK*. Antwerp: Maklu, 125–46.

Trautwein, H.-M. and Rönnau, A. (1993) 'Self-Regulation of the Medical Profession in Germany: A Survey', in Faure, M., Finsinger, J., Siegers, J., and Van den Bergh, R. (eds.), *Regulation of Professions: A Law and Economics Approach to the Regulation of Attorneys and Physicians in the US, Belgium, The Netherlands, Germany and the UK.* Antwerp: Maklu, 249–306.

Tullock, G. (1975) 'The Transitional Gains Trap', *Bell Journal of Economics and Management Science,* 6: 671–8.

Van den Bergh, R. (1986) 'Belgian Public Policy towards the Retailing Trade', in Graf von der Schulenburg, J. M. and Skogh, G. (eds.), *Law and Economics and the Economics of Legal Regulation.* Dordrecht: Kluwer, 185–205.

Van den Bergh, R. (1993) 'Self-Regulation in the Medical and Legal Professions and the European Internal Market in Progress', in Faure, M., Finsinger, J., Siegers, J., and Van den Bergh, R. (eds.), *Regulation of Professions: A Law and Economics Approach to the Regulation of Attorneys and Physicians in the US, Belgium, The Netherlands, Germany and the UK.* Antwerp: Maklu, 21–43.

Van den Bergh, R. and Faure, M. (1991) 'Self-Regulation of the Professions in Belgium', *International Review of Law and Economics,* 11: 165–82.

Zohlnhöfer, W. and Schmidt, P.-G. (1985) 'Preisbildung für kassenärztliche Leistungen im ambulanten Bereich in der Bundesrepublik Deutschland', in Adam, D. and Zweifel, P. (eds.), *Preisbildung im Gesundheitswesen.* Gerlingen: Bleicher, 101–50.

Zweifel, P. and Eichenberger, R. (1988) 'Der Korporatismus der niedergelassenen Ärzte', in Gäfgen, G. (ed.), *Neokorporatismus und Gesundheitswesen.* Baden-Baden: Nomos, 159–79.

6

Barriers to entry and the self-regulating professions: evidence from the market for Italian accountants

BERNARDO BORTOLOTTI AND GIANLUCA FIORENTINI

The exclusive privileges of corporations, statutes of apprenticeship, and all those laws which restrain, in particular employments, the competition to a smaller number than might otherwise go into them, ... are a sort of enlarged monopolies, and may frequently, for ages together, and in a whole classes of employment, keep up the market prices of particular commodities above the natural price, and maintain both the wages of the labor and the profits of the stock employed about them somewhat above their natural rate.

Adam Smith, *The Wealth of Nations*, I:7

1. Introduction

The self-regulating profession displays a substantial discretion to restrict entry into the market; indeed, it is often successful in imposing additional requirements in terms of training programmes and human capital and plays an active role in the selection of perspective candidates. The rationale for that lies in the fact that active professionals should be better suited to establishing the educational profiles and to evaluate the quality of the applicant. Comparative evidence about legal, accountancy, and engineering professional services clearly indicates that this institutional arrangement is prevalent across countries; furthermore, legislation often allows the professions to operate in non-competitive regimes (OCDE 1995).

Starting from the seminal work by Friedman and Kuznets (1945), economists have raised the issue of whether these institutional barriers to entry were successful not only in preserving the average quality of the member, but also in raising the rate of return of the profession up to supernormal levels. In this case, self-regulation could limit competition within the industry and raise the concern of anti-trust authorities. Some studies have collected evidence that the American Medical Association restricted the supply of physicians by lobbying successfully to reduce the number of accredited medical schools (Curran 1993). In a related study, Becker (1986) has shown that additional requirements tend to increase professional incomes and that states are more prone to being 'captured' the lower is voter participation in elections, and the higher is the level of education.

Some tests have been developed to establish also the welfare effects of admission policies; analysing in cross-section US states, Svorny (1987) has found a negative correlation between the number of physicians and the level of qualification imposed by regulation. Interpreting the former as a proxy for the equilibrium demand for professional services, a more restrictive regulation has reduced consumer surplus; indeed, consumers did not increase demand despite the higher qualification of operating professionals.

While the effects of input regulation have raised the attention of economists, quite surprisingly the economic literature about the impact on the competitiveness of the industry of admission rates is very limited. Professional boards generally display substantial control on the pass-to-fail ratio that may reveal a powerful instrument for manipulating the supply side of the market and generate undue economic rents. As Maurizi (1974) has shown, a large number of self-regulating professions failure rates appear to be correlated to prevailing economic conditions. Demand fluctuations indeed seem responsible for manipulative activity by the boards: admissions are restricted to respond to a decrease in activity or to prolong a period of high incomes.

The aim of the present paper is essentially twofold; first, we try to carry out a descriptive analysis of the Italian accountancy market. In this area the urge for quantification is compelling, since separate figures for the professional service market are not reported in national accounting statistics. Secondly, we build two different specifications of a dynamic panel data model for the demand for and supply of accountancy services, explicitly taking into account admission rates as crucial determinants for the equilibrium emerging in the market.

Two major stylized facts emerge from the descriptive analysis: first, the convergence in the last few years in incomes of the two professions operating with different licensing requirements, namely *Ragionieri* and *Commercialisti*; secondly, the existence of a substantial earning differential between the two professions despite the recent trends. We claim that the rate of entry, and in particular, the admission policy in the profession implemented each year by professional boards, provides some interesting insights to explain this evidence.

From an empirical analysis in a dynamic setting, we obtain the following results: first, lagged admission rates represent an important factor to explain professional incomes. In particular, we find a strong negative correlation between the two variables, confirming the view that institutional barriers to entry are successful in creating economic rents. Secondly, and maybe more importantly, admission rates are an endogenous variable and are deeply influenced by past levels of income.

Indeed, a negative correlation between admission rates and accountants' income might indicate that consumers are just paying higher prices for a more qualified service which is warranted by professionals with higher skills, namely those who survived the hard selection process. In this case, the anti-competitive effect of institutional barriers to entry has to be weighted with the increase in consumer surplus due to the higher quality of the good exchanged.

Our findings provide some evidence that on average the admission policy by boards is more influenced by past market conditions than by the average quality of the candidate. Furthermore, despite our results being far from conclusive, we suspect that, where implemented, the quality-inducing policy via entry restriction has failed to restore efficiency to a market pervaded by information asymmetries.

The paper is organized as follows: Section 2 provides a descriptive analysis of the Italian market for accountancy services and characterizes the details of the institutional setting; Section 3 presents our specification for the market for accountants; Section 4 presents the empirical results of our panel data simultaneous equations estimation. Section 5 concludes.

2. The accounting profession in Italy

In this section we provide a brief analysis of the working of the market for accounting services over the period 1980–91. In Italy such services can be supplied by professionals from two official bodies (*Ragionieri* and *Commercialisti*). The main difference between the two concerns the length of the academic curriculum required to practise. In the period under observation, to become a *Commercialista*, after a four-year university degree in economics, one had to pass an examination controlled—to some extent—by representatives of the professional body. To enter the professional exam to become a *Ragioniere* one needed only three years of apprenticeship but no university degree.[1]

Once the professional examination is passed, the new professionals can enter the market without further constraints in terms of freedom of settlement which are not uncommon for other professions in Italy (e.g. public notaries). Moreover, excepting the above differences in terms of educational requirements, there are no constraints on either profession in dealing with specific groups of clients or in providing specific types of services. As a consequence, there are no functional differences in the market for the two professions such as those in England and Wales for solicitors and barristers.[2]

In this respect, the Italian market for accounting services represents a good setting in order to test the hypothesis according to which self-regulating professional bodies, which are given some discretion over the procedures to enter the market, use it more to establish and protect rents than to raise quality standards.

2.1. Trends in the two professions

The following analysis draws from two main data sets. The first is the Archivio delle Professioni built by INPS, the Italian state-owned company managing the compulsory pension schemes. The Archivio includes personal data and reported incomes of all Italian professionals from 1980 to 1991.[3] Over the period, the records for the two professions are between 20,000 and 37,000.

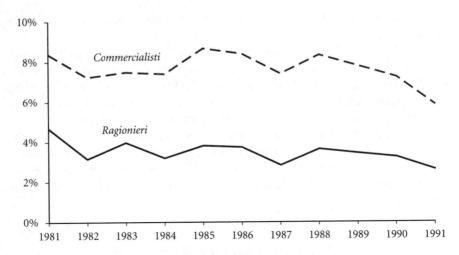

Figure 6.1. Rates of entry for *Commercialisti* and *Ragionieri,* 1980–1991

The second data set, ANCITEL, includes about 250 socio-economic variables at the city/town level (about 8,000 observations for each year). Such data are collected from several official sources such as ISTAT (the national agency for statistics), the Bank of Italy, the Ministry of Finance, other regulatory agencies, providers of public services such as telephone services, electricity, and so on. This second data set is used to better understand how the economic fundamentals of the market for accounting services are related with the economic environment in which they are provided.

The two professions under investigation are in the middle range of the Italian professions as for the number of registered members. To get a comparative idea, the largest profession is that of the medical doctors with some 300,000 registered members in 1991, followed by the engineers (about 100,000), and the lawyers (60,000). Much smaller professional bodies are the architects (9,000) and the public notaries (4,000).[4]

Commercialisti and *Ragionieri* started from a very similar membership in 1980 (approximately 10,000) with the *Commercialisti* slightly below the *Ragionieri,* but followed a different pattern of growth. By 1991, the *Ragionieri* reached about 15,000, while the *Commercialisti* went up to over 22,500. This difference is particularly remarkable if one recalls that the two professions supply the same type of services and that there is no further regulation on entry except the state examination where the professional bodies play a significant role. Moreover, among the rapidly growing service industries, the market for accountants would not appear to have experienced technological changes of such magnitude to justify such a rapid shift from one group of suppliers to the other.

For these reasons one is encouraged to look for institutional explanations of such a rapid growth in the proportion of accountants with a university education. There are two main factors which can explain such differences: First, on the supply side, Italy in the late 1970s and early 1980s witnessed a large increase in the university population due to a dramatic increase in the supply of courses at the public universities character-ized by very low fees. Therefore, to explain the relatively low proportion of accountants with a university degree at the beginning of the 1980s one can refer to a generally low share of the population with such a degree. Secondly, on the demand side, the average Italian firm size is much smaller than that prevailing in other developed countries and this, in its turn, had a negative influence on the demand for highly specialized account-ing services (Barca and Visco 1992).

Taking into account these two institutional factors, however, one can only partially understand the differences in growth rates of the two professions (see Figure 6.1). While the reduction in the opportunity costs of a university degree can explain the higher growth rates of the number of *Commercialisti* through the 1980s, since uni-versity reform takes time to influence the market for professional services, it is less clear what the impact of the second factor is. Indeed, the Italian industrial structure has not experienced major changes in the average firm size during the period, so a structural shift in the demand for accounting services by firms is rather unlikely. As a very preliminary conclusion, one can explain the differences in the growth rates more in terms of supply rather than demand variables.

The drop in the rate of growth for the *Commercialisti* can be interpreted as the beginning of a period in which, after about 10 years in which the supply of accountants with a degree had grown to compensate the previous scarcity, the market adjusted to a lower equilibrium. Alternatively, the drop in growth rates can be seen as a signal of a greater control by the professional body over entry, perhaps justified by the growing competition in the market for accounting services. In comparison, the entry for the *Ragionieri* follows a much smoother pattern possibly for symmetric reasons: there had been no comparable shock on the supply side due to institutional reasons, and there-fore there was less urge to take measures in order to restrict entry after a large inflow of new members.

2.2. Regional distribution of professionals

In this section we look at the regional distribution of the members of the two profes-sions in order to see whether they are active in different markets although we have seen that there are no institutional differences in the services they are allowed to supply. This is because in Italy, the main areas (north, centre and south) have distinct economic features so that a different geographic distribution of the professionals may, to some extent, provide insights on their functional characteristics. To explore this idea, we assume that there are at least two components in the demand for accounting services. First a basic demand, expressed by individuals and small firms, and distributed uni-formly across regions and, second, a demand for more sophisticated services expressed by larger firms or firms operating in international markets.

In Figure 6.2 the Italian regions are geographically ranked on the horizontal axis from north (left) to south (right). The more heavily industrialized northern regions

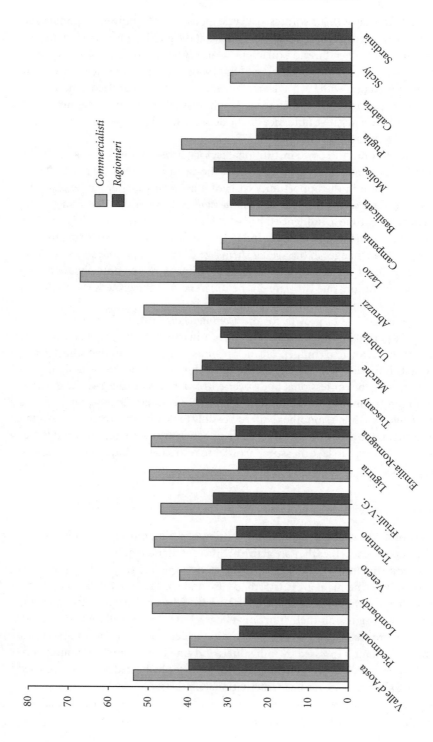

Figure 6.2. Density of *Commercialisti* and population (× 10,000) regional distribution, average values, 1980–1991

witness only a slightly higher density of *Ragionieri* than the southern ones. In this respect the highest density of *Ragionieri* is to be found in the regions of the centre which are characterized by a relatively large number of small firms.

A rather different picture emerges in the regional distribution of the *Commercialisti*. With the exception of Lazio—the region which includes Rome, and therefore the Ministries and the central bureaucracies—the more industrialized northern regions witness a much higher average density than the central, and especially the southern ones.

If one looks at the difference between the density of *Commercialisti* and of *Ragionieri* as a proxy for the size of the market for specialized accounting services, the data summarized in Figure 6.2 clearly support the idea that such a different market exists, and that is heavily concentrated in the northern regions.

2.3. The distribution of income

As we have seen, in the 1980s *Ragionieri* and *Commercialisti* exhibited quite different growth rates, with the *Commercialisti* increasing more rapidly than the *Ragionieri* and covering more specialized areas of the market. These two elements should have played some role in explaining the trend of the income levels for the two professions, shown in Figure 6.3, which are clearly symmetric to those of the membership. For the *Commercialisti*—whose number more than doubled in the period—the average income went up from 40 millions in 1980 to nearly 50 millions in 1991.[5] For the *Ragionieri*—whose membership grew less than 50 per cent over the same period—the average income went up from 23 millions to over 50 millions, overcoming in the last year that of the *Commercialisti*.

The comparative growth of the incomes for the *Ragionieri* is quite surprising even in comparison with other professions, and it can hardly be justified only in terms of the

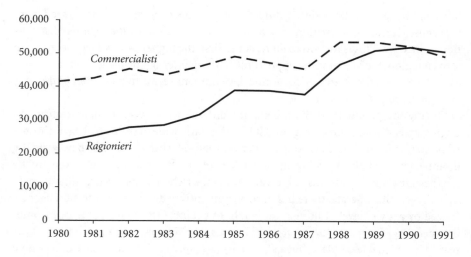

Figure 6.3. Average income for *Commercialisti* and *Ragionieri*, 1980–1991

particularly low rate of entry into the profession. Indeed, taking into account their lower level of human capital we assumed that the *Ragionieri* on average supply less sophisticated accounting services than the *Commercialisti* so that they might face problems in defending their incomes in a more competitive setting. As the opposite is the case, one is led to see these preliminary data as *prima facie* evidence that the degree of institutional control over entry is not irrelevant in explaining the profitability of the markets for professional services.

However, there is at least another institutional factor which must be considered in order to evaluate this inverse relation between rate of entry and rate of growth of income. In fact, the demand for basic accounting services is mainly expressed by small firms, which after 1983 have been subjected to a new fiscal regime that made it less profitable not to include the fees for the accounting services in the income report. On its turn this new incentive for small firms to ask for a regular fiscal receipt from the *Ragionieri* forced the latter to increase their reported income. Such change in the fiscal legislation would have little or no effect on larger firms who were given relatively strong incentives to report their accounting fees even before 1983.

The above hypothesis is at least partially supported by the data in Figure 6.3, since one of the sub-periods of more dramatic growth of the incomes of the *Ragionieri* occurs precisely in 1984 and 1985, that is right after the change of the fiscal regime. Moreover, that period is followed by two years of slightly declining incomes. However, a similar argument cannot be used to explain the upward trend observed in 1987. Therefore, at least for the late 1980s, a possible explanation for the differences in income trends of the two professional groups can be framed in terms of different admission policies.

2.4. The regional distribution of incomes

Since the Italian market is clearly differentiated across geographical areas (see Figure 6.2) some relevant information may come from the analysis of the regional distribution of income. This is for two main reasons. First, the higher the average income is in a given region, the higher is the opportunity cost of entering the profession. Secondly, as we have seen, the degree of economic development seems to be related to the type and quality of professional services.[6]

During the period 1980–85, the income differential between *Commercialisti* and *Ragionieri* is still large on average and it is particularly wide in the more heavily industrialized northern regions. During the period 1986–91, such differences have virtually disappeared, and the catching up has taken place almost completely even in the northern regions. This seems to indicate that in the richest areas of the country, where most large firms operate, there has been a competitive edge to the profession characterized by a lower level of human capital. In this respect the convergence of incomes between *Ragionieri* and *Commercialisti* is not surprising only for the relatively short period in which it takes place, but also because it is more evident in those regions where one would have expected the opposite trend to prevail.

Owing to this lack of a convincing explanation for the above convergence, in the following sections we will try to identify other factors which cannot be observed at the regional level, but which might shed some more light on this effect at the city/town level. However, working on the results of the previous sections, at a less aggregated level, we will still take into account the rate of entry as one of the main candidates to explain the different trends in incomes.

2.5. Entry and the profitability of the local market

The plots in Figure 6.4 describe the relationship between the cumulative entry rate in local markets[7] and the average professional incomes in those markets. The local markets are sorted into four classes each including one quarter of the total markets from those with the lowest income level (1) to those with the highest (4). As one can see, for both professions, the analysis of the local markets confirms a rather neat inverse relationship between entry rate and income levels.

As for the *Commercialisti* the cumulative entry rate is 74 per cent for the lowest income class, and goes down to about 55 per cent for the highest income class. Moreover, while the median entry rate is well above the mean for the first three income classes, it becomes lower for the highest one. This indicates that by far the majority of local areas with the highest incomes is characterized by yearly entry rates below 48 per cent.

In Figure 6.4 one should also notice that the interquartile differential increases significantly going from the lower income class to the higher ones. This larger variance in the local markets with high incomes can be explained in terms of differences in the first part of the distribution of the entry rates. Indeed, in class 4 the first quartile is at a cumulative entry rate of 20 per cent, while in all other classes it is above 50 per cent. This means that the greatest proportion of local markets with very low entry rates is also characterized by high income levels.

A rather different picture emerges from Figure 6.4 looking at the income distribution for the *Ragionieri*. First of all, and not surprisingly, the rate of entry is on average lower than that for the *Commercialisti* in all income classes. In this respect, in classes 1 and 4 one half of the local markets has a zero entry rate, and in classes 2 and 3 one quarter respectively. However, the main difference with the *Commercialisti* is the lack of a clear negative relationship between incomes and average entry rates. This would point to a minor relevance of the entry conditions in determining the income levels in the local markets.

Summing up, the analysis of the entry–income relationship in the local markets partly supports the evidence at the regional and national level discussed in the previous sections. A negative relationship between the two variables is however less controversial for the *Commercialisti* whose incomes seem more heavily affected by the entry of new competitors. Recalling Figure 6.1, the convergence between income levels might be more due to the lack of control on entry on the part of the *Commercialisti* rather than a successful policy of entry restriction by the *Ragionieri*. Hence, the low rate of entry for the *Ragionieri* can alternatively be explained in terms of a reduction in the

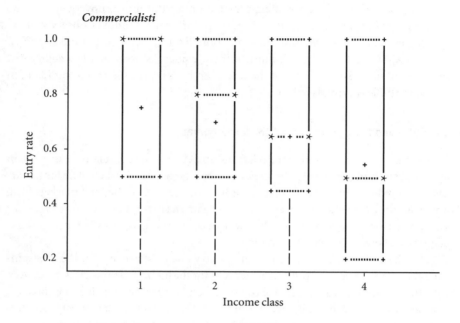

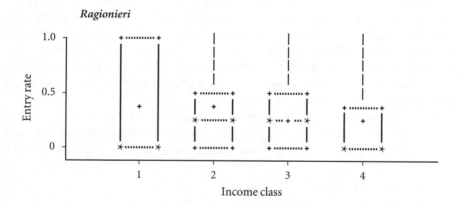

Figure 6.4. Cumulative entry rates and income in local markets, average values, 1980–1991

Notes: Some outliers have been removed from the plot to allow a relatively neat presentation. The distribution in the plot has not been otherwise modified. In Figures 6.4 and 6.5 there is a plot for each class of the variable described along the horizontal axis. Each box plot includes several elements describing the shape of the distribution of the variable described along the vertical axis:

- a central cross for the average value of the distribution;
- a lower dotted line with two crosses for the first quartile;
- an upper dotted line with two crosses for the third quartile;
- an internal dotted line with two stars for the median;
- vertical lines (I), zeroes (0), and asterisks (*) for outliers further away from the average value.

number of candidates, preferring instead to invest more heavily in human capital anticipating a higher return and discounting a lower cost of higher education.

2.6. Age-earning profiles

The last section introduces the question of the expected profitability of the investment in higher education as a possible explanation for the different entry rates in the two professions. Hence, it becomes relevant to acquire more information about the differences in the earning profiles of the two professions.

In Figure 6.5 we show the distribution of incomes (along the vertical axis) in different classes of age. Such classes are built splitting the membership into four groups of

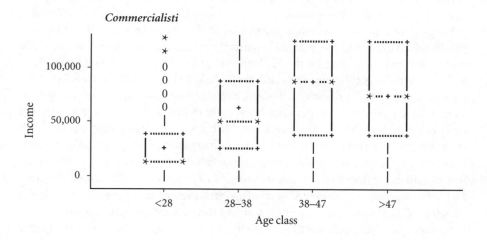

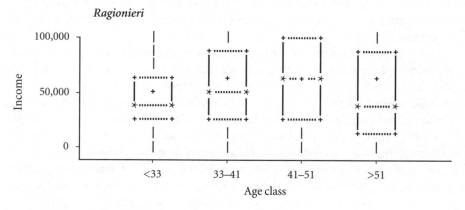

Figure 6.5. Age–earnings profiles, average values, 1980–1991

Notes: See notes to Figure 6.4.

equal membership, and attributing each member the age he had in 1986, the median year of the period. Accordingly, the first quartile of the age distribution for the *Commercialisti* is at 28, the median at 38, and the third quartile at 47, while the analogous values for the *Ragionieri* are 4 to 5 years higher with the first quartile at 33, the median at 41, and the third quartile at 51. The high entry rates of the *Commercialisti* have therefore a clear impact on the age structure of the membership.

In order to better understand how this different age structure influences the incomes at the local level, one can also observe in Figure 6.5 the income distributions for each class of age. For the *Commercialisti*, the average income in the first class is relatively low (about 25 millions), but it grows rapidly over 50 millions in the second, reaches the highest level in the third, and falls back to about 60 millions in the fourth.

To understand the differences between *Commercialisti* and *Ragionieri* one must keep in mind that for the latter the age classes are shifted forward by about five years. Taking this into account, one is not surprised to detect only relatively small differences in terms of average income comparing similar classes of age. However, if one looks at the dynamics of the income, one notices that there is a much steeper ascending trend for the *Commercialisti* than for the *Ragionieri* in terms of both means and medians.

This difference is coherent with the different level of human capital available to the members of the two professions. Indeed, the *Ragionieri* in class 1 (below age 33) already have considerable experience (they enter the market on average at 22), and therefore have had the opportunity to establish relatively strong relationships with their clients. On the other hand, the *Commercialisti* in class 1 (lower than 28) who enter the market on average at 26 have no time to establish the above relationships and therefore to reap the returns from the higher investment in human capital. When the *Commercialisti* reach approximately 35 years of age their average incomes are very similar to those of the *Ragionieri*, and when they reach 40 their advantage starts to widen.

Summing up, although the *Commercialisti* have a delayed entry due to the higher requirements in terms of human capital, the rate of return on such capital seem to be significant even in the first ten years of their professional life. It follows that the entry of new professionals in the market has a relevant negative effect on the average income of the competitors.

The variance of the income distribution differs significantly over the classes, so that the younger professionals witness an interquartile difference of less than 25 millions, while in the other classes the differential is over 50 millions. This reflects a process of specialization which takes place as the experience accumulates, and which explains why the variance for the *Ragionieri* in the first class is larger than for the *Commercialisti*. Moreover, the degree of asymmetry in the distribution is quite different across the classes with the first two with a much greater density of incomes towards the lower end of the distribution (the median is far below the average value). Only from the third class onwards do both professions assume a more symmetric distribution which signals that most members have reached a high degree of income stability.

In this section we have provided some comments on the evidence related to the earning profile in the two professions. Such evidence shows that while it takes about ten years of professional activity for the *Commercialisti* to overcome the income levels of the *Ragionieri*, the former manage to reach relatively high income level in a short period after entry. This points to the fact that the entry of new professionals represents an immediate competitive threat for those already established.

In this respect, looking at the average incomes in the first eight years of professional life, for the *Commercialisti* one can notice a steady growth of the average value and a much steeper trend of the median.[8] This is due to the fact that in the first years of professional life few newcomers succeed in reaching relatively high levels of income while the vast majority experiences very low levels. Once the professionals get more established, due to the quasi normal distribution of talents and disutilities from work, the distribution of incomes tend to become more symmetric around the central values. Furthermore, as the mean–median differential gets smaller, the interquartile differential becomes larger possibly due to a progressive process of specialization and differentiation. Alongside this process, the first quartile grows at a much slower rate than the third quartile showing a consistent minority of new professionals who are left at the margin by the competitive process.

The new *Ragionieri* start from slightly higher income levels in the first three years of professional life and witness thereafter slower rates of growth. What makes the case of the *Ragionieri* particularly interesting is that the mean–median differential does not close up even after a relatively high number of years of professional life. This is mostly due to the very slow growth of the first quartile (a large group, characterized by very low income levels with respect to the mean of the professionals of equal experience) and points to the fact that this is a group of professionals who are working only part-time or are at the margin of the competitive process.

2.7. Admission rates for professional examinations

If the educational requirements are met, in order to enter the market for professional services a candidate must pass a state examination. Although the rules of such examinations vary across professions, on average the members of the adjudicating commission are representatives of the professional bodies (40 per cent), civil servants (40 per cent) and university professors (20 per cent). However, as many university professors, and sometimes even some civil servants are also, directly or indirectly, suppliers in the professional services market place, the professional bodies manage to keep a high degree of control over admission rates.

The evidence presented in the previous sections has focused on the link between entry rates and income levels as measured by the actual earnings reported by the new professionals. It is, however, clear that the rate of entry is determined by several economic and institutional factors, among which it is not at all easy, at this stage of the analysis, to single out the specific role played by the professional bodies in establishing higher barriers to entry.

In this respect, we were able to collect systematic data only for the *Commercialisti*, whose state examination is organized by the Faculty of Economics of the public

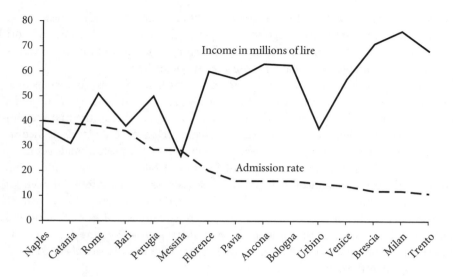

Figure 6.6. Average incomes and admission rates for *Commercialisti* in selected cities, 1984–1991

universities. The data refer to the period 1984–91 and to fifteen universities. Figure 6.6 shows the average admission rate for the professional examination of *Commercialisti* over the aforesaid period and the average income of the *Commercialisti* in the cities where the examinations take place every year.[9] In Figure 6.6 one observes a clear inverse relation between income levels and admission rates. The cities with lowest average incomes are those in which the admission rates are higher. Moreover, this relation becomes, on average, more clear-cut as the income levels rise, with only one exception.[10]

Looking at the trend in the admission rates between 1984 and 1991 one can see that the last year featuring relatively high admission rates is 1987. After that year, there is a clear decrease in the admission rates so that the average rate for the period 1984–87 is 29 per cent while the same average for the period 1988–91 is 24 per cent. We then conjecture that the professional boards are responding to the declining incomes by increasing the level of the institutional barriers to entry.

These data—although rather rough—make it difficult to accept *prima facie* the idea that such systematic differences in the admission rates over a relatively long period are purely the result of differences in evaluation procedures and/or in the performances of the candidates. This notwithstanding, the above evidence is difficult to interpret, because it is not clear in which direction one might establish a causal link between the two variables or whether there is a mutually reinforcing relationship. The higher income levels might be the result, among other factors, of a more restrictive entry policy to keep a high quality standard in the profession, and/or the admission rates could be seen as the result of a deliberate strategy of the professional bodies to keep those incomes high.

Even if we assume that there is a mutually reinforcing relation between admission rates and incomes, there are further interpretative problems. While it might be sensible to assume that in areas where professional incomes are higher there are higher incentives to deter entry, it is not completely clear why professional bodies in low income areas should be less ready to defend their incomes by restricting entry. One possible interpretation is that the benefits from restricting access to the market are higher when the perspective candidates will swiftly reach a relatively high income level.[11]

The descriptive evidence shown so far repeatedly points to a strong negative relationship between rates of entry in the local markets and professional incomes. This is particularly true for that profession (the *Commercialisti*) for which one needs to invest more heavily in human capital and the earning profile rises rather rapidly after entry. Moreover, we have seen that the ability of the professional bodies to control entry might be a crucial variable in order to stabilize incomes at a higher level. On this basis, in the next sections, we will estimate a demand and supply model of the market for accounting services where we also treat the admission rates at the professional examinations as an endogenous variable.

3. The market for *Commercialisti*

We estimate two different econometric models for the market for *Commercialisti*; the first is a simultaneous equations model for the demand and supply in which admission rates in the profession are considered exogenous. The second specification explicitly takes into account the possible endogeneity of this variable in a three simultaneous equations system.

3.1. A demand and supply model

The demand and supply equation for a professional service can take many forms; it is however customary in the literature to consider the number of professionals and their incomes as proxies for quantities and prices of professional services respectively (Pashigian 1977, Noether 1986, Kantor and Legros 1993). We therefore propose the following model:

$$y_{it} = \alpha_0 + \alpha_1 q_{it} + \sum_{j=0}^{2} \alpha_{2+j} a_{i(t-j)} + \alpha_5' X_{it} + \varepsilon_{it}, \tag{1}$$

$$y_{it} = \beta_0 + \beta_1 q_{it} + \sum_{j=0}^{2} \beta_{2+j} a_{i(t-j)} + \beta_5' Z_{it} + \eta_{it}. \tag{2}$$

Equation (1) represents the structural form of a semi-log inverse demand function, where y_{it} is the (natural) log of *Commercialisti* incomes, q_{it} the number of active *Commercialisti*, a_{it} the admission rates, X_{it} the vector of exogenous demand determinants, and ε_{it} the error term. Equation (2) describes the supply side of the market, where Z_{it} is the vector of exogenous supply determinants and η_{it} the error term; y_{it} and q_{it} are therefore the only endogenous variables in this system. Subscripts refer to cross-sectional units observed at time *t*.

This specification deserves some comment. If accountancy services are a normal good, we would expect a downward sloping demand curve, but we do not have any *a priori* reason to conclude that it might not exhibit non-standard functional forms. The literature has stressed that in a market pervaded by information asymmetries prices convey information about quality; therefore demand functions might be upward sloping along some critical intervals (Stiglitz 1987).

The admission rates are a crucial variable to explain how institutional barriers to entry influence equilibrium quantities and prices in the market for accountants. Let us consider the supply side first; when candidates decide to train and to try the examination in a local market where boards are very restrictive in their selection, entrants know that this will require a career-specific investment. In particular, the high probability of failure, the extended period of study—given the several trials needed before success—will raise opportunity costs. Incumbent *Commercialisti* are therefore protected from competition so that incomes can rise to provide a fair return on an investment that is at least partly sunk. Under the assumption that restrictive Boards are benevolent institutions who strive to admit only highly skilled and educated candidates, and that after the examination there are no spill-overs among board jurisdictions, institutional barriers to entry may prove effective in providing quality and a premium to operating professionals at equilibrium.

As it has been stressed by Svorny (1987), for a given supply of *Commercialisti*, we should therefore find in the demand equation a positive relation between board restrictiveness and income. We believe that this argument can be more fully understood in a dynamic specification, so we have introduced two lagged values for admission rates.

The vector of exogenous determinants include socio-economic and anagraphic variables that are described in detail in Table 6.1. Instead, the vector of exogenous variables in the supply equation conveys information about the competitiveness of the local market in which professionals operate, namely entry, exit, and the standard deviation of incomes. An ongoing debate in the theoretical literature on professional services is trying to establish the effects of an increase or decrease in the number of competitors on fees. Obviously, the conclusions of competing explanations depend on the assumption about the prevailing regime within the industry. In monopolistically competitive regimes, the increasing monopoly model posits that when the number of professionals is larger, search costs increase; this makes consumers less sensitive to prices so that equilibrium professionals' fees increase too (Satterthwhite 1979). The target income theory claims that professionals may respond to an increase in competition by stimulating internally the demand for their services and then maintaining constant or even increasing levels of incomes (Evans 1974).[12] If instead some degree of intra-professional competition is displayed, entry will plausibly push downward incumbents' incomes.

In this respect, the standard deviation of incomes can be interpreted as a proxy for the prevailing market condition on the industry. If a market for a professional service

Table 6.1. Description of the variables

Balanced panel:	
Cross-sectional units: 4228 towns/cities	
Time period: 1984–91	
Q^a	*Commercialisti* operating at the town/city level
Y^a	Reported *Commercialisti* incomes (natural log) (averages at the town/city level)
ADM^b	Admission rate at the professional examination
$BANK^c$	Bank offices over population (average in the time dimension)
POP^c	Population at the town/city level (average in the time dimension)
$PROD^c$	Industrial plants over population (average in the time dimension)
$INCOME^c$	Per capita income at the town/city level (average in the time dimension)
$CAREER^a$	Years after entry into the profession
AGE^a	Years of age
$AGE2^a$	Squared years of age
$STDY^a$	Standard deviation of incomes
$ENTRY^a$	Per year percentage of new *Commercialisti* over the stock
$EXIT^a$	Per year percentage of *Commercialisti* exiting the market over the stock
SEX^a	Dummy variable taking value 1 for males and 0 for women
$SOUTH^a$	Dummy variable taking value 1 for southern regions and 0 otherwise
1987	Year dummy

Sources: [a] Archivio INPS delle Professioni; [b] Università degli Studi; [c] ANCITEL.

is characterized by a low variation in incomes, the professionals in general sell an homogeneous good and, if similar technologies are adopted, one would expect price-taking behaviour. Vice versa, a high variance in incomes might be a signal of high product differentiation and of the presence of scattered monopolistic rents in the market. All this causes a substantial deviation from the ideal of a perfectly competitive regime.[13]

3.2. Endogenous barriers to entry

In the second model, we explicitly take into account the possible endogeneity of admission rates. In this specification, we therefore assume that boards, in establishing admission rates, do not only evaluate the average quality of the candidate, but also the prevailing market conditions. We propose the following three simultaneous equations model:

$$q_{it} = \alpha_0 + \alpha_1 y_{it} + \sum_{j=0}^{2} \alpha_{2+j} a_{i(t-j)} + \alpha_5' X_{it} + \varepsilon_{it}, \tag{3}$$

$$y_{it} = \beta_0 + \beta_1 q_{it} + \sum_{j=0}^{2} \beta_{2+j} a_{i(t-j)} + \beta_5' Z_{it} + \eta_{it}, \tag{4}$$

$$a_{it} = \gamma_0 + \sum_{j=0}^{2} \gamma_{1+j} y_{i(t-j)} + \gamma_4' W_{it} + \omega_{it}. \tag{5}$$

Essentially, equations (3) and (4) are the same demand and supply of the previous model except for the fact that we model a direct demand equation. Equation (5) provides our specification of the barriers to entry function; as customary in the industrial organization literature, barriers to entry are put in relation with the profitability of the market: where economic rents are present, one could argue that incumbents endeavour to preserve them.[14] Entry restrictions have a lasting effect on incumbents' income which is stronger if the profession operates in a monopoly regime and if boards can directly manipulate pass-to-fail ratios in response to market conditions. The vector W_{it} therefore includes the same exogenous variables about the competitiveness of the market that were present in the previous specification and other useful control dummies.

This model represents a logical step forward with respect to the simple demand and supply since it provides a more appropriate setting to evaluate the counterbalancing welfare effects of entry restrictions and to investigate the possible determinants of admission entry under an alternative behavioural assumption by the boards.

4. Empirical results

Estimates of the first model are obtained by two-stage least squares. By the order condition, both equations are over-identified. We estimate therefore the reduced form of the supply equation and replace quantity with its predicted value in the demand equation. This allows us to obtain consistent estimates despite the correlation between endogenous variables and the error term.

We performed a plain ordinary least squares for unbalanced panel data in the first and second stage assuming constant slopes and intercepts. More sophisticated procedures that could be useful for testing the existence of individual or random effects could not be adopted since some variables are averages in the time dimension.

Table 6.2 contains the empirical results for the first model; our estimates confirm the existence of a downward sloping inverse demand curve in the market for *Commercialisti*; the contemporaneous and lagged values coefficient of admission rates are highly significant and negative; this indicates that institutional barriers to entry are indeed effective in raising accountants' income.

According to the theory we mentioned in Section 3.1, this indicates the existence of a substantial premium for the *Commercialista* operating in a regime where entry is limited by the boards. Supply being equal, consumers therefore seem willing to pay for the increase in the quality of the service.

Excluding per capita income and the number of banks operating in the cross-sectional area, socio-economic variables have the expected sign and are significant. As far as the anagraphic variables are concerned, seniority and male sex are positively correlated to income; using a quadratic expression for the variable age we capture the peculiarity of the age-earnings profile that we observed in the descriptive analysis in Section 2.6. Incomes are indeed increasing in age but at decreasing rates. The time dummy is not significant despite the observed upward trend in incomes in 1987. The

Table 6.2. Semi-log 2SLS estimates of accountants' income (*t*-values in parentheses)

	First stage equation	Second stage demand equation
Dependent variable:	Q	Y
CONSTANT	1.09338	9.36394**
	(.259628)	(178.070)
FITQ		−.408113**
		(−24.9610)
ADM	−.027008	−.012433**
	(−.794723)	(−15.9529)
ADM(−1)	−.856303E-02	−.216172E-02**
	(−.219600)	(−2.78711)
ADM(−2)	−.324451E-02	−.325490E-02**
	(−.104437)	(−5.31947)
BANK	.011888	.244692E-02
	(.130302)	(1.35738)
PROD	.764622E-02**	.313313E-02**
	(18.2989)	(25.0802)
POP	.649886E-04**	.265200E-04**
	(5.10614)	(24.4024)
INCOME	−.213055E-05	−.836044E-06**
	(−.810252)	(−13.6495)
CAREER	.872897**	.411912**
	(3.75720)	(29.8931)
AGE	−.191680**	−.072768**
	(−2.84835)	(−20.6887)
SEX	−.498593	.067862
	(−.266595)	(1.80330)
SOUTH	2.06695*	.217159**
	(2.07253)	(5.38349)
STDY		−.296767
		(−.833911)
ENTRY		1.73374
		(.748770)
EXIT		−1.31815
		(−.489219)
YEAR4		−.133349
		(−.145918)
N	4228	4228
Adjusted R^2	.808918	.522500

Key: * statistically significant at the 5% level; ** statistically significant at the 1% level.

regional dummy instead is significant, but has the wrong sign. As a matter of fact, southern Italian accountants are characterized by far lower level of income with respect to their northern and central Italian colleagues.

As we stated in the introductory section, the boards display substantial discretion in the admission of new members to the profession. One can hypothesize that boards might take income levels into account to manipulate entry and therefore supply,

Bernardo Bortolotti and Gianluca Fiorentini

neglecting the average quality of the candidate as the primary variable during the selection. If admission rates were an endogenous variable, the estimates of the simple demand and supply model would be inconsistent.

In this direction, we have performed a Hausman (1978) test adopting the omitted variable interpretation; as Table 6.3 shows, we could reject the exogeneity of admission

Table 6.3. Hausman test for endogeneity of the admission rates (*t*-values in parentheses)

	First stage equation	Second stage demand equation
Dependent variable:	ADM	Y
CONSTANT	57.1968**	11.1354
	(24.3452)	(117.481)**
FITQ		−.168135**
		(−8.87088)
ADM		−.574993E-02**
		(−7.20050)
FITADM		−.054300**
		(−21.9680)
ADM(−1)		−.121690E-02
		(−1.65335)
ADM(−2)		−.144871E-02
		(−2.47448)*
BANK		.620272E-03
		(.362785)
PROD		.128594E-02**
		(8.85782)
POP		.109492E-04**
		(8.75984)
INCOME		−.306058E-06**
		(−4.87040)
CAREER		.215127**
		(13.58847)
AGE		−.027113**
		(−6.90405)
SEX		.148490**
		(4.14331)
SOUTH		−.192954**
		(−4.53692)
YEAR4		−.950605E-02
		(−.556053)
STDY	−3.16514**	
	(−13.6549)	
ENTRY	.638667	
	(.448497)	
EXIT	7.26263**	
	(3.96456)	
N	4228	4228
Adjusted R^2	.045343	.571474

Key: * statistically significant at the 5% level; ** statistically significant at the 1% level.

rates at the 1 per cent significance level. We therefore turn to our second specification that explicitly takes into account the endogeneity of admission rates. Three-stage least squares estimates for the second model are reported in Table 6.4.[15]

In the demand equation, the equilibrium quantity of accountancy services are positively related to prices; this result contradicts the information of the previous model, where the demand function was downward sloping. If the services provided by *Commercialisti* are a search or credence good, consumers are not able to evaluate quality properly and tend to infer it from prevailing fees (Nelson 1970, Darby and Karni 1973). Therefore, where fees are higher, consumers tend to expand their demand since the information asymmetry is partially fulfilled. The supply equation is instead a conventional upward sloping function; as fees increase, a larger quantity of professional services will be supplied.

Now we turn to the main variable of interest of our analysis. Indeed, when treated as an endogenous variable in the system, admission rates result in a very interesting variable to explain the equilibrium quantities in the market for *Commercialisti*. First of all, we claim that the lagged values for the admission rates deserve closer attention; even if it is necessary to include contemporaneous values for that to be a proper simultaneous equation system, there are well-grounded economic reasons to discard the theory that admission rates could have an immediate impact on incomes and quantities. As far as incomes are concerned, it is not sensible to establish any economic effect between the rate of new admissions in one year and income in the same year; *Commercialisti* who have passed the examination cannot immediately generate any real effects on incumbents' incomes. The same argument applies for the quantity of accountancy services actually demanded. Once again, it is problematical that consumers perceive instantaneously any variation in the average quality of the professional. These effects are more tangible in the following years after some consumption activity has been carried out.

Given these *caveats*, we observe first of all a strong negative correlation between past admission rates and incomes in the supply equation; this indicates quite clearly that the institutional barrier to entry is successful in creating rents. On the same line of reasoning as the previous model, the rationale for this economic rent can be found in the higher human capital investment that is necessary to facilitate joining the profession in a local market where boards are quite selective. At this juncture, it is fundamental to establish whether the selection of candidates is not biased by other factors, namely the profitability of the local market or the competitiveness of the industry. A close inspection of the admission rates equation clarifies the fact that past incomes within the profession seem to be an important variable to explain the restrictiveness of the professional boards. The negative correlation we find between past incomes and admission rates indicates clearly that the profitability of the market at least partly explains the admission policy. Boards are indeed restrictive where incumbents enjoy economic rents; in addition, the sign on the standard deviation of incomes confirms the fact that less competitive markets exhibit lower admission rates in the market for *Commercialisti*.

It is however possible to find a rationale for this anti-competitive behaviour by the

Table 6.4. 3SLS estimates for the simultaneous equations model (t-values in parentheses)

Demand equation
Dependent variable: Q
Mean of dependent variable = 13.6414
Std. dev. of dependent var. = 48.717555
Sum of squared residuals = .178445E+08

Variance of residuals = 4220.55
Std. error of regression = 64.9658
R^2 = .242149

Parameter	Estimate	Error	t-statistic	P-value
ALPHA0	−241.774	49.4698	−4.88731	** [.000]
Y	−14.7089	6.67423	−2.20384	* [.028]
Y(−1)	24.2823	5.02220	4.83498	** [.000]
Y(−2)	17.1388	2.21827	7.72619	** [.000]
ADM	−6.02334	.874295	−6.88936	** [.000]
ADM(−1)	2.43034	.392997	6.18412	** [.000]
ADM(−2)	.958059	.162973	5.87863	** [.000]
POP	.816485E-04	.214303E-04	3.80996	** [.000]
INCOME	.164839E-04	.542170E-05	3.04036	** [.002]
PROD	.464306E-02	.757837E-03	6.12673	** [.000]
BANK	−.400079	.169252	−2.36380	* [.018]
SOUTH	69.9407	7.44177	9.39839	** [.000]

Supply equation
Dependent variable: Y
Mean of dependent variable = 10.6460
Std. dev. of dependent var. = .605971
Sum of squared residuals = 1804.67

Variance of residuals = .426837
Std. error of regression = .653328
R^2 = .177292

Parameter	Estimate	Error	t-statistic	P-value
BETA0	9.99688	.267852	37.3224	** [.000]
Q	.324292E-02	.228857E-03	14.1701	** [.000]
ADM	.042773	.013367	3.19992	** [.001]
ADM(−1)	−.016911	.589235E-02	−2.87005	** [.004]
ADM(−2)	−.997954E-02	.253180E-02	−3.94167	** [.000]
ENTRY	−.797864	.067773	−11.7725	** [.000]
EXIT	−.027319	.069472	−.393244	[.694]
STDY	.052238	.018807	2.77759	** [.005]
SOUTH	−1.01615	.096428	−10.5379	** [.000]
1987	.735596	.158539	4.63984	** [.000]

Admission rates equation
Dependent variable: ADM
Mean of dependent variable = 25.7264
Std. dev. of dependent var. = 15.1772
Sum of squared residuals = .122330E+07

Std. error of regression = 17.0098
Variance of residuals = 289.333
R^2 = .119708

Parameter	Estimate	Error	t-statistic	P-value
GAMMA0	183.726	17.2343	10.6605	** [.000]
Y	14.0539	3.13717	4.47979	** [.000]
Y(−1)	−21.3050	2.19443	−9.70867	** [.000]
Y(−2)	−4.44057	.842037	−5.27361	** [.000]
STDY	−3.64995	.501937	−7.27172	** [.000]
SOUTH	7.93829	1.35227	5.87033	** [.000]

boards; in fact the policy of creating and preserving rents may be functional to provide a relatively high return for those skilled *Commercialisti* who are the only ones admitted to the professional society. This argument does not seem too convincing; first, it is not at all clear that a policy of entry restriction should make consumers better off if their demand is upward sloping. Secondly, from our estimates the equilibrium consumption of services is *lower* in local markets where boards have been restrictive. The co-efficient on lagged admission rates in the demand equation are in fact both significant and positive. One could therefore argue that the quality-inducing policy has not been successful in increasing consumers' willingness to pay for quality, as consumers are peculiarly inclined to infer quality by the prevailing fees.

Some other interesting results are apparent from our estimation; in the demand equation, with the exclusion of the number of banks, the vector of socio-economic variables is significant and has the appropriate sign. The regional dummies confirm some of the stylized facts that emerged from the descriptive analysis: in the southern regions, income levels are substantially lower and admission rates much higher. In the supply equation, more entrants reduce the profitability of the market, and this indicates that competition tends to dissipate rents. Finally, despite the relatively lower significance of the coefficient on standard deviation of incomes in the supply equation, we claim that a lower variability in incomes is associated with lower prices and higher admission rates. This result confirms that the competition operates in downsizing profits and that, where economic rents are not tangible, the boards are not concerned to restrict entry.

5. Conclusions

In this paper, we have provided a systematic study on the market for Italian accountants; this market deserves close attention since the same service is provided by two distinct professions (*Commercialisti* and *Ragionieri*) which differ in terms of input regulation. By law, only *Commercialisti* must have a university degree to be allowed to practise. The paper has shown the existence of a substantial earning differential over the professional life-cycle; we claim that this differential and the competitive threat exercised by new entrants and by the less-qualified *Ragionieri* lie at the basis of the admission policy administered by incumbent *Commercialisti* who are widely represented in the examining body.

Our empirical results indicate clearly that entry sensibly reduces the profitability of the market and that the institutional barrier to entry, namely the professional examination, is effective in preserving monopoly rents in the market. Furthermore, we have shown that the admission policy itself is endogenous and deeply influenced by market conditions. Indeed, the cross-sectional variance in admission rates all over the country can be only partially explained by differences in education or the professional ability of the candidates. Our analysis indicates that, once treated as an endogenous variable, admission rates are highly negatively correlated with past levels of income. As far as

Italian *Commercialisti* are concerned, this result casts some doubts on the view that professional boards are benevolent institutions who strive to preserve high quality standards of active professionals and posits the question whether it might represent a possible guideline for an intervention by anti-trust authorities.

This analysis can obviously be extended in many directions; first, it would be extremely interesting to collect data on admission rates for *Ragionieri*. A comparative analysis between the two segments of the market for accountants would allow any relation between the differences in admission policies and the profitability of the two professions to be put into context. In addition, it would be possible to estimate properly the degree of inter-professional competition and of substitutability between the services provided by *Commercialisti* and *Ragionieri*.

Finally, our estimates will probably be improved if we could have available a panel where all the variables were not averages in the time dimension; in this case we could test for fixed or random effects in the cross-section. Furthermore, it would be useful to carry out other diagnostics to test the robustness of our specification. We leave all this to further research.

Notes

We would like to thank Roger Van den Bergh and Steve Magee for helpful comments and suggestions.

1. After the period under observation, the procedures for entering the market have been changed and made significantly more demanding. For the *Ragionieri*, to be admitted to the professional exam one now needs a three-year degree in economics, and a further three years of experience in a partnership with a registered *Ragioniere*. For the *Commercialisti* three years of apprenticeship are required in a partnership with a registered *Commercialisti*. In other words, for both professions the two requirements—university education and working experience—have now been made compulsory.
2. Although this is not the purpose of the present paper, the existence of two legally recognized professions in the market for accounting services, with different levels of human capital, might allow for a comparative analysis of the returns from the investment in higher education.
3. After 1991, the Archivio was dismantled because the data on the compulsory contribution to the National Health System, for which it was originally organized, passed under the administrative control of the Ministry of Finance.
4. The number of professionals in Figures 6.1 and 6.2 refer to those active in the market and paying a specific contribution to the health service. Such contribution is proportional to earned income.
5. Incomes are expressed in Lire 1992.
6. These data are available from the authors.
7. The cumulative entry rate is defined as the total number of new professionals who entered during the period over the stock of professionals at the beginning of the period. The local markets coincide with the administrative area of the town/city.
8. As a result, the income distribution, which starts off asymmetric with the average values

almost twice as large as the median, becomes progressively less skewed, so that in the eighth year of professional life the difference is less than 2 millions. These data are available from the authors.

9. Cities are ranked from the highest average admission rate (Naples) to the lowest (Trento).
10. Alternatively, one might say the admission rates are influenced by other factors directly or indirectly linked with the degree of economic development as there is a strengthening of the relationship as we move from the economically less-developed southern regions to the more advanced northern ones.
11. Such a cost might be approximated by the risk of being subjected to a disciplinary action or a civil suit on the part of one of the candidates, or the opportunity costs of refusing bribes.
12. For an empirical testing of increasing monopoly vs. target income theory see Pauly and Sattherwhite (1981).
13. For an intriguing interpretation of the variability of fees in a market for experts in a Bertrand equilibrium, see Emons (1994).
14. As Stigler (1971) points out, regulations limiting entry are even preferred to direct subsidies, since these will be dissipated by competition in the market.
15. It may be useful to reiterate here that three-stage least squares involves the application of generalized least squares to the system under the assumption that error terms of each equation are correlated for identical cross-sectional units. Once the two-stage least squares parameters are obtained, the residuals of each equation are used to estimate cross-equation variance and covariances. In the third stage, generalized least squares parameter estimates are obtained (Pyndick and Rubenfeld 1981).

References

Akerlof, G. (1970) 'The Market for Lemons: Quality, Uncertainty, and the Market Mechanism', *Quarterly Journal of Economics*, 60: 488–500.

Arrow, K. (1963) 'Uncertainty and the Welfare Economics of Medical Care', *American Economic Review*, 53: 941–73.

Barca, F. and Visco, I. (1992) 'L'economia italiana nella prospettiva europea: terziario protetto e dinamica dei redditi', *Temi di discussione del Servizio Studi*, Banca d'Italia.

Becker, G. (1986) 'The Public Interest Hypothesis Revisited: A New Test of Peltzman's Theory of Regulation', *Public Choice*, 46: 223–34.

Coate, M. B. (1989) 'Horizontal Restraints in the Professions', *Antitrust Bulletin*, Winter: 774–96.

Curran, C. (1993) 'The American Experience with Self-Regulation in the Medical and Legal Professions', in in Faure, M., Finsinger, J., Siegers, J., and Van den Bergh, R. (eds.), *Regulation of Professions: A Law and Economics Approach to the Regulation of Attorneys and Physicians in the US, Belgium, The Netherlands, Germany and the UK*. Antwerp: Maklu.

Darby, M. R. and Karni, E. (1973) 'Free Competition and the Optimal Amount of Fraud', *Journal of Law and Economics*, 16: 67–88.

Emons, W. (1994) 'Credence Goods and Fraudulent Experts', mimeo, Univesitat Bern.

Evans, R. (1974) 'Supplier-Induced Demand', in Perlman, M. (ed.), *The Economics of Health and Medical Care*. London: Macmillan, 162–73.

Friedman, M. and Kuznets, S. (1945) 'Income from Independent Professional Practice', NBER.

Gabzewicz, J. J. and Grilo, I. (1993) 'Price Competition when Consumers Are Uncertain about which Firm Sells which Quality', *Journal of Economics and Management Strategy*, 1: 629–50.

Gale, D. and Rosenthal, R. W. (1994) 'Price and Quality Cycles for Experience Goods', *RAND Journal of Economics*, 25: 590–607.

Hausman, A. (1978) 'Specification Tests in Econometrics', *Econometrica*, 46: 1251–71.

Kantor, S. E. and Legros, P. (1993) 'The Economic Consequences of Legislative Oversight: Theory and Evidence from the Medical Profession', NBER Working Paper no. 4281.

Klein, R. and Leffler, K. (1981) 'The Role of Market Forces in Assuring Contractual Performance', *Journal of Political Economy*, 89: 615–41.

Kleiner, M. (1989) 'Are There Economic Rents for More Restrictive Occupational Licensing?', mimeo, University of Georgia.

Latham, R. and Schechter, M. C. (1979) 'The Price of the Legal Service Industry: Minimum Fee Schedules and Price Discrimination', *Antitrust Bulletin*, Spring: 42–62.

Leland, H. E. (1979) 'Quacks, Lemons, and Licensing: A Theory of Minimum Quality Standards', *Journal of Political Economy*, 87: 1328–46.

Love, J. H., Stephen, F. H., Gillanders, D. D. and Paterson, A. A. (1992) 'Spatial Aspects of Deregulation in the Market for Legal Services', *Regional Studies*, 26: 137–47.

Maddala, G. S. (1992) *Introduction to Econometrics*. New York: Macmillan.

Matthews, R. C. (1991) 'The Economics of Professional Ethics', *Economic Journal*, 101: 737–50.

Maurizi, A. (1974) 'Occupational Licensing and the Public Interest', *Journal of Political Economy*, 82: 399–413.

Miller, J. C. (1985) 'The FTC and Voluntary Standards: Maximising the Net Benefits of Self-Regulation', *The Cato Journal*, 4: 897–903.

Nelson, P. (1970) 'Information and Consumer Behavior', *Journal of Political Economy*, 78: 311–29.

Noether, M. (1986) 'The Growing Supply of Physicians: Has the Market Become More Competitive?' *Journal of Labour Economics*, 4: 503–37.

OCDE (1995) *Professions, activités et reglementation dans la zone de l'OCDE*. Paris: OECD.

Pashigian, P. (1977) 'The Market for Lawyers: The Determinants of the Demand and Supply of Lawyers', *Journal of Law and Economics*, 20: 53–85.

Pauly, M. V. and Satterthwite, M. A. (1981) 'The Pricing of Primary Health Care Physicians' Services: A Test for the Role of Consumer Information', *Bell Journal of Economics*, 12: 488–506.

Pindyck, R. S. and Rubenfeld, D. L. (1981) *Econometric Models and Economic Forecasts*. New York: McGraw Hill.

Polachek, H. and Siebert, W. S. (1993) *The Economics of Earnings*. Cambridge: Cambridge University Press.

Rosen, S. (1992) 'The Market for Lawyers', *Journal of Law and Economics*, 35: 215–45.

Satterthwhite, M. A. (1979) 'Consumer Information, Equilibrium Industry Price, and the Number of Sellers', *Bell Journal of Economics*, 10: 483–502.

Shaked, A. and Sutton, J. (1981) 'The Self-Regulating Profession', *Review of Economic Studies*, 48: 217–34.

Shapiro, C. (1986) 'Investment, Moral Hazard, and Occupational Licensing', *Review of Economic Studies*, 53: 843–6.

Stephen, F. (1994) 'Advertising, Consumer Search Costs and Prices in a Professional Service Market', *Applied Economics*, 26: 1177–88.

Stigler, G. J. (1971) 'The Theory of Economic Regulation', *Bell Journal of Economics and Management*, 2: 3–21.

Stiglitz, J. (1987) 'The Causes and Consequences of the Dependence of Quality on Price', *Journal of Economic Literature*, 25: 1–48.

Svorny, S. (1987) 'Physician Licensure: A New Approach to Examining the Role of Professional Interests', *Economic Inquiry*, 25: 497–509.

Van den Bergh, R. (1993) 'Self-Regulation in the Medical and Legal Professions and the European Internal Market in Progress', in Faure, M., Finsinger, J., Siegers, J., and Van den Bergh, R. (eds.), *Regulation of Professions: A Law and Economics Approach to the Regulation of Attorneys and Physicians in the US, Belgium, The Netherlands, Germany and the UK*. Antwerp: Maklu.

7
Imperfect competition in certification markets

LUIGI ALBERTO FRANZONI

1. Introduction

Increasingly, independent bodies are engaged to certify firms' compliance with existing laws, regulations, or production standards. Certification intermediaries are found in a great variety of areas, ranging from security markets, where underwriters and auditors play a crucial role, to quality and safety assessments, where accredited bodies guarantee the conformity of products, production units, and laboratories to specified standards.

This paper provides a theoretical analysis of the market for certification services with imperfect competition *à la* Cournot. We assume that certifiers sell their services to 'judgement proof' firms that intend to start a particular activity (enter a regulated market) and that need to produce evidence of compliance with standards. As firms are reluctant to invest the resources needed to meet the standard, certifiers serve as 'gate-keepers of the market', with the task of challenging, detecting, and stopping the non-compliant.

In the model, certifiers are called upon to perform a test of conformity with given standards, loosely denoted as 'compliance with the relevant rules'. The actual nature of the standard is extraneous: we simply assume that one exists and that it reduces the negative externalities produced by operating firms (this will allow us to conduct normative analysis).[1] Services of this sort are normally provided by auditors and CPAs with respect to compliance with specific laws and regulations ('compliance and attestation audits')[2] and by accredited certification bodies with respect to safety and health standards ('conformity assessment').[3] Compliance certification by a third party is required, for example, from recipients of major federal financial assistance in the USA (Single Audit Act and Circular A-128), and certification of conformity (to EN standards) of products and manufacturers is mandatory in many industries and procurement settings in Europe. Registration in the European Eco-Management and Audit Scheme (EMAS) requires the 'validation' of the firm's own environmental statement by an accredited independent verifier. Third party verification is also required from firms claiming compliance with environmental standard ISO 14001.

We assume that certifiers are profit-maximizing agents which compete in the market for certification services. An important postulate is that certifiers' effort is not observable to third parties. This poses a problem of moral hazard, as certifiers will exert effort only insofar as they risk liability for erroneous certification.

The main result of this paper is the demonstration that the interaction between certifiers and firms generates a market equilibrium that can be approached with the techniques of ordinary oligopoly theory. That is, competing certifiers face a 'demand curve' for certification services that is independent of each certifier's level of effort. The equilibrium certification fee will thus be determined by the total certification capacity arising from conventional quantity competition, while the fraction of non-compliant firms among those demanding a certificate will be proportional to certifiers' liability.

The involvement of private actors in the enforcement of regulatory standards raises such important issues as the optimal level of gatekeepers' liability and the need for regulation of the certification market. As noted, we address these issues under the assumption that gatekeepers' function is to prevent firms from producing a negative externality (social harm). We show that the greatest possible liability is likely to be socially desirable, whereas market regulation turns out to be very problematic. In fact, despite the formal analogy with conventional markets, the market for certification services has significant peculiarities. The most important is that the expected amount of social harm produced by non-compliant firms depends on the equilibrium price in the certification market. It turns out that an increase in competition or the imposition of a price cap may not be socially desirable.

So far, very little theoretical research has been devoted to certification intermediaries. Kraakman (1986) gives an interesting description of the possible role of third parties in the enforcement of rules and regulations and derives a useful distinction between 'gatekeeping' and 'whistle blowing'. The former enforcement strategy requires private parties to prevent misconduct by withholding their cooperation from wrong-doers; the latter requires them to report information of wrong-doing to enforcement agencies or potential victims.

Choi (1996) provides a full-fledged if informal analysis of the role that certification intermediaries play in information signalling. Choi points out that certifiers may differ from generic gatekeepers, as they do not necessarily prevent firms from selling in the market. Furthermore, certifiers may signal their information without a formal pronouncement, but solely by means of their association with the primary actor (as in the case of underwriters). As such, certification turns out to be less disruptive of markets and may exist in market settings where gatekeeping is not feasible. Our analysis, however, concentrates on the true gatekeeping function, as we assume that certification is necessary to engage in a regulated activity. Yet, most of our analysis (but not the normative part) can be extended to the case in which the standard is not set up to deal with an externality but relates to product quality. In this case, firms failing to win certification would still be allowed to initiate the activity but would necessarily be relegated to the lower tail of the market.

Lizzeri (1995) investigates the optimal disclosure policy for profit maximizing certification intermediaries. The author develops a sophisticated adverse selection model in which certifiers may find out the firm's type with perfect accuracy and without expense. They sell their services to producers of goods of unobservable quality, where 'service' means any kind of (verifiable) information disclosure. The author shows that, under some conditions, the equilibrium may entail no revelation and monopolistic profits for the certifiers. Albano and Lizzeri (1997) consider the choice of the optimal disclosure rule by a monopolistic certifier, assuming moral hazard on the side of producers. They show that the certifier will elect to provide noisy disclosures able to maximize buyers' surplus.

The role played by gatekeepers in tax enforcement has been investigated by Franzoni (1998). The present paper extends my previous work by focusing on the enforcement of generic regulations instead of income taxes. This means that individuals' decisions are not restricted to the amount of taxable income to report, but involve the choice of whether to start up an activity, and whether or not to comply with the regulation. Here, in contrast to Franzoni (1998), individuals have differing compliance costs and are distributed over a continuum. Further, the certification fee is assumed not to be refunded. This highlights a different aspect of gatekeeping, namely the possibility that high certification fees themselves constitute an entry barrier.[4]

Finally, a good deal of research has been carried out in the accounting literature with respect to financial audits, which allow third parties to provide 'reasonable assurance about whether the financial statements of an audited entity present fairly the financial position, results of operation, and cash flows in conformity with generally accepted accounting principles'. The audit market is known to be dominated by the Big 6, and hence seems to be better captured by imperfect competition models. Starting with De Angelo (1981), however, the bulk of the auditing literature has concentrated on price competition, disregarding auditors' capacity choice.[5] Financial audits can be likened to the verification technology adopted in this paper. An unqualified opinion (a full certification) usually represents a means of obtaining cheap resources on the capital market. Inaccurate audits do not end up with an externality as is assumed in this model, but rather with direct damage to the purchaser (the firm's financiers). The normative analysis of Section 4 is hence ill fitted for this kind of gatekeeping.

In very brief summary, Section 2 introduces the model and presents a full characterization of the equilibrium of the game; Section 3 illustrates how the parameters of the model affect the players' behaviour; Section 4 addresses the main policy issues attendant upon a certification system; finally, Section 5 provides a summary and some final remarks.

2. The model

Let us consider the problem of enforcement of a particular law or regulation placing special constraints on the firms that intend to engage in a particular activity. To get an idea of the situation, one may think of safety and environmental regulations prescribing that firms in a certain industry must comply with specified production standards.

Compliance with the regulation is costly. The actual cost of compliance to the firm depends on its type, as it may be more or less close to the prescribed standard. Compliance costs are assumed to be uniformly distributed on the interval [0, 1].[6] The benefit to each firm from engaging in the activity subject to regulation is equal to b, with $b < 1$; the benefit from not engaging in the activity is normalized to 0. A firm that starts up the activity without abiding by the regulation is expected to produce social harm of amount h. For simplicity, we assume that firms are perfectly 'judgement proof' and that they cannot be sanctioned for the harm caused.[7] In the absence of specific impediments, all firms would start the activity, none would comply with the regulation, and social harm would result.

In an ideal situation with full information, though, only compliant firms would be allowed to enter the activity (as $h > b$), and hence only firms with a small compliance cost would do so. This situation can be fruitfully used as a benchmark for analysis.

REMARK 1. *In the first best outcome, firms with compliance cost $c < b$ comply with the standard and engage in the activity. The other firms do not engage in the activity.*

In the presence of asymmetric information, compliance is fostered by requiring entering firms to produce a certification. The certification service is provided by independent intermediaries, which compete *à la* Cournot. Once engaged, the certifier exerts effort to ascertain whether the firm respects the standard or not. If the certifier detects a compliance failure, it does not issue certification and the firm cannot start the activity. Conversely, if the certifier detects no failure, it gives the go-ahead for the activity to be carried out. We assume that certifiers cannot deny a compliance certification when the firm is effectively compliant.

The probability that the certifier will detect a non-compliant firm depends on the level of effort exerted. The effort cost is assumed to be proportional to the 'quality' of the certification, that is to be equal to sa, where s is the marginal detection cost and a the probability that a non-compliant firm will be detected. By exerting a sufficiently great effort, the certifier learns the firm's compliance level with certainty. We assume that random events lead the firm's actual compliance behaviour to become common knowledge with probability α (e.g. through a government inspection, a change of ownership, or an accident). In that case, if the certification proves to be erroneous, the certifier is liable to a monetary penalty P.

The sequence of moves in this game is as follows.

1. Firms know their compliance cost and decide whether to engage in the regulated activity.
2. Certifiers compete on quantities in the certification market.
3. Firms that enter the activity hire a certifier to get a certification of compliance.
4. Upon engagement, certifiers decide the level of effort to exert.
5. Firms that fail to get a certification cannot initiate the activity.
6. With probability α, miscertifications are detected and sanctioned.

The game is solved through the Bayes–Nash equilibrium concept. We consider the firm's problem first, then the certifier's optimal choice of effort. The results will allow us to derive the 'demand' for the certification services, which will then be used to determine the market equilibrium.

Let us start from the problem faced by the single firm. It has to make two decisions: (1) whether to engage in the activity (and, hence, hire a certifier), and (2) whether to comply with the regulation.

Consider a firm that intends to engage in the activity. It will prefer to comply with the regulation only if

$$b - c > (1 - a)b,$$

that is, only if the net benefit from compliance is greater that the expected benefit from non-compliance (recall that $(1 - a)$ is the probability of not being detected by the certifier). For simplicity, we assume that random detection occurs *after* the firm has reaped the benefit from the activity and has produced expected social harm h.[8] Given the expected certification quality a, only firms with compliance costs

$$c \leq ab \tag{1}$$

will comply.

Let us turn to the entry decision. Firms with a compliance cost below ab will enter the activity only if

$$b - c \geq p. \tag{2}$$

Firms with a compliance cost above ab will make an attempt to start the activity (and risk being rejected by the certifier) only if

$$(1 - a)b \geq p, \tag{3}$$

where p is the certification fee.

Note that the benefit to compliant firms from participation is decreasing in c. If non-compliant firms make an attempt to enter, then the marginal type, that is the one indifferent between complying and not, will enter the activity too, and so will all firms with compliance costs less than ab.

The optimal behaviour of firms can be summarized as follows.

LEMMA 1. *If $(1 - a)b > p$, then all firms will seek to enter the activity. Only those with compliance cost $c < ab$ will comply with the regulation.*

If $(1 - a)b < p$, then the activity will be started only by firms with compliance cost $c < b - p$, which will all comply with the regulation.

Let us now turn to the certifier's problem. N identical certifiers are operating in the certification market. Each decides his own certification capacity and, upon engagement, the amount of effort to devote to the discovery of the firm's compliance status.

The profit for each certifier i can be written as

$$\Pi_i = [p - sa_i - (1 - a_i)v_i \alpha P]Q_i,$$

which includes the certification fee p, less the detection cost sa_i, less the expected liability associated with a miscertification, times the number of tests performed, Q_i. v_i is a probability measure that represents the certifier's belief that its customers are non-compliant. Note that if the test reveals that the firm is non-compliant, the certifier has an incentive to deny certification.[9]

Let us consider the choice of detection effort. Differentiation with respect to the certification quality a_i yields

$$\frac{\partial \Pi_i}{\partial a_i} = [-s + v_i \alpha P] Q_i.$$

Hence, depending on the probability that tested firms are non-compliant, the certifier's effort will be such that

$$\begin{cases} a_i^* = 0 & \text{if } v_i < \frac{s}{\alpha P}, \\ a_i^* \in [0,1] & \text{if } v_i = \frac{s}{\alpha P}, \\ a_i^* = 1 & \text{if } v_i > \frac{s}{\alpha P}. \end{cases} \tag{4}$$

We assume that the expected liability associated with an erroneous certification is sufficient to motivate accurate testing at least when all firms are non-compliant: $\alpha P > s$.

The expected cost of each test is: $s a_i + (1 - a_i) v_i \alpha P$, and, hence, at the optimum:

$$\text{marginal certification cost} = \begin{cases} v_i \alpha P & \text{if } v_i \le \frac{s}{\alpha P}, \\ s & \text{if } v_i \ge \frac{s}{\alpha P}. \end{cases} \tag{5}$$

In order to calculate the optimal certification quantity provided by each certifier, we first need to derive the market 'demand' for certifications. In other terms, we must derive firms' behaviour as a function of the market price p and the expected certification quality provided by each certifier.

As a first step, one may want to establish whether, in equilibrium, certifiers may provide certifications of different quality. The following lemma makes sure that no differentiation can effectively arise *ex post*.

LEMMA 2. *In equilibrium, all certifiers will exert the same detection effort.*

PROOF. From equation (4), we know that the certifier's effort is greater if the fraction of non-compliant firms among those it serves is larger. As non-compliant firms prefer not to be detected, they will all demand the service of the certifier with the lowest expected quality. This means that non-compliant firms would all 'herd' towards the certifier with the smallest fraction of non-compliant firms unless this fraction is the same for all. As a result, in equilibrium, the mix between compliant and non-compliant firms, as well as the detection effort, will be the same for all certifiers.[10] ∎

In equilibrium, we thus have $v_i = v$ and $a_i = a$ for all certifiers.

Let us now consider the firms and certifiers' behaviour given the market price p.

If the certification fee exceeds the private benefit from the activity, $p \geq b$, then clearly nobody enters the activity and $Q^D(p) = 0$.

If $p < b$, we have to consider firms' entry and non-compliance decisions together. We have two possible cases: either all non-compliant firms enter the market or only a fraction do so.

Consider first the case in which all non-compliant types enter the activity. The fraction among those demanding certification will be $v = 1 - ab$ (from Lemma 1). If certifiers exerted no detection effort, no one would comply with the regulation and $v = 1$. Since $\alpha P > s$, certifiers would then exert full effort, $a^* = 1$, and non-compliant firms would prefer not to enter the activity. In equilibrium, the detection probability has to be such that the probability of non-compliance given engagement leaves each certifier indifferent about the level of effort: $a_i = \bar{a}$ for all i, with

$$(1 - \bar{a}b)\alpha P = s.$$

Hence,

$$\bar{a} = \frac{1}{b}\frac{\alpha P - s}{\alpha P}. \tag{6}$$

In equilibrium, firms with a compliance cost less than $\bar{c} \equiv \bar{a}b = (\alpha P - s)/\alpha P$ will comply, while the others will not. The demand for certification services is equal to 1.

Note that this equilibrium can occur only if non-compliant firms find it profitable to enter the activity, that is only if (from equation 3): $\bar{a} \leq (b - p)/b$, that is only if

$$p \leq b - \bar{c}.$$

When the certification fee is high or $b < \bar{c}$, the previous inequality is not satisfied. Non-compliant types will not find it profitable to apply for certification unless the certification quality is set below $\bar{a}$. They will be indifferent between doing it and not if $a = (b - p)/b$. In turn, certifiers will be indifferent about detection effort if non-compliant firms randomize and enter with a probability x such that

$$\frac{x[1 - (b - p)]}{x[1 - (b - p)] + (b - p)}\alpha P = s.$$

In equilibrium, we will hence have

$$x^* = \frac{b - p}{1 - b + p}\frac{s}{\alpha P - s}. \tag{7}$$

In this case, the certification demand will be equal to

$$Q^D(p) = b - p + [1 - (b - p)]x^* = \frac{\alpha P}{\alpha P - s}(b - p).$$

To sum up, the certification demand can be written as:

$$Q^D(p) = \begin{cases} 0 & \text{for} \quad p \geq b \\ \frac{\alpha P}{\alpha P - s}(b - p) & \text{for} \quad b - \bar{c} \leq p < b \\ 1 & \text{for} \quad p \leq b - \bar{c} \ (\text{if } b - \bar{c} > 0). \end{cases}$$

Figures 7.1 and 7.2 illustrate the certification demand on the assumption that $b < \bar{c}$ and $b > \bar{c}$, respectively.

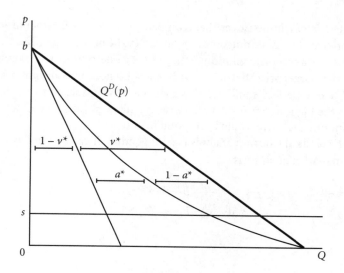

Figure 7.1. Unconstrained demand: $b < \bar{c}$

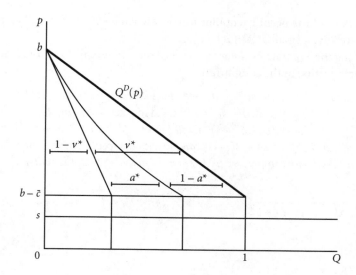

Figure 7.2. Constrained demand: $b > \bar{c}$

The demand function together with the marginal certification cost determine the market configuration. Note that in any continuation equilibrium we have $v^* = s/\alpha P$. Hence, from equation (5), the expected marginal certification cost for each certifier is equal to s. Further, it can be seen that the certifier's profit is independent of a_i:

$$\Pi_i^* = \left[p(Q) - sa_i^* - (1 - a_i^*)v_i^* \alpha P \right] Q_i = \left[p(Q) - v_i^* \alpha P - a_i^*(s - v_i^* \alpha P) \right] Q_i =$$
$$= \left[p(Q) - v_i^* \alpha P \right] Q_i = \left[p(Q) - s \right] Q_i.$$

In the market, N symmetric certifiers compete in quantities. In order to account for the widest range of possible outcomes, we allow N to be non-integer: $N \in [1, \infty)$.

In order to get a complete solution to the market game, one has to make an assumption about the market price that occurs when $Q^D = 1$. The only assumption compatible with a sub-game perfect equilibrium is that the price associated with full market coverage is the highest: $p = b - \bar{c}$. Otherwise, certifiers' payoffs would not be upper-hemicontinuous and there would be no equilibrium.

Through standard Cournot analysis (see Appendix), it can be established that the equilibrium market quantity is

$$
\begin{cases}
Q^* = \frac{N}{N+1}(b - s)\frac{\alpha P}{\alpha P - s} & \text{if} \quad \frac{N}{N+1}(b - s)\frac{\alpha P}{\alpha P - s} \le 1 \\
Q^* = 1 & \text{if} \quad \frac{N}{N+1}(b - s)\frac{\alpha P}{\alpha P - s} > 1
\end{cases}
$$

with

$$
\begin{cases}
p^* = s + \frac{1}{N+1}b & \text{if} \quad \frac{N}{N+1}(b - s)\frac{\alpha P}{\alpha P - s} \le 1 \\
p^* = b - \frac{\alpha P - s}{\alpha P} & \text{if} \quad \frac{N}{N+1}(b - s)\frac{\alpha P}{\alpha P - s} > 1
\end{cases}
$$

Recall that $Q^* = 1$ can occur in equilibrium only when $b - \bar{c} \ge 0$, that is when certifiers' liability is relatively small: $P \le s/(\alpha(1 - b))$.

By nesting the equilibrium values into the players' best reply functions, we obtain a full characterization of the equilibrium.

PROPOSITION 1. *The unique sub-game perfect equilibrium is characterized as follows.*

If $(N/(N+1))(b-s)(\alpha P/(\alpha P - s)) < 1$ (partial market coverage), *then certifiers serve* $Q^* = (N/(N+1))(b-s)(\alpha P/(\alpha P - s))$ *firms for a fee* $p^* = s + (1/(N+1))b$. *Firms with compliance cost* $c^* \le (N/(N+1))(b-s)$ *comply with the regulation and enter the activity, while the others do not comply and try to enter the activity with probability*

$$x^* = \frac{s}{\alpha P - s} \frac{1}{\frac{N+1}{N}\frac{1}{b-s} - 1}.$$

A fraction

$$a^* = \frac{b - p^*}{b} = \frac{N+1}{N}\frac{b-s}{b}$$

of non-compliant firms are detected by their certifier and denied certification. Each certifier earns a profit equal to

$$\Pi_i^* = \left[\frac{1}{N+1}(b-s) \right]^2 \frac{\alpha P}{\alpha P - s}.$$

If $(N/(N+1))(b-s)(\alpha P/(\alpha P-s)) > 1$ (full market coverage), then certifiers serve all firms, $Q^* = 1$, for a fee $p^* = b - ((\alpha P - s)/\alpha P)$. Firms with compliance cost $c^* \leq ((\alpha P - s)/\alpha P)$ comply with the regulation and enter the activity, while the others do not comply and try to enter the activity with probability 1. A fraction

$$a^* = \frac{1}{b} \frac{\alpha P - s}{\alpha P}$$

of non-compliant firms are detected by their certifier and denied certification. Each certifier earns a profit equal to

$$\Pi_i^* = \frac{1}{N} \left(b - \frac{\alpha P - s}{\alpha P} \right).$$

We have identified two types of equilibrium: in the first, the certification fee is high enough to discourage some firms from hiring a certifier and trying to enter the activity. In the second, all firms hire a certifier and try to enter. The second type can occur only when certifiers' liability is relatively small, $P \leq s/(\alpha(1 - b))$, and the number of operating certifiers is large, $N \geq (\alpha P - s)/(\alpha P(b-s) - (\alpha P - s))$.

3. Equilibrium properties

In this section, we use Proposition 1 to assess how the equilibrium is affected by changes in the underlying parameters.

3.1. Number of certifiers

This variable is relevant only when the equilibrium entails partial coverage.

Suppose that the number of certifiers in the market increases. As competition intensifies, certifiers perform more tests for a lower price. Certifiers' profits decrease. Thanks to the reduction in the certification fee, more firms can afford to comply with the regulation. As this would reduce certifiers' incentive to exert effort in detection, a larger number of non-compliant firms try to initiate the activity. Further, the detection rate has to rise so as keep non-compliant firms indifferent between entering and not. As a result, the detection rate is higher.

As the number of certifiers grows to infinity, we have two possible outcomes. If $s > b - \bar{c}$, then the Cournot equilibrium converges to the Bertrand equilibrium. We have,

$$\lim_{N\to\infty} p^* = s \quad \text{and} \quad \lim_{N\to\infty} Q^* = (b-s)\frac{\alpha P}{\alpha P - s} < 1.$$

At the limit, certifiers earn zero profits and serve all firms willing to pay at least the marginal certification cost s.

If $s < b - \bar{c}$, the perfect competition outcome is not approximated. In fact, we have

$$\lim_{N\to\infty} Q^* = 1 \quad \text{and} \quad \lim_{N\to\infty} p^* = b - \bar{c}.$$

With quantity competition, the equilibrium price cannot drop below $b - \bar{c}$. At the limit, the profit per test equals $b - \bar{c} - s > 0$. Certifiers serve all firms and exhaust their certification capacity.

3.2. Certifiers' liability

Consider now an increase in certifiers' liability for miscertification. Let us start with the partial coverage equilibrium. As P increases, miscertification becomes more costly and certifiers have an incentive to increase the detection probability. Non-compliant firms offset this increased incentive by reducing their entry probability. The certification demand curve thus rotates to the left. In equilibrium, the certification fee will be the same, but the quantity of the tests will be lower. The detection probability will not be affected, as firms' incentives to comply are unaltered.

Let us now consider the full coverage equilibrium, recall that this equilibrium emerges only when P is relatively small. An increase in certifiers' liability increases their incentive to perform thorough tests. This factor is offset by a rise in the compliance level: some firms that were not compliant turn compliant. However, this means that both the equilibrium compliance cut-off level and the detection probability are lower. Somewhat paradoxically, therefore, an increase in certifiers' liability reduces their detection effort.

3.3. Detection cost

Let us consider the effect of an increase in the marginal detection cost s on the partial coverage equilibrium. Due to the decreased incentive for accurate testing, non-compliant firms try to enter the market with a higher probability: the certification demand curve rotates to the right. Since the marginal certification cost is now higher, the effect on the equilibrium quantity may be of either sign: Q^* increases if and only if $b > \alpha P$. Whatever the sign of the variation in Q^*, the effect on the certification fee is positive. Certifiers' profits decrease if and only if $b > 2\alpha P + s$. Since a higher fee discourages non-compliant firms from entering, the compliance cut-off is lowered and the detection probability decreases.

Consider the equilibrium with full market coverage. An increase in s reduces the certifiers' incentive for accurate testing. This leads a fraction of compliant firms to turn non-compliant, restoring the certifiers' incentive. In equilibrium, the compliance cut-off c^* and the detection probability a^* will be lower. Faced with a lower detection probability, firms will be willing to pay more for certification, and both the certification fee and certifiers' profits will be higher.

3.4. Private benefit

When firms' private benefit from engaging in the regulated activity is greater, a higher detection rate is required to keep non-compliant firms out. In the partial coverage equilibrium, both the detection probability and the certification demand will be higher. As a result, the certification fee will be higher and the certification capacity will be lower. Thanks to the rise in the certification fee, certifiers' profits will be higher. More firms will prefer to comply.

In the full coverage equilibrium, non-compliant firms cannot be kept out. The increase in the private benefit does not affect certifiers' incentives and has no effect on the compliance rate. Firms' additional incentive to comply are offset by a reduction in the detection probability. Finally, since firms are willing to pay more for certification, the fee will be higher.

The comparative statics is summarized by Tables 7.1 and 7.2.

Table 7.1. Direction of change: partial coverage equilibrium

Endogenous variable	Exogenous parameters to be increased			
	Number of certifiers N	Certifiers' liability P	Detection cost s	Private benefit b
Certification capacity	+	−	[a]	+
Ratio of non-compliant applicants	0	−	+	0
Certification fee	−	0	+	+
Detection rate	+	0	−	+
Individual certifier's profits	−	−	[b]	+

[a] Positive if and only if $b > \alpha P$.
[b] Positive if and only if $b > 2\alpha P + s$.

Table 7.2. Direction of change: full coverage equilibrium

Endogenous variable	Exogenous parameters to be increased		
	Certifiers' liability P	Detection cost s	Private benefit b
Ratio of non-compliant applicants	−	+	0
Certification fee	−	+	+
Detection rate	+	−	−
Individual certifier's profits	−	+	+

4. Policy analysis

This section addresses two policy issues attendant upon the certification market: the optimal level of certifiers' liability and the quest for price regulation.

Social welfare is defined as the sum of net private benefits to firms from engaging in the regulated activity ('consumer surplus'), less detection costs, less social harm associated with non-compliance. As usual, no weight is attached to monetary transfers between parties.

We have

$$W = \underbrace{\int_0^{c^*} (b-c)dc + (1-a^*)x^*(1-c^*)}_{\text{net benefit from the activity}} - \underbrace{[c^* + x^*(1-c^*)]sa^*}_{\text{detection costs}} - \underbrace{x^*(1-a^*)(1-c^*)h}_{\text{social harm}},$$

where the compliance threshold c^*, the entry probability x^* and the detection rate a^* are determined in equilibrium (Proposition 1).

Let us now consider the welfare effect of an increase in P. In the partial coverage equilibrium, the only relevant variable affected by P is x^*, which decreases. Social welfare is therefore greater, thanks to the reduction in the number of non-compliant firms entering the activity:

$$\frac{\partial W^{Part.}}{\partial P} = -(1-a^*)(1-c^*)(h-b)\frac{\partial x^*}{\partial P} > 0,$$

where '*Part.*' stands for 'partial coverage'. If certifiers' liability were stretched to infinity, we would get

$$\lim_{P \to \infty} W^{Part.} = \int_0^{c^*} (b-c)dG(c) - c^*sa^*,$$

with $a^* = ((N+1)/N)((b-s)/b)$ and $c^* = (N/(N+1))(b-s)$. We would still be far from the first best outcome (described in Remark 1): not all the potential gains from compliance would be reaped (some firms are put off by the certification fee) and costly detection would take place.

For low levels of certifiers' liability, the equilibrium entails full market coverage, and the effect of a variation in P is more complicated. In fact, an increase in P yields higher certification quality and induces a larger fraction of firms to comply:

$$\frac{dW^{Full}}{dP} = [(b-c^*)b + (h-b)(1+b(1-2a^*)) - s]\frac{\partial a^*}{\partial P},$$

with $\partial a^*/\partial P = -s/\alpha P^2$.

Hence,

$$\frac{dW^{Full}}{dP} > 0 \Leftrightarrow s < (b-c^*)b + (h-b)(1+b(1-2a^*)). \tag{8}$$

Owing to the attendant increase in detection costs, an increase in certifiers' liability is socially desirable only if the marginal detection cost is not too high. Note that equation (8) is more likely to hold when a^* is high, that is when P is relatively small.

Let us now consider the effect of a variation in the number of operating firms. As the effect of an increase in N is a reduction in the certification fee, comparative statics can be used to assess the desirability of direct price regulation. Note that variations in N and p are relevant only when the equilibrium entails partial coverage.

To start with, let us rewrite the equilibrium variables in terms of Q. By substitution, we obtain $c^* = (1-v)Q$, $x^*(1-c^*) = vQ$, $p = b - (1-v)Q$, and $a^* = (1-v)(1/b)Q$. Hence,

$$W^{Part.} = \int_0^{(1-v)Q} (b-c)dc + b(1-a^*)vQ - sa^*Q - h(1-a^*)vQ, \tag{9}$$

with

$$\frac{\partial W^{Part.}}{\partial Q} = (1-v^*)(b-(1-v^*)Q) + bv^*(1-a^*) - sa^* - h(1-a^*)v^*$$

$$+ \frac{\partial a^*}{\partial Q}[(h-b)v^* - s]Q =$$

$$= (1-v^*)p^* + v^*p^* - sa^* - h(1-a^*)v^* + \frac{1-v^*}{b}[(h-b)v^* - s]Q.$$

Hence, through further simplification

$$\frac{\partial W^{Part.}}{\partial Q} = \underbrace{p^*}_{\text{increase in net benefit}} - \underbrace{sa^*}_{\text{increase in detection costs}}$$

$$- \underbrace{(1-a^*)v^*h}_{\substack{\text{increase in social harm due to} \\ \text{more non-compliant applicants}}} + \underbrace{a^*[(h-b)v - s]}_{\substack{\text{decrease in net social harm and} \\ \text{increase in detection costs due to} \\ \text{increased detection probability}}}.$$

An increase in certification capacity has four effects: (1) it increases the 'consumer surplus', as a greater share of the certification demand is satisfied; (2) it increases detection costs; (3) it increases social harm, as more non-compliant firms apply; and (4) it increases the detection probability and hence reduces social harm and increases detection costs.

This formulation highlights the features marking a difference between the certification market and conventional markets.

First, variations in certification capacity affect the amount of social harm attendant on non-compliance. This occurs through two means: the increase in the fraction of non-compliant applicants and the increase in the equilibrium detection probability. When deciding the amount of certification services to provide, firms disregard these effects because they do not affect their profits: the first relates to an externality, while the second is mediated by a variation in a, which does not enter into the firms' *ex ante* payoff function.[11] The net effect is equal to $-h(1-a^*)\,v^* + a^*[(h-b)v^* - s]$ and may be of either sign.[12]

Second, firms' perceived marginal certification cost, s, is greater than the real marginal social cost, as, as firms account their prospective liability payments as costs, while they are merely transfers.

In view of these two effects, the social optimum does not necessarily correspond to the point at which price equals marginal costs. This means, specifically, that an increase in competition in the industry, due to the entry of additional certifiers, is not necessarily socially desirable.

To specify, the perfect competition outcome with $p = s$ is *not* desirable if

$$\left.\frac{\partial W^{Part.}}{\partial Q}\right|_{p=s} = (1-a^*)s - h(1-a^*)v^* + a^*[(h-b)v^* - s] =$$

$$= \frac{s}{\alpha P}[-(1-a^*)(h-\alpha P) + a^*(h-b-\alpha P)] =$$

$$= s + \left(1 - \frac{s}{b}\right)\frac{s}{\alpha P}[2h - b - 2\alpha P] < 0,$$

that is, if (upon simplification)

$$b(h - b - \alpha P) < s(2h - b - 2\alpha P). \tag{10}$$

Note, for instance, that inequality (10) holds (and perfect competition is *not* desirable) when certifiers' liability is infinite and $b > 2s$.

Conversely, if

$$\left.\frac{\partial W^{Part.}}{\partial Q}\right|_{p=s} > 0,$$

a certification capacity greater than that arising from perfect competition is likely to be desirable. In particular, the government should *subsidize* a competitive certification industry if

$$\left.\frac{\partial W^{Part.}}{\partial Q}\right|_{p=s} > 0 \text{ and } \frac{\partial^2 W^{Part.}}{\partial Q^2} \le 0,$$

where

$$\frac{\partial^2 W^{Part.}}{\partial Q^2} = \frac{\partial}{\partial p}\left[\frac{\partial W^{Part.}}{\partial Q}\right]\frac{\partial p}{\partial Q} = -\left[1 - \frac{s}{\alpha P}\frac{1}{b}(2h - b - 2\alpha P)\right]\left(1 - \frac{s}{\alpha P}\right).$$

Both conditions are satisfied, for instance, when certifiers' liability is infinite and $b < 2s$.

The presence of the two 'additional' effects mentioned above makes welfare maximization a surprisingly complex problem, whose solution is strictly dependent on the configuration of the parameters.

5. Final remarks

The model developed in this essay provides a theoretical analysis of imperfect competition in the market for certification services. It is based on the assumption that firms are required to produce evidence of compliance with a given standard in order to engage in a regulated activity. Our main result shows that the certification market can be analysed with the tools of ordinary oligopoly theory, as certifiers' effort of choice can be separated from their decision on capacity. When certifiers' liability is high, they serve only a fraction of the firms potentially interested. When liability and the marginal detection cost are low, certifiers serve all firms. In both cases, the fraction of non-compliant firms among those demanding a certificate is constant, and depends on the ratio between certifiers' expected liability and the marginal detection cost.

The model is deliberately sketchy about the exact content of the certification: only the normative analysis of Section 4 is based on the assumption that miscertifications lead to negative externalities. In fact, the model can be extended to quality certification, on the assumption that the upper, and most lucrative, tail of the market is served by certified firms only. In such a setup, firms' benefit from certification would supposedly relate inversely to the number to firms that obtain it, due to the increased competition in the downstream market.[13] The demand for certification services would then be bent downward, as firms' willingness to pay for certification would decrease more than proportionally to the number of applicants. The ratio between compliant and non-compliant applicants, whoever, would not change, and the qualitative properties of our analysis would remain unaltered.

Appendix
Derivation of the Cournot equilibrium

Suppose first that $b < \bar{c}$ and consider the unconstrained demand function:

$$Q^D(p) = \begin{cases} 0 & \text{for} \quad p \geq b \\ \frac{\alpha P}{\alpha P - s}(b - p) & \text{for} \quad 0 \leq p < b \end{cases}.$$

The marginal certification cost is s.

The best reply function of firm i is obtained by maximizing the profit function:

$$\Pi_i = [p(Q) - s]Q_i,$$

with $p(Q) = b - ((\alpha P - s)/\alpha P)Q \equiv b - kQ$.

By setting marginal profits equal to zero, we get

$$Q_i^* = \frac{b - s - kQ_{-i}}{2k},$$

with $Q_{-i} \equiv Q - Q_i$. Since the equilibrium is symmetrical, we have $Q_i = Q/N$ and $Q_{-i} = Q(N-1)/N$. Hence

$$Q^* = \frac{N}{N+1}\frac{b-s}{k} = \frac{N}{N+1}(b-s)\frac{\alpha P}{\alpha P - s},$$

and

$$p^* = b - kQ^* = b - \frac{N}{N+1}(b-s).$$

Suppose now that $b > \bar{c}$, and that the demand function takes the form

$$Q^D(p) = \begin{cases} 0 & \text{for} \quad p \geq b \\ \frac{\alpha P}{\alpha P - s}(b-p) & \text{for} \quad b - \bar{c} \leq p < b \\ 1 & \text{for} \quad p \leq b - \bar{c} \end{cases}.$$

If $s > \bar{c}$, the previous analysis carries through and the market is only partially served.

If $s < \bar{c}$, then competition among certifiers may drive the certification fee so low that the whole market is served. When deciding their capacity, certifiers know that the market demand cannot exceed 1. When the demand is effectively constrained, certifiers have no incentive to conduct additional tests. The constraint is binding when the number of certifiers is so high as to yield an unconstrained Cournot equilibrium quantity greater that 1:

$$\frac{N}{N+1}(b-s)\frac{\alpha P}{\alpha P - s} > 1.$$

Since the unconstrained equilibrium quantity cannot be completely sold, firms will not be able to meet their optimal production quantity. In theory, the equilibrium could be asymmetrical, as firms could be differently affected by the constraint. For simplicity, we restrict our attention to the symmetrical equilibrium in which all (identical) firms produce the same quantity, $Q_i^* = 1/N$. For a continuity argument, the equilibrium price has to be equal to $b - \bar{c}$: any other price (less than $b - \bar{c}$) would cause a discontinuity in the firms' payoff functions, thus yielding discontinuous best replies and non-existence of the equilibrium (as firms might prefer not to meet the constraint and produce an aggregate quantity equal to $1 - \varepsilon$, with ε infinitely small).

Notes

I am grateful to Fabrizio Zecchin for precious insights on the European certification system, and seminar participants in Bologna, Marco Trombetta, and two anonymous referees for helpful comments. Aura and Leonardo provided enduring support.

1. Quality and safety standards applying to the most variegated industries are regularly produced by public and private agencies alike. Among the best known are those produced by the

International Organization for Standardization (ISO standards) and the CEN–CENELEC–ETSI triad, a set of European bodies endorsed by the European Commission (EN standards).

2. Compliance and attestation audits are wider in scope than financial audits, as they can result in any sort of engagement in which the auditor is asked to provide an assertion 'capable of evaluation against reasonable criteria' and 'capable of reasonably consistent estimation or measurement using such criteria' (AT 3, US Auditing Standards Board).

3. Accreditation usually results from the recognition by official committees like the American National Standards Institute and the Registrar Accreditation Board (in the USA), and the European Organization for Testing and Certification.

4. Choi (1996) reports that ISO 9000 certification may cost from $15,000 to several hundred thousand dollars for mid-sized US companies. In view of the recent proliferation of certification intermediaries, the fees for the same sort of certification in Italy have plummeted, reaching an average level of 10 million lire (roughly $7,000).

5. Auditors' expropriable wealth has represented one of the key variables for the explanation of their quality choice. See, for instance, Dye (1993). Doogar and Easley (1998) develop (and test) an interesting model in which auditors' cost functions depend on their 'size' (endowment of a fixed production factor).

6. The uniform distribution yields a linear certification demand function and simplifies the analysis of the market equilibrium.

7. This means that neither a Pigovian remedy (a sanction for non-compliance) nor a Coasian remedy (a liability rule) can be applied.

8. This assumption does not affect the qualitative features of our results.

9. Contingent fees are not admitted.

10. This argument is based on the assumption that the certification price is unique. Yet it also extends to the case in which certifiers can quote different prices (in a model *à la* Kreps and Scheinkman 1983). In this case, it would be sufficient to recall that only non-compliant firms would be willing to pay a premium for low certification quality. Any certifier offering low quality would then face non-compliant firms only, and would be led to exert full effort.

11. In view of the envelope theorem, the latter result applies whenever the detection cost function is weakly convex.

12. Note that even if h were negligible, the net effect would not vanish. However, it would collapse to zero if s were negligible. In the latter case, the first best outcome would be achieved for $N \to \infty$.

13. This effect may, however, be countered by an increase in final buyers' willingness to pay due to the higher average rate of compliance (to prescribed standards) of certified firms (as the detection rate increases with Q).

References

Albano, G. L. and Lizzeri, A. (1997) 'A Monopolistic Market for Certification', Discussion Paper 9737, C.O.R.E., Louvain, Belgium.

Choi, S. (1996) 'Certification Intermediaries', mimeo, University of Chicago.

De Angelo, L. (1981) 'Auditor Size and Audit Quality', *Journal of Accounting and Economics*, 3: 183–99.

Doogar, R. and Easley, R. (1998) 'Concentration without Differentiation: A New Look at the Determinants of Audit Industry Structure', mimeo, University of Notre Dame, Indiana.

Dye, R. (1993) 'Auditing Standards, Legal Liability, and Auditor Wealth', *Journal of Political Economy*, 101: 887–915.

Franzoni, L. A. (1998) 'Independent Auditors as Fiscal Gatekeepers', *International Review of Law and Economics*, forthcoming.

Kraakman, R. (1986) 'Gatekeepers: The Anatomy of a Third-Party Enforcement Strategy', *Journal of Law, Economics, and Organization*, 2: 53–104.

Kreps, D. and Scheinkman, J. (1983) 'Quantity Precommitment and Bertrand Competition Yield Cournot Outcomes', *Bell Journal of Economics*, 14: 326–37.

Lizzeri, A. (1995) 'Information Revelation and Certification Intermediaries', mimeo, Northwestern University.

Part III

Private Ordering and Self-Regulation

8

Trust under endogenous
transaction costs

PIER LUIGI SACCO

1. Introduction

The enforcement of cooperation between firms for the achievement of a common endeavour is an issue of increasing relevance in the post-Fordist era of vertical disintegration and subcontracting. As the large scale production of standardized items has become less and less viable in increasingly segmented markets, firms have gradually discovered the virtues of productive flexibility and of fine-tuned differentiation of their product lines. The firms' concern for cooperation is then clear: under vertical disintegration, the establishment of actual coordination and cooperation between partners is crucial for productive efficiency. In addition, the need of frequent product and process innovation makes it very costly and risky for a single firm to develop resource- and time-consuming R&D investment programmes on its own, thereby looking for joint ventures with firms with similar or complementary R&D interests. The ability of building and preserving cooperative relationships is therefore going to become (and possibly is already) a key component of a firm's competitive potential. But then the issue becomes enforceability, in that cooperative advantages are typically medium/long-run ones whereas any of the involved firms ordinarily faces a large number of short-run defectionist temptations that might be hard to resist, especially in view of the uncertainty about the eventual outcome of the cooperative deal. In this context, firms clearly have a strong incentive to learn to evaluate the reliability of a potential cooperative partner but have to carry the costs that derive from the gathering and processing of the relevant information.

In this context, transaction costs play an undeniable role. As long as the monitoring of potential partners' reliability is easy and cheap, it is reasonable to expect that most firms will do it and that eventually reliability will become a social standard of behaviour as would-be defectors are systematically detected and kept out of business. Conversely, if monitoring is difficult and costly, most firms will do without it and consequently the viability of cooperation will be at a serious risk. The above line of reasoning, however, sounds disturbingly close to a plain truism insofar as the monitoring costs are thought of as exogenous. If on the other hand such costs are exclusively traced back to 'technical' factors like the ease of access to, and use of, information databases, a rather immediate implication is that the promotion of social cooperation has to rely essentially upon technical progress in informational highways and in information-processing technologies and that, *a fortiori*, technologically sophisticated societies should be the most cooperative, an intuition that finds little empirical support. Indeed, many researchers have pointed out that the reliability issue has an intrinsic social dimension, which amounts to saying that societies with a comparative level of technical development may display remarkably different propensities to the creation and maintenance of cooperative relationships.

A pioneering series of studies stressing the importance of socially systemic factors for the enforceability of single cooperative relationships is the well-known volume edited by Gambetta (1988), which focuses upon the notion of trust. The link between propensity to cooperation and trust is clear: trusting others means essentially relying upon their responsibility in taking a pro-social course of action in situations where they face defectionist temptations. As a matter of fact, one can cooperate with others in the absence of trust: this is exactly what happens when economic agents monitor each other to learn about their respective reliability; the opposite, however, cannot be true: trust may only emerge as a consequence of a relatively long and successful past record of cooperation that leads economic agents to give up monitoring. The diffusion of trust as a social standard of behaviour can therefore be taken as a good observable proxy of a successful and lasting enforcement of cooperation at the social level. In a recent book, Fukuyama (1995) draws a distinction between high- and low-trust societies that is mainly based on sociological factors pointing out that even G7 countries like Italy and France can be characterized by a weak propensity to trust and thus, more fundamentally, to cooperation. Another recent study that is worthy of mention in this respect is Putnam's (1993) study on Italy showing that, even in a country that is being labelled by other authors as low-trust, there are substantial regional differences as to cooperative reliability and pro-social propensity that again can be traced back to huge differences in the respective social contexts.

The implications of the previous considerations for our discussion of transaction costs are twofold: in the first place, the actual relevance of transaction (monitoring) costs for the viability of a cooperative relationship depends heavily on the social context in which such a relationship is embedded, and specifically on whether or not reliability and responsibility have the status of a social standard of behaviour; moreover, the level of monitoring costs may itself be influenced by the social context in that, given the information technology in use, in a situation of generalized compliance a habitual defector is much more 'visible' and recognizable than in a situation of low compliance, due to the action of social mechanisms like stigma and ostracism which actually work as social channels of transmission of the relevant information.

The paradoxical implication is that once this social dimension is taken into account, one can have a situation where economic agents are willing to buy monitoring about partners when its costs are relatively (but not exceedingly) high but not when they are low: the reason is that in the first case cooperation is problematic at the social level and low trust results, and therefore it is wise to monitor potential partners even if at some cost; on the other hand, when trust is high defectors are very visible and easily detectable so that the cost of monitoring is low, and nevertheless economic agents tend to economize on it because defection becomes exceptional. If not to a complete reversal, this amounts to a deep modification of the intuition coming from a transaction cost analysis entirely focused on technological factors. In a recent and insightful retrospective essay, Coase (1988) himself stresses how reductive interpretations of transaction costs like the 'technological' one in the present context often miss the point and that social factors may play an important role in determining the actual level of such costs in many situations of interest, for example through their effects on the structure of contractual agreements.

A natural way to accommodate for the role of such social forces within a formal model of strategic interaction between firms is by means of an evolutionary game theoretic model. Evolutionary game theory is one of the most rapidly growing areas of research in contemporary economic theory, and the social selection of cooperative (and more generally pro-social) behaviours is one of the outstanding issues in this new body of literature. A widely chosen line of attack has been that of justifying the emergence of cooperation in social selection processes by assuming that self-interested players may be willing to act according to some pseudo-altruistic set of preferences rather than according to their own self-serving preferences if other self-interested players rationally choose to do the same and if this leads to the enforcement of otherwise unattainable (or to the more likely emergence of previously attainable) 'desirable' outcomes (think, e.g., of the cooperative outcome in prisoners' dilemma games) (see Sen 1974, 1985, Mueller 1986, Raub and Voss 1990, Hechter 1990, Kliemt 1990, Guth and Kliemt 1994, Menicucci and Sacco 1996a, b, Sethi 1996; for a more conventional 'business-oriented' view about the viability of pro-social behaviour see Maitland 1985). If pseudo-altruistic play has to be viable and rewarding, it is necessary that such players are able to anticipate correctly the strategy of the opponent (and therefore to recognize each other) and to optimally adjust their behaviour to the anticipated behaviour of the opponent. When such foresight may be obtained at a cost, choosing to buy it is, however, not necessarily optimal (see Guth and Kliemt 1994, Sethi and Franke 1995). Molander (1992) shows that, in the special context of prisoners' dilemma games, the enforcement of cooperation via conditional cooperation is more difficult in n-wise interaction than it is in pairwise interactions that are typically considered in the previously cited literature.

Sugden (1993) takes an alternative approach justifying cooperation on the basis of the superposition of individual and group incentives. Kranton (1996) studies a model where firms can form stable cooperative partnerships but with an 'exit' option that they can choose should they have doubts about the future viability of the actual relationship; however, firms have to take into account that the establishment of a new relationship entails a cost. Kranton finds that stable cooperative relationships can be formed in this context if the value of the actual partnership can be increased through time via specific investments that would be lost if quitting the relationship.

Finally, in Landi and Sacco (1997) the cooperative relationship requires a costly two-stage specific investment and entails an opportunity cost that in some cases may be larger than the relationship's completion value; in this context, if actual cooperation does emerge as a social standard of behaviour, it is of the conditional (viz. 'cautious') type: trust is too risky because of the large stake that players have to put to enter the relationship and because of the large opportunity costs. Nevertheless, a certain amount of trust may emerge even in this somewhat 'hostile' environment under particular conditions.

This very brief and inevitably partial survey suggests that cooperative relationships can emerge as a result of a social selection process under suitable conditions. Other interesting inputs come from the experimental literature in which the role of social factors in determining individual attitudes toward cooperation has been clearly established. Of particular interest is the study of Parks and Vu (1994) showing that, in experimental prisoners' dilemma interactions, people coming from cultures with a strong collectivist bias tend to cooperate much more often than people from cultures with an individualistic bias; the cooperative attitude of people with a collectivist cultural orientation was not undermined even in the face of a perfectly defectionist opponent, which seems to imply that the cooperative norm at work is one of pure trust without any monitoring or conditioning on the expected behaviour of the opponent. A useful survey of cross-cultural research on social norms of cooperation may be found in Smith and Bond (1993, ch. 7). Other recent experimental results by Hackett (1994) and Berg *et al.* (1995) point out, respectively, that social norms of equity are an important factor for the explanation of sharing rules in actual partnerships even in the absence of reputational effects and of repeated interaction, and that people show a propensity to participate in reciprocity-oriented cooperative schemes provided that even weak evidence of the viability of such schemes is available.

In this paper we pick up some of the suggestions coming from the previously discussed literature to build a model where transaction costs are endogenously determined by their co-evolution with the social pattern of cooperative vs. defectionist behaviours in a context where a large number of firms interact to carry out, say, R&D joint ventures. Firms have access to a monitoring technology whose cost depends on the actual diffusion of cooperative behaviour across the economy. The model explores whether, and if so under what conditions, trust emerges as the eventual social standard of behaviour, that is under what conditions firms find it optimal to cooperate with partners without having to monitor them. The behaviour of firms is assumed to evolve through time according to a social selection process that is indexed by three parameters: one for the order of magnitude of transaction costs, another for the actual completion value of the joint venture, and the last for a cooperation externality that increases with the number of successfully completed joint ventures: in other words, the value of being cooperative is greater the better the past record of cooperation (this may be due to knowledge spillovers, to network externalities, to technological complementarities, etc.). The interplay of the three parameters is complex and gives rise to non-trivial patterns of social dynamics. Results are not easily summarized in a few sentences, because the complexity of the social dynamics mandates resolution by means of simulation analysis. However, some interesting stylized facts emerge.

First, and unsurprisingly, if the completion value of the joint venture is large enough, plain trust always emerges as the social standard of behaviour, that is cooperation is so rewarding that everybody finds it optimal to comply without the need to monitor the opponent's behaviour (on the other hand, when the whole economy is made of cooperators the costs of monitoring would drop to zero anyway). Convergence to cooperation is quicker the larger the completion value; however, for relatively small but still sensible levels of the completion value, cooperation may eventually emerge even after a first transitional phase in which it seems to die out. When the initial distribution of behaviours across the population prescribes an even splitting between cooperators and non-cooperators, cautious cooperation (i.e. cooperation with monitoring of the opponent) does not play a major role in the establishment of the cooperative norm, and the emergence of unconditional cooperation (i.e. of trust) is observed. If the completion value is positive but relatively low, cooperation dies out eventually.

As to transaction costs, their order of magnitude may play a very important role when the completion value is low. When the cost of monitoring is low enough, the existence of cautious cooperators who monitor their opponent may help to bring about trust (i.e. unconditional cooperation) in that their presence lowers the value of defectionist behaviour; once defection begins to decline, unconditional cooperation becomes rewarding and cautious cooperation dies out. In a sense, then, cautious co-operation seems to have the role of 'breaking the path' toward the eventual emergence of trust. The effect of the cooperation externality is symmetrically opposite to that of transaction costs: when the externality is relatively low, cooperators and defectionists can coexist for moderate levels of the completion value and the latter prevail for low enough levels. The comparative strength of transaction costs vs. cooperation externality as critical parameters for the eventual selection of cooperative behaviours seems to be roughly equal for a uniform initial distribution of behaviours, that is the effects of a simultaneous decrease of the two parameters by the same amount tend to cancel each other out.

If we consider an initial distribution of behaviours in which defectionist players are a large majority, a very interesting dynamic pattern emerges for moderate levels of the completion value. If the order of magnitude of transaction costs is very low, one has a two-stage dynamics such that, at stage one, cautious cooperators spread over whereas unconditional cooperators die out; as a consequence of this, defectionists, who can hardly find someone to exploit, die out as well; but then phase two suddenly takes over: once the proportion of defectionist players has been cut, the proportion of cautious cooperators drops and that of unconditional cooperators 'explodes' bringing about a social standard of behaviour based on plain trust. If however the completion value is too low, cautious cooperators do not manage to set the stage for unconditional co-operators and defectionist behaviour spreads over.

These results are of course but a preliminary investigation of the dynamic patterns generated by the social selection process. Further work will be needed to arrive at a complete characterization for arbitrary initial distributions of behaviours and arbitrary parameter constellations.

The remainder of the paper is organized as follows: Section 2 is devoted to the exposition of the basic model; Section 3 introduces the social dynamics; Section 4 presents and discusses the results; while Section 5 concludes.

2. The basic model

Consider a cooperative relationship (e.g. an R&D joint venture), the successful completion of which requires a sequence of incremental investments to be made by two parties; we will refer to these parties as players I and II, respectively. For simplicity, we assume that both players have to make two investments: player I begins, then it is the turn of player II and then again I and finally II. Such investments are, however, not entirely specific to the project being undertaken. At each stage players may choose to defect, selling the asset being built so far to a third party—a possibility that the existing structure of property rights does not allow one to rule out. Keeping in mind the R&D joint venture as the reference case, defection may be interpreted as one firm selling the knowledge produced in the R&D joint venture to a third firm; it is then difficult for the partner being cheated to prove that the illegal transaction has taken place and that the third party has not acquired such knowledge through its own R&D activity. Once one player has defected, the value of the project for the other player drops to zero and investment previously made amounts to a net loss. As to the defecting player, the value of selling out knowledge to a third party is of course higher the larger is the aggregate amount of investment put in the project: that is to say, the project has an opportunity cost that increases as the project advances.[1] We can therefore represent the strategic interaction between players I and II by means of the following extensive form game with perfect information:

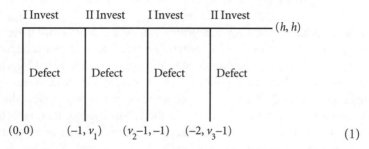

$$(1)$$

where h is the *net* completion value of the relationship (i.e. actual completion value minus investment costs) and the v_is are the opportunity costs at the various stages of the project, that is the amount that can be obtained by the defecting player selling the asset to a third party when the aggregate level of realized investment is i, $i = 1, 2, 3$, respectively; one has $v_1 < v_2 < v_3$. Clearly, the payoff to the defecting player is equal to the net opportunity cost, that is the amount v_i minus the cost of the player's own past investment, if any.

In this paper we assume that the roles of players I and II are not interchangeable, that is that the two roles, which we will henceforth call positions I and II, respectively, correspond to two distinct sets of specific skills (for example, technological or informational skills). That is to say, players I and II are not distinguished only by their timing of play, but also by some intrinsic characteristics; one can think that the two kinds of firms give complementary, and unsubstitutable, contributions, and that the sequence of play reflects the order in which the specific skills of the two partners are to be supplied for the eventual, successful completion of the project.[2] We associate with both players I and II a set of strategic types, that will be denoted as (I, r) and (II, s). By (I, r) we clearly mean a position I player whose strategic type is r, $r = 1, \ldots, R$, and accordingly (II, s) is a type s position II player, $s = 1, \ldots, S$. All players of a given strategic type are characterized by the same behaviour. In this paper we will consider four strategic types for each position, such that $R = S = 4$. Moreover, we assume that the behavioural types for each position are suitable specifications of a common behavioural repertoire. We can therefore index without ambiguity the set of behavioural types as 1, 2, 3, 4 without having to bother about the position; clearly, the actual interpretation of the behavioural type will still depend on the position. We consider the following types:

- explicit opportunists (type 1);
- cooperative screeners (type 2);
- pure cooperators (type 3);
- subtle opportunists (type 4).

By 'explicit opportunist' we mean a player type that defects as soon as he or she is called upon to play. If playing at position I, this type of player quits the cooperative relationship at the very beginning. If playing at position II and if the position I player did actually invest, he or she sells out the investment to a third party, and more specifically to a position I explicit opportunist. In conclusion, position I explicit opportunists are not interested in cooperative relationships and prefer to buy assets from other defectionist players. Position II explicit opportunists are among those who sell out; more precisely, they specialize in 'raw' assets, that is sell out assets whose level of incorporated investment is low and never make any investment themselves.

'Cooperative screeners' were called 'cautious cooperators' in the discussion in Section 1. They are willing to cooperate but do not trust their partner; therefore, they monitor the partner's actual strategic type (carrying the corresponding cost) and play a best reply to the partner's strategy. Specifically, if the partner is a cooperator, they cooperate; if he is a defectionist, they quit (i.e. defect themselves). For this strategic type, positions I and II vary only in the amount of risk that has to be taken. A position

I cooperative screener must protect him- or herself from the possibility that the partner defects immediately and from the possibility that he or she defects at the last stage of the game, when the cooperative position I player has already provided two units of investment. A position II cooperative screener must face only one possibility of defection: that of the position I player at stage 3 of the game, which would imply a net loss of one unit of investment; indeed, if the position I player did not invest at stage 1, the position II cooperative screener would never be called upon to play.

'Pure cooperators' are cooperative players who rely on the cooperative attitude of their partner and therefore do not monitor him or her; in other words, their behaviour is based on trust. By doing so, pure cooperators economize upon the cost of monitoring but run a substantial risk of being cheated. As for cooperative screeners, the level of risk is different for positions I and II. Position I pure cooperators may be cheated twice losing up to two investment units, position II pure cooperators only once. In a well-defined sense, the kind of trust being implied by the behaviour of position I pure cooperators is therefore a deeper one.

Finally, 'subtle opportunists' are players whose aim is to cheat their partner but, unlike explicit opportunists, they specialize in selling out assets with a high level of incorporated investment. (Clearly, potential buyers are again position I explicit opportunists.) As a consequence, subtle opportunists behave as follows. First of all, they monitor the behavioural type of their partner; if she or he is a defectionist player (i.e. an explicit or subtle opportunist) or a cooperative screener, they defect immediately to prevent the partner's defection. If conversely the partner is a pure cooperator, they make their investment so as to defect at the next stage they are called upon to play, in order to build a high-valued saleable asset. In other words, subtle opportunists disguise themselves as cooperators in order to exploit the trust of pure cooperators as much as possible. Position II players obviously have more rewarding opportunities, in that they can sell out assets that incorporate as many as three units of investment, whereas position I players can only sell out assets carrying two units of investment at most.

In the remainder of the paper we will indicate the proportion of players of type (I, r) as x_r and the proportion of players of type (II, s) as z_s, respectively, with $r, s = 1, 2, 3, 4$. Of course, $\sum_{r=1}^{4} x_r = \sum_{s=1}^{4} z_s = 1$.

At this point we introduce the structure of transaction (monitoring) costs and of cooperation externalities discussed in Section 1; as explained, the level of monitoring costs is assumed to be endogenous and in particular to depend on the distribution of behavioural types. Specifically, the larger the number of 'cheaters', the more costly it is to monitor the partner's type, in that defections are more 'visible' and sanctionable (e.g. through social stigma and bad reputation) when defective behaviour is exceptional than when it is the norm. We differentiate between explicit and subtle opportunists as to their impact on monitoring costs and assume that the incidence of subtle opportunists on costs is twice as much as that of explicit opportunists; the rationale of the assumption should be clear: the unreliability of the former type of player is more difficult to detect than that of the latter, in that only subtle opportunists disguise themselves as cooperators whereas explicit opportunists do not. As a consequence we write (fixed) monitoring costs $M(x, z)$ as follows (where x, z are the four dimensional vectors $(x_r), (z_s)$):

$$M(x, z) = \eta(2 - x_2 - x_3 - z_2 - z_3 + x_4 + z_4) \tag{2}$$

where $\eta > 0$. Notice in particular from equation (2) that if all players are cooperators, monitoring costs drop to zero. The different incidence on costs of opportunists players can be easily checked noting that $2 - x_2 - x_3 - z_2 - z_3 = x_1 + x_4 + z_1 + z_4$.

As to the cooperation externality $E(x, z)$, it is assumed that the value of cooperation increases with the number of successfully completed projects. In a large population where the matching of partners is random one can therefore write:

$$E(x, z) = \varepsilon(x_2 + x_3)(z_2 + z_3), \tag{3}$$

where $\varepsilon > 0$. The existence of this externality may bring about a 'bandwagon effect' that amplifies the rewards from cooperation as the proportion of cooperators increases, thereby inciting more players to cooperate, and so on.

Finally, we must specify the structure of the side markets for the assets sold by defecting players. On the demand side we find only one type of player: position I explicit opportunists. On the supply side we find, respectively, position II explicit opportunists selling an asset that incorporates one unit of investment, position I subtle opportunists selling an asset that incorporates two units of investment, and position II subtle opportunists selling an asset that incorporates three units of investment. We will assume that when markets clear all three assets give a constant profit, that we fix equal to 1, to position I explicit opportunists (clearly, the return on the three parallel markets must be the same at equilibrium). When supply is large with respect to demand (i.e. when the number of defectionist players selling out assets is large with respect to the number of players buying them) the profit for position I explicit opportunists increases, and conversely when supply is small with respect to demand. Of course, defectionist players selling more valuable assets make larger profits; once again, however, the actual profit earned by defectionists depend on the relative size of supply vs. demand. We assume that the equilibrium profits for a player selling an asset that incorporates i units of investment (henceforth we will denote it as i-asset for short) are equal to i. We are now in a position to compute the values of the opportunity costs v_i, $i = 1, 2, 3$. Let us begin by v_1. In this case (1-asset), the level of demand is equal to the proportion of position I explicit opportunists, whereas that of supply is equal to $x_3 z_1$: in order to have one 1-asset supplied it is necessary that a position I pure cooperator is matched to a position II explicit opportunist. So far for the price being paid for a 1-asset; but if the position II explicit opportunist must actually sell such an asset, he or she has to be matched to a position I pure cooperator and has to find a position I explicit opportunist buying it; otherwise, he or she does not make any profit. We assume that the probability of finding a buyer for a defecting player selling out an asset is equal to the frequency of prospective buyers, namely x_1: the market for i-assets is then characterized by out-of-equilibrium trade and mismatching between suppliers and demanders. If the defecting player is unlucky and does not find a buyer, the asset is lost and his or her profit is zero; when x_1 is relatively low this may happen rather frequently.

Denoting by p the parameter that measures the impact of the excess demand/supply on the market price, we can then write:

$$v_1 = [1 + p(x_1 - x_3 z_1)] x_1 x_3. \tag{4}$$

Following the same line of reasoning it is easy to show that v_2 and v_3 are equal, respectively, to:

$$v_2 = [2 + p(x_1 - x_4 z_3)] x_1 z_3; \tag{5}$$
$$v_3 = [3 + p(x_1 - x_3 z_4)] x_1 x_3. \tag{6}$$

3. Social dynamics

We are now in a position to compute the payoff earned by the various player types conditional on the current distribution of player types across the economy. We will denote by $\pi(I, r)$ the payoff earned by player type (I, r) and by $\pi(II, s)$ the payoff earned by player type (II, s).

As to position I explicit opportunists, by always quitting the cooperative relationship at first stage they always get a zero payoff apart from cases in which they trade with defectionist players selling out assets. Remembering that their equilibrium profit on all i-assets is equal to 1, by the same logic followed in the derivation of equations (4–6), it is easy to check that:

$$\pi(I, 1) = [1 + p(x_3 z_1 - x_1)] z_1 x_3 + [1 + p(x_4 z_3 - x_1)] z_3 x_4 + [1 + p(x_3 z_4 - x_1)] z_4 x_3. \tag{7}$$

Position I cooperative screeners must pay the cost of monitoring $M(x, z)$ as measured by equation (2) above, but also enjoy the cooperation externality $E(x, z)$ as determined by equation (3) above. In addition, they immediately quit the relationship when matched to defectionist players, whereas when they are matched to cooperative players (position II cooperative screeners or pure cooperators) they stay in and eventually get the completion value h; therefore, we have that:

$$\pi(I, 2) = h(z_2 + z_3) - M(x, z) + E(x, z). \tag{8}$$

The case of position I pure cooperators is more complex. They always make their investment and therefore may be cheated; on the other hand, they do not have to pay monitoring costs. Like cooperative screeners, they always get the completion value h when matched to a cooperative position II player. However, if they are matched to a position II explicit opportunist they lose one investment unit, whereas if they are matched to a position II subtle opportunist they lose two investment units. Summing up, we have:

$$\pi(I, 3) = -z_1 + h(z_2 + z_3) - 2z_4 + E(x, z). \tag{9}$$

Position I subtle opportunists are very easily handled. They only invest and make profits when matched to position II pure cooperators (provided that they find a buyer); in addition they have to pay monitoring costs. Therefore,

$$\pi(I, 4) = [2 + p(x_1 - x_4 z_3)]x_1 z_3 - z_3 - M(x, z). \tag{10}$$

Coming now to position II explicit opportunists, matters are once again quite simple: they only earn non-zero payoffs if matched to position I pure cooperators (and if finding a buyer). That is to say,

$$\pi(II, 1) = [1 + p(x_1 - x_3 z_1)]x_1 x_3. \tag{11}$$

As to position II cooperative screeners, their payoffs are exactly analogous to those of their position I colleagues:

$$\pi(II, 2) = h(x_2 + x_3) - M(x, z) + E(x, z) \tag{12}$$

and the same can be said for position II pure cooperators with respect to their position I counterparts (notice that position II pure cooperators cannot be cheated by position I explicit opportunists):

$$\pi(II, 3) = h(x_2 + x_3) - x_4 + E(x, z). \tag{13}$$

And finally, position II subtle opportunists have to pay monitoring costs and once again make profits (and invest) only if matched to a position I pure cooperator (and if finding a buyer), from which it follows

$$\pi(II, 4) = [3 + p(x_1 - x_3 z_4)]x_1 x_3 - x_3 - M(x, z). \tag{14}$$

At this point the payoff structure of all player types is fully specified. To determine how the proportion of the various types evolves through time we have now to introduce the social dynamics. In this respect we are faced with a multiplicity of possible choices; in the evolutionary game-theoretic literature the main trend is that of modelling social dynamics by means of the so-called 'replicator dynamics', which has initially been used by biologists in their modelling of Darwinian selection processes (see, e.g., Hofbauer and Sigmund 1988). The basic feature of the replicator dynamics is that of assuming that the rate of growth of the frequency of a certain strategy within a given population is equal to the difference between the actual performance of that strategy and the average performance of all strategies that are present in the population. In other words, the more a certain strategy does 'better than average', the more it grows; the more it does 'worse than average', the more it dies down. As we have argued elsewhere (see Sacco 1994), this dynamic specification also has some rationale in the case of cultural rather than biological selection processes where transmission of strategic types takes place via purposeful human choice rather than via biological reproduction.

Various authors question the use of replicator dynamics in economic applications as a sensible model of social selection processes (see, e.g., van Damme 1994). Nevertheless, it has been shown that this dynamics can be rigorously derived as an aggregation of a large number of interactions between boundedly rational agents (see Bjornerstedt and Weibull 1996 and also the comments in Sacco 1996) so that choice of the replicator selection mechanism is not entirely *ad hoc* but has some factual content in that it implies clear cut restrictions on the information gathering and processing routines adopted by the players. Moreover, it turns out that a large class of selection mechanisms may be represented as a suitable (generally state-dependent) time rescaling of the replicator mechanism (see Samuelson and Zhang 1992), which therefore obtains a somewhat 'focal' position in the choice space of the model maker interested in social selection processes.

In view of the above considerations, in this paper we will adopt the replicator selection mechanism, which can be written as follows:

$$\dot{x}_r = x_r[\pi(I, r) - \pi(I, m)];$$
(15)

$$\dot{z}_s = z_s[\pi(II, s) - \pi(II, m)].$$
(16)

Here dots denote first derivatives with respect to time; moreover $r, s = 1, 2, 3, 4$ and the $\pi(\cdot, m)$ are the average payoffs relative to positions I and II, respectively, which are given by

$$\pi(I, m) = \sum_{r=1}^{4} \pi(I, r)x_r;$$
(17)

$$\pi(II, m) = \sum_{s=1}^{4} \pi(II, s)z_s.$$
(18)

Notice that the restriction that both the xs and the zs have to sum up to one implies that both equation sets (15) and (16) include a redundant equation. The phase space of the dynamical system (15–16) is therefore given by the Cartesian product of two three-dimensional unit simplexes, one for each position.

Equations (15–16) then describe the social dynamics of behaviours in the economy. Its intuitive rationale is the following: players sample the relative profitability of the various strategies and tend to switch from less to more rewarding ones. The better the performance of a strategy with respect to the average, the more outstanding it is from the point of view of players, and therefore the more likely it is that it is adopted (see Bjornerstedt and Weibull 1996 for a precise characterization of the sampling and decision-making process). In this way, some types of behaviour are selected at the expense of others and the dynamics eventually lead to the establishment of a social standard, that is to a set of behaviours (possibly a singleton) that players find it convenient to adopt in that, *given the current distribution of behaviours across the population*, no feasible alternative proves to be more rewarding, or at least equally rewarding. In general, therefore, reaching a social standard of behaviour does not imply that the selection process lands on a stationary distribution: when the selected behaviours are more than one, the social dynamics may keep on wandering within an invariant set (i.e. a subset of the whole phase space) (see Weibull 1995). In several cases, however, single behaviours are actually selected; in particular, it has been proved that strict Nash equilibria are always attractors for the replicator dynamics (as well as for a more general class of selection processes) and that, in addition, in multi-population models as it is the one studied in this paper, *only* strict Nash equilibria may be point attractors for such processes (see Weibull 1995). In conclusion, under the replicator selection mechanism a homogeneous standard of behaviour will be selected if and only if it is a strict Nash equilibrium for the underlying game.

The search for social standards of behaviour then amounts to the search for point- or set-attractors of the dynamics described by equations (15–16).

4. Results

As already remarked, the dynamic process described by equations (15–16) takes place in a six-dimensional space; an analytical characterization of the dynamics as depending on the whole set of parameters of the model is therefore very demanding and, in principle, not necessarily feasible. For this reason we will rather present and discuss some simulations, which provide us with a first clue of the (presumably much larger) set of behaviours that can be generated by the model, and whose fuller characterization will require further work.

The model of Section 2 contains four parameters that can be of potential interest as to their bearings on the social dynamics: η, namely, the order of magnitude of transaction (monitoring) costs; ε, the level of the cooperative externality; h, the (net) completion value of the project, and p, the parameter that measures the sensitivity of prices to the disequilibria that can emerge in the parallel markets for assets that are sold out by defectionist players. We choose to conduct our analysis in terms of the first three parameters only, normalizing p to 1, thereby focusing on the impact of 'fundamental' variables on the social dynamics. The issue of the impact of technical and institutional facets of the structure of the parallel markets for assets (which, as we shall discuss in the final section, are not characterized exhaustively by p) is somewhat away from the main concern of the present paper and is again left for future work.

Intuitively, one can expect that a highly non-linear, high-dimensional dynamics, as it is the one studied in this paper, is likely to produce behaviours that display non-trivial sensitivities to the choice of the initial conditions. For this reason, and in lack of a complete analytical characterization of the dynamics, meaningful simulations require that initial conditions are selected according to sensible criteria. In this paper we will consider two sets of initial conditions. The first, corresponding to baricentric coordinates (i.e. all behavioural types are present in equal proportions at the beginning of the story), is a natural and somewhat obliged choice, in that it provides information about the social dynamics in a context where no behavioural type can exploit possible advantages deriving from its under- or over-representation in the current distribution of behaviours: for example, the potential payoff to cooperation is increasing in the proportion of cooperators whereas the payoff to defection is decreasing in the number of defectionists of the same type (in that the corresponding side of the market grows 'longer' thereby cutting the profit margin). The choice of the second set of initial conditions is more subtle and refers to a context where, initially, one of the parallel markets for assets is potentially well developed because both its supply and demand sides are well represented in the population. Specifically, we have focused upon the situation where position I explicit opportunists and position II subtle opportunists are preponderant in the initial population, with all other types being present in very modest amounts. This is to say that the market for high-value assets (those incorporating three units of investment) should be very active. Moreover, in this situation it is very dangerous for pure cooperators to rely upon trust, that is on non-monitored cooperation, in that the potential risk of being exploited is very high. This set of initial conditions is therefore a very severe test for the viability of trust as a social standard of behaviour: if trust can eventually emerge as a rewarding option in a context in which there is initially a very high probability that such trust is ill posed, one can conclude that there is a strong evolutionary argument for the social viability of trust.

Formally, we denote initial conditions by $x_r(0)$ and $z_s(0)$, respectively, $r, s = 1, 2, 3, 4$. The first set of initial conditions will then be given by $x_1(0) = x_2(0) = x_3(0) = x_4(0) = z_1(0) = z_2(0) = z_3(0) = z_4(0) = 0.25$ and will henceforth be referred to as the baricentric scenario. The second set of initial conditions will be given by $x_1(0) = z_4(0) = 0.76$, $x_2(0) = x_3(0) = x_4(0) = z_1(0) = z_2(0) = z_3(0) = 0.08$ and will henceforth be referred to as the exploitation scenario. In this latter situation, then, position I explicit opportunists and position II subtle opportunists initially represent (slightly more than) three-quarters of the respective populations, with the remaining shares equally distributed among all other types.

4.1. Baricentric scenario

The most sensible strategy for the investigation of the impact of the three parameters h, η, ε on the social dynamics is to begin by isolating the effect of single parameters and then to clarify their interactions. First we focus our attention on the role of h. Setting $\varepsilon = \eta = 1$ as a reference, we find the following pattern. As one could expect, when h is low enough, that is when the continuation value is small, cooperation dies out. Specifically, one can check that there is a value h' between 0.3 and 0.46973 below which position I explicit opportunists gradually spread over[3] until immediate defection becomes the standard of behaviour for position I players. However, the low relative value of the critical level of the continuation value h' with respect to the transaction cost η implies that monitoring is expensive enough to imply the eventual disappearance of all player types of *both* positions who monitor their opponents. This implies that the eventual equilibrium distribution for position II players is a mix of explicit opportunists and pure cooperators. Clearly, at the eventual equilibrium such distribution is irrelevant for the final outcome in that, being all position I players explicit opportunists, no project ever goes beyond stage 1 and so position II players are never called upon to play. But during the transition toward the equilibrium, the distribution of position II players is indeed relevant because cooperation is still possible (although less and less likely as position I explicit opportunists spread over). Perhaps rather surprisingly, it turns out that even when h is as low as 0.3, the equilibrium distribution of position II players contains 40 per cent of pure cooperators.

As monitoring players die out because of the high relative level of transaction costs, as far as position II is concerned the competition is between explicit opportunists and pure cooperators. Now, the payoff of position II explicit opportunists entirely comes from the exploitation of position I pure cooperators. Since the latter die out, the former must die out as well, despite a first transitory phase in which their proportion increases because of the still high number of easily exploitable position I pure cooperators. At this point one could object that the disappearance of position I pure cooperators is also harmful to position II pure cooperators whose chances of successful completion of a project decrease as the proportion of reliable partners vanishes. One must note, however, that the level of the cooperation externality ε is again very high relative to those of the other parameters and therefore, despite the modest stock of successfully completed projects, it is enough to make a difference and to allow position II pure cooperators to make bigger profits from the cooperation with their position I colleagues than position II explicit opportunists do by exploiting them.[4]

The more the continuation value h drops below 0.3, and the lower the value of the cooperation externality ε, the larger the relative proportion of position II explicit opportunists at the equilibrium. Notice the subtlety and complexity of dynamic interactions between cooperator and defectionist player types emerging from the pattern just analysed: the decline of a cooperator player type in one population may bring about the success of the same type in the other population, and conversely the success of a defectionist player type in one population may bring about the decline of the same type in the other, and this despite the strong complementarities existing between couples of homogeneous player types belonging to different populations.

If however h rises even slightly above h' (e.g. for $h = 0.46973$), the social dynamics changes entirely. Because of the high relative level of the cooperation externality ε, this apparently negligible increase in the continuation value is enough to bring about trust as the eventual social standard of behaviour. The success of pure cooperators, however, is not straightforward; once again there is a first transitory phase where position I and II explicit opportunists spread over whereas position I pure cooperators decline (as before, all monitoring player types quickly die out). The trend is however quickly inverted for position II explicit opportunists in that the slight increase in h, together with the high value of ε, causes the steady increase of the already strong position II pure cooperators (see the above analysis for $h = 0.3$); as a consequence, position II pure cooperators always increase more quickly than explicit opportunists and, from a certain point on, even increase at the expense of explicit opportunists. This trend reversal in the position II population is, at least in a first phase, not strong enough to invert the trend in the position I population, where explicit opportunists keep on growing at the expense of pure cooperators; at a certain point their proportion almost reaches 70 per cent.

After a relatively long phase in which the position I population seems to have stabilized at a distribution with a modest presence of pure cooperators, the changes in the position II population suddenly become relevant: the quick growth of position II pure cooperators creates strong new opportunities for cooperation and as a consequence the relative shares of position I explicit opportunists and pure cooperators 'swap' very quickly. After this sudden change of regime the dynamics enters into the final phase of the transition where explicit opportunists slowly but steadily die out and trust gradually becomes the social standard of behaviour (Figure 8.1). Further increases in h imply a more and more steady affirmation of trust. For $h = 0.6$, for instance, the continuation value is large enough to allow the shares of both position I and II pure cooperators to grow from the beginning, thereby cancelling the initial phase in which defectionist player types seemed to prevail for $h = 0.46973$.

Finally, it is interesting to point out how even further increases in h cause the survival of a positive share of position II cooperative screeners at the equilibrium. The reason is once again intuitive after some reflection: as the payoff from cooperation grows larger, position I pure cooperators wipe out all rival types almost immediately; as a consequence, despite the relatively high level of η, transaction costs drop to nearly zero very quickly, thereby leaving room for those few position II cooperative screeners who have not yet disappeared: once monitoring costs nothing, the performance of pure cooperators and cooperative screeners becomes identical (remember that defectionist types have previously died out). Thus we have once again an apparently paradoxical result: the quick affirmation of position I pure cooperators favours the survival of position II cooperative screeners at the expense of position II pure cooperators. The effect is however a modest one, at least for small increases in h. For example, when $h = 0.7$, the equilibrium proportion of position II cooperative screeners is less than 0.05. But as h diverges, the equilibrium proportion of the latter type of players consequently increases: the more and more sweeping affirmation of position I pure cooperators quickly cancels any difference between position II pure cooperators and cooperative screeners by dropping transaction costs at once to almost zero. In the limit, as h tends to infinity, the two types become practically equivalent and a fifty–fifty equilibrium share is observed.

With this reference analysis in mind, we can now explore the impact of the other model parameters. As to transaction costs η, it is not surprising to find that a decrease in the order of magnitude of transaction costs causes the survival at the equilibrium of larger shares of position II cooperative screeners for given (high enough) levels of h such that position I pure cooperators prevail, with respect to the case where η was higher. For example (with ε still fixed at 1), when $\eta = 0.4$, $h = 0.4$ implies a positive even if very small equilibrium share of position II cooperative screeners, whereas such share was still null for $h = 0.6$ when η was set to 1. Consequently, as h tends to infinity one has

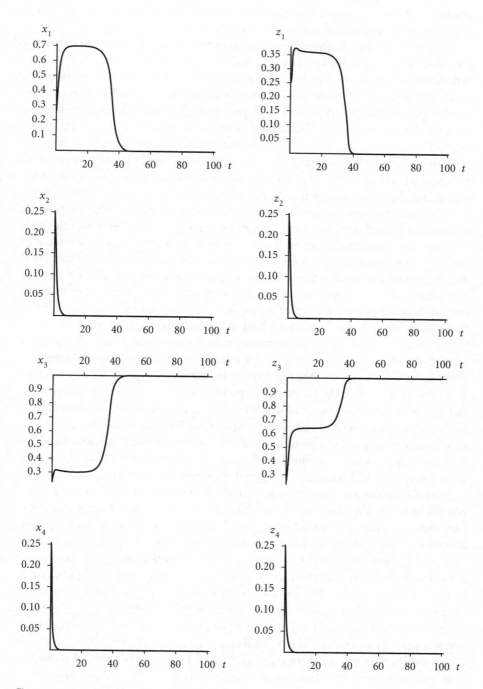

Figure 8.1. Baricentric scenario, $\varepsilon = \eta = 1$, $h = 0.46973$

again that the equilibrium distribution in the position II population tends to a fifty–fifty state, even more quickly than in the case with $\eta = 1$.

Another important consequence of the fall of transaction costs is the widening of the range of values of h that cause the eventual prevalence of cooperation. A first interesting, and somewhat 'intermediate' case is that with $\eta = 0.4$, $h = 0.3$. In this instance, position I explicit opportunists still prevail but there is an intriguing effect on the equilibrium distribution of position II players. The fall in the order of magnitude of transaction costs, although still causing the eventual extinction of monitoring player types, drastically changes the transitional dynamics. On the one hand, position I cooperative screeners decline steadily because of the low level of the completion value. On the other hand, the share of position I subtle opportunists has a sudden 'burst' after an initial decline: the reason is that the lower level of transaction costs makes it profitable for them to exploit the large and increasing share of position II pure cooperators that builds up together with that of position I explicit opportunists. However, this state of things does not last: as position II pure cooperators decrease as a consequence of their heavy exploitation by position I subtle opportunists, the size of the 'suckers' pool' shrinks; in addition, the decrease of position II pure cooperators causes the expansion of position II explicit opportunists, which in turn advantages position I explicit opportunists because of the mutually favourable trading opportunities that derive from the exploitation of the (although vanishing) position I pure cooperators.

One cannot help noticing the complexity of the dynamic interactions: the low level of transaction costs advantages position I subtle opportunists thereby damaging position II pure cooperators; the result is that the equilibrium proportion of position II pure cooperators then decreases with respect to the case $\eta = 1$ for $h = 0.3$, despite the fact that, on intuitive grounds, one would expect that the decrease of transaction costs would *facilitate* the eventual viability of cooperation. The reason why this intuition is misplaced here is that the completion value is too low to grant the survival of cooperative screeners and therefore the reduction of transaction costs basically benefits those player types which use monitoring to better exploit cooperators.

The fall of transaction costs from $\eta = 1$ to $\eta = 0.4$ for $h = 0.3$ does not alter the final equilibrium outcome which is still the extinction of cooperation. However, the complex dynamic effects just described suggest that further decreases of η might bring about more radical changes. This conjecture is easily verified for $\eta = 0.15$ (with h still fixed at 0.3): here the level of transaction costs is so low that position I cooperative screeners survive long enough to seriously undermine the profitability of position II explicit opportunists. In addition, and for the same reasons, position II cooperative screeners stabilize on a positive equilibrium share (which is above 0.35). The rapid decline of defectionist position II players creates strong opportunities for position I pure cooperators which (after a brief initial phase of transitory decline) eventually wipe out all rival types. One can check that, as for the analogous cases analysed above, the divergence of h implies the (fast) convergence toward a fifty–fifty equilibrium distribution for position II players.

Coming now to the impact of the cooperation externality ε, consider the case

$h = 0.74703$ when ε drops to 0.4 (η then switches back to 1). Here, given the relatively high level of the completion value, the small size of the cooperation externality is enough to grant the eventual success of position I pure cooperators. A small share of position I explicit opportunists coexists with pure cooperators for a while but then dies out. As to position II, pure cooperators prevail (as happened for larger values of ε). Further falls in ε would then push the fading of position I explicit opportunists further away in time. Dropping h to 0.2 for ε at 0.4 causes a further change of regime: position I explicit opportunists now prevail, whereas in position II there is a relatively balanced coexistence between naive opportunists and pure cooperators: the joint reduction of h and ε thus reduces the profitability of position II pure cooperators to the advantage of naive opportunists; on the other hand, the high level of monitoring costs causes the extinction of all monitoring types.

Given the above discussion, the effect of a joint reduction of η and ε should now be foreseeable: for example, when $h = 1$ and $\eta = \varepsilon = 0.3$, position I pure cooperators prevail because the relative size of the completion value with respect to η and ε is large, whereas the low level of η causes the coexistence of position II cooperative screeners and pure cooperators. Dropping η further to 0.1 brings about an increase of the share of position II cooperative screeners; if h increases then the familiar pattern of convergence to the fifty–fifty equilibrium distribution emerges. On the other hand, for $\eta = \varepsilon = 0.3$ and $h = 0.5$, the effect of the reduction of the cooperative externality tends to prevail on that of the reduction of transaction costs: in the position I population there is the co-existence of a small share of explicit opportunists and a large share of pure cooperators (which rises above a 0.8 equilibrium share after an initial first phase of decline well below 0.3), whereas in the position II population only pure cooperators eventually remain (Figure 8.2).

4.2. Exploitation scenario

In the baricentric scenario, pure cooperation (viz. trust) and cooperative screening (viz. 'cautious' cooperation) play substitute rather than complementary roles: there is no synergetically reinforcing interaction between the two types of cooperators to bring about the final prevalence of cooperation. The exploitation scenario provides different insights. We will confine our attention to the parameter constellations which give rise to new instances of dynamic regimes.

Starting from a reference situation in which $\eta = \varepsilon = 0.7$, and $h = 1$, the resulting behaviour is analogous to that observed in Figure 8.2: coexistence of position I explicit opportunists and pure cooperators and prevalence of position II pure cooperators. However, if η drops to figures such as 0.1, a new and unprecedented effect emerges: due to the relatively high level of h and to the relatively low level of η, position I cooperative screeners initially prevail whereas pure cooperators nearly disappear; the reason is simple: given that in the initial population there is a very high share of dangerous exploiters, cooperators who rely on trust do badly whereas cooperators who monitor

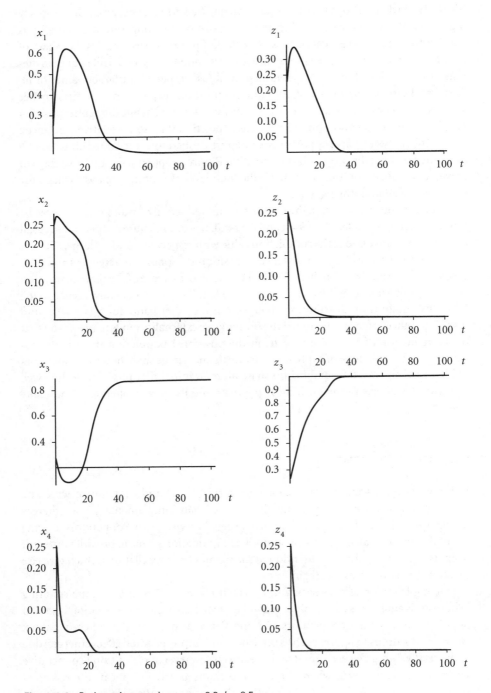

Figure 8.2. Baricentric scenario, $\varepsilon = \eta = 0.3$, $h = 0.5$

do very well. As a consequence, defectionist types die out. It is interesting to remark that the low initial level (and the steady decline) of position I subtle opportunists, i.e. the only potential exploiters for position II pure cooperators, implies that the latter are not penalized as their position I colleagues increase their share up to 0.8 (they are advantaged with respect to position II cooperative screeners in that they economize on monitoring costs).

However, the really interesting phase emerges as position I cooperative screeners (through their interaction with position II cooperators) drive out all defector types. At this point, position I pure cooperators no longer run the risk of being heavily exploited and therefore they 'burst out' and in a very short time completely wipe out cooperative screeners themselves. In other words, we observe here an endogenous two-phase transition toward the establishment of trust: first cautious cooperation 'opens the way' wiping out potential exploiters, and then the less expensive trust suddenly and completely takes over when the risk of exploitation becomes negligible: in other words, the two types of cooperators now work in a complementary rather than substitute way for the establishment of cooperation. As h drops to 0.85 and η is set at 0.2, the viability of position II cooperative screeners is seriously compromised in that the completion value is no longer sufficient to cover transaction costs. As a consequence, position II pure cooperators eventually stand almost alone whereas at position I one still observes the two-stage transition to trust through cautious cooperation. As h drops down to 0.7, the first phase of the transition toward trust becomes more complex and troubled: it takes a longer time for position I cooperative screeners to wipe out defection, also because the low completion value and the low level of transaction costs initially create remarkable opportunities for position I subtle opportunists (who can exploit a raising stock of position II pure cooperators) and for position II explicit opportunists (who exploit position I pure cooperators). However, the near-extinction of position I pure cooperators in this first phase 'kills' position II explicit opportunists whereas position I subtle opportunists are eliminated by the joint effect of a sudden 'burst' of position II cooperative screeners that lowers the opportunities of exploitation, and the parallel diffusion of position I cooperative screeners and position II pure cooperators which gradually increases the profitability of cooperation through the cooperation externality. Whereas phase one of the transition becomes very long, phase two becomes extremely short: a spectacular switch (as to both its quickness and its size) from 'cautious cooperation' to trust suddenly occurs.

Moving further down to $h = 0.5$ and easing down η at 0.1, the continuation value becomes too small for position I pure cooperators to recover eventually: after a long and complex transient phase, cooperation prevails; specifically, 'cautious' cooperation prevails in position I and trust prevails in position II (with a small minority of cautious position II cooperators): once defectionists have been wiped out from position I, monitoring in position II can be dispensed with and pure cooperators spread over (Figure 8.3). A parallel increase of η back to 0.2 and of h to 0.6209835 produces an analogous effect but with a even longer transient: now the relatively higher cost of monitoring causes the eventual disappearance of position II cooperative screeners;

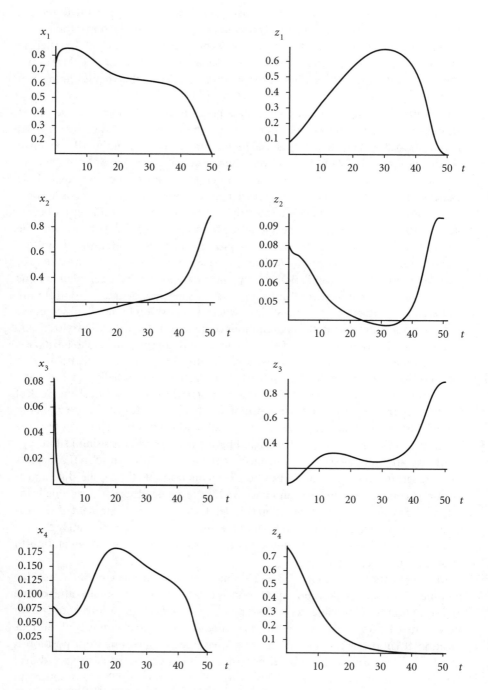

Figure 8.3. Exploitation scenario, $\varepsilon = 0.7$, $\eta = 0.1$, $h = 0.5$

moreover, position I and II explicit opportunists are still substantially present after as many as 200 periods.

When the drop in h is less drastic, however, the two-stage transition toward coopera-tion emerges again and with even more spectacular characteristics. Setting $\eta = 0.2$ and $h = 0.67$ (with ε still fixed at 0.7), we find that, as the share of position I cooperative screeners rises to almost 1 in the first phase, it is once again suddenly and entirely substituted by the, since then, virtually extinct pure cooperators. When $h = 0.6209834$, the transition becomes extremely quick and it follows an initial period in which de-fectionist players predominate; a three-stage pattern then emerges: defection, then cautious trust, and finally pure trust. The transition to the latter phase is almost in-stantaneous.

Compare this case with the already discussed case $\eta = 0.2$, $h = 0.6209835$: now, a marginal *drop* in the continuation value h with respect to the latter case causes the eventual emergence of *pure* cooperation, in that it favours an earlier affirmation of position I cautious cooperators and *therefore*, once the latter have spread over soon enough, creates a 'last minute' opportunity for pure cooperators to take over before they go irreversibly extinct. Interestingly, a marginally lower continuation value is then conducive to pure trust whereas a marginally higher one is not. In these last cases the dynamic patterns become more and more complex in their transitional behaviour, which is characterized by non-monotonic transitions and by intriguing dynamic in-teractions among player types. Notice also how the 'parallel market' effect never works in these cases: the proportion of position II subtle opportunists always quickly falls from the initial figure of 0.76 to zero. The reason is that, because of the low level of transaction costs, the parallel market is always killed by the action of position I cooperative screeners. An increase in transaction costs would hurt subtle opportunists as well as cooperative screeners and therefore would not help the former to enhance their survival chances.

If h goes down to 0.62095, cooperation suddenly crumbles down: the point is that the completion value is too low and position I pure cooperators die out during the former 'phase one' of the process, whereas position I cooperative screeners do not manage to sustain transaction costs. As a consequence, position I explicit opportunists take over, whereas in position II a mix of (preponderant) explicit opportunists and (minoritarian) pure cooperators emerges according to a logic similar to that of the case $\varepsilon = \eta = 1$, $h = 0.3$ of the baricentric scenario.

Finally, the crucial role of transaction costs in the exploitation scenario should not be understated. Starting from the case just discussed where cooperation is eventually wiped out, even a very small drop of η from 0.2 to 0.1999 becomes enough to restore the two-phase pattern toward the emergence of pure trust. As η drops further to 0.16, the transition to 'phase two' of pure trust becomes quicker and easier. At $\eta = 0.12$ one finds in addition that position II cooperative screeners are now observed at the equilib-rium after a transitional phase in which their share 'plunges down' temporarily: interestingly, this dynamic pattern is the opposite of that of their position I colleagues (Figure 8.4).

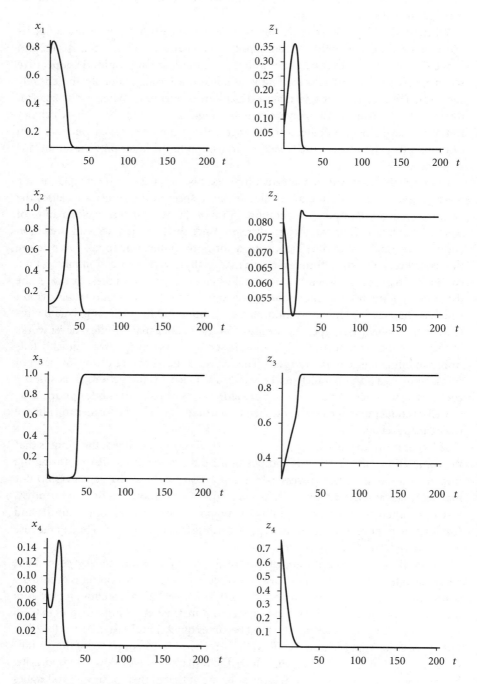

Figure 8.4. Exploitation scenario, $\varepsilon = 0.7$, $\eta = 0.13$, $h = 0.62095$

5. Conclusions

Although it provides some interesting and somewhat surprising results, the simulative analysis presented in this paper is only a preliminary stage toward a full understanding of the dynamic behaviour of the model of Sections 2–3. Although demanding in itself, this fuller simulative analysis is in turn but a first step within the broader framework that emerges by relativizing some of the key hypotheses of the model.

A first point is the relatively minor role played by parallel markets for assets in the simulation runs discussed in the previous section. This may depend among other things on the structure of such markets, and in particular on the fact that mismatching can occur: defectionist players cannot be sure to sell their assets in that they must find a buyer and this is often not the case. Assuming that the market is more transparent and that consequently mutually advantageous trades are always carried out might substantially increase the profitability of subtle cheating, thereby leading to more developed and durable parallel markets.

Another open and important point has to do with the legal enforcement system. In the present model, cooperative players who are exploited by defectionists have no way to punish them, neither they can ask for guarantees *a priori* against the possibility of defection of a partner. One could, for example, imagine the possibility of legal action against defectors; then, depending on the probability with which defectors are punished and on the time delay with which a decision is reached, the payoffs to defectionist behaviours might change; more specifically, the parameters describing the characteristics of the judicial system may add to the ones considered in this paper as factors that have a bearing on the social dynamics. As for the guarantees issue, one could imagine a precommitment arrangement in which partners who agree to carry out the cooperative project pay a bonus that they will lose in the case of defection (this type of mechanism has been explored in Landi and Sacco (1997), although with different motivations and with a different characterization of player types).

Finally, as pointed out by many authors, replicator dynamics is a sensible specification for the modelization of social dynamics in the medium–long run but not in the very long run where the possibility of random disturbances of various kinds should be taken into account; this aspect is particularly relevant for 'centipede' games like the one studied in this paper. It is clear, for example, that in the exploitation scenario the eventual diffusion of pure cooperators creates an ideal context for defectionists; therefore, if for whatever reason a small fraction of defectionists 'invades' the equilibrium population it may spread over at the expense of trustful cooperators. But this makes room for the diffusion of cautious cooperators who can successfully monitor defectors, and so on: a complex cyclical pattern emerges, as has been noted by Ho (1991) following a different but somewhat related evolutionary approach.

A fair evaluation of the descriptive and explanatory potential of the model requires that all these possibilities be explored on their own and in a comparative perspective: a busy but promising research agenda for the understanding of the impact of transaction costs on the social dynamics of cooperation and trust.

Notes

I am deeply grateful to Marco Sandri for his help with the computer simulations. The usual disclaimer applies.

1. In Kranton (1996) the opportunity cost for the involved firms *decreases* as the project advances because of the specificity of the investment decision. Here cooperation seems more difficult to enforce than in Kranton's framework, because the saleability of realized investments on the side-market implies that the temptation to defect grows as the relationship goes on.
2. Antoci *et al.* (1996) study an analogous partnership model in which the roles of the two kinds of firms are interchangeable.
3. Here and in the following, expressions like 'players of type *t* spread over' or 'die out' do not mean that they actually add to, or leave, the players pool. As explained in Section 3, the social dynamics studied in this paper are a cultural selection process driven by imitation of successful strategies rather than a natural selection process driven by physical replication and extinction of players. Therefore, the above expressions have to be meant as 'an increasing proportion of players adopt strategy *t*' or 'dismiss strategy *t*', respectively.
4. For a detailed visual account of the simulation results see Sacco (1997).

References

Antoci, A., Sacco, P. L., and Scarpa, C. (1996) 'Endogenous Partnership Formation in a Transitional Economy', *Economic Systems*.

Berg, J., Dickhaut, J., and McCabe, K. (1995) 'Trust, Reciprocity, and Social History', *Games and Economic Behaviour*, 10: 122–42.

Bjornerstedt, J. and Weibull, J. W. (1996) 'Nash Equilibrium and Evolution by Imitation', in Arrow, K. J. *et al.* (eds.), *The Rational Foundations of Economic Behaviour*. London: Macmillan, 155–71.

Coase, R. (1988) 'The Nature of the Firm. 1. Origin, 2. Meaning, 3. Influence', *Journal of Law, Economics and Organization*, 4: 3–17.

Fukuyama, F. (1995) *Trust*. New York: The Free Press.

Gambetta, D. (ed.) (1988) *Trust: Making and Breaking Cooperative Relations*. Oxford: Basil Blackwell.

Guth, W. and Kliemt, H. (1994) 'Competition or Co-operation: On the Evolutionary Economics of Trust, Exploitation and Moral Attitudes', *Metroeconomica*, 45: 155–87.

Hackett, S. C. (1994) 'Is Relational Exchange Possible in the Absence of Reputations and Repeated Contact?' *Journal of Law, Economics and Organization*, 10: 360–89.

Hechter, M. (1990) 'The Emergence of Cooperative Social Institutions', in Hechter, M., Opp, K.-D., and Wippler, R. (eds.), *Social Institutions: Their Emergence, Maintenance and Effects*. Berlin: de Gruyter.

Ho, T.-H. (1991) 'An Evolutionary Analysis of the Centipede Game Using Classifier Systems with Genetic-Algorithm Reproduction', Decision Sciences Working Paper, Philadelphia: University of Pennsylvania.

Hofbauer, J. and Sigmund, K. (1988) *The Theory of Evolution and Dynamical Systems*. Cambridge: Cambridge University Press.

Kliemt, H. (1990) 'The Costs of Organizing Social Cooperation', in Hechter, M., Opp, K.-D., and Wippler, R. (eds.), *Social Institutions: Their Emergence, Maintenance and Effects.* Berlin: de Gruyter.

Kranton, R. E. (1996) 'The Formation of Cooperative Relationships', *Journal of Law, Economics and Organization*, 12: 214–33.

Landi, M., and Sacco, P. L. (1997) 'Norms of Cooperation in a Partnership Game', CITG Working Paper no. 29, Florence.

Maitland, I. (1985) 'The Limits of Business Self-Regulation', *California Management Review*, 27: 132–47.

Menicucci, D. and Sacco, P. L. (1996a) 'Evolutionary Dynamics with λ-players', CITG Working Paper no. 19, Florence.

Menicucci, D. and Sacco, P. L. (1996b) 'Rawlsian Altruism and Efficiency', *Studi e discussioni* no. 102, Florence: Department of Economics, University of Florence.

Molander, P. (1992) 'The Prevalence of Free Riding', *Journal of Conflict Resolution*, 36: 756–71.

Mueller, D. (1986) 'Rational Egoism versus Adaptive Egoism as a Fundamental Postulate for a Descriptive Theory of Human Behaviour', *Public Choice*, 51: 3–23.

Parks, C. D. and Vu, A. D. (1994) 'Social Dilemma Behaviour of Individuals from Highly Individualist and Collectivist Culture', *Journal of Conflict Resolution*, 38: 708–18.

Putnam, R. D. (1993) *Making Democracy Work.* Princeton, NJ: Princeton University Press.

Raub, W. and Voss, T. (1990) 'Individual Interests and Moral Institutions: An Endogenous Approach to the Modification of Preferences', in Hechter, M., Opp, K.-D., and Wippler, R. (eds.), *Social Institutions: Their Emergence, Maintenance and Effects.* Berlin: de Gruyter.

Sacco, P. L. (1994) 'Selection Mechanisms in Economics', *Behavioural Science*, 39: 311–25.

Sacco, P. L. (1996) 'Comment on Bjornerstedt and Weibull', in Arrow, K. J. *et al.* (eds.), *The Rational Foundations of Economic Behaviour.* London: Macmillan, 172–81.

Sacco, P. L. (1997) 'Self-Regulation and Trust with Endogenous Transaction Costs', *Nota di lavoro*, 39/97, Milan: Fondazione ENI Enrico Mattei.

Samuelson, L. and Zhang, J. (1992) 'Evolutionary Stability in Asymmetric Games', *Journal of Economic Theory*, 57: 363–91.

Sen, A. K. (1974) 'Choice, Orderings and Morality', in Korner, S. (ed.), *Practical Reason.* Oxford: Basil Blackwell.

Sen, A. K. (1985) 'Goals, Commitment and Identity', *Journal of Law, Economics and Organization*, 1: 341–55.

Sethi, R. (1996) 'Evolutionary Stability and Social Norms', *Journal of Economic Behaviour and Organization*, 29: 113–40.

Sethi, R. and Franke, R. (1995) 'Behavioural Heterogeneity under Evolutionary Pressure: Macroeconomic Implications of Costly Optimization', *Economic Journal*, 105: 583–600.

Smith, P. B., and Bond, M. H. (1993), *Social Psychology across Cultures.* Hemel Hempstead: Harvester.

Sugden, R. (1993) 'Thinking as a Team: Towards an Explanation of Nonselfish Behaviour', *Social Philosophy and Policy*, 10: 69–89.

van Damme, E. (1994) 'Evolutionary Game Theory', *European Economic Review*, 38: 847–58.

Weibull, J. W. (1995) *Evolutionary Game Theory.* Cambridge, MA: Mit Press.

9

Self-regulation of pollution: the role of market structure and consumer information

DEVON GARVIE

1. Introduction

The purpose of this paper is to provide an analytical framework to assess the efficiency, distributional, and environmental consequences of voluntary codes in pollution-generating industries. In particular, we identify the conditions under which voluntary regimes are likely to be a viable alternative to mandatory regimes. Attention focuses upon the complex interaction among market structure, demand, and environmental factors including imperfect competition among pollution-generating firms and imperfect consumer knowledge of the environmental consequences of production.

Voluntary codes are a form of *self-regulation.* Any regulatory regime—whether it be voluntary or mandatory—consists of a target and institutional arrangements which provide incentives to attain the target. Institutional arrangements include a rule (for example, a voluntary or mandatory code for emissions) and an *ex post* governance structure (monitoring and sanctioning activities) which ensure compliance with the rule. A key difference between voluntary and mandatory regimes is that the choices of target and institutional arrangements are private rather than public decisions. In particular, since the choice of rule is a private decision, the rule is not backed up by the force of law and hence compliance with the rule is voluntary rather than mandatory. Voluntary codes can be chosen at either the firm or industry level.[1]

Four potential sources of market failure are present in our analysis of voluntary compliance regimes: (1) imperfect competition; (2) pollution byproducts; (3) imperfect consumer information regarding the environmental impact of production; and (4) pollution abatement is a public good. These sources of market failure interact and determine firm and industry incentives to adopt voluntary codes.

In an oligopolistic market structure with pollution-generating firms, the first two sources of market failure work in conflicting directions. The oligopoly itself tends to restrict output relative to the socially efficient (and perfectly competitive) level. In contrast, the presence of an unpriced pollution externality leads to overproduction and hence excessive environmental damage relative to the social optimum. Whether the imperfect competition effect or the externality effect dominates will depend upon the degree of concentration in the industry, technology and demand conditions, the type of pollutant being emitted and the current assimilative capacity of the environment (the degree of environmental damage). For instance, the imperfect competition effect will tend to dominate the externality effect in a highly concentrated industry which emits pollutants that tend to break down fairly quickly, while the opposite will hold in a less concentrated industry which emits persistent pollutants.

In the absence of legal sanctions, the primary source of compliance incentives in voluntary regimes is consumers. Consumers can effectively sanction firms by reducing demand for pollution-generating products. Clearly, the ability of consumers to sanction firms depends critically on the quality of the information they possess regarding (or attitudes toward) industrial environmental performance. Poorly informed consumers possess weak sanctioning power and, hence, compliance incentives are diminished.

Finally, the public good nature of pollution abatement efforts leads to an under-provision of abatement technology; firms cannot be excluded from benefiting from competitors' abatement efforts since consumer demand depends upon industry environmental performance. Consequently, a free-rider problem in abatement effort emerges. The free-rider problem is particularly pronounced when consumers are well informed and can lead to a significant gap in the performance of firm vs. industry codes; an industry association is better placed to resolve free-rider problems since it makes decisions in the industry interest.

Simulation results are presented for two broad categories of pollutants—cumulative and non-cumulative pollutants.[2] The identity of winners and losers in voluntary compliance regimes is highly dependent upon the respective levels of consumer sanctioning power and market power: for instance, in the case of cumulative pollutants, we find that voluntary regimes perform best when consumer sanctioning power and market power are strong.

The paper is organized as follows. An overview of alternative solutions to the externality problem is presented in Section 2. In Section 3, a graphical analysis of voluntary compliance is presented. An algebraic example is derived in Section 4. A simulation welfare analysis is presented in Section 5; concluding remarks are presented in Section 6.

2. Alternative solutions to the externality problem

The idea of fully privatizing or delegating traditional regulatory tasks to a polluting industry may initially seem to be a perversion of economic logic. It is certainly a radical departure from conventional economic thought on solutions to the externality problem. During the last 75 years, two broad schools of thought—Pigovian and Coasian—have dominated the economic analysis of externalities and hence policymaking.[3] While Pigovians and Coasians agree that externalities are caused by market failure and that correction requires government intervention, they disagree on the scope and degree of public intervention which is required. Neither school of thought suggests full delegation or decentralization as a viable solution.

Pigovians believe that the source of market failure is the missing market for pollution, that is, environmental assets are not priced. A Pigovian prescription for government intervention entails centralized choice of targets and institutional arrangements; for example, command-and-control regimes based on performance or design standards and incentive-based regimes based on taxes or marketable permits are both centralized solutions to the externality problem—they are centralized solutions because targets, rules, and *ex post* governance structures are chosen by central authorities even though individual emission decisions may be decentralized under incentive-based regimes. The regulatory agency, acting in the public interest, acquires and processes information about the costs and benefits of pollution control and chooses a set of institutional arrangements which maximizes social welfare. Pigovian solutions implicitly define a set of property rights for polluters.[4] Incentive-based rules are based on a *polluter pays principle*, forcing polluters to internalize external costs imposed on others as a result of their polluting activities.

In contrast, Coasians maintain that the source of market failure is ill-defined property rights. They argue that if property-rights are well defined over environmental assets, then decentralized bargaining between polluters and victims will lead to a Pareto-improving and self-enforcing agreement consisting of a mutually acceptable level of pollution and compensatory payment. Moreover, if transaction costs are zero, then the self-enforcing agreement will attain the social optimum. A Coasian prescription for government intervention is restricted to the definition of property rights. While the initial assignment of property rights does not have allocative consequences —even if property rights are not assigned efficiently, decentralized bargaining will lead to an efficient allocation of property rights—it does have distributional consequences. For instance, if a polluter has the right to pollute, then correction of the externality requires that the victim pays the polluter to restrict emissions; in contrast, if the victim has the right to a pollution-free environment, then the polluter must compensate victims for any pollution generated. Thus, unlike incentive-based Pigovian rules which require that a polluter always pays for the right to pollute, the identity of who pays under decentralized bargaining is determined by the initial assignment of property rights.[5]

In theory, Pigovian and Coasian solutions can both sustain competitive equilibria characterized by externalities as Pareto optimum under well-specified conditions. Again, although there are no efficiency consequences of choosing one solution over the other, there will be distributional consequences.

In practice, the implementation of Pigovian and Coasian solutions in Western economies has met with limited success. As predicted by innumerable non-Coasians, Coasian solutions are not well suited to many environmental problems. Many environmental assets are either public goods or common property resources for which property rights cannot be defined. In addition, many environmental problems involve large numbers of polluters and victims, leading to substantive coordination problems, free-riding, and high transaction costs. Finally, imperfect information regarding the opponent's bargaining curve can result in missed Pareto-improving bargains.[6] In short, decentralized bargaining cannot resolve the externality problem because of multiple sources of market failure.

Centralized Pigovian solutions have also failed to solve the externality problem because of multiple sources of regulatory failure. Regulators have imperfect knowledge about the costs and benefits of pollution abatement which result in errors in the target and rule-setting process and, consequently, welfare losses. Regulatory capture by interest groups such as environmental groups or industry itself also leads to suboptimal outcomes. In addition, limited regulatory resources for monitoring and enforcement leads to underprovision of compliance incentives and hence incomplete enforcement of environmental laws.

Neither decentralized bargaining nor mandatory compliance regimes have been effective choices for managing the environment. In addition, mandatory compliance regimes, particularly the prevalent command-and-control regime, have proven to be prohibitively expensive. It is not surprising that debt-ridden governments are searching for more cost-effective solutions to the externality problem. The key question which this paper addresses is whether or not voluntary compliance regimes can provide sufficient incentives for the correction of externalities in a cost-effective manner.

The success or failure of voluntary and mandatory regimes is, in large part, determined by the strength of compliance incentives provided by the regime. In traditional Pigovian analysis, incentives to comply with mandatory codes are provided in the form of expected financial penalties for non-compliance with the law. The source of compliance incentives is the government—the regulatory agency and statutory law.[7] In contrast, incentives to comply with voluntary codes are primarily provided by consumers of the pollution-generating product and, in the case of industry codes, the industry association.

Our analysis departs from traditional Pigovian analysis by explicitly recognizing the role that consumers play in the environmental protection process. In the absence of an agency acting in the public interest, consumers can both acquire and process information regarding the environmental consequences of industrial activities as well as exercise a powerful sanctioning role in the market place through reduced demand or consumer boycotts. Depending upon preferences, quality of information, and budget constraints, consumers will, to some extent, internalize the externality in their consumption decisions; in this sense, the role of consumers in a voluntary compliance regime may play a similar role to pollution victims in a Coasian bargaining situation. The key difference between the role of consumers in a voluntary compliance regime and victims in a Coasian bargaining situation is that the behaviour of agents in a voluntary compliance regime is mediated by prices.

3. A graphical analysis

3.1. Environmental preferences and consumer demand

Consumers can play a pivotal role in the provision of incentives for firms to voluntarily reduce emissions in the absence of regulatory directives. A growing empirical literature in environmental benefit measurement identifies a positive willingness to pay on the part of consumers for improvements in environmental quality.[8] A positive willingness to pay for environmental improvements is a monetary indicator that consumers hold preferences over different states of the environment. As a result, consumer demand depends, in part, on the environmental consequences of production. Let us suppose, for the sake of argument, that consumers' willingness to pay for a pollution-generating good, Q, is given by the following relationship:

$$P(Q, Z) = f(Q) - MD(Z) \tag{1}$$

where Z is the industry level of pollution emitted during the production process and $MD(Z)$ is the monetized value of the environmental damage caused by an additional unit of pollution—in other words, the marginal damage curve. If consumers do not care about the environmental consequences of production, then willingness to pay for a good depends solely upon the quantity consumed, $f(Q)$; $P = f(Q)$ is a standard inverse demand curve so that willingness to pay is decreasing in the level of consumption, Q, due to diminishing marginal benefits of consumption. When consumers care about environmental consequences of production, then their willingness to pay for a product is also decreasing in the level of pollution which the industry generates. More formally, willingness to pay is strictly decreasing in industrial pollution levels when the environmental damage function $D(Z)$ is strictly convex in $Z - P_Z = -D_{ZZ}(Z) < 0$ since $D_{ZZ}(Z) > 0$. Most pollutants are characterized by convex environmental damage functions as damages generally increase at an increasing rate as pollution levels rise. Thus, consumer demand will be dampened in pollution-intensive industries and enhanced in environmentally friendly industries.

3.2. Impact of industrial pollution abatement on consumer demand

Firms can, to some extent, control their pollution emission levels. In particular, several options for reducing pollution may be available to firms: firms' may be able to reduce pollution emissions by reducing output, shifting their product mix toward low pollution-intensive goods, changing their production process or by installing pollution abatement equipment which lowers the level of waste residuals created per unit of output. Let us suppose, for simplicity, that a firm is restricted to two options for reducing pollution emissions: a firm can reduce output and/or install an emission control input. For instance, a public utility could reduce sulphur dioxide emissions by reducing electricity generation and/or by installing scrubbers in their tall stacks or switching to low sulphur coal. The total level of emission control input used by the industry is denoted by E. Pollution is thus generated by a process involving output and emission control inputs—$Z = Z(Q, E)$—where pollution levels are increasing in the level of industry output and declining in the industry's level of emission control input usage.

Firm level choices of output and emission control input usage directly affect the level of pollution and, hence, consumer demand. To see this, let $f(Q) = A - Q$ and $MD(Z) = Z$ so that consumer demand is given by $P(Q, Z) = A - Q - Z$, where $A > 0$. Suppose further that the pollution production function (and, for this example, the

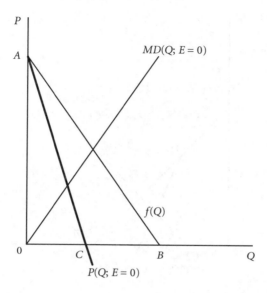

Figure 9.1. No installation of emission control inputs

marginal damage function) is described by $Z = Q - \gamma E$, where $\gamma < 1$ parameterizes the efficiency level of the emission control input. The pollution production function assumes that a unit of production increases pollution by one unit while installation of a unit of emission control input reduces pollution by less than one unit γ. As the abatement technology becomes more efficient, γ increases and a higher proportion of a unit of pollution can be reduced. Substituting $Z = Q - \gamma E$ into $P(Q, Z)$ yields $P(Q, E) = A + \gamma E - 2Q$. We can now see that consumer demand or willingness to pay, $P(Q, E)$ is a function of Q and E; willingness to pay for a good is decreasing in the level of output and increasing in the industry's usage of abatement technology.

Figure 9.1 illustrates consumer demand, $P(Q; E = 0)$, when the industry does not install any emission control inputs. Note that $P(Q; E = 0)$ is simply the difference between $f(Q)$ and $MD(Q; E = 0)$—consumers' willingness to pay for a pollution-generating good is net of the value of any environmental damage costs generated during the production process. In other words, consumers internalize the value of environmental damage costs in their consumption decisions. Pollution emissions cause the demand curve to pivot inward towards the origin, resulting in a steeper demand curve, and a lower willingness to pay for any given level of production; the total reduction in consumers' willingness to pay for Q is given by the area ABC.

By installing emission control inputs, the industry can reduce the level of emissions per unit of output, hence the level of environmental damage for any given level of output. The marginal damage curve for a fixed level of industry emission control input usage, $\bar{E}$, is labelled $MD(Q; \bar{E})$ in Figure 9.2. The installation of $\bar{E}$ shifts the marginal damage curve $MD(Q; E = 0)$ down and to the right to $MD(Q; \bar{E})$; the downward shift

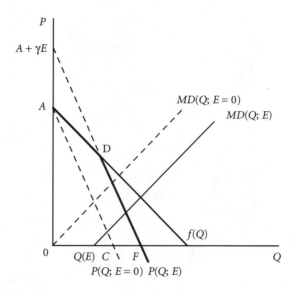

Figure 9.2. Installation of emission control inputs

is equal to $\gamma\overline{E}$—the amount of waste residuals removed and the environmental damage prevented by the emission control inputs. Notice that when production is below $Q(\overline{E})$, no environmental damage is incurred when $\overline{E}$ units of emission control inputs are installed. Environmental damage is increasing for levels of production in excess of $Q(\overline{E})$. As the industry's level of emission control input usage is increased, $Q(\overline{E})$ is increasing and the marginal damage curve shifts to the right. Thus, the industry effectively chooses the location of the marginal damage curve through its choice of E. Substituting the marginal damage curve $MD(Q; \overline{E})$ into the inverse demand curve given by equation (1) yields the following kinked demand curve:

$$P(Q; \overline{E}) = \begin{cases} A + \gamma\overline{E} - 2Q & \text{if} \quad Q \geq Q(\overline{E}) \\ A - Q & \text{otherwise.} \end{cases} \tag{2}$$

$P(Q; \overline{E})$ is illustrated in Figure 9.2. Note that the $\gamma\overline{E}$ downward shift in the marginal damage curve leads to an $\gamma\overline{E}$ upward shift in the demand curve for levels of production in excess of $Q(\overline{E})$. Further, by installing $\overline{E}$, the industry can lower the reduction in consumers' willingness to pay by the area $ADFC$. Thus, industry output and emission control input usage affect consumer demand in two ways. First, pollution emissions cause environmental damages which reduce consumers' willingness to pay for a good (inward pivoting of the demand curve). Secondly, firm investment in pollution abatement technology can reduce the level of emissions per unit of output and hence environmental damages, thereby offsetting the reduction in consumers' willingness to pay (outward shift of the demand curve).

3.3. Impact of pollutant type and consumer knowledge on consumer demand

Two additional factors affect the shape and location of the consumer demand curve: the type of pollutant emitted as a byproduct of production and the extent of consumer knowledge about the environmental consequences of production.

Pollutants can be grouped into two broad categories—cumulative and non-cumulative pollutants. Cumulative pollutants accumulate in the environment as the environment has no assimilative capacity to break them down. Examples of cumulative pollutants include inorganic chemicals, minerals, plastics, and radioactive waste. In contrast, the environment has some natural assimilative capacity to break down non-cumulative pollutants. Provided that the absorptive capacity of the environmental medium is high enough relative to the emission rate, non-cumulative pollutants may not accumulate in the environment at all. For instance, degradable wastes such as organic residuals are attacked and broken down by bacteria in a body of water while the atmosphere has some capacity to absorb carbon dioxide emissions. If the assimilative capacity of the environment is exceeded, non-cumulative pollutants can become cumulative. In order to distinguish between cumulative and non-cumulative pollutants, we parameterize the marginal damage curve as $MD(Z) = \delta Z$, where $\delta > 0$. Cumulative pollutants are characterized by high values of δ while non-cumulative pollutants causing gradual, steady environmental degradation are characterized by low values of δ.

Consumer knowledge about the true environmental consequences of production also plays a major factor in the determination of demand for pollution-generating products. Consumer knowledge about environmental consequences is captured by the parameter $\theta \in [0, 1]$ in the inverse demand curve $P(Q, Z) = f(Q) - \theta MD(Z)$. In other words, willingness to pay for a pollution-generating good depends upon how well informed consumers are about the true marginal damage curve.[9] For instance, consumers of paper products are relatively well informed (high θ) about clear-cutting practices in the British Columbia lumber industry and the consequent environmental impacts due largely to the public education efforts of Greenpeace. In contrast, consumers were relatively poorly informed (low θ) about the environmental impact of unlined oil sumps used in Alberta during the oil boom in the 1980s.

Taking into account the type of pollutant and the extent of consumer knowledge about the environmental consequences of the pollutant, we can rewrite consumer demand given by equation (2) as follows:

$$P(Q; \overline{E}, \theta, \delta) = \begin{cases} A + \theta\delta\gamma\overline{E} - (1 + \theta\delta)Q & \text{if} \quad Q \geq Q(\overline{E}) \\ A - Q & \text{otherwise.} \end{cases} \tag{3}$$

Referring again to Figure 9.2, if consumers are well informed about the environmental consequences of highly toxic emissions (high θ and δ), then the inward pivoting (measured by $\theta\delta$) and the outward shift (measured by $\theta\delta\gamma\overline{E}$) in the demand curve will be large. If consumers are poorly informed about the environmental impact of relatively benign emissions (low θ and δ), then the impact of environmental preferences on consumer demand will be small.

In the following two subsections, we present a graphical analysis of the social optimum, monopoly and perfect competition outcome to provide an intuitive feel for the model of voluntary codes. Algebraic examples of the alternative regimes are presented in the next section, followed by a simulation analysis.

3.4. Socially optimal pollution control

The social optimum is a useful benchmark for evaluating industry choices of output and emission control input levels and the resulting level of environmental quality in voluntary regimes. A benevolent, perfectly informed social planner will choose industry levels of output and emission control inputs to maximize social welfare, where social welfare is the sum of gross surplus less producer and environmental damage costs.

Social welfare maximization requires choosing an activity level so as to equate the social marginal benefit of the activity with the social marginal cost. The social marginal benefit of installing emission control inputs, $MB_E^* = -D_Z Z_e$, is equal to the reduction in environmental damages which can be obtained by installing an additional unit of emission control input. Referring to Figure 9.3, notice that the social marginal benefit of emission control inputs is downward-sloping, reflecting diminishing marginal returns from the installation of emission control inputs; diminishing marginal returns arise because the marginal benefit accruing from emission reductions is falling. The social marginal cost of installing emission control inputs, MC_E, is simply the marginal

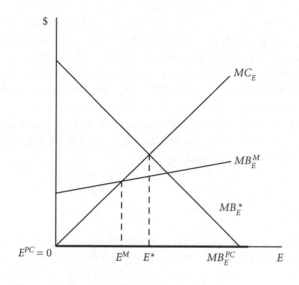

Figure 9.3. Investment in pollution abatement technology

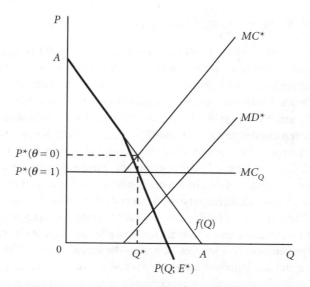

Figure 9.4. Socially optimal output choice

cost of installation; MC_E is assumed to be upward-sloping, reflecting increasing marginal costs of abatement. The socially optimal level of emission control input usage, E^*, is found at the intersection point of MB_E^* and MC_E. Note that E^* is independent of θ.

The socially optimal output choice, given installation of E^*, is illustrated in Figure 9.4. As noted earlier, the choice of E determines the location of the marginal damage curve. Installation of E^* shifts the marginal damage curve southeast to MD^*. When consumers fully internalize the externality ($\theta = 1$), the demand curve is given by $P(Q, E^*)$ which is simply the difference between $f(Q)$ and MD^*; $P(Q, E^*)$ measures the net social marginal benefit of output, that is, the marginal benefit of consumption net of environmental consequences. The socially optimal level of output, Q^*, is found at the intersection point of $P(Q, E^*)$ and MC_Q, where MC_Q measures the marginal cost of producing Q. The socially optimal price of Q when consumers fully internalize the externality is denoted by $P^*(\theta = 1)$. If consumers do not internalize the externality ($\theta = 0$), then the demand curve is given by $f(Q)$. The socially optimal level of output is now the intersection point of $f(Q)$ and MC^*, where MC^* is the social marginal cost incurred with the production of Q; MC^* is the vertical summation of MD^* and MC_Q.

Notice that while there are no allocative consequences associated with the value of θ—Q^* is independent of θ—the price of Q does vary with θ. When consumers do not internalize the externality in their consumption decisions, then the socially optimal price of Q is $P^*(\theta = 0)$; clearly, $P^*(\theta = 0) > P^*(\theta = 1)$. The socially optimal price of Q is monotonically decreasing in θ. It can also be seen in Figure 9.4 that consumer surplus is increasing in θ, that is, consumers are better off the more informed they are about the environmental consequences of production.

3.5. Industrial incentives to adopt voluntary codes

What incentive do firms have to voluntarily install emission control inputs? Suppose that there is a single producer of the product who has the power to set prices. A profit-maximizing monopolist will choose a level of emission control input usage by equating the private marginal benefit of an additional unit of input to the marginal cost of installation. The marginal benefit to the monopolist of installing the input, MB_E^M, is the incremental revenue earned; $MB_E^M = P_E Q$, where $P_E = \theta \delta \gamma$ is the value of the reduction in the marginal damage when an additional unit of the emission control input is installed. Alternatively, P_E is the increment which consumers are willing to pay for a unit of a more environmentally friendly good. Referring to Figure 9.2, each additional unit of emission control input installed results in an outward shift in the demand curve of $\theta \delta \gamma$. Thus, the incentive for a monopolist to install abatement technology is a pecuniary one—the monopolist can increase profits by exploiting consumers' environmental preferences to raise consumers' willingness to pay. It is important to emphasize that the monopolist's decision to install abatement technology is a purely *voluntary decision*. The decision is motivated by self-interest and does not require government intervention in any form, including mandated technology-based standards wherein regulations require the installation of a particular kind or level of emission control input.

The monopolist's privately optimal choice of emission control input is illustrated in Figure 9.3. Note that, in contrast to MB_E^*, MB_E^M is upward-sloping. The monopolist's profit-maximizing choice of E is found at the intersection point of MB_E^M and MC_E and is denoted by E^M. It can be shown that MB_E^M will always cut MC_E below MB_E^*, hence a monopolist will install too low a level of emission control inputs relative to the social optimum—$E^M < E^*$.

Underprovision of abatement technology results in a higher level of environmental damages for any given level of output. The marginal damage curve associated with E^M is labelled MD^M in Figure 9.5. Note that MD^M lies everywhere above and to the left of MD^*.

When $\theta = 1$, market demand for the monopolist's output Q is given by $P(Q, E^M)$. The monopoly output level is the level of output which equates the private marginal benefit of output, $MR(Q, E^M)$, with the marginal production cost, MC_Q. It is easy to see in Figure 9.5 that the monopolist restricts output below the socially optimal level—$Q^M(\theta = 1) < Q^*$. In addition, the monopoly price, $P^M(\theta = 1)$, is higher than the socially optimal price, P^*.

The divergence between Q^* and Q^M is decreasing in θ. In other words, as consumers become better informed about the environmental consequences of production, a monopolist will adopt more environmentally friendly production processes, raising consumers' willingness to pay for its product and hence enhancing the monopolist's incentive to produce output. As θ decreases, consumers' willingness to pay for the product is less responsive to the monopolist's choice of abatement technology, reducing both the incentive to adopt more environmentally friendly production

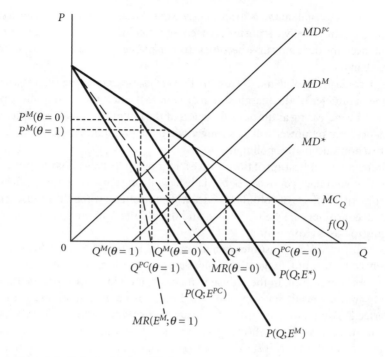

Figure 9.5. Output market equilibria

processes and to expand output. For instance, when $\theta = 0$, any pecuniary advantage of installing emission control inputs is removed as demand is no longer responsive to environmental performance. Consequently, $MB_E^M = 0$ and hence $E^M = 0$. Referring to Figure 9.5, demand is now given by $P(Q, E^M = 0)$. The monopolist's optimal output choice is restricted further to $Q^M(\theta = 0)$. Notice, however, that the monopoly price which emerges when $\theta = 0$, labelled $P^M(\theta = 0)$, is lower than $P^M(\theta = 1)$. When $0 < \theta < 1$, Q^M and P^M will lie in the respective intervals $[Q^M(\theta = 0), Q^M(\theta = 1)]$ and $[P^M(\theta = 0), P^M(\theta = 1)]$.

The monopolist's ability to mark-up prices derives directly from its market power. Figure 9.5 illustrates a paradox—a monopolist's market power is increasing in consumer knowledge about the environmental consequences of production. To see this, observe that the monopolist's market power or ability to mark-up prices is directly related to the price elasticity of the demand curve, ε:

$$\frac{P - MC_Q}{P} = \frac{1}{|\varepsilon|} \tag{4}$$

where $0 < |\varepsilon| \leq 1$. As the price elasticity of demand declines, demand becomes less responsive to price changes and the monopolist's ability to mark-up prices increases.

The price elasticity of demand is strictly decreasing in θ, hence, market power is strictly increasing in θ. Intuitively, as consumers become better informed about environmental consequences, the demand curve becomes steeper and hence demand is less responsive to price changes.

The price elasticity of demand (market power) is also decreasing (increasing) in δ, the slope parameter of the marginal damage curve. Hence, the monopolist's market power will be increasing as the hazardousness of the pollution emissions is increasing; for instance, market power will be stronger when the pollutant is a cumulative as opposed to a non-cumulative pollutant.

An important implication of the positive relationships between market power and θ and δ is that voluntary codes can potentially have strong anti-competitive effects. The anti-competitive effects of voluntary codes will be strongest when the industry is concentrated, consumers are well informed and the pollutant in question is particularly damaging to the environment.

The extent to which consumers' environmental preferences affect firm choice of emission control input usage also depends upon the level of competition in the industry. As competition in the industry increases, individual firm's market power is declining and, as a result, incentives to install emission control inputs are diminished. In a perfectly competitive industry, for instance, firms are sufficiently small so that individual decisions will not affect market prices. When firms are price-takers, there is no incentive to voluntarily install emission control inputs since firms cannot capture the pecuniary benefit. In other words, the marginal benefit to a perfectly competitive firm of installing abatement technology is zero and, given positive costs of installation, profit maximization requires that no technology be installed. The perfectly competitive output equilibria $Q^C(\theta = 0)$ and $Q^C(\theta = 1)$ are shown in Figure 9.5. When $0 < \theta < 1$, the competitive outcome will lie somewhere between these two solutions.

4. An algebraic example

For simplicity, we adopt a linear-quadratic model of homogeneous firms.[10] The number of firms, n, is fixed, hence there is no entry or exit into the industry. Each firm produces a pollution-generating good q, where $Q = nq$ is industry output. Individual producers may choose to install an emission control input e to reduce emission levels z, where $z = q - \gamma e$; industrial emission control usage and pollution emissions are given by $E = ne$ and $Z = nz$, respectively. An individual producer's cost of production and abatement is assumed to be $C(q, e) = bq + (k/2)e^2$, where $b, k > 0$. Pollution generated by the industry causes environmental damage $D(Z) = (\delta/2)Z^2$, where $\delta > 0$. Consumer inverse demand is given by equation (3). Finally, in order to satisfy the *Second Law of Thermodynamics*, we make the following parameter assumption:[11]

$$\gamma < \sqrt{\frac{k}{\theta\delta}}. \tag{5}$$

4.1. Social optimum

We assume that the social planner has full information about the environmental consequences of production. The social planner will choose levels of q and e to maximize social welfare $SW(Q, E; n)$, where social welfare is the sum of gross surplus, $U(Q, E) = \int_0^Q f(t)dt - \theta D(Z(Q, E))$, less environmental damage costs not internalized by consumers, $(1 - \theta)D(Z(Q, E))$, and industry production and abatement costs, $C(Q, E)$:

$$\max_{q,e} SW(Q, E; n) = \int_0^Q f(t)dt - D(Z(Q, E)) - C(Q, E).$$

Note that social welfare is independent of θ since the social planner takes into account the full environmental consequences of production. The social planner's decision rules for output and emission control input are characterized by the following pair of equations:

$$q^* : f(Q) - D_z Z_q - C_q = 0, \tag{6}$$
$$e^* : - D_z Z_e - C_e = 0. \tag{7}$$

Substituting the assumed functional forms and after some algebraic manipulation, we can derive the Pareto optimal decision rules as:

$$q^* = (k + n\delta\gamma^2)F, \tag{8}$$
$$e^* = n\delta\gamma F, \tag{9}$$
$$z^* = kF, \tag{10}$$

where

$$F = \frac{A - b}{n[k(1 + \delta) + n\delta\gamma^2]}. \tag{11}$$

Again, note that the Pareto optimal decision rules do not depend upon θ. Further, the environmental damage parameter δ is negatively correlated with output and pollution and positively correlated with the level of emission control input. Firm (industry) level quantities are strictly decreasing (increasing) in n.

4.2. Uncoordinated industry equilibrium: company codes

Following convention, we adopt the standard assumption that firms behave as Cournot–Nash competitors, that is, each producer chooses output and emission control input levels to maximize his or her own profits, π_i, taking as given that the other producers are also choosing their best actions:

$$\max_{q_i, e_i} \pi_i(q_1, ..., q_n, e_1, ..., e_n; n) = P\left(\sum_{i=1}^n q_i, \sum_{i=1}^n e_i\right)q_i - C(q_i, e_i).$$

An individual firm's decision rules are characterized by the following equations:

$$q_i^c : P + P_q q_i - C_q = 0, \tag{12}$$

$$e_i^c : P_e q_i - C_e = 0. \tag{13}$$

An individual firm's private incentive to undertake abatement, $P_e = \theta \delta \gamma$, is strictly increasing in the level of consumer information, θ. If consumers are uninformed about the industry's environmental performance, then $\theta = 0$ and the marginal benefit to a firm from abating pollution vanishes since price no longer varies with e. As a result, firms do not have any incentive to adopt pollution control methods and $e^c = 0$. If consumers have knowledge about industrial environmental performance, then $0 < \theta \leq 1$ and consumers can exercise their power to discipline an industry, providing firms with a positive price incentive to voluntarily undertake abatement efforts to reduce emission levels. Note that the incentive to voluntarily comply is also related to a firm's market power: if firms are price-takers, then the positive price effect and, hence, the incentive to voluntarily comply are absent.

Equation (13) also illustrates that a free-rider problem exists in the choice of abatement effort. Abatement effort or emission control input usage is a public good. No firm can be excluded from the positive benefits (outward shift in the demand curve) of an individual firm's installation decision—non-exclusivity leads to a free-rider problem. Since firms cannot be excluded from the benefits of competitors abatement efforts, their own incentive to invest in abatement technology is diminished when investment choices are uncoordinated. Individual producers do not internalize the benefits to others of their adoption level. An individual producer only takes into account the private marginal benefit of adoption, $P_e q_i$, when choosing a level of abatement rather than the social marginal benefit, $P_e Q$, which is the increase in industry marginal revenue.

Turning to equation (12), we can observe that an individual producer's output level also depends upon consumer knowledge about the industry's environmental performance as well as his or her own and competitors' abatement efforts and competitors' output levels. The direction of the distortion in output levels will largely depend upon the relative magnitudes of the imperfect competition effect and the externality effect. Output levels will be too low if the imperfect competition effect dominates and too high if the externality effect dominates.

To determine which output effect dominates—the imperfect competition effect or the externality effect—we evaluate equation (6) at Q^c and E^*. Let $P = P(Q^c, E^*)$. The imperfect competition effect dominates if and only if the following inequality holds:

$$P - (1 - \theta)D_Z Z_q - C_q > 0. \tag{14}$$

Define the Cournot equilibrium price as $P^c = P(Q^c, E^c)$. Equation (14) can be rewritten as:

$$\frac{P^c - C_q}{P^c} > \frac{P^c - P - (1-\theta)D_z Z_q}{P^c},$$

or, alternatively, as:

$$\frac{s}{|\varepsilon|} > \frac{P^c - P(\theta = 1)}{P^c},\tag{15}$$

where s measures the market share and ε measures the price elasticity of the demand curve at the Cournot–Nash equilibrium. The left-hand side of equation (15) measures the degree of market power at the Cournot–Nash equilibrium while the right-hand side measures the proportion of uninternalized damage in the market price. Equation (15) is more likely to hold when θ is large and n or δ is small.

In equilibrium, since firms are symmetric, $q_i^c = q_j^c = q^c$ and $e_i^c = e_j^c = e^c$. Substituting the symmetry conditions and the assumed functional forms into equations (12) and (13) and after some algebraic manipulation we can derive the following solutions:

$$q^c = kG,\tag{16}$$

$$e^c = \theta\delta\gamma G,\tag{17}$$

$$z^c = (k - \theta\delta\gamma^2)G,\tag{18}$$

where

$$G = \frac{(A - b)}{k(1 + n)(1 + \theta\delta) - n(\theta\delta\gamma)^2}.\tag{19}$$

Output and pollution levels are strictly decreasing and emission control inputs are strictly increasing in θ and δ. Firm (industrial) quantities are strictly decreasing (increasing) in n.

Comparing equations (9) and (17), it is easy to show that $e^c < e^*$, that is, abatement effort will always be underprovided relative to the social optimum. Comparing equations (8) and (16), we can show that $q^c < q^*$ whenever equation (15) holds.

4.3. Coordinated industry equilibrium: industry code

Industries have the legal option of coordinating on pollution control efforts. Although firms cannot explicitly collude on output levels without violating anti-trust laws, they can coordinate on pollution levels by cooperatively choosing abatement technologies. The irony is clear—choice of an industry code results in price collusion since the industry association effectively holds price-setting power. Accordingly, we model a coordinated industry equilibrium as a two-stage game. In the first stage of the game, an industry association chooses a level of emission control input, e, to maximize joint or industry profits, given individual firm output levels. In the second stage of the game, firms non-cooperatively choose output levels, q_i, taking the emission control input level as fixed at e. The nature of the game captures two features of the competitive environment. First, as mentioned above, while firms can legally collude on an industry voluntary code, they cannot collude on output levels, hence output levels must be chosen at the individual firm level. Second, the sequential moves of the industry association and firms introduces the ability of the industry association to commit to a voluntary code. We adopt the equilibrium concept of sub-game perfection and, accordingly, solve the game backwards.

In the second stage of the game, an individual producer chooses an output level to maximize own profits, taking the voluntary code as fixed:

$$\max_{q_i} \pi_i(q_1, ..., q_n; e, n) = P\left(\sum_{i=1}^{n} q_i; e, n\right) q_i - C(q_i; e).$$

An individual firm's output decision rule is characterized by the following equation:

$$\frac{\partial \pi_i}{\partial q_i} = P + P_q q_i - C_q = 0. \tag{20}$$

Equation (20) implicitly defines an individual producer's output level as a function of competitors output levels, q_j^J, where $j \neq i$, and the industry voluntary code, e. Given firm symmetry, $q_i^J = q_j^J = q^J$, and substituting the assumed functional forms, we can write an individual producer's output rule or voluntary code response function as

$$q^J(e) = \frac{A - b + n\theta\delta\gamma e}{(n-1)(1+\theta\delta)}. \tag{21}$$

Equation (21) reveals that firm level output is strictly increasing in the industry voluntary code, e. Once again, the positive relationship between q and e derives from the demand externality—installation of abatement technology shifts the demand curve outward, enhancing the incentive to produce.

In the first stage of the game, the industry association chooses an emission control input level, e, to maximize industry profits subject to firms' voluntary code response function $q^J(e)$. Clearly, the ability to choose and commit to a voluntary code effectively gives an industry association price-setting power. The industry association's decision problem can be written as:

$$\max_{e} \Pi = n\pi = n[P(nq^J(e), ne)q^J(e) - C(q^J(e), e)].$$

The industry association's decision rule is characterized by the following equation:

$$\frac{\partial \Pi}{\partial e} = \frac{\partial \pi}{\partial q^J} \frac{dq^J}{de} + \frac{\partial \pi}{\partial e} = 0. \tag{22}$$

Note that $\partial \pi / \partial q^J = \partial \pi_i / \partial q_i + P_q q^J(n-1)$, where $\partial \pi_i / \partial q_i$ is defined by equation (20). Applying the Envelope Theorem, equation (22) reduces to:

$$\frac{\partial \Pi}{\partial e} = P_q q^J(n-1)\frac{dq^J}{de} + \frac{\partial \pi}{\partial e} = 0. \tag{23}$$

Substituting for $\partial\pi/\partial e$ yields:

$$e^J : \left[P_q \frac{(n-1)}{n} \frac{dq^J}{de} + P_e \right] Q^J - C_e = 0. \tag{24}$$

Two key results emerge from equation (24). First, an industry association can resolve the free-rider problem which characterizes uncoordinated firm choice of abatement technology. When an industry code is adopted, the industry association chooses a level of installation which maximizes the benefits to all members of the industry, that is, the increase in industry marginal revenue due to higher demand for environmentally friendly products, $P_e Q^J$. In other words, the industry association fully internalizes the benefits accruing to all members from any given level of installation. In contrast, when firms choose voluntary codes non-cooperatively, they only consider the private benefits of installation. Since industry benefits of emission control input installation always exceed individual benefits, underprovision of abatement technology will be less pronounced in the case of company codes.

Second, the industry association takes into account the strategic costs associated with the indirect effect on industry output. Comparing equations (24) and (13), we observe that an industry association takes into account the indirect output effect on industry marginal revenue, $P_q((n-1)/n)(dq^J/de)Q^J$; the indirect output effect is a cost associated with increasing the level of a voluntary code—an additional cost of increasing e is the loss in marginal revenue due to movement down the demand curve.

Substituting the assumed functional forms into equation (24) and after some algebraic manipulation, we can derive the following solutions:

$$q^J = k(1+n)H, \tag{25}$$
$$e^J = 2n\theta\delta\gamma H, \tag{26}$$
$$z^J = [k(1+n) - 2n\theta\delta\gamma^2]H, \tag{27}$$

where

$$H = \frac{(A-b)}{k(1+n)^2(\alpha+\theta\delta) - 2(n\theta\delta\gamma)^2}. \tag{28}$$

Comparing equations (17) and (26), it can be shown that an industry association will choose a higher level of emission control input usage than an uncoordinated industry, that is, $e^J > e^c$. The gap between levels of company and industry codes is increasing in θ and δ, that is, when consumers are well informed and pollution emissions are cumulative; incentives to adopt voluntary codes are strongest under these conditions and hence the free-rider problem will be most pronounced. In addition, since $dq/de > 0$, it follows that $q^J > q^c$. Further, it can be shown that pollution levels are lower and market prices are higher when industry codes are implemented, that is, $z^J < z^c$ and $P^J > P^c$.

Summarizing, a stable and credible industry association can resolve the free-rider problem, resulting in higher overall levels of abatement efforts which enable firms to produce higher levels of output and emit lower levels of pollution.[12] However, although firms do not explicitly collude on output choice when industry codes are adopted, output and emission control input decisions are interdependent. As a result, market power is enhanced when industry codes are adopted, resulting in higher market prices.

5. Simulation analysis

Simulation of the oligopoly models of company and industry voluntary codes provide important insights into the conditions under which a voluntary compliance regime is likely to be a viable alternative to a mandatory regulatory regime for protecting the environment. The simulations focus on the roles of three critical parameters in the model: θ (consumer knowledge), n (market structure), and δ (environmental damage). Numerical simulation results on quantities and welfare measures are presented in Tables 9.A1–A3 in the Appendix. Discussion of the simulation results are presented below.

We first discuss the role of consumer information, parameterized by θ. As consumers become better informed about the environmental consequences of production, firm incentives to reduce pollution levels are enhanced; as θ increases, pollution abatement is achieved by installing increasingly higher levels of emission control inputs and reducing production levels. Although emission control inputs are under-provided in both industry and company code regimes, higher levels are installed when firms coordinate; the gap between installation levels in industry and company code regimes is increasing in θ and is particularly large when the free-rider problem is significant (high θ, δ and n). Output levels are also higher when firms coordinate on abatement technology choices. When consumers are poorly informed, pollution levels will be excessive, particularly in competitive industries, leading to market prices which do not reflect the full social costs of production. However, as θ increases, higher levels of emission control input usage and output levels in highly concentrated industries can lead to a reduction in pollution below the socially optimal level. This strategic manipulation of pollution levels enhances market power, leading to high mark-up pricing. Referring back to Figure 9.4, recall that the socially efficient price is declining in θ. When $\theta = 0$, the socially efficient price equals the full social marginal cost of production. As θ increases, consumers internalize an increasingly higher level of the externality in their consumption decisions and hence, the socially efficient price is falling. When $\theta = 1$, the socially efficient price reflects only the marginal production cost. In contrast, in a market economy, price is an increasing function of θ. Thus, the proportionate change in price between a voluntary regime and the social optimum is increasing in θ.

Given that the adoption of pollution reduction practices is voluntary and that firms are profit-maximizers, firms will always gain as a result of the introduction of voluntary regimes. Producer surplus will also be higher when firms can coordinate and resolve the free-rider problem. We find that producer gains are highest when consumers are well informed (as market power is increasing in θ) and are particularly high in concentrated industries. Consumer surplus, on the other hand, is strictly decreasing in θ in a voluntary regime—knowledge makes consumers worse off; in contrast, consumer surplus evaluated at the socially efficient levels of output and emission control inputs in strictly increasing in θ, that is, knowledge does make consumers better off in a first-best world. Declining consumer surplus is due to the strategic manipulation of prices in voluntary regimes. Consumer losses are particularly high when industry is concentrated and lowest when industry codes are implemented in competitive markets. In general, there is a transfer of surplus from consumers to producers in voluntary regimes.

The environmental consequences of voluntary regimes is also highly dependent on the level of consumer information. In general, environmental damages are declining as θ increases. However, damages will be excessive (and perhaps catastrophic) in competitive industries. Environmental damages will also be excessive in concentrated industries when consumers are poorly informed. However, as consumer knowledge increases, strategic behaviour will result in substantially reduced emission levels and damage levels below the socially optimal level.

Welfare losses will always arise in voluntary regimes but are declining in θ. Welfare losses will be substantively higher in company code regimes whenever the free-rider problem is significant. In addition, welfare losses will be high when consumers are poorly informed about the environmental consequences of cumulative pollutants and in the case of a competitive industry emitting a non-cumulative pollutant. Notably, welfare losses are relatively small when consumers are well informed and the industry is highly concentrated.

We next discuss the role of market structure, parameterized by n. As the level of competitiveness in a pollution-generating industry increases, the ability of firms to exploit consumer environmental preferences declines. As a result, the capacity of a voluntary regime to control emission quantities, a fundamental concern of environmental regulators, rapidly deteriorates. Excessive emissions lead to the highest level of damages and the highest welfare losses when pollutants are cumulative and consumers are poorly informed. Welfare losses are not significant when there is a small degree of competition in industries which emit non-cumulative pollutants and in industries which adopt industry codes to limit emissions of cumulative pollutants. In general, voluntary regimes will not perform well in highly competitive industries. However, welfare losses may potentially be small for sufficiently high levels of competition.

Finally, we discuss the role of pollutant type, parameterized by δ. We find that voluntary regimes result in relatively small welfare losses when consumers have strong sanctioning power (high θ) and producers have strong market power (low n) for a wide range of pollutants. In contrast, voluntary regimes result in relatively large welfare losses whenever producers have weak market power; the exception is the case of strong consumer power and an extremely benign pollutant. Voluntary regimes also perform well in the case of non-cumulative pollutants, weak consumer power and strong producer power.

The simulation results are conveniently summarized in Tables 9.1 and 9.2. Conclusions, derived from the simulation tables presented in the Appendix and Tables 9.1 and 9.2, are summarized in Tables 9.3 and 9.4.

Whether voluntary regimes provide efficient and cost-effective arrangements for protecting the environment depends upon the relative performances of voluntary and mandatory regimes. As discussed in Section 2 of the paper, there is considerable evidence that current regulatory structures are neither efficient nor cost-effective. Measures of welfare losses incurred under current regulatory structures are not available but anecdotal evidence suggests that losses may potentially be quite large. We adopt the rather arbitrary rule-of-thumb that if welfare losses under a voluntary

Table 9.1. Voluntary compliance with cumulative pollutant

Cumulative pollutant (high δ)		Consumer power		
		Weak (low θ)	Strong (high θ)	
Producer power	Weak (high n)	• externality dominates imperfect competition • free-rider problem not significant • prices too low	• externality dominates imperfect competition • free-rider problem significant • prices too low • producer gains major	
		• output restriction significant to major • input underprovision major • emissions overprovision catastrophic • consumer losses significant to major • producer gains major • damages catastrophic • welfare losses major	Industry code • output restriction significant • input underprovision major • emissions overprovision catastrophic • consumer losses major • damages catastrophic • welfare losses major	Company code • output restriction higher • input underprovision higher • emissions overprovision higher • consumer losses higher • damages significantly higher • welfare losses higher
	Strong (low n)	• externality dominates imperfect competition • free-rider problem not significant • prices too low	• imperfect competition dominates externality • free-rider problem significant • prices too high • consumer losses major • producer gains major	
		• output overprovision significant • input underprovision major • emissions overprovision major • consumer gains major • producer gains not significant • damages major • welfare losses major	Industry code • output restriction significant • input underprovision significant • emissions underprovision significant • damages even lower • welfare losses not significant	Company code • output restriction higher • input underprovision major • emissions underprovision significant • damages too low • welfare losses significant

Table 9.2. Voluntary compliance with non-cumulative pollutant

Non-cumulative pollutant (low δ)		Consumer power	
		Weak (low θ)	Strong (high θ)
Producer power	Weak (high n)	• externality dominates imperfect competition • free-rider problem not significant • prices too low • output restriction not significant • input underprovision major • emissions overprovision major • consumer gains/losses very small • producer gains major • damages catastrophic • welfare losses significant	• externality dominates imperfect competition • free-rider problem not significant • prices too low • output restriction small to significant • input underprovision major • emissions overprovision major • consumer losses small to significant • producer gains major • damages catastrophic • welfare losses small to significant
	Strong (low n)	• imperfect competition dominates externality • free-rider problem not significant • prices too high • output restriction significant • input underprovision major • emissions overprovision significant • consumer losses significant • producer gains significant • damages significant • welfare losses very small	• imperfect competition dominates externality • free-rider problem not significant • prices too high • output restriction significant • input underprovision significant with industry code and major with firm code • emissions underprovision significant • consumer losses major • producer gains major • damages too low • welfare losses not significant

regime are less than 12–15 per cent, then voluntary regimes are potentially a viable alternative to mandatory regulation. Applying this rule-of-thumb to our simulation results we find that there are indeed conditions under which voluntary regimes should be seriously considered as a viable alternative to mandatory regulation.

Referring to Table 9.3, we conclude that voluntarism or self-regulation should not generally be considered as a viable means of dealing with cumulative pollutants except in an environment where consumers are well informed and an industry code can be successfully implemented in a highly concentrated industry. In this case only, the imperfect competition effect dominates the externality effect, leading to small welfare losses overall. However, it must be recognized that in such an environment, self-regulation will result in a large transfer of surplus away from consumers to producers. Consumers will experience large losses in surplus relative to the social optimum due to the anti-competitive effects of voluntary codes in this environment.

Referring to Table 9.4, we conclude that self-regulation should be considered as a viable alternative to mandatory regulation for non-cumulative pollutants except in an environment where consumers are poorly informed and the industry is relatively competitive. When both consumers and producers are weak, voluntarism can potentially

Devon Garvie

Table 9.3. Mandatory (M) versus voluntary (V) compliance

Cumulative pollutant (high δ)		Consumer power	
		Weak (low θ)	Strong (high θ)
Producer power	Weak (high n)	M $\succ$ V	M $\succ$ V
	Strong (low n)	M $\succ$ V	V $\succ$ M iff industry codes • consumers lose • producers win • environment wins

Table 9.4. Mandatory (M) versus voluntary (V) compliance

Non-cumulative pollutant (low δ)		Consumer power	
		Weak (low θ)	Strong (high θ)
Producer power	Weak (high n)	M $\succ$ V	V $\succ$ M iff δ and n sufficiently small • consumers lose • producers win • environment loses
	Strong (low n)	V $\succ$ M • consumers lose • producers win • environment loses	V $\succ$ M • consumers lose • producers win • environment wins

have disastrous environmental and welfare implications. Whether voluntarism may potentially dominate mandatory regulation in a competitive environment as consumers become better informed depends largely on how rapidly environmental damages escalate. If consumers are strong and producers are weak, voluntarism should be considered if and only if damages from the pollutant are rising slowly and gradually and competition is not too strong. In contrast, when producers are strong, the models analysed and simulated above predict that overall welfare losses are well contained in voluntary regimes. Again, there are distributional and environmental consequences associated with the adoption of voluntarism. Voluntary regimes lead to a transfer of surplus away from consumers to producers. In addition, whenever there is an asymmetric distribution of power between consumers and producers, the environment loses. The environment wins only in the case of strong producers and strong consumers.

6. Conclusions

An analytical framework for assessing the efficiency, distributional and environmental consequences of voluntary codes is derived and presented in the paper. The analysis shows that conditions do exist under which welfare losses incurred under voluntary regimes can be relatively small. For instance, voluntary regimes may provide viable alternatives to mandatory regulation when consumers are well informed and producers have significant market power. In addition, if pollutants are of a non-cumulative nature, voluntary regimes can be a viable alternative even when there is an asymmetry in producer and consumer power.

A number of important issues emerge from the foregoing analysis. When firms have price-setting power, market incentives do exist for firms to voluntarily reduce pollution emissions in the absence of regulatory directives. Moreover, market incentives are enhanced the better informed consumers are regarding the environmental consequences of production. We find that firms will strategically exploit consumers environmental preferences to raise profits and that market power is positively related to the level of consumer informedness. Ironically, when the anti-competitive effects of voluntary codes are the strongest, overall welfare losses from voluntary regimes are the lowest. Anti-competitive effects can, however, have potentially strong distributional consequences—namely a large transfer of surplus away from consumers to producers.

A direct implication of the positive relationship between consumer knowledge and producer power is that government strategies which focus exclusively on public information provision to enhance the efficiency of voluntary regimes may have the unexpected and undesired effect of strengthening the anti-competitive effects of voluntary codes. The analysis strongly suggests that delegation of environmental regulation to the private sector should be subject to some form of government oversight. For instance, voluntary codes should be subject to vigorous scrutiny or monitoring by the government agency charged with the task of enforcing anti-trust laws since voluntary codes may have strong anti-trust implications.

The analysis also emphasizes the importance of understanding the role of market structure when deciding among alternative approaches for protecting the environment. Although the analysis presented above focuses on an oligopolistic model of industry structure, preliminary analysis of a dominant firm–competitive fringe market structure shows that voluntary regimes can potentially have less extreme distributional consequences when a firm with strong market power is subject to the pressure of a competitive fringe.[13] The presence of the competitive fringe restricts the ability of the dominant firm to exploit consumers environmental preferences and hence the exercise of market power. In particular, consumers may actually gain from a transition to voluntarism. In addition, a model with entry and exit could be examined to determine whether the adoption of voluntary codes can act as a strategic barrier to entry. Thus, further analyses of alternative market structures should be undertaken to obtain additional insights into the workings of voluntary regimes.

Although the above analysis focuses on the use of voluntary codes for controlling pollution, the framework could, with the appropriate modifications, be used to analyse the use of voluntary codes in other areas. For instance, the analysis could be fruitfully applied to the adoption of voluntary codes in the area of industrial health and safety practices as well as industrial labour practices. The framework presented above is useful for understanding the efficiency and distributional consequences of voluntary codes whenever a demand externality is present, that is, whenever consumer demand is dependent upon industrial practices. In addition, the analysis clearly shows that the success of voluntary regimes is environment or industry dependent; the outcome of voluntary regimes is highly dependent on technological, demand, and environmental factors. An important advantage of the above framework is that it enables policy-makers to identify the key determining factors which must be present to ensure that adoption of voluntary codes will be a viable alternative to mandatory regulation.

Appendix

Simulation results for different values of θ, δ, and n are presented in the Tables 9.A1–A3. Each table provides data on proportionate changes in market price (P) and industry quantity variables (output, Q, emission control input usage, E, and pollution discharges, Z) which emerge under company codes (labelled c) and industry codes (labelled J) relative to the socially optimal variables. In addition, proportionate changes in consumer surplus (CS), environmental damages (D) and social welfare (W) relative to the social optimum are also reported for the two regimes to facilitate analysis of the distributional and efficiency consequences of voluntary codes. We do not report proportionate changes in producer surplus since profit-maximization always results in higher firm profits in voluntary regimes and strictly higher profits in coordinated voluntary regimes.

Table 9.A1 reports the simulation results regarding the role of consumer information, θ. Results are reported for four different environments: (1) cumulative pollutant emitted by highly concentrated industry ($\delta = 4$, $n = 2$); (2) cumulative pollutant emitted by highly competitive industry ($\delta = 4$, $n = 250$); (3) non-cumulative pollutant emitted by highly concentrated industry ($\delta = .5$, $n = 2$); and (4) non-cumulative pollutant emitted by highly competitive industry ($\delta = .5$, $n = 250$).

Table 9.A2 reports the simulation results regarding the role of market structure, n.

Table 9.A1. Role of consumer information[a]

θ	%Pᶜ[b]	%Pᴵ	%Qᶜ	%Qᴵ	%Eᶜ	%Eᴵ	%Zᶜ	%Zᴵ	%CSᶜ	%CSᴵ	%Dᶜ	%Dᴵ	%Wᶜ	%Wᴵ
Case 1: $\delta = 4$; $n = 2$														
0.00	−0.5	−0.5	1.03	1.03	−1.00	−1.00	2.97	2.97	3.11	3.11	14.79	14.79	−3.70	−3.70
0.25	−0.3	−0.3	0.06	0.07	−0.74	−0.65	0.82	0.76	0.26	0.29	2.32	2.11	−0.41	−0.34
0.50	0.1	0.1	−0.24	−0.21	−0.63	−0.49	0.13	0.05	−0.35	−0.31	0.27	0.10	−0.16	−0.09
0.75	1.1	1.2	−0.38	−0.33	−0.55	−0.35	−0.22	−0.32	−0.58	−0.55	−0.40	−0.54	−0.16	−0.11
1.00	8.5	9.6	−0.46	−0.38	−0.47	−0.20	−0.44	−0.57	−0.70	−0.68	−0.69	−0.81	−0.21	−0.17
Case 2: $\delta = 4$; $n = 250$														
0.00	−0.3	−0.3	0.03	0.03	−1.00	−1.00	124	124	0.06	0.06	15500	15500	−4.07	−4.07
0.25	−0.3	−0.3	−0.45	−0.42	−0.93	−0.86	57	53	−0.42	−0.35	3394	2890	−1.09	−0.93
0.50	−0.2	−0.1	−0.59	−0.50	−0.90	−0.76	37	31	−0.54	−0.38	1407	1006	−0.72	−0.51
0.75	−0.0	0.0	−0.65	−0.45	−0.87	−0.60	26	18	−0.57	−0.28	741	359	−0.61	−0.29
1.00	0.1	0.3	−0.67	−0.14	−0.84	−0.17	20	4	−0.58	−0.06	439	20	−0.56	−0.02
Case 3: $\delta = .5$; $n = 2$														
0.00	0.1	0.1	−0.04	−0.04	−1.00	−1.00	0.08	0.08	−0.07	−0.07	0.17	0.17	−0.04	−0.04
0.25	0.4	0.4	−0.14	−0.14	−0.88	−0.84	−0.05	−0.06	−0.26	−0.26	−0.10	−0.11	−0.04	−0.04
0.50	0.9	0.9	−0.23	−0.22	−0.78	−0.71	−0.16	−0.17	−0.40	−0.40	−0.29	−0.30	−0.06	−0.06
0.75	2.0	2.0	−0.29	−0.29	−0.70	−0.60	−0.24	−0.25	−0.50	−0.50	−0.43	−0.44	−0.09	−0.09
1.00	6.4	6.4	−0.35	−0.35	−0.64	−0.51	−0.31	−0.33	−0.57	−0.57	−0.53	−0.55	−0.12	−0.12
Case 4: $\delta = .5$; $n = 250$														
0.00	−0.3	−0.3	0.03	0.03	−1.00	−1.00	15.4	15.4	0.06	0.06	269	269	−0.48	−0.48
0.25	−0.2	−0.2	−0.09	−0.08	−0.99	−0.97	13.4	13.2	−0.07	−0.07	207	201	−0.38	−0.36
0.50	−0.2	−0.2	−0.17	−0.17	−0.97	−0.95	11.8	11.5	−0.17	−0.16	164	156	−0.32	−0.30
0.75	−0.1	−0.1	−0.24	−0.23	−0.96	−0.93	10.6	10.2	−0.25	−0.23	133	123	−0.30	−0.27
1.00	0.1	0.1	−0.30	−0.29	−0.96	−0.91	9.5	9.0	−0.31	−0.28	109	100	−0.29	−0.26

[a] Parameter values set at $A = 200$, $b = 10$, gamma $= .6$, $k = 3$.
[b] % = Proportionate change with respect to social optimum, e.g. $\%P^c = (P^c - P^*)/P^*$.

Table 9.A2. Role of market structure[a]

n	%P^c(b)	%P^J	%Q^c	%Q^J	%E^c	%E^J	%Z^c	%Z^J	%CS^c	%CS^J	%D^c	%D^J	%W^c	%W^J
Case 1: $\delta = 4$; $\theta = .2$														
1	-0.1	-0.1	0.05	0.05	-0.69	-0.69	0.41	0.41	0.15	0.15	1.0	1.0	-0.19	-0.19
2	-0.3	-0.3	0.16	0.17	-0.77	-0.69	1.05	1.00	0.50	0.52	3.2	3.0	-0.58	-0.51
5	-0.5	-0.5	0.04	0.07	-0.86	-0.76	2.21	2.06	0.40	0.46	9.3	8.4	-1.06	-0.90
20	-0.6	-0.6	-0.24	-0.21	-0.92	-0.84	6.28	5.84	-0.10	-0.03	52	46	-1.27	-1.09
500	-0.2	-0.2	-0.41	-0.38	-0.94	-0.88	127	119	-0.38	-0.33	16450	14401	-1.28	-1.12
Case 2: $\delta = 4$; $\theta = .8$														
1	2.2	2.2	-0.48	-0.48	-0.39	-0.39	-0.53	-0.53	-0.74	-0.74	-0.8	-0.8	-0.24	-0.24
2	1.5	1.7	-0.40	-0.35	-0.53	-0.32	-0.28	-0.38	-0.61	-0.58	-0.5	-0.6	-0.17	-0.12
5	0.7	1.1	-0.43	-0.27	-0.69	-0.34	0.20	-0.11	-0.53	-0.41	0.4	-0.2	-0.27	-0.08
20	0.1	0.4	-0.57	-0.33	-0.82	-0.46	1.83	0.89	-0.56	-0.30	7.0	2.6	-0.49	-0.15
500	-0.0	0.0	-0.66	-0.42	-0.87	-0.55	49.7	31.6	-0.58	-0.24	2565	1061	-0.61	-0.25
Case 3: $\delta = .5$; $\theta = .2$														
1	0.8	0.8	-0.33	-0.33	-0.86	-0.86	-0.30	-0.30	-0.55	-0.55	-0.5	-0.5	-0.11	-0.11
2	0.3	0.3	-0.12	-0.12	-0.90	-0.87	-0.03	-0.03	-0.23	-0.23	-0.1	-0.1	-0.04	-0.04
5	-0.2	-0.2	0.05	0.05	-0.95	-0.91	0.35	0.34	0.11	0.11	0.8	0.8	-0.09	-0.08
20	-0.5	-0.5	0.06	0.06	-0.98	-0.96	1.31	1.29	0.16	0.17	4.3	4.2	-0.24	-0.24
500	-0.2	-0.2	-0.08	-0.08	-0.99	-0.98	27.3	27.0	-0.07	-0.07	798	781	-0.40	-0.39
Case 4: $\delta = .5$; $\theta = .8$														
1	3.8	3.8	-0.47	-0.47	-0.55	-0.55	-0.47	-0.47	-0.72	-0.72	-0.7	-0.7	-0.22	-0.22
2	2.4	2.4	-0.30	-0.30	-0.69	-0.58	-0.26	-0.27	-0.52	-0.51	-0.5	-0.5	-0.10	-0.09
5	1.0	1.1	-0.17	-0.16	-0.83	-0.71	0.03	0.00	-0.29	-0.28	0.1	0.0	-0.06	-0.05
20	0.1	0.1	-0.15	-0.14	-0.93	-0.86	0.77	0.71	-0.22	-0.20	2.1	1.9	-0.16	-0.13
500	-0.0	-0.0	-0.27	-0.26	-0.96	-0.93	20.7	19.9	-0.26	-0.24	469	435	-0.30	-0.28

[a] Parameter values set at $A = 200$, $b = 10$, gamma $= .6$, $k = 3$.

[b] % = Proportionate change with respect to social optimum, e.g. $\%P^x = (P^x - P^*)/P^*$.

Table 9.A3. Role of pollutant type[a]

δ	%P^c(b)	%P^J	%Q^c	%Q^J	%E^c	%E^J	%Z^c	%Z^J	%CS^c	%CS^J	%D^c	%D^J	%W^c	%W^J
Case 1: θ = .2; n = 2														
0.1	2.1	2.1	−0.28	−0.28	−0.93	−0.90	−0.27	−0.27	−0.49	−0.49	−0.46	−0.46	−0.08	−0.08
0.5	0.3	0.3	−0.12	−0.12	−0.90	−0.87	−0.03	−0.03	−0.23	−0.23	−0.06	−0.06	−0.04	−0.04
1.0	−0.1	−0.1	0.01	0.01	−0.88	−0.83	0.22	0.21	0.02	0.02	0.48	0.46	−0.08	−0.08
5.0	−0.3	−0.3	0.14	0.15	−0.75	−0.66	1.20	1.13	0.51	0.54	3.84	3.54	−0.67	−0.58
10.0	−0.3	−0.3	−0.02	0.02	−0.67	−0.54	1.53	1.36	0.38	0.45	5.42	4.57	−0.75	−0.56
Case 2: θ = .8; n = 2														
0.1	4.5	4.5	−0.32	−0.32	−0.72	−0.63	−0.31	−0.31	−0.54	−0.54	−0.53	−0.53	−0.10	−0.10
0.5	2.4	2.4	−0.30	−0.30	−0.69	−0.58	−0.26	−0.27	−0.52	−0.51	−0.45	−0.47	−0.10	−0.09
1.0	1.8	1.8	−0.31	−0.30	−0.66	−0.54	−0.23	−0.25	−0.52	−0.51	−0.40	−0.43	−0.11	−0.10
5.0	1.6	1.9	−0.41	−0.34	−0.48	−0.22	−0.33	−0.48	−0.63	−0.61	−0.55	−0.72	−0.18	−0.12
10.0	3.1	6.1	−0.32	0.21	−0.08	1.19	−0.91	−2.15	−0.85	−2.20	−0.99	0.32	−0.21	−1.78
Case 3: θ = .2; n = 250														
0.1	−0.2	−0.2	0.00	0.00	−1.00	−0.99	3.0	3.0	0.01	0.01	15	15	−0.07	−0.07
0.5	−0.3	−0.3	−0.07	−0.06	−0.99	−0.98	13.8	13.6	−0.05	−0.05	217	213	−0.39	−0.38
1.0	−0.3	−0.3	−0.14	−0.14	−0.98	−0.96	25.0	24.5	−0.12	−0.12	676	649	−0.68	−0.65
5.0	−0.3	−0.3	−0.45	−0.42	−0.93	−0.86	71.7	66.1	−0.41	−0.35	5286	4502	−1.32	−1.12
10.0	−0.3	−0.3	−0.59	−0.50	−0.90	−0.76	92.3	78.0	−0.53	−0.37	8713	6233	−1.28	−0.91
Case 4: θ = .8; n = 250														
0.1	−0.0	−0.0	−0.05	−0.05	−0.99	−0.98	2.7	2.7	−0.07	−0.06	13	13	−0.07	−0.07
0.5	−0.0	−0.0	−0.26	−0.25	−0.96	−0.92	10.3	9.9	−0.26	−0.24	127	118	−0.29	−0.27
1.0	−0.0	−0.0	−0.40	−0.38	−0.94	−0.88	15.7	14.6	−0.39	−0.34	278	244	−0.43	−0.38
5.0	0.0	0.2	−0.67	−0.14	−0.84	−0.17	25.2	4.7	−0.57	−0.05	684	32	−0.59	−0.02

[a] Parameter values set at $A = 200$, $b = 10$, gamma $= .6$, $k = 3$.

[b] % = Proportionate change with respect to social optimum, e.g. $\%P^c = (P^c - P^*)/P^*$.

Simulation results are reported for four different environments: (1) consumers poorly informed about cumulative pollutant ($\theta = .2$, $\delta = 4$); (2) consumers well informed about cumulative pollutant ($\theta = .8$, $\delta = 4$); (3) consumers poorly informed about non-cumulative pollutant ($\theta = .2$, $\delta = .5$); and (4) consumers well informed about non-cumulative pollutant ($\theta = .8$, $\delta = .5$).

Table 9.A3 reports the simulation results regarding the role of pollutant type, δ. Simulation results are reported for four different environments: (1) poorly informed consumers, highly concentrated industry ($\theta = .2$, $n = 2$); (2) well-informed consumers, highly concentrated industry ($\theta = .8$, $n = 2$); (3) poorly informed consumers, highly competitive industry ($\theta = .2$, $n = 250$); and (4) well-informed consumers, highly competitive industry ($\theta = .8$, $n = 250$).

Notes

1. While polluters will always adopt self-enforcing voluntary codes at the firm level, a free-rider induced compliance problem may arise in the case of industry voluntary codes; if firms cannot credibly commit to comply with an industry code, the industry association must provide sufficiently strong compliance incentives or an *ex post* governance structure to prevent instability. Although enforcement issues are potentially important, we restrict attention to an analysis of the *incentives* to adopt voluntary codes at both the firm and industry level.
2. In general, the environment has some assimilative capacity for breaking down non-cumulative pollutants while cumulative pollutants, as the name suggests, accumulate in the environment. As a result, environmental damages tend to escalate much more rapidly for cumulative as opposed to non-cumulative pollutants.
3. I broadly classify the Pigovian school of thought to include the literature on mandatory regulatory regimes. See Pigou (1920) and Coase (1960).
4. Under a command-and-control regime, the public holds the right to a socially acceptable level of pollution. Polluters may freely pollute up to the socially acceptable level of pollution but must pay for the right to pollute beyond that point in the form of penalties for non-compliance. In contrast, the public holds the right to a clean environment under an incentive-based regime and polluters must pay for the right to pollute any level of pollution.
5. Under Pigovian solutions, the extent to which pollution control costs are passed on to consumers in the form of higher prices depends upon the elasticity of the demand curve.
6. See Farrell (1988) and Maskin (1994).
7. The levying of financial penalties requires that the regulatory agency undertake two costly activities—monitoring and sanctioning activities. Monitoring entails site visits to obtain measurements of emission or concentration levels and testing to determine whether or not the firm is in compliance with the law. If a firm is found to be out of compliance, then regulators often have a range of sanctioning options available, ranging from administrative hassling or fines to criminal prosecution. For a detailed analysis of regulatory choice of monitoring and sanctioning activities see Garvie and Keeler (1994).
8. See generally Braden and Kolstad (1991).
9. An alternative interpretation of θ is that θ represents the weight that a fully informed consumer places on the environmental consequences of production.

10. See Garvie (1998) for a more general analytical treatment.
11. The *Second Law of Thermodynamics* states that entropy increases. In other words, it is physically impossible to eliminate all waste, hence $z > 0$ for all $q > 0$.
12. We note that an assurance problem may exist, leading to cartel stability and commitment issues. However, analysis of such issues is beyond the scope of this paper.
13. See Garvie (1998).

References

Braden, J. and Kolstad, C. (eds.) (1991) *Measuring Demand for Environmental Quality.* Amsterdam: North-Holland.

Coase, R. (1960) 'The Problem of Social Cost', *Journal of Law and Economics*, 3: 1–44.

Farrell, J. (1988) 'Information and the Coase Theorem', *Journal of Economic Perspectives*, 1: 113–29.

Garvie, D. (1998) 'Voluntary Codes: The Role of Market Structure and Consumer Information', mimeo, Queen's University.

Garvie, D. and Keeler, A. (1994) 'Incomplete Enforcement and Endogenous Regulatory Choice', *Journal of Public Economics*, 55: 141–62.

Maskin, E. (1994) 'The Invisible Hand and Externalities', *American Economic Review*, 84: 333–7.

Pigou, A. (1920) *The Economics of Welfare.* London: Macmillan.

10

The theory of quality regulation and self-regulation: towards an application to financial markets

CARLO SCARPA

1. Introduction

After years in which price regulation has been at the centre of attention of the theoretical as well as the empirical debate, that attention is now shifting towards a greater concern for quality. This is largely due to the conviction that although regulation is quite powerful in controlling prices, an excessive emphasis on prices runs the risk of neglecting quality issues that at least in the medium–long run become equally important. While price changes are immediately visible and can be easily monitored, the perception of quality levels typically takes much longer, but is not less relevant. The recent experience of the water industry in England or of several types of public procurements in Italy seems to indicate that strict price controls are often self-defeating, in that firms tend to cut costs at the expense of quality levels, and hence of consumers.

In this paper we want to build on the existing microeconomic literature to study to what extent market failures exist in the provision of quality, and to what extent different types of regulation can actually contribute to a solution. In particular, we will focus on self-regulation (SR) as an alternative to more traditional types of public interventions. More precisely, we want to analyse:

1. in what sense the market may not lead to optimal quality level(s) (the market failure);
2. what problems public intervention might run into (regulatory failure);
3. what features self-regulation has in different market situations;
4. under what conditions some of the previous problems may thus find a solution in self-regulation.

Our interest in self-regulation is due to its relevance in the stock market, which in some countries has a relevant tradition of self-regulation (the UK in the first place), and where proposals of regulatory reforms often try to strike a balance between external regulation and self-determined rules (the recent privatization of the Italian stock market being a pertinent example). In so doing we hope to give a contribution to the present debate, helping to single out some likely consequences of a (more) systematic reliance on SR.[1]

One of the main problems faced by any attempt to apply the theory is the actual definition of quality, a characteristic of the good such that all consumers agree that 'more is better than less'. In general, each good is characterized by features on whose desirability consumers agree ('quality') and others on which their preferences differ (these features distinguish 'varieties' of a good) and product differentiation can take place along each of these dimensions. Furthermore, quality is multi-dimensional, that is quality is a vector and not just a number, which is the common assumption of theoretical models, which makes it even harder, to define what the expression 'better product' means.

The application of principles of self-regulation to financial markets entails additional problems, that we do not want to hide. First of all we have to determine the real difference between 'industrial' markets and 'financial' markets; although there may be several answers to this question, we do not feel that the issue is completely settled. Markets for different securities show different problems, which is the reason why here we have decided to focus on one type only, that is the stock market. However, even in such a market 'quality' can mean different things to different categories of customers, so that one may want to distinguish between large professional customers and small ones, whose protection is a more problematic issue. The microstructure of the stock market also makes a difference; for instance, self-regulation with market makers is different from self-regulation of match makers (who in a way operate with less transparent prices); in the same way, it matters whether intermediaries have the 'dual capacity' or possibly the permission to manage their clients' portfolios (in which case, regulatory problems become much more severe). And so on.

These practical problems do not imply that theoretical analysis is powerless. In our view, the greater the complexity of the issue, the greater the need to use theory to look for some guidance and to 'organize' such complexity. The fact the policy conclusions cannot be as clear cut as in other cases is only an indication that not enough theory has been developed in the area so far.

Probably the best way to organize this discussion of the literature is to follow the traditional distinction, introduced in the theory of asymmetric information, between models with hidden information and models with hidden action. Thus, it becomes crucial to understand whether the quality of service depends mainly on intrinsic features of the financial intermediary or rather on his or her actions. The relative weight of these two aspects determines whether the asymmetric information that we typically face should be considered mainly a problem of hidden characteristic (adverse selection), or one of hidden action (moral hazard). As the two aspects are typically present together, we have another problem of applying theoretical models that (correctly) concentrate on one issue at a time.

As the quality of service depends both on the ability of the intermediary and on his or her effort,[2] we can have different regulatory problems. The first one has mainly to do with conditions of access to the profession and with the training of financial intermediaries—issues that seem to be relatively settled. Probably the second type of problem is the more important one when it comes to the policy debate, in that controlling the behaviour of intermediaries, checking that transactions are carried out in a fair way and that the operator is actually working in the interests of his or her client are among the main issues on the present agenda.

These issues will be analysed in the attempt to study the feasibility of SR and to compare its outcome with the outcomes of different regulatory constraints. In line with the prevailing modelling strategy, the definition of SR we adopt in this paper is that of a regulation of (potentially) rival firms run by the group of firms itself (e.g. intermediaries in financial markets). As analyses of SR exerted by a coalition of sellers, buyers and intermediaries have not yet been carried out, the desirability of involving other agents in the management of regulation will emerge from the limitations of the type of SR studied, and will be considered only in the conclusions.

The paper is organized as follows. Section 2 addresses the problem of (unregulated) quality choice asking whether a market failure really exists with and without asymmetric information. Section 3 reviews some of the main forms of intervention on quality, pointing out the limitations that public intervention inevitably faces. Section 4 turns to the theory of self-regulation, showing to what extent the few existing results and some additional arguments can really help to find a role for SR in financial markets. Section 5 concludes the paper, trying to derive from the theory some extremely tentative policy indications.

2. How firms determine quality levels: do we have a market failure?

Unfortunately, even in the simplest contexts very little can be said about the comparison between market equilibrium and social optimum. If we start from a full information set-up, we know from Spence (1975) that the quality level a monopolist chooses might be either higher or lower than the socially optimal one. This depends on whether the *marginal* valuation of quality given by consumers—the relevant parameter for profit maximization—is higher or lower than the *average* valuation of quality—crucial for welfare maximization.

The Spence paper shows how this condition boils down to a condition on how the marginal valuation of quality varies with income. Let $p(q, x)$ be the inverse demand function, where p is price, q is quality and x is quantity. When $\partial p/\partial q$ (the marginal valuation of quality) decreases with x ($p_{qx} < 0$), the monopolist produces too low a quality level for each given output level; this happens when the choices of consumers with the higher willingness to pay are more sensitive to quality than the choices of low-income consumers. Although this condition—that we will use later on—seems quite plausible, in general nothing can be said with certainty.[3]

When we move from a monopoly to an oligopoly, we see that typically firms differentiate their products in order to relax price competition. Unfortunately, these models tend to be quite complex, so that—in order to study market equilibrium—heavy assumptions are introduced, that lead to fairly model-specific results;[4] this makes it difficult to draw general conclusions on the comparison between equilibrium and optimum. At least two separate issues should be tackled: first, how many firms (i.e. types of product) we observe; secondly, which quality levels are produced.

As regards the number of firms, there are two opposite effects. On the one hand, as entry requires a fixed cost, in a free entry equilibrium we tend to have 'too many' firms, with a duplication of fixed costs;[5] on the other hand, the tendency in vertically differentiated oligopolies is to have a limited number of firms, because competition in quality levels increases their fixed costs and sets an upper limit to the number of firms that can survive in equilibrium (Shaked and Sutton 1983).

The indeterminacy that we see in a monopoly regarding the choice of quality levels carries over to the oligopoly equilibrium. Although the models that are usually analysed show that equilibrium quality levels are lower than would be desirable, it is hard to tell to what extent this result—obtained under the assumption that $p_{qx} < 0$—can be generalized.

2.1. Asymmetric information

The issue of quality levels becomes more 'delicate' when we consider asymmetric information.[6] This term can refer to a number of different situations, and we will focus in particular on two of them, depending on whether the quality is produced before the product is purchased (unknown characteristic) or after it (unknown action, particularly common in services and thus relevant to our problem).

The case in which the (predetermined) characteristic of the good is unknown to the buyer was first studied by the classic paper by George Akerlof (1970). Let us quickly review his result.

Consider a market where quality levels are given, but cannot be observed by customers before purchasing the goods; in such a situation, no customer will accept paying a price higher than 'normal', so that all goods are sold at the same price. As high quality firms receive an insufficient reward, they are not willing to sell what they would sell otherwise. This leads Akerlof to conclude that asymmetric information reduces (1) the volume of transactions and (2) the average quality of goods exchanged. The existence itself of the market for high quality goods is put into question. As such a situation penalizes high quality goods, we talk of 'adverse selection', which is one of the main (potential) market failures regarding quality choices; the pervasiveness of informational problems in financial markets makes it necessary to focus on these issues in particular detail.

The main question is: to what extent is the market by itself able to overcome the main consequences of informational problems? The answer must by necessity be complex, as it largely varies with the features of the good sold. Given the type of uncertainty we are considering, three types of goods can be distinguished:[7]

- search goods, for which asymmetric information on a good's features can be eliminated before consumption takes place, paying a 'search' cost;
- experience goods, for which only by consuming the good can one become aware of its features;[8]
- credence goods, for which neither before, nor after consumption can the quality of the good become fully known to consumers.

In all cases, some inefficiency, at least in the short run, will emerge.[9] However, the main issue is whether the market itself is able to give producers the correct incentives to provide quality, inducing potential customers to buy.

With search goods, the existence of asymmetric information creates an additional cost for consumers; because of this, the search process typically stops before full information is achieved and firms have a lower incentive to produce quality, proportional to the difficulty of search. This is a pretty obvious and 'banal' distortion, and we will not devote much attention to it. From the policy viewpoint, however, notice that when a good's quality can be detected before consumption consumer protection can be achieved at a well-defined cost, and the only issue is the definition of benefits and their comparison with such a cost. The relevance of this scheme is probably high when it comes to information on aspects of a product which can be objectively and precisely defined: it is no surprise that the main application of this idea is to situations where certain goods can be offered at different prices which a consumer can discover by 'shopping around'.

Notice that often these models indicate how 'informative' advertising, by increasing consumers' information, can increase welfare. Furthermore, as advertising reduces product differentiation, it also reduces firms' market power and profits. Thus, the prohibition of advertising in certain professional services can be seen as a device to help collusion, rather than something inspired to protect consumers.

The cases when the product's characteristics cannot be discovered before consumption are certainly the more relevant ones, especially as the most interesting features of a product are probably difficult to define without a (more or less direct) experience of it. Notice that very often in the case of financial services the quality of the good purchased is not observable before the customers decide to buy it; indeed, in that case production itself typically takes place after the service is acquired, which is the most extreme case of (*ex ante*) unobservability.[10]

What several 'experience' models indicate is that there is a plethora of equilibria, one of which is a full-revelation equilibrium, in which—in the long run—an equilibrium is achieved where qualities become known to consumers and producers earn a quality premium (pricing above marginal cost) (Klein and Leffler 1981, Shapiro 1983). A similar result emerges in signalling models, or when the producer can provide warranties.

The reason why firms have an incentive to produce goods of a consistent quality is that whenever they 'cheat', consumers will punish them by refusing to repeat the purchase. It is important to stress that—for this mechanism to work—repeated purchase must be possible. In other terms, the product cannot be too expensive, and the poor performance of a purchase must not eliminate the possibility of the customer buying again, which is not a banal condition in financial markets, where agents must leave the market when they have no money to invest. However, the main limitations of these results are that

1. many other equilibria exist;
2. the result holds only in the long run.

Let us analyse the two problems in sequence. Following Stiglitz (1988), the punishment of a firm is a sort of public good, that raises the usual free-rider issue. The punishment is individually rational only if a consumer is convinced that the firm keeps 'cheating'; otherwise, given that all other customers are punishing a certain firm a consumer would not have any reason to do so. The issue of expectations formation is crucial, as the equilibria analysed—for instance—by Shapiro (1983) are 'bootstrap' equilibria, based on self-fulfilling expectations: producers behave in a certain way because consumers' expectations are what they are, and vice versa. The multiplicity problem is obviously intrinsic to this type of model. However, these models say very little on how expectations are built. Following Stiglitz (1988) once again, we could observe that

If one constructs a model in which no one ever cheats and sells lousy commodities, then how are individuals to form expectations . . .? . . . Moreover, firms, in deciding whether to cheat, must form expectations concerning the consequences of their cheating. To do this, they must guess how consumers will respond. Again, if in equilibrium no shoddy commodities or no cheating ever occur, they have no basis for forming their expectations. (Stiglitz 1988, 824–5).

In the presence of multiple equilibria, a selection device is required, possibly based on an explicit learning mechanism. However, given the interaction between the learning processes on both sides of the market, it is difficult to see how this could eliminate the multiplicity problem. Using concepts from evolutionary game theory would probably represent a preferable alternative, in that it often allows a considerable narrowing of the set of 'reasonable' outcomes, allowing one to link the final equilibrium to well-defined initial conditions. This latter aspect is potentially the main weakness and—at the same time—the strength of this approach; only if one is able to 'tell a story' on where market dynamics starts from, do evolutionary arguments really help understand the future evolution of the market itself. As our focus in on financial markets and more precisely on the (Italian) stock market, this line of research might provide quite useful insights. We will go back to this approach later in the paper.

Even if we really believe that the 'efficient' equilibrium will eventually be reached, we have to admit that this might be the case only 'in the long run'. The vagueness of this expression calls for careful use especially for policy purposes. One problem that has only recently attracted the attention it deserves is the speed of convergence towards an equilibrium. This requires specifying an explicit learning process and clarifying what has to be learnt. The latter is typically the trickiest problem; indeed, while we already know something about the convergence when only one parameter is initially un-known,[11] we still know very little about situations in which economic agents have to learn several parameters, whose values change over time, which is unfortunately the most plausible representation of numerous markets.

Secondly, the population changes, and this interferes with any learning process. This is true of agents on both sides of the market, but is particularly a problem for sellers. It is not very useful to know that in (say) ten years you will learn everything about people who are now in the market, if these people are not going to be in the market in ten years' time. The mobility from one market to another is considerable, and we know that reputation does not always spread from market to market. One agent could be tempted to 'cheat' the market as long as possible, and then to abandon it by moving to a different activity, or trying to 'reappear' in the same market under a different commercial label (even if firms' names are usually well known, their administrators' are often not). Another reason for population changes is that if the convergence process takes too long, people might be tempted to drop from the market because they have lost confidence. This is also related to the Grossman–Stiglitz (1980) problem of the im-possibility of informationally efficient markets: if people tend to free-ride and not to acquire information in the short run, who will lead the learning process?

Finally, there is the intertemporal problem we have already mentioned. First of all, before we learn we run the risk of incurring losses, and the expected loss may be larger that the future discounted gain (when we learn 'who is who'). Without adequate guar-antees, the incentive to engage in a costly learning process may be absent. Moreover, future gains depend on the sum we can invest. If we have losses in the short run, we may not be able to invest anything later. Thus, full information might arrive 'too late'.

Therefore, knowing that in the long run the learning process leads to full informa-tion may not be enough to convince investors to remain in the market. The 'short run' problem thus remains crucial. This supports the conclusion that we have a market failure which *potentially* justifies some form of public intervention.[12]

3. Quality regulation

Very little is written on the theory of quality regulation, and there are probably good reasons for this. In the first place, we have seen that we cannot even be 100 per cent sure that with symmetric information a real market failure exists and in which direction it operates. Secondly, modelling quality competition in oligopoly is extremely complex and most models in the field simply by-pass the issue. Finally, all alternatives are intrinsically imperfect ones, and comparing second-best outcomes is quite hard.

The (apparently) most straightforward and reasonable type of intervention is the introduction of a minimum quality standard (MQS), that prevents firms from selling products of a quality level lower than the MQS.

The effects of the introduction of an MQS in an oligopoly have been studied within a complete information set-up and even in this context they are not yet well understood. With two firms, if the MQS is not too high social welfare increases (Ronnen 1991). However, a more plausible representation of market competition should allow for a larger number of firms, and the presence of intermediate-quality firms changes some relevant features of market competition in the presence of an MQS. The position of these firms is particularly difficult, in that when the lowest quality increases because of the MQS, they face a dilemma: if they do not increase their quality levels, they are 'too similar' to the worst product, but if they do, then the distance from higher quality goods decreases. Whatever their decision, price competition increases, and might reduce or destroy the incentive to produce high quality goods.

In a three firm set-up, the MQS decreases top quality, average quality and firms' profits to such an extent, that social welfare is reduced (Scarpa 1998). This result can be interpreted as offering theoretical backing to the common suspicion that under certain conditions 'excessive' competition can represent a negative incentive to supply high quality goods. This also shows how public intervention could be a self-defeating remedy for imperfect market competition.

Other attempts to study quality regulation with asymmetric information typically avoid the complications arising from an explicit modelling of oligopolistic behaviour and concentrate on market structures where the only market power arises from informational problems and where firms' strategies never come to the forefront.[13] The focus is typically on long-run equilibria where quality levels are eventually revealed and on the role of different types of intervention on such equilibria.

In particular,[14] Shapiro (1986) compares licensing and certification. Licensing is defined as a form of *input* regulation[15] whereby only producers that satisfy a certain requirement on investment are allowed into the market; such investment is assumed to facilitate the production of high quality goods. 'Certification' instead requires the public authority to provide consumers with the relevant information on the amount invested (e.g. the length of the training period).

Therefore, licensing sets a minimum level of quality related investment that all producers must make. Certification reduces the informational asymmetry which remains as long as quality levels are not fully revealed; this reduces the incentive to make only a 'small' investment, and, again, induces more producers to provide high quality goods. Both policies increase the average quality level,[16] but the cost of doing so may be so high as to reduce total surplus; furthermore, consumers with a low willingness to pay are typically worse off. Not surprisingly, even the results of the comparison are extremely mixed and yield no definite result.

An alternative—and indeed very traditional—tool for controlling quality is to impose liability on the producer in case the quality of the product/service provided is 'not sufficient'. Polinsky and Rogerson (1983) analyse the relationship between liability rules[17] and market power; the latter is important in that an industry where firms have market power will react to the imposition of liability rules by restricting output to an excessive extent. Only with market power do liability rules have such a distortionary effect, so that in a competitive environment a strict liability is optimal; with less competitive markets, liability rules should be made less stringent so as not to trigger a welfare reducing reaction of firms.[18]

In a richer set-up, however, Shavell (1984) points out that neither liability rules nor the regulation of product quality may be sufficient. In this context, regulation is defined as a minimum care that the firm should exert (in this sense, it is a sort of input regulation); however, this is an imperfect tool, in that the regulator cannot observe the magnitude of the harm each customer suffers in case the product 'fails'. In general, thus, the joint use of both means of controlling quality turns out to be advantageous, a conclusion widely in accordance with observed arrangements.

To sum up, none of the alternatives considered seems to guarantee the effectiveness of public interventions. There is little guarantee that quality regulation increases social welfare or the average quality of the products; distributional problems may arise, in that consumers with a lower willingness to pay are often penalized by a quality-increasing regulation; when informational asymmetries involve the regulator's ability to observe quality levels or to enforce rules, the power of regulation is reduced even further. Furthermore, notice that the previous results are based on the assumption that regulation is carried out by benevolent policymakers, whose objective function is nothing but social welfare. The literature on regulation, however, reminds us that the regulator might be captured by the producers (Stigler 1971) or at least that he might have private objectives, and that the interventions of the political authority might be at least partially determined by the influence of pressure groups (Becker 1983). It seems pretty obvious that in such cases public regulation will achieve even less impressive results, and—although we will not elaborate further on these well-known arguments— we will have to keep these possibilities in mind when drawing any policy conclusions.

4. The theory of self-regulation

Asymmetric information problems do not involve consumers only, but the regulator as well; producers know their business better than anybody else and regulating a market means giving substantial power to a body that may not have sufficient information to use that power properly. Furthermore, regulation is a formal process where sanctions may be imposed on to firms only if there is sufficient evidence that they have not complied with some norm; many variables, although somehow observable, are not easily verifiable by a third party, so that a court may not be able to punish improper behaviour. Finally, the formal process of regulation may not be flexible enough to keep up with the pace of change in particularly dynamic markets.

The first question one should try and answer is: to what extent can an agreement among producers themselves overcome the limitations that market competition and regulation inevitably suffer from? The traditional arguments that might support SR as a sensible alternative to outside regulation can be obtained by looking at the above list of limitations of formal regulatory processes. Insiders have better information on market conditions and on the behaviour of other firms; SR can be designed as a less formal process, with the double advantage of a lower level of reliance on formal procedures and evidence and of a greater ability to adapt to exogenous market changes.[19]

This important issue, however, has been the object of formal analysis only very few times. To the best of our knowledge, the relevant formalized literature on the subject consists of little more than four published papers and an unpublished dissertation,[20] which mainly look at the consequences of SR considering some—although not all—of the relevant aspects of the problem.

The first point to bear in mind is that self-regulation will never go against the interest of the (self-) regulator, that is of the firms involved. Indeed, on many occasions SR is simply seen as the intervention of producers either as a cartel (whose objective function is joint profit maximization) or as a cooperative (maximizing profits per firm): the latter is probably a more reasonable alternative if the number of firms is predetermined when SR is introduced.

Finally, notice that the term self-regulation might mean either the self-determination of rules or else the self-management of the application of exogenous rules. Although no rule is probably so complete that it does not leave sufficient margins of discretion in its application, the difference might turn out to be important when drawing some conclusions.

4.1. Self-regulation when quality levels are exogenous

The first—and probably easier—issue tackled by the theoretical literature is the one of SR in the presence of exogenous quality levels on which there is asymmetric information between consumers and producers. In this set-up, the most natural issue to address is the one of fixing a quality level that allows potential producers actually to act in the market, that is the problem of setting a minimum quality standard, such that only producers whose quality is above it are allowed to sell. The relationship between the MQS set by a self-regulating organization (SRO) and the socially optimal one thus comes to the forefront.

The first model that explicitly addresses this issue is Leland (1979) within a typical Akerlof-type model. As individual quality levels are not observable, consumers' willingness to pay depends on *average* quality. On the supply side, it is assumed that the opportunity cost of supplying a good of given quality increases with quality itself. In the unregulated equilibrium, we have underprovision of quality (adverse selection).

The two main results Leland obtains are the following. First of all, the fixation of a minimum quality standard (L) increases welfare (relative to $L = 0$) if (1) the willingness to pay (i.e. price) is very low for low quality levels and (2) is very sensitive to quality changes, if (3) demand is rigid and if (4) cost does not increase too rapidly with quality. Under these quite intuitive conditions, then 'some' MQS improves welfare. The second result regards the comparison between the MQS that emerges with SR and the optimal one. If the opportunity cost is convex in q and $p_{xq} \geq 0$, then the self-regulated MQS is too high.

These results are thus not very clear cut, which is not necessarily a problem, given the intrinsic complexity of the problem at hand. However, it is important to point out that some of the underlying assumptions raise some perplexity. The convexity of the opportunity cost in q is far from obvious, if one considers that it cannot be considered a real production cost, but rather the income a producer can obtain (i.e. the price he or she can command) in another market. Such remuneration is more likely to be concave in q, and this already weakens the previous result. Furthermore, the assumption $p_{xq} \geq 0$ is not at all convincing, so that one should conclude that the MQS might well be too low, rather than too high from a social viewpoint.

Following some of these criticism, Shaked and Sutton (1981) develop a miniature general equilibrium model with two sectors, and in this way they endogenize the opportunity cost of supplying a good of given quality. One input (labour) must be allocated between the two sectors; there are N workers, whose labour supply is inelastic. Their skills (quality) are uniformly distributed in the interval $[0, N]$, so that all workers are different and can be ranked according to quality.

The differences in skills translate into actual differences in output quality depending on the sector where labour is employed. People working in sector A (called 'lawyers') differ in the quality of their output, while all those working in sector B (call them 'workmen') produce a homogeneous output which does not depend on their skill.[21] Self-regulation (of 'lawyers') consists of the determination of the minimum quality standard for lawyers, that is of a skill level L such that only the best $N - L$ people can exercise the profession, while the remaining L have to go and work as generic labour force. This structure contains an important assumption on the effects of SR: as quality levels are given, setting an MQS is equivalent to deciding the number of competitors in the sector. This means that any increase in the MQS entails a reduction in output (a price increase).[22]

The demand for professional services depend on the quality of the service provided. Consumers have identical utility functions, which eliminates the element ambiguity intrinsic in the sign of p_{xq}. While other lawyers can observe whether a worker's quality is higher or lower than L, consumers cannot observe this, and demand for professional services depends on the *expected* quality of the profession $\bar{q}(L, N)$, which is assumed to increase in both arguments (a slightly more general formulation than Leland's). Thus the higher the MQS, the higher the quality level consumers expect.[23]

The MQS is decided autonomously by the self-regulating organization in order to maximize per seller the earnings of its members. This implies that the monopolist SRO works as a labour managed firm, and we know that this type of firm has a tendency to reduce output even more than a profit-maximizing monopolist would.

Thus, it is not surprising that the main result obtained by Shaked and Sutton is that the MQS set by the SRO is too high from a social viewpoint. Indeed, notice that an increase in L by one unit has two effects on social welfare. On the one hand, it reduces the output of lawyers by one unit, while on the other hand it increases the average quality of the profession. The incentives of the SRO to increase L are such that in equilibrium the former, welfare reducing effect dominates the latter.

Notice that the assumption that the opportunity cost of suppliers in sector A does not depend on quality is crucial to this result. Indeed, we cannot have any problem of adverse selection: given L, all producers whose quality is above L will stay in the sector, and none will be tempted to take an outside option (which might be the case if the opportunity cost of staying in the market increases with the skill of the producer). Another crucial aspect is the fact that all consumers are identical, which assumes away all ambiguities on the demand side, that instead were present in Leland's model.[24]

4.2. Self-regulation with endogenous quality levels and moral hazard

As argued in the introduction, the issue of controlling *behaviour* and not just innate *characteristics* is at least as important, and probably more challenging. In this set-up the main issue is no longer the study of the consequences of SR, but the analysis of the conditions under which an SRO is able to enforce control on its members.

The above-mentioned paper by Shapiro (1983) does not contain any indication on the activity of an SRO, but can be used as a basis for understanding the role of self-regulation with moral hazard when experience matters. In that set-up, regulation may only serve two purposes—it may accelerate the detection of quality and increase the minimum quality level. Notice that both things reduce the quality premium, that is the price–cost margin that firms obtain in equilibrium as an incentive to produce goods of a quality higher than zero. Indeed, if quality is detected immediately there is no need to provide incentives not to cheat and competition should drive prices down to marginal costs; in the same way, the higher the minimum quality that can legally be produced, the lower the risk run by consumers, and the lower the compensation that firms obtain in equilibrium. Therefore, it is easy to conclude that the SRO would not help in the detection of high quality products and that it would set too low a standard.

Two more instruments for regulation are suggested by Mayer and Neven (1991), who consider an industry where N potential firms have innate quality levels θ_i. The quality of the product they offer can be either θ_i or zero (which identifies cheating). Firms are endowed with a capital C_i which is positively correlated to θ_i. In order to control quality, it is assumed that there are two instruments, capital requirement (CR), which represent the prerequisite all active producers must satisfy, and a fine (of fixed amount U) imposed on cheating firms. The rationale of the capital requirement lies in the relationship between capital and quality; eliminating all firms whose capital is lower than a certain level entails eliminating 'intrinsically bad' producers.

If a firm cheats, it earns a higher gross profit, but by assumption it is discovered with probability 1, it loses its capital C and must pay the fine U; moreover, there is a positive probability that the same loss is wrongly imposed on firms who are not cheating. This imposes a trade-off, in that honest firms cannot be sure that they are not going to be penalized; thus, increasing CR means eliminating from the market some firms that are going to cheat, but some honest ones as well. Raising CR to the level where no cheating takes place means excluding too many honest producers, and thus using the fine as well is necessary.

With SR, firms may join an SRO by paying CR and committing not to cheat consumers. If they cheat, they lose their capital and pay the fine (as above). Is the SRO going to enforce these penalties, and is SR going to require less or more capital than standard regulation? On this point, the analysis leaves a lot of questions open,[25] while the discussion probably becomes too informal.

External regulation may be inferior to SR because it also requires the third party verifiability of cheating, while with SR its generic 'observability' can be sufficient,[26] given the more informal nature of the procedures adopted; this aspect is only mentioned by Mayer and Neven, while it is at the core of the analysis by Fletcher (1993) with a clearer microeconomic foundation. In particular, quality levels θ_i are assumed to be observable by market operators but not verifiable by an external regulator, and the SRO—unlike the regulator—is able to impose different fines to firms of different innate quality levels. In this case, regulation entails welfare maximization under the constraint that quality levels are non-verifiable, while SR involves profit maximization under appropriate incentives that the regulator can give to the SRO.

Without going into the formal details of the model, which extends and clarifies some features of Mayer and Neven (1991), it is worth noting that this paper introduces an explicit distinction between 'cheating on quality' (i.e. providing a service of zero quality when innate quality is higher) and fraud (an additional damage consumers may suffer, for instance, because the firm runs away with its money). These ways to exploit consumers are substantially different, in that cheating on quality gives a reward equal to the price paid by consumers,[27] while fraud entails a reward independent of price.

This allows one to distinguish different cases. When cheating on quality is the main problem, the highest level of regulation would be required by high quality firms, in that the price they can get (i.e. the reward they would get from cheating) is higher, and so is their incentive to cheat. On the contrary, when fraud is the main problem, it is the low quality firms that need the toughest regulation. Thus, the ability of the SRO to observe quality makes the SRO better equipped to design an 'optimal' structure of fines.

Given that optimal fines can be made conditional on quality, it is also fairly intuitive that SR may achieve a better result in terms of the range of quality levels admitted in the market; quality is observed, so that low quality firms can be given better incentives. With external regulation, punishing cheats on quality is more difficult, and it may be optimal to restrict product variety, while the better ability of the SRO to observe behaviour may allow it to admit a wider range of firms (which is socially beneficial, given the heterogeneity of consumers' willingness to pay).

Finally, it is interesting to see that SR is more likely to be welfare improving relative to external regulation for the following reasons:

1. Fraud becomes more important. This is a consequence of previous remarks; in this case low quality firms should be monitored more closely, and the ability of the SRO to condition its decisions on θ is socially advantageous.
2. Sellers are more homogeneous. This depends on the fact that the SRO maximizes the profits of its members; intuitively, the idea is that when the members' interests tend to coincide, its job is easier.

3. The observation lag is longer. In this case, consumers are less able to punish cheats by refusing to repeat the purchase, and so the role of SR and its ability to intervene taking θ into consideration become more important.

4. Demand is more elastic. This latter condition is easily understood, in that the SRO pursues profit maximization, and the output reduction is smaller when demand is more elastic.

Another model that addresses similar issues is the one by Gehrig and Jost (1995), where N producers operate in N separate markets (a device to by-pass the problem of competition among firms); in each market there is an identical number of potential consumers (normalized to 1). The structure of the game is the following. If t indicates time, in $t = 0$ firms decide their quality levels (q) that are known to all firms, but unknown to consumers; this choice cannot be reversed. In $t = 1$, consumers decide whether to buy one unit of the good or not to enter the market. Only after consumption do consumers become aware of the quality of the product they have consumed. Direct experience is the only means of learning. In $t = 2$ each consumer knows the quality of the good it has consumed. The market game is repeated, but with an important change: a proportion λ of consumers of each market 'migrates' to other markets (mobility from one firm to another); therefore, in each market we now have consumers who know the quality of the product, and others who have no experience of the product offered in their 'new' market.[28]

This highly stylized structure captures a few interesting elements. The first one is the mobility of consumers (the 'migration'). The second one is the relevance of reputation. The third one is the assumption that the learning process is imperfect, such that in period 2 each firm faces some consumers who 'know', but others who 'don't know'; therefore individual reputation is not the only thing that matters, and collective reputation acquires relevance. Unfortunately the proportion of mobile consumers is totally exogenous, and in particular it does not depend on how happy consumers are with their initial choice, that is on the behaviour of producers; this is probably the least acceptable assumption of the model.

Then the paper analyses SR, which is managed by an SRO, which declares that to accept as members all those producers who supply a good whose quality is at least equal to some minimum standard, q_{SR}, and perfectly monitors its members.

In the first period, consumers observe whether a firm is part of an SRO or not. If it is, they expect $q = q_{SR}$. Otherwise, they expect $q = q^*$, the individual profit maximizing level. Their demand for financial services and hence the price they pay depend on expected quality.

In $t = 2$, non-migrant consumers already know the quality provided by their supplier, and do not need anything else. On the other hand, migrants' expectations are partly determined by the reputation of the SRO. The crucial issues are (1) whether in period one their expectations on a SRO member proved to be correct and (2) in case an SRO member provided $q^* < q_{SR}$, what the reaction of the SRO was.

If no cheating occurred in period one, consumers will maintain their trust in the

SRO. If some consumers have been cheated but the SRO has not expelled the firm, they will lose their faith in the SRO, and will believe that the new firm will supply only quality q^*. This behaviour of the consumers gives complying firms an incentive to expel deviant firms; notice that this is purely a reputational effect, as the structure of the model assumes away any direct competition.[29]

Thus, SR functions if for each producer the incentive to expel deviant firms is large enough relative to the reward from cheating himself. This indicates that SR is 'feasible' when the mobility of consumers is large enough (so that the SRO's reputation is important to each 'obedient' firm) and when the number of firms is not too large; indeed, if N is very large the number of dissatisfied consumers will be excessively 'diluted',[30] in the sense that in $t = 2$ each firm will face a very small number of consumers coming from each other market, and the punishment of a specific deviant firm becomes less crucial. Notice that this way of reasoning resembles very closely the classic argument against competition in the production of public goods (Oakland 1987).

Another relatively straightforward result is that SR is likely to be preferable to regulation if the regulator's uncertainty about the firms' costs is substantial enough. In such a case, the strong point of SR would be a greater ability to observe firms' characteristics.

The difference between models with exogenous quality (Leland and Shaked–Sutton) and these models (where quality is a choice variable) is that here the strong result that the self-imposed MQS is set too high from a social viewpoint disappears. This is no surprise, in that if quality is costly we have a force operating in the opposite direction.

Which type of model is more relevant, however, is an open issue. If SR is introduced when the professional group is already in place, it is possible that quality levels were chosen a long time ago, so that at the time when SR begins they are given. Thus, the real question mark is to what extent quality choices of already established producers may or may not be changed.

As for the comparison between regulation and self-regulation, we are dealing with imperfect alternatives so that only with highly specific assumption is it possible to say something precise. The more relevant conditions for the 'feasibility' (or effectiveness) of SR are probably those emerging from the Gehrig and Jost (1995) paper, but even in their framework the comparison with standard regulatory schemes does not go much beyond the analytical proof of a fairly common intuition.[31]

4.3. Self-regulation in financial markets

Although not directly linked to the formal literature on SR, two more papers have particular relevance to the present discussion as they refer more directly to financial markets. The paper by Fischel and Grossman (1984) is probably the first one to develop (although very informally) the theme of SR in securities markets. Their analysis relies on a clear and almost dogmatic 'Chicago view' that customers are in principle perfectly able to defend themselves, despite the fact that informational problems are formidable ('those who are uninformed always have the ability to become informed', Fischel and

Grossman 1984, 289), and in particular that the measurability of the intermediaries' service is extremely difficult.[32]

In their view, the stock market naturally provides incentives to coordination, in that 'the ability of any single firm to attract customers depend on the overall quality of transaction services provided by the exchange' (p. 290). Thus, Fischel and Grossman argue that SR could be a natural answer to the problem of customer protection. This is because they assume that the exchange's interest is to maintain its reputation for fairness and thus to maximize the possibility of competition among intermediaries. Fischel and Grossman's answer to the problems of self-regulation is that if there is enough competition among exchanges, all attempts to restrain competition within a stock market will be self-defeating.

One problem is that we still know very little about how competition among markets takes place and what efficiency properties it has. Furthermore, the quality of a stock market largely depends on how many traders operate in it, which determines market liquidity; this implies that it is extremely difficult to challenge the leadership of a market (as long as many traders are there, many others will stick to it) even if the service provided by its intermediaries may not be satisfactory on other aspects. On the other hand, the common perception among practitioners is that competition among exchanges—at least within Europe—represents a substantial pressure over national markets. A deeper understanding of these processes will certainly facilitate an understanding of the proper role of national and supra-national regulatory approaches.[33]

A further problem with the Fischel and Grossman's set-up is that it is not clear who actually decides on regulation. Although they admit that the self-interest of individual members of the stock market might conflict with collective interest, their assumption is that such a problem 'is resolved by the members bargaining among themselves until a strategy that maximizes the sum of their wealth is achieved' (p. 293). This pseudo-answer is extremely unsatisfactory, in that—by ruling out *a priori* any inefficiency—it assumes away most interesting issues.[34]

The second paper with relevance to the issue under discussion is by Hart and Moore (1996), who model the stock market as a firm. They compare two different governance structures, the cooperative one (which seems very close to the idea of self-regulation) and some (not better determined) form of outside ownership. The output of the firm is the volume of transactions; on each transaction a price (intermediation fee) is paid and this decides the firm's income. The cooperative structure is assumed to have an informational advantage, in that monitoring of individuals' behaviour is assumed to be easier than in a profit maximizing firm.

Building on fairly standard (possibly, too standard) arguments of theory of the firm, they conclude that outside ownership is relatively better (i.e. more efficient) as the distribution of the members' characteristics becomes more skewed, and that it is preferable as the stock exchange faces more competition. The idea is that profit oriented firms are better able to reach efficient decisions when the interests of the cooperative members are highly diversified, and that they are better at facing competition than cooperatives. Hart and Moore's conclusion can be interpreted as saying that SR can work if the group of agents running the stock exchange is sufficiently cohesive, but that in the presence of increasing competition among exchanges a more profit-oriented management seems to guarantee a better performance.

The framework by Hart and Moore is a useful reference point, but it does not seem completely satisfactory. In the first place, if we have outside ownership (when the exchange is not controlled by intermediaries) we do not have the informational benefit of self-regulation, and there seems to be little guarantee that no outside regulation is needed. Furthermore, the analogy between a stock exchange and a firm is not completely convincing. Unlike a workers' cooperative, the income (and in general) the utility of the members does not only depend on the firm's performance and on individual effort, but also on competition among the members of the market. A stock exchange can be modelled as a cooperative firm only if workers' remuneration is determined on a competitive basis (on the basis of rather extreme relative incentive schemes); this is not true in general, however, and even less in workers' cooperatives. Thus the incentive structure we ought to consider is different, and should take into account the competition among intermediaries. To what extent and in what sense this might change the conclusions is an issue that at present is still unexplored.

4.4. Possible extensions of the present literature

What is missing from the present literature? The gap between theoretical models and application for policy purposes is often substantial, and it would be easy as well as uninteresting to point out the limitations of the stylized models we have analysed. However, (at least) a few points are worth mentioning.

Although several authors agree that financial services probably represent a case of credence good, the models on SR (even when they have financial markets in mind) introduce some assumptions on observability of quality that clearly contradict this opinion. This attitude could be justifiable on the grounds of the difficulty in dealing with credence goods, but seriously undermines some of the policy implications.

The definition of the incentives for the SRO to punish 'cheats' is still not satisfactory. So far, it has been assumed that an SRO will punish the deviant for fear of losing its reputation *vis-à-vis* the consumers. Although this is correct, we believe this is not the whole story. When the SRO punishes a member's behaviour, it makes public the fact that a member has kept a line of conduct that SRO members declare to refuse. In so doing, the SRO gives a signal to the market, in that it says something on what can be considered acceptable, and what cannot. The problem is that it cannot tell the market how far that member's 'actual' behaviour was from 'acceptable' behaviour; in other terms, investors, observing that one firm's behaviour, might revise (downward) their expectation of what other firms might be doing, that is of the *general practice* of the profession.

In a similar way, following Vickers (1991), one could argue that by informing all customers that a particular firm does certain things, the SRO informs all customers of what a member could hope to do without being detected or punished: 'exposure might be a negative signal about the average quality of remaining members' and 'a sign that the fraudulent member thought that vigilance was low enough for there to be a reasonable chance of getting away with it'. Thus, an SRO might have an incentive to cover-up deviations of its members for fear that public knowledge of such deviations might harm even its honest members.

In our view, a satisfactory representation of an SRO's incentives to intervene should comprehend both effects, representing the SRO's decisions as emerging from the attempt to strike a balance between (1) the risk that the information spreads anyway, which would damage the reputation of the SRO and (2) the risk that all SRO's members suffer from a reputational externality when the fraudulent behaviour of one member is made public. Furthermore, the issue of membership to an SRO and possibly of competition among different SROs should be paid more attention.[35] The two aspects are closely related. As for membership, there can be different cases, such as

1. (compulsory) membership of the SRO as a requirement for operating in the market (this is the implicit assumption in Leland (1979) and Shaked and Sutton (1981)); in this case, the SRO plays a semi-public role with relevant formal power;
2. optional membership, in which case the SRO simply guarantees the quality of member firms (as in Gehrig and Jost (1995)); here the SRO plays a relevant role with respect to consumers, but a firm can operate without being member;
3. obligation to join one of several competing SROs (as under 1);
4. possibility of joining one of several competing SROs (as under 2).

The implications of each arrangement are still largely unexplored terrain, and further analysis—although far from easy—would be extremely helpful to focus on the policy issues at stake.

5. Conclusions

We already pointed out in the introduction how difficult the application of theoretical principles can be. This is even more true in this case, as the contribution that economic theory can give so far to the analysis of self-regulation is still preliminary. Therefore, most of the present discussion of the results and of any attempt to draw some conclusions will have to bring together some carefully developed specific arguments, some arguments borrowed from other fields of economics, and at the same time indicate some directions for future research. We hope that this attempt will at least stimulate some further reflections on behalf of scholars who are better equipped to argue about institutional aspects of securities markets and their possible regulatory reforms.

At present, countries that traditionally relied very heavily on SR (e.g. the UK) are going in the direction of a re-balancing of powers, given the increasing dissatisfaction with the recent performance of SR. It is interesting to see that this is not a phenomenon peculiar to the UK or to financial markets;[36] many markets are probably becoming increasingly open to competition, and this seems to be in conflict with self-regulation.

The experience in Italy after unification[37] and in Britain during the last decades seems to suggest that SR may work as long as the group of agents exerting this power is relatively small and cohesive. The models by Mayer and Neven, Fletcher, Hart and Moore, and Gehrig and Jost, although for different reasons, all reach a common conclusion: SR is more difficult and less effective when it involves a large and heterogeneous group of agents. Liberalization entails a break-up of previous equilibria, and—at least at the beginning—an increase in the number of agents; given the already mentioned reputational externalities and the nature of the public good of SR, this increase in competition is likely to worsen the ability of intermediaries to keep control of the market. The recent move in Italian legislation towards a heavier reliance on SR when the European directive increases the number of intermediaries allowed to operate in Italy will certainly require great attention on behalf of stock market authorities.

Furthermore, situations in which reputation, and particularly *collective* reputation, matters typically lead to multiple equilibria: what agents do depend on what others do and expect, and so on. Knowing that there exist equilibria with certain features does not mean that other equilibria with less desirable properties do not exist. Where does the market go? How can we decide which equilibrium is more plausible?

Arguments borrowed from the theory of evolutionary games suggest that the starting point is crucial ('history matters') in that what agents do and expect now largely determines the relative profitability of different types of behaviour, and hence the direction in which the market is going to move. In other terms, when considering whether to give more room to SR, one should ask: given current features, habits and expectations of agents, is self-regulation likely to favour the agents who immediately accept the new rules? Or is the attitude of agents such that opportunistic behaviour is more likely to be rewarding and to prevail, pushing the 'snowball' in the wrong direction? Clearly, this has to do with the current 'culture' of agents on all sides of the market, and we cannot expect such culture to change promptly when a new regulatory regime is introduced. A gradual and cautious approach is thus preferable.

As for the allocation of competencies between SRO and the stock exchange authority,[38] the theory seems to indicate that delegating to the SRO the control of the criteria for the admission to the profession is not an enormous problem, as long as quality is endogenous.[39] As for the opportunity to give the SRO the control of market operations and functioning, the theory does not say much. To the extent that these operations are really 'neutral', financial intermediaries could well be fully in charge of market management, while in other cases involving representatives of other interest groups (e.g. listed firms, potentially listed firms, buyers) might be desirable.[40] When the direct representation of a category seems particularly difficult (e.g. small investors) the role of the public authority remains particularly important.[41] This is even more true in general, given the existing question marks on the incentives of an SRO to enforce its own rules.

As for investors' protection, theoretical models indicate a number of pros and cons but—not surprisingly—never provide a definite answer. SR might be a solution only if one believes quite firmly in the ability of the market to learn product quality within a reasonable time, on the ability of investors and of the SRO to effectively punish deviations and thus discourage such behaviour. We cannot conceal a substantial scepticism on these points, which again induces us to stress the relevance of maintaining some public supervision over the SRO.

What type of power should an SRO be given? The question is not banal, in that one of the advantages of SR is the possibility of intervening in 'not-so-formal' ways that a public body would not be able to use. But endowment of formal power and ability to use informal procedures are difficult to reconcile.

In many cases, it might be helpful to have a form of SR that operates with the support of state sanctions,[42] a useful solution, which however raises problems of accountability; this is another crucial and in practice extremely delicate issue, in that the control over the operations of the SRO must be sufficient to ensure fairness, but must not be so heavy as to neutralize self-regulation.[43] Moreover, the existence of multi-tier regulation has problematic aspects. In the first place, when there are overlapping competencies it might be difficult to identify actual responsibilities, which represents a major risk. Furthermore, having different hierarchical levels might be justifiable, but it entails the cost implicit in any complex agency relationship.

However, every time an SRO is endowed with formal power, its ability to use informal procedures is probably substantially reduced. If this is the case, its advantage on external regulation gets very small, and it might be worth considering the possibility of favouring the formation of professional associations which simply certify the quality of their members without much formal power. In this case, having different competing organizations would seem to be a preferable solution.

A closely related point is to determine when it is more appropriate to rely on a complete self-determination of rules or rather the self-management of publicly decided rules. In the case of state-sanctioned SR, we often see systems which work on the self-management of rules set from above, and the actual power of the SRO depends on the degree of 'incompleteness' of the general norm. In turn this partially depends on a decision by the policymaker, sometimes on exogenous conditions (e.g. observability, predictability of states of the world, etc.).

The historian Braudel introduces a distinction between public and private markets. In the present context, we can say that public markets are those where buyers and sellers meet within a public framework (regulation), while private ones are those where professional intermediaries manage the transactions. Braudel also claims that the latter type tends to favour 'asymmetric exchanges' where capital accumulation is spurred. Basically, both the limited theoretical results and reflections on history indicate that public regulation emphasizes guarantees and fairness, while private control (and possibly self-regulation) tend to favour high (but risky) returns and capital accumulation.

This trade-off can hardly be escaped, as we have tried to argue, and the choice of the regulatory regime probably depends on a more or less implicit evaluation of what a country needs in a certain moment. For instance, given the current underdevelopment of the Italian stock market, probably the main worry should be to attract investors and firms, that so far have not trusted the stock market. It is hard to see how a heavy reliance on self-regulation could serve this purpose.

Notes

I would like to thank L. Caprio, M. Da Rin, G. Ferrarini, G. Galli, G. Nicodano, two referees and the participants to a Consob conference in Milan for helpful comments on an earlier draft. The usual, obvious, disclaimer applies.

1. One topic that we will barely touch is whether we actually need so much regulation in financial markets. As we stress in the next section, quality regulation is not always needed, and the impression that some aspects of financial markets are over-regulated is not ill founded.
2. Furthermore, the quality of service depends on the 'quality of the market', its organization, its functioning, the conditions of competition among intermediaries, listing procedures, and so on. Whether any of these matters should be left to self-regulation is also an important point. Although we will not directly address this issue in the formal analysis, we will try and go back to it in the concluding section.
3. Notice that this also depends on the extent to which monopoly entails a restriction in output relative to its welfare maximizing level (Spence 1975).
4. In particular, a detailed analysis of the equilibrium in models with more than two firms is quite complex without introducing specific assumptions on technology and income distribution; unfortunately, when more than two firms are present, some well-known results can be reversed.
5. See Suzumura and Kiyono (1987).
6. Stiglitz (1994) correctly stresses how asymmetric information should be considered the normal reference point, while situations of complete and symmetric information should be treated as highly 'special'.
7. See Nelson (1970) and Darby and Karni (1973). The distinction between these categories is not as clear cut as the definition might suggest. A search might be possible, but in practice is too costly. Personal experience does not help unless purchase is sufficiently frequent; other consumers' viewpoints are irrelevant when tastes are not correlated. Some degree of uncertainty over a good's (objective) quality is probably always present even after consumption, so that the distinction between 'experience' and 'credence' goods is more a matter of how much uncertainty consumption can really dissipate. To say the least, the application of this taxonomy will require considerable care.
8. Notice that this can be either through personal experience or—in certain cases—through 'word of mouth'.
9. Tirole (1988) points out that equilibria are not even efficient in the sense of constrained Pareto efficiency, i.e. given the distribution of information among individuals.
10. Several authors—quite rightly, in our view—agree in classifying financial services as credence goods (e.g. Mayer and Neven 1991, Gehrig and Jost 1995).
11. Jun and Vives (1996).
12. In line with this conclusion, see Tirole (1988).
13. This is obviously a weak point, in that the existence of informational problems is known as the source of market power (Arrow 1973), so that talking of perfect competition with informational asymmetries is somehow a contradiction in terms. Unfortunately, an analysis of oligopolistic competition with asymmetric information is not yet available.
14. Many other contributions are not reviewed here, both because this is not the centre of our

analysis, and because the qualitative conclusions one can reach (in the direction we are interested in) would not be affected by enriching the list of references.

15. Notice that this contrasts with Leland's (1979) definition, which considers a direct output regulation through a minimum quality standard (on output quality).

16. Notice that producers simply choose whether to produce high or low quality goods, but these quality levels are exogenous. What is endogenous is only the number of producers who decide to provide each quality level. Thus, the only effect of these interventions is to affect the product mix supplied, and not to affect quality levels as such. As there is no competition in quality levels, we do not observe any of the previously mentioned effects.

17. These authors distinguish between strict liability, which fully insures consumers, and a no-negligence rule, which requires a firm to compensate consumers only if it can be shown that firms did not exert 'sufficient' care in providing their service.

18. The conclusion that seems to emerge is thus, that the law should be strong against the weak, and weak against the strong. Although formally correct, one wonders to what extent such principle can really be implemented.

19. Last, but not least, as regulation has a cost, SR has the advantage of internalizing this cost, and probably the ability to minimize it. Unfortunately, so far this aspect is absent from the theoretical literature.

20. Early empirical studies of quality self-regulation in trade associations, the farm machinery industry, the computer industry and entertainment television can be found in Caves and Roberts (1975).

21. Thus, unlike Leland (1979), the opportunity cost of producing in sector A is independent of quality. Notice that this entails a *loss* of generality.

22. Scarpa (1998) shows how this assumption may not hold when quality levels are chosen by the producers and are not given.

23. Notice that when quality levels are endogenous and information is symmetric the average quality of the product does not necessarily increase with the MQS (Scarpa 1998).

24. Furthermore, the assumption that the SRO works as a cooperative means that the tendency to reduce output is stronger than in Leland's model; however, this assumption is probably more plausible than joint profit maximization.

25. We refer to Fletcher (1993) for several criticisms on this part.

26. An action may be observable by some people but not 'verifiable', when a third party—e.g. a court—cannot find sufficient evidence on what has been done. Usually, formal legal procedures require the latter, more stringent feature.

27. The reason is that the price paid is in line with the intrinsic quality of the seller, and consumers would have been willing to pay zero for a zero quality product.

28. The distribution of 'migrants' to other markets is such, that the number of potential consumers in each market remains constant: a number $\lambda/(N-1)$ of consumers goes from market 1 to each other market, and so on.

29. In a way, this mechanism anticipates the idea of collective reputation, later introduced by Tirole (1996).

30. In period 2 each firm (in particular, those belonging to the SRO) 'receives' $\lambda/(N-1)$ consumers coming from each other market.

31. To compare the different alternatives, one other possibility would be to generalize the framework suggested by Shapiro and Willig (1990) in the attempt to compare regulation and privatization, but even their set-up does not seem terribly promising.

32. We have already stressed how many authors agree on considering financial services as

credence goods, i.e. goods whose quality may remain unknown to the customer even after purchase. In this situation even greater information acquisition is not very valuable, and the ability of customers to monitor intermediaries is limited. This possibility is never mentioned by these authors.

33. A first step in this direction is the paper by Gehrig (1998).

34. The problem of customer protection is usually seen as a problem of guaranteeing 'fair trade', but the definition of 'fairness' itself is not easily provided. Grossman (1986) insists that 'fair trading is trading which is volume enhancing'. If we accept this definition, self-regulation can be optimal in that intermediaries are (*ceteris paribus*) interested in increasing the volume of trade. Of course, however, there is a potential free-riding problem, in that if an intermediary 'cheats', he enjoys the profit of his activity, but does not bear the whole cost, in that he runs the risk of reducing the *global* volume of trade. This externality, pointed out by Gehrig and Jost, might seriously hinder the possibility of reaching an agreement among intermediaries.

35. Fletcher (1993) provides a first attempt to model this important aspect.

36. Moran and Wood (1993) stress how a similar problem is emerging in Germany with the SR of the medical profession.

37. Baia Curioni (1995) gives a good account of the history of Italian securities markets since unification in 1861. Self-regulation was an important feature of that system until Fascism.

38. We believe we can take for granted that not everything can be delegated to the SRO. Notice that in other sectors as well (e.g. the medical profession; see Moran and Wood 1993) whenever some SRO is involved, there are other agents that intervene in regulating the market. In some cases the 'countervailing power' is not a public one, but—especially in the USA—it is an organization representing interests conflicting with those of the SRO (e.g. doctors vs. insurance companies, in the specific case of the health sector).

39. A common feature of SR systems even in other contexts is that entry regulation is typically quite formal, while other aspects of regulation are tackled in a much more informal way, probably as they are less easy to tackle than a simple in-or-out decision (Moran and Wood 1993).

40. The control of competitive practices is probably one of the more delicate points in this respect.

41. The direct representation of other interests is particularly relevant in systems where the protection provided by the legal system is weak (e.g. remember the outrageous length of time most legal cases need in Italy before their settlement). This is even more important with respect to small investors, with less bargaining power and worse information.

42. Moran and Wood (1993) call this situation a 'state-sanctioned SR', pointing out how sometimes this form of distribution of power developed out of independent 'pure' SR systems, that often face serious problems of control.

43. We are perfectly aware that the practical application of this principle is far from obvious.

References

Akerlof, G. (1970) 'The Market for Lemons', *Quarterly Journal of Economics*, 84: 488–500.

Arrow, K. J. (1973) 'Information and Economic Behaviour', mimeo, reprinted in Arrow, K. J. (1984), *The Economics of Information*. Oxford: Basil Blackwell.

Baia Curioni, S. (1995) *Regolazione e competizione: storia del mercato azionario in Italia (1808–1938)*. Bologna: Il Mulino.

Becker, G. (1983) 'A Theory of Competition among Pressure Groups for Political Influence', *Quarterly Journal of Economics*, 98: 371–400.

Caves, R. and Roberts, M. (eds.) (1975) *Regulating the Product: Quality and Variety*. Cambridge, MA: Ballinger.

Darby, M. and Karni, E. (1973) 'Free Competition and the Optimal Amount of Fraud', *Journal of Law and Economics*, 16: 67–88.

Fischel, D. and Grossman, S. (1984) 'Customer Protection in Futures and Securities Markets', *Journal of Futures Markets*, 4: 273–95.

Fletcher, A. (1993) 'Theories of Self-Regulation', unpublished D.Phil. Thesis, Nuffield College, Oxford University.

Gehrig, T. (1998) 'Competing Markets', *European Economic Review*, 42: 277–310.

Gehrig, T. and Jost, P. (1995) 'Quacks, Lemons, and Self-Regulation: A Welfare Analysis', *Journal of Regulatory Economics*, 7: 309–25.

Grossman, S. (1986) 'Analysis of the Role of "Insider Trading" on the Futures Market', *Journal of Business*, 59: S129–S146.

Grossman, S. and Stiglitz, J. (1980) 'On the Impossibility of Informationally Efficient Markets', *American Economic Review*, 70: 461–84.

Hart, O. and Moore, J. (1996) 'The Governance of Exchanges: Members' Cooperatives versus Outside Ownership', *Oxford Review of Economic Policy*, 12: 53–69.

Jun, B. and Vives, X. (1996) 'Learning and Convergence to a Full-Information Equilibrium are not Equivalent', *Review of Economic Studies*, 63: 653–74.

Klein, B. and Leffler, K. (1981) 'The Role of Market Forces in Assuring Contractual Performance', *Journal of Political Economy*, 89: 615–41.

Leland, H. (1979) 'Quacks, Lemons, and Licensing: A Theory of Minimum Quality Standards', *Journal of Political Economy*, 87: 1328–46.

Mayer, C. and Neven, D. (1991) 'European Financial Regulation: A Framework for Policy Analysis', in Giovannini, A. and Mayer, C. (eds.), *European Financial Integration*. Cambridge: Cambridge University Press.

Moran, M. and Wood, B. (1993) *States, Regulation and the Medical Profession*. Buckingham: Open University Press.

Nelson, P. (1970) 'Information and Consumer Behaviour', *Journal of Political Economy*, 78: 311–29.

Oakland, W. (1987) 'Theory of Public Goods', in Auerbach, A. and Feldstein, M. (eds.), *Handbook of Public Economics*. Amsterdam: North-Holland.

Polinsky, M. and Rogerson, W. (1983) 'Products Liability, Consumer Misperception and Market Power', *Rand Journal of Economics*, 14: 581–9.

Ronnen, U. (1991) 'Minimum Quality Standard, Fixed Costs and Competition', *Rand Journal of Economics*, 22: 490–504.

Scarpa, C. (1998) 'Minimum Quality Standards with More than Two Firms', *International Journal of Industrial Organization*, 16: 665–76.

Shaked, A. and Sutton, J. (1981) 'The Self-Regulating Profession', *Review of Economic Studies*, 48: 217–34.

Shaked, A. and Sutton, J. (1983) 'Natural Oligopolies', *Econometrica*, 51: 1469–83.

Shapiro, C. (1983) 'Premiums for High Quality Products as Rents to Reputation', *Quarterly Journal of Economics*, 98: 659–80.

Shapiro, C. (1986) 'Investment, Moral Hazard and Occupational Licensing', *Review of Economic Studies*, 53: 843–62.

Shapiro, C. and Willig, R. (1990) 'Economic Rationales for the Scope of Privatization', Discussion Paper, Department of Economics, Princeton.

Shavell, S. (1984) 'A Model of the Optimal use of Liability and Safety Regulation', *Rand Journal of Economics*, 15: 271–80.

Spence, M. (1975) 'Monopoly, Quality and Regulation', *Bell Journal of Economics*, 6: 417–29.

Stigler, G. (1971) 'The Theory of Economic Regulation', *Bell Journal of Economics*, 2: 3–21.

Stiglitz, J. (1988) 'Imperfect Information in the Product Market', in Schmalensee, R. and Willig, R. (eds.), *Handbook of Industrial Organization*, vol. 1. Amsterdam: North-Holland.

Stiglitz, J. (1994) *Whither Socialism?* Cambridge, MA: MIT Press.

Suzumura, K. and Kiyono, K. (1987) 'Entry Barriers and Economic Welfare', *Review of Economic Studies*, 54: 157–67.

Tirole, J. (1988) *The Theory of Industrial Organization*. Cambridge, MA: MIT Press.

Tirole, J. (1996) 'A Theory of Collective Reputations (with Applications to the Persistence of Corruption and to Firm Quality)', *Review of Economic Studies*, 63: 1–22.

Vickers, J. (1991) 'Discussion of Mayer and Neven', in Giovannini, A. and Mayer, C. (eds.), *European Financial Integration*. Cambridge: Cambridge University Press.

Index

abatement costs, marginal 215
abatement effort 220
accelerated declining support hypothesis 69
access, conditions of 238
accountancy, *see* barriers to entry: accountancy in
   Italy
admission
   entry 148
   policies 138
   rates 8, 132, 146–7, 150–1, 153–4
adverse selection 108, 159–60, 237, 239, 245, 247
advertising 110, 240
   restrictions 100, 103–4, 106–7, 114–15, 117, 122
Africa 54
after-tax allocations 37
age-earning profiles 141–3, 148
agents 32–3, 41, 42, 43–4, 46
Akerlof-type model 245
Alpine Investment case 107
American Medical Association 131
anagraphic variables 148
ANCITEL 134
anti-competitive effects 132, 218, 229
anti-trust
   authorities 104, 131, 154
   control 105
   laws 229
   scrutiny 101, 102, 106
architects 134
Archivio delle Professioni 133
Articles, *see* European Community Treaty
Asia–Pacific 54
assets 185, 186, 187, 188, 191, 192, 203, 208
association rights 21
asymmetric information 120, 146, 150, 161
   medical and legal professions 108, 110, 114, 115,
     117, 118, 119, 120
   quality regulation and financial markets 237,
     239–42, 243, 244, 245

bandwagon effect 187
Bank of Italy 134
Bar Association 122
baricentric scenario 192–7, 198, 201
barriers to entry: accountancy in Italy 131–55
   admission rates for professional examinations
     143–5
   age-earning profiles 141–3
   Commercialisti 145–8; demand and supply
     model 145–7; endogenous barriers 147–8

empirical results 148–53
entry and profitability of local market 139–41
income distribution 137–9
regional distribution 135–9
trends 133–5
Bayes–Nash equilibrium concept 161
behavioural types 185, 186, 190, 191, 192
Belgium 52, 64
   Arbitration Court 105
   medical and legal professions 89, 92, 99, 104–5,
     114, 115–16, 121
Bertrand equilibrium 167
bias 21–2; *see also* ideological bias
bloc size 57
boards 149–50
bootstrap equilibria 241
boycotting 102
British Code of Advertising Practice 104
Broekmeulen case 92
Brussels Tariff Nomenclature (BTN) 64, 65
business structure rules 100

Canada 114, 213
capital
   deepening 55, 56, 73, 74
   –labour endowment ratio 56
   losses 111
   requirement 247
cartels 105, 245
cautious cooperation 197, 199, 201, 203; *see also*
   cooperative screeners
certification 90, 118–19, 120, 243
   capacity 171, 172
   cost 166, 168, 172, 173
   fee 162, 167, 168, 169, 171, 174
   markets, *see* imperfect competition in
     certification markets
certifiers' liability 170, 173
Chamber of Architects 102
'Chambers' 89
cheating 247–8, 249, 250, 252
Circular A–128 158
civil law tradition 98
civil servants 143
coalition size 113
Coasian bargaining 209
Coasians 207, 208
coercion 17, 113
Cohen Commission 112
cold calling 107

Colegio Oficial de Agentes de la Propriedad Industrial 106
collective action 17, 25
collective decision-making 32, 37, 46
Commercialisti 132, 133, 134, 135, 151, 153, 154
  admission rates for professional examinations 144
  age-earning profiles 141, 142, 143
  entry and profitability of local market 139, 140
  income distribution 137, 138
  market for 145–8
  regional distribution 136, 137
Commission v France 100
common external protection 60
common external tariff 51, 53, 68, 72, 73, 74, 75
  endogenous 52
  endogenous regionalism 54, 55, 56, 57
  endogenous tariff creation/diversion with trade bloc formation 62, 63
  lobbying 59
  trade creation/diversion versus tariff creation/diversion 58
common law tradition 98
Communal State 16
company codes 219–21, 223, 225, 230
comparative advantage 47, 59, 73
compensation effect 55, 56, 57, 69
competition 59, 193, 252, 253, 254
  accountancy in Italy 146, 147, 150, 153, 154
  between interest groups 35–40
  electoral rules and interest groups 31, 32, 36, 37, 42
  import 57, 58, 63, 69, 73
  inter-professional 123
  law 90, 101–6; EC law 105–6; France 102–3; Germany 101–2; Italy, Belgium and Netherlands 104–5; United Kingdom 103–4
  market 243, 244
  medical and legal professions 91, 110, 111, 117, 121
  perfect 172
  pollution: market structure and consumer information 218, 225, 228, 230
  quality regulation and financial markets 252, 253, 254
  restrictions 105, 122
  settings 26
  stock markets 251
  see also imperfect competition
Competition Council 105
completion value 183–4, 188, 196, 197, 199, 201
compliance 161, 162, 168, 169, 173, 180, 206
  and attestation audits 158
  costs 160–1, 162, 164, 166, 167
  incentives 207, 209
  with relevant rules 158
  threshold 170
  see also voluntary compliance
conformity assessment 158

Consiglio nazionale degli spedizionieri doganali 106
constitutional constraints 31, 37
constitutional rules 2–3, 4, 47
constitutions 4
consumer 207
  demand 209–14
  information 206, 225, 231
  information, *see* pollution
  knowledge 224, 225, 229
  participation 122
  surplus 170, 171, 225, 230
consumption 62, 63, 65, 210
continuation value 192, 193, 194, 199, 201
continuity and novelty in political history 15–16
cooperation 45–7, 245, 251, 252
  cautious 183, 184
  conditional 181, 182
  externalities 186, 187, 188, 191, 193, 196–7
  trust under endogenous transaction costs 179–83, 187, 192–5, 199–200, 203
  unconditional 183, 184
  see also cautious cooperation; cooperative screeners; pure cooperators
cooperative screeners 185, 186, 188, 189, 194, 196, 197, 199, 201
coordination 179, 208, 221–4
corporatist bias 21
cost–benefit analysis 118
country size 55, 68, 73
Cournot
  analysis 166
  equilibrium 167, 173–4, 220
  oligopoly 38
Cournot–Nash competitors 219
Cournot–Nash equilibrium 221
Courts and Legal Services Act 1990 90
credence goods 115, 240, 252
cumulative pollutants 213, 218, 223, 225, 226, 227, 230, 234
customs unions 51–2, 54–9*passim*, 62, 63

damage
  costs 219
  curve 212, 213, 215, 216, 218
  function 210, 211
Dassonville, Cassis de Dijon 96
dead-weight costs 31
decentralized bargaining 208, 209
defectionists 182, 183, 203
  basic model 184, 185, 186, 187
  results 191, 192, 193, 194, 196, 199, 201
  social dynamics 188, 189
demand 31, 32, 162, 187, 249
  accountancy in Italy 132, 135, 145–7, 148, 150, 153
  for certification 164
  constrained 165
  curve 159, 168, 211–13, 215–18, 221–3
  elasticity 218
  equation 150

externality 222
  function 146, 166, 173, 174, 238
  generation 108
  lobbies 24–5
  market 163
  pollution: market structure and consumer information 213, 214, 216, 230
  trust under endogenous transaction costs 188, 192
  unconstrained 165
Denmark 64, 66
deregulation movement 90, 118
detection
  costs 162, 168–9, 170, 171, 173
  effort 163, 164
  probability 168, 169, 171
  rate 167, 169
diplomas 92, 93–5
Directive
  75/362 (mutual recognition of medical qualifications) 92, 93–4
  75/363 (training requirements) 94
  77/249 (provision of services) 94–5
  77/2489 (representation) 95
  89/48 99
  98/5 95, 97–8, 99
  on mutual recognition of higher education diplomas 93, 94, 98
  right of establishment 118
Director's Law 21
disclosure policy 159–60
distributive justice considerations 106
divide and rule pattern 17
doctors, *see* medical and legal professions

earning differential 132
economic development 138
economic institutions 1
economic policymaking 3
economic rents 132, 150
economies of scale 59
education programmes 113
educational requirements 133, 141; *see also* examinations
efficiency 9
electoral competition 32, 36, 37
electoral constituencies 22
electoral equilibrium 41–2, 44, 46
electoral rules and interest groups: direct and indirect taxation 24, 30–49
  background literature 31–2
  basic model 32–40
  competition between interest groups 35–40
electoral competition 33–5
  cooperative setting 45–7
  non-cooperative setting 42–5
  regulated setting 40–2
emission control input 210, 212, 215–25*passim*, 230
employment 66

EN standards 158
endogenous barriers to entry 147–8
endogenous quality levels 247–50
endogenous regionalism and free-trade bias 51–81
  data 63–6; concentration 66; tariffs 64–5; trade creation and trade diversion 65–6
  empirical results 74–5
  endogenous tariff creation/diversion with trade bloc formation 61–3
  endogenous tariff with endogenous free-riding 60–1
  European Economic Community formation 54–7
  literature review 52–4
  preliminary estimation results 67–74; tariff creation estimates 73; tariff diversion estimates 72–3; terms of trade estimates and endowment effects 73–4
  trade creation/diversion versus tariff creation/diversion 57–60
endogenous tariff 7, 56, 57, 60–1
endogenous transaction costs, *see* trust
endowment effects 55, 73–4
enforcement strategy 159, 160
engineers 134
entry barriers 115, 122, 160
Envelope Theorem 222
environmental damage 224, 225, 230; *see also* pollution
environmental preferences 209–10
environmental self-regulation 9
equilibrium 174
  Bayes–Nash 161
  Bertrand 167
  bootstrap 241
  electoral 41–2, 44, 46
  full coverage 168, 169
  general 7, 246
  market 159, 162
  mixed-strategy 51
  multiple 254
  partial coverage 168, 169, 170, 171
  price 159
  tax rates 46
ethical rules 92, 100–1, 106–8, 110, 114–17, 120, 122
Europe 5, 7, 21, 251
European Commission 94, 100, 104, 105–6
European Community concentration index 7
European Community Treaty 91, 101, 117, 118
  Article 30 (free movement of goods) 90, 96, 106, 107, 117
  Article 52 (freedom of establishment) 90, 92, 93, 96, 97, 99, 100
  Article 57 93
  Article 59 (freedom to provide services) 90, 91, 92, 94, 96, 100, 106–7, 117
  Article 85 101, 105, 106
  Article 86 101, 105

European Court of Justice 90, 92, 95–6, 99–100, 104, 106–7, 117, 121
European Customs Union 61
European Eco-Management and Audit Scheme (EMAS) 158
European Economic Community formation 54–7
European Economic Community Industrial Classification (NACE) 64, 65
European Free Trade Area 54
European Free Trade Association 65
evaluation procedures 144
evolutionary game theory 9, 181, 189, 241, 254
examinations 134, 154
exogenous quality levels 245–7
expenditure taxation 36, 41, 47
experience goods 240–1
explicit opportunists 192, 193, 194, 196, 197, 199, 201
   basic model 185, 186, 187
   social dynamics 188, 189
exploitation scenario 192, 197, 199–202, 203
exports 59, 72, 73
   intensity variable 69, 72
externality 108–9, 110, 118, 119, 120, 187
   effect 206, 207, 220, 227
   problem, alternative solutions to 207–9

Faculty of Economics 143
Fair Trading Act 103
fairness 9
Federal Supreme Court 102
fees 102–3, 104
   regulation 100, 103, 109, 114, 115, 120, 122–3
financial audits 160
financial markets 237, 250–2
fines 247–8
first-past-the-post 24
fiscal burden 37
fiscal constraint 36
fiscal equilibrium 37, 41, 42, 44, 46, 47
fiscal rules 37
fixed costs 239
Flawed State 16, 17
France 180
   endogenous regionalism and free trade bias 52, 63, 64, 66, 72
   medical and legal professions 89, 97, 100, 102–3, 116
   Paris Bar Council 102–3
fraudulent behaviour 248, 253; *see also* cheating
free movement of capital 96
free movement of goods (Article 30 EC Treaty) 90, 96, 106, 107, 117
free movement of persons 96
free trade
   areas 52, 54, 55, 57, 58
   bias 56
   see also endogenous regionalism and free-trade bias
freedom of choice 119

freedom of establishment (Article 52 EC Treaty) 90, 92, 93, 96, 97, 99, 100
freedom of settlement 133
freedom to provide services (Article 59 EC Treaty) 90, 91, 92, 94, 96, 100, 106–7, 117
free-riding 113, 114, 241, 242
   electoral rules and interest groups 39, 40, 47
   endogenous regionalism and free-trade bias 51–4, 58, 60–3, 69, 70, 73
   political institutions as screening devices 16, 17, 18
   pollution: market structure and consumer information 207, 208, 220, 223–4, 225
full coverage equilibrium 168, 169
functional lines 22

gatekeepers 8, 159, 160
Gebhard case 95–6, 97
General Agreement on Tariffs and Trade 64, 68, 73, 74
   Article XXIV 58
   Kennedy Round 67
general equilibrium model 7, 246
General Medical Council 104
geographical constituencies 22
Germany 52, 56, 89, 92, 96, 97, 99, 100, 116
   Berlin Court of Appeal 102
   Chamber of Pharmacists 106
   competition law 101–2
globalization 52
goods case law 106
governance structure 206
government intervention 122, 207, 208
grandfather clauses 116
Greece 64
Greenpeace 213
group utility function 45
growth rates 135, 137
guarantees 9, 203
Guidelines of the Bar 105
Gullung case 96–7

Harberger triangles 112
Hausman test 73, 77, 150
Herfindahl index 64, 66, 67, 69, 72, 73
hidden action 237
hidden information 237
High Court 104
higher education 141
horizontal exchanges 23, 24–5
human capital 142, 145, 150
Hünermund case 90, 106

ideology/ideological 19, 20, 23
   bias 33–4, 35
   lines 22
   syntax 22, 26
imperfect competition 206, 207, 220, 227; *see also* imperfect competition in certification markets

imperfect competition in certification markets
158–75
Cournot equilibrium, derivation of 173–4
equilibrium properties 167–9; certifiers' liability
168; certifiers, number of 167–8; detection
cost 168–9; private benefit 169
model 160–7
policy analysis 170–2
imports 56, 59, 65, 66, 68, 73
competition 57, 58, 63, 69, 73
duties 64
protection policy 72
incentive-based rules 208
income 116, 144, 145, 146, 147, 148, 149, 150
classes 139
distribution 137–9, 142
levels 153
taxation 41
industry
associations 5, 207, 209, 221–2, 223
codes 209, 221–4, 227, 230
concentration 64, 70, 73
decline 69
markets 237
production and abatement costs 219
information
consumer 225, 231
costs 26
issue 17
lack 109
measures 118
provision 113
symmetric 242
technology 180
see also asymmetric information
INPS 133
institutional
architecture 26
arrangements 206
effects 39, 43, 44, 45
framework 31–2
rules 6, 19, 47
interest-groups 53; *see also* electoral rules and
interest groups
intermediation fee 251
internal export ratio 69
internal imports ratio 69
inter-professional competition 123
intra-professional transfers 116
investment 184, 186, 187, 188, 189, 192, 243
costs 185
specific 182
Ireland 64, 66
ISO 14001 158
ISTAT 134
Italy 16, 89, 92, 96, 121, 180, 254
competition law 104–5
electoral results 22
endogenous regionalism and free-trade bias 52,
56, 63, 64, 66, 72

pharmacies 21
public procurements 236
stock market 237, 241, 255
see also barriers to entry: accountancy in Italy

judgment-proof problem 110, 161

Keck case 106, 107
Klopp case 100
Kraus case 96

labour adjustment costs 67
Law Society 104, 112
leaders' opportunism 17
Legal Aid 104
legal enforcement system 203
legal profession, *see* medical and legal professions
legislative process 30, 32
liability
expected 162–3
rules 109, 110, 243, 244
licensing 119–20, 121, 122, 132, 243
linear utility function 40
lobbying 55, 56, 61, 62, 72, 73, 113, 114
common external tariff 59
free-riding 60
opportunity costs 69
protectionist 63
tariff 57
Lord Chancellor's Advisory Committee on Legal
Education 122
loyalty links 22
loyalty trap 20, 24
Luxembourg 52, 64

mandatory regulation 206, 209, 224, 226, 227, 228,
229, 230
marginal abatement costs 215
marginal production cost 216, 224
marginal valuation of quality 238
mark-up prices 217
market
competition 243, 244
demand 163
equilibrium 159, 162
failure 206, 208, 236, 238–42
power 207, 217, 218, 220, 224, 225, 229, 230,
243
regulation 244
structure, *see* pollution
medical and legal professions: barriers to
competition and legislation 89–127, 134
access to professions, rules regarding 91–100;
diplomas 93–5; nationality discrimination
92–3; professional titles and compulsory
membership of professional bodies 95–9;
second office 99–100
conduct, rules regarding 100–7; competition
law 101–6; freedom to provide services
106–7

medical and legal professions (*cont.*):
  economic analysis 108–16; self-regulation and private interests, pursuit of 111–16; self-regulation and public interest 108–11
  legal and economic approaches combined: proportionality requirement 117–21
Middle East 54
migration (mobility of consumers) 249, 250
minimum quality standard 242–3, 245, 246, 250
Ministry of Finance 134
mixed-strategy equilibrium 51
monitoring 179, 181, 182, 183, 185, 192, 196, 199
  costs 36, 180, 186–7, 188, 189, 191
Monopolies and Mergers Commission 103
monopoly 112, 116, 146, 216, 218, 238, 246
  price 217
  rents 153
  rights abolition 90
moral hazard 109, 159, 160, 237, 247–50
Most Favoured Nation 64, 65
multiple equilibria 254
mutiplicity problem 241
mutual recognition principle 121

NACE 64, 65
Nash equilibrium 35, 38–9, 40, 191
National Health bill 21
nationality 91–3
Netherlands 52, 64
  Dutch General Practitioners Registration Committee 92
  medical and legal professions 89, 90, 104–5, 107, 112, 114, 116
  Order of Attorneys 120–1
new institutional economics 4
non-compliance 163–4, 167, 168, 169, 170, 171, 173
non-cooperation 42–5, 46, 47
non-cumulative pollutants 213, 225, 227, 229, 230, 234
North American Free Trade Agreement 53, 54

Office of Fair Trading 103–4
Official Journal of the European Communities 64
oligopoly 159, 173, 224, 229, 239, 242, 243
opportunists 25, 187; *see also* explicit opportunists; subtle opportunists
opportunity costs 245, 246–7
  accountancy in Italy 135, 138, 146
  endogenous regionalism and free-trade bias 55, 56, 72, 73
  lobbying 69
  trust under endogenous transaction costs 182, 184, 185, 187
optimal disclosure rule 160
optimal output choice 217
Order of Architects 103
Order of Attorneys 105, 112
Order of Dentists 103

Order of Pharmacists 103
'Orders' 89, 104, 121
organizational effect 39, 43, 44, 45, 46
organized interests 5
output 210, 212, 214, 215, 219, 221, 225, 230
  choice 224
  decision rule 222
  effect, indirect 223
  levels 220
outside ownership 251, 252

parallel markets 201, 203
Pareto
  efficiency 9
  improvement 208
  optimality 208, 219
  superiority 58
partial coverage equilibrium 168, 169, 170, 171
payoffs 188, 189, 190, 192, 193, 194, 203
pension schemes 113
Pigovians 207, 208, 209
pledge bias 21
policy suppliers 17
politics/political 57, 58
  economy 1–4
  exchange 23
  institutions as screening devices 1, 6, 15–28; continuity and novelty in political history 15–16; horizontal exchanges and demand lobbies 17, 18, 24–5; political information 25–7; political parties, rise and decline of 22–4; public action 17–18; structural features 18–20; vertical dimension of politics 17, 18, 20–2
  macroeconomics 3
  preferences 31
pollutant type 233; *see also* cumulative; non-cumulative
polluter pays principle 208
pollution: market structure and consumer information 206–35
  algebraic example 218–24; coordinated industry equilibrium: industry code 221–4; social optimum 219; uncoordinated industry equilibrium: company codes 219–21
  consumer information role 206, 225, 231
  externality problem, alternative solutions to 207–9
  graphical analysis 209–18; environmental preferences and consumer demand 209–10; industrial incentives to adopt voluntary codes 216–18; industrial pollution abatement and consumer demand 210–12; pollutant type and consumer knowledge impact on consumer demand 213–14; socially optimal pollution control 214–15
  market structure role 224, 225, 229, 230, 232, 243
  pollutant type role 233
  simulation analysis 224–9

pollution
  abatement 206, 207
  byproducts 206
  discharges 230
production function 210–11
population changes 242
pressure groups 26
pretended invisibility bias 21
price 236
  agreements 102
  cap 159
  competition 160
  –cost margin 63, 66, 247
  fixing 102, 104, 106
  recommendations 102
  regulation 170
principal–agent problem 108, 110
prior approval 119, 120, 121
prisoners' dilemma games 181, 182
private benefit 169
private interests 111–16
private marginal benefit of adoption 220
private markets 255
producer power 229
product quality 159
production 62
  cost, marginal 216, 224
professional associations 5, 7, 8, 21
  accountancy in Italy 133, 134, 143, 144, 145,
    154
  compulsory membership 92, 95–9, 113–14, 118,
    122
  fee scales 123
  medical and legal professions 89–90, 98–9, 102,
    104, 108, 111–13, 120–1
  membership 120
professional titles 92, 95–9, 119, 120
profit 187, 188, 189, 190, 193, 203
  maximization 248, 249
  seeking 112
property-rights 207, 208
proportional rule 24
proportionality requirement 117–21, 122
protection 51–8 *passim*, 60, 64, 65, 68, 72, 74
  industry concentration 70
  lobbying 63
  trade 61
  trade creation 68
  trade diversion 67, 68
public
  action 15, 17–18
  interest 108–11
  intervention 207
  markets 255
  notaries 134
  procurements 236
pure cooperators 192–4, 196–7, 199, 201,
    203
  basic model 185, 186, 187
  social dynamics 188, 189

quality 110, 121, 153
  average 238, 245, 246
  checks 116
  endogenous 247–50
  exogenous 245–7
  expected 246
  levels 109
  marginal valuation 238
  product 159
  of services 108, 114, 115
  standards 119, 122; *see also* minimum quality
    standard; quality regulation and
    self-regulation
quality regulation and self-regulation 109–10, 115,
    236–58
  quality levels determination: market failures
    238–42; asymmetric information 239–42
quality regulation 242–4
  theory of self-regulation 244–53; endogenous
    quality levels and moral hazard 247–50;
    exogenous quality levels 245–7; financial
    markets 250–2

Ragionieri 132, 133, 153, 154
  age-earning profiles 141, 142, 143
  entry and profitability of local market 139,
    140
  income distribution 137, 138
  regional distribution 137
  trends 134, 135
rate of entry 143
reduced form model 1, 47
referral system 117
regional distribution 135–7, 138–9
regionalism, *see* endogenous regionalism
registration 118–19, 120
regular sector 30, 35–6, 41
regulated activity 161
regulated setting 40–2, 46, 47
regulatory failure 236
rent-seeking 18, 112, 113, 114–16
replicator dynamics 189–90, 191, 203
reputational effect 249, 250, 254
research and development 182, 184
Restraints of Competition Act (GWB) 101
restrictive practices 102, 103; *see also* advertising
    restrictions
reverse democracy bias 22
right of establishment 91, 94, 95, 97, 98, 117
right to conduct litigation 112
rights of audience 112
riskiness 9
rule, choice of 206
rule of double ethics 95
rule of law 19, 23
rule of reason 96, 97, 106, 107, 117, 121–2
rules of competition law 100
rules of conduct 95, 102

sanctions 207, 209, 225, 244, 255

screening devices, *see* politics/political institutions
    as screening devices
search goods 240
Second Law of Thermodynamics 218
second office 99–100
selling modalities rules 106, 107
Service State 16
services case law 106
services, quality of 108, 114, 115
shadow sector 30, 35, 41, 44, 47
shipments 63, 69, 72
Shipments Ratio 77
Single Audit Act 158
size of the interest 113
size-of-country effect 53
skills, specific 185
social
    dynamics 189, 191, 192, 193
    factors 181, 182
    harm 159, 161, 162, 170, 171
    marginal benefit 214, 215
    marginal cost 172, 214, 215, 224
    planner 219
    selection process 182, 184, 190, 191
    standard of behaviour 190–1
    welfare 35, 170, 214, 219, 230, 243, 244, 246
socially efficient price 224
socio-economic variables 148, 153
standards 109, 110
state action doctrine 101
Stigler–Peltzman capture theory of regulation 3
stock markets 236, 237, 241, 251, 254, 255
Stolper–Samuelson factor prices effects 55
subtle opportunists 185, 186, 187, 189, 192, 196,
    199, 201
supply 31, 32, 187, 188, 192, 245
    accountancy in Italy 132, 134–5, 145–7, 148,
        149, 150
    equation 150, 153
    of services 107
    Sweden 26
symmetric information 242

tariff 64–5
    1983/tariff 1968 65
    creation 7, 52, 57–60, 72, 73, 74, 75; endogenous
        61–3; regression results 71, 78
    customs unions 63
    declines 68
    diversion 7, 52, 57–60, 72–3, 74, 75; endogenous
        61–3; regression results 71, 78
    endogenous 7, 56, 57, 60–1
    external 69
    reduction 64, 68, 74
    see also common external tariff
taxation, *see* electoral rules and interest groups:
    direct and indirect taxation
terms of trade 53, 56, 73–4
Thieffry case 92

trade bloc formation 61–3
trade creation 51, 57–60, 65–6, 68, 69
trade diversion 51, 57–60, 65–6, 67, 68
trading blocs 57, 58
training 238
transaction costs 31, 33, 37, 40, 45, 47, 208; *see also*
    trust
transitional gains trap 111
trust under endogenous transaction costs
    179–204
    basic model 184–8
    results 191–202; baricentric scenario 192–7,
        198; exploitation scenario 197, 199–202
    social dynamics 188–91
two counsel rule 103

uncoordinated industry equilibrium: company
    codes 219–21
undertakings 101, 102, 104
unemployment rate 53
United Kingdom 22, 64, 90, 112, 116, 122, 253, 254
    competition law 103–4
    employment 66
    water industry 236
United States 99, 114, 116, 132, 158
    anti-trust laws 101
    endogenous regionalism and free-trade bias 55,
        56, 61, 63, 69, 73
    political institutions as screening devices 22,
        24–5
    tariff reductions 67, 68, 74
    university professors 143
unknown action 239
unknown characteristic 239
utility function 37, 38, 40–1, 42, 45

vertical framework 23, 24, 25, 26
voluntary codes 206, 209, 216–18, 222, 223, 224,
    229, 230
voluntary compliance 209, 224, 225, 226, 227, 228,
    229
voting 26, 31

water industry 236
welfare 245
    effects 132, 148
    gain 57, 111
    implications 58
    improvement 248
    losses 57, 225, 226, 227, 229; *see also* social
        welfare
Welfare State 16
West Germany 64, 68
whistle blowing 159
willingness to pay 210, 211, 212, 213, 216, 238, 243,
    244, 248
world trade 58

zero cost 36

DATE DUE

			Printed in USA

HIGHSMITH #45230